Creation *ex nihilo*

Creation
ex nihilo

Origins, Development,
Contemporary Challenges

edited by
GARY A. ANDERSON
and
MARKUS BOCKMUEHL

University of Notre Dame Press
Notre Dame, Indiana

University of Notre Dame Press
Notre Dame, Indiana 46556
undpress.nd.edu

Copyright © 2018 by the University of Notre Dame

Paperback edition publlished in 2021

All Rights Reserved

Published in the United States of America

The Press gratefully acknowledges the generous support of
the McGrath Institute for Church Life, University of Notre Dame,
in the publication of this book.

Library of Congress Cataloging-in-Publication Data

Names: Anderson, Gary A., 1955– editor.

Title: Creation ex nihilo : origins, development, contemporary challenges /
edited by Gary A. Anderson and Markus Bockmuehl.

Description: Notre Dame : University of Notre Dame Press, 2017. |
Includes index. |

Identifiers: LCCN 2017030399 (print) | LCCN 2017036040 (ebook) |
ISBN 9780268102555 (pdf) | ISBN 9780268102562 (epub) | ISBN
9780268102531 (hardcover : alk. paper) | ISBN 9780268102548 (paperback :
alk. paper) |

Subjects: LCSH: Creation—History of doctrines. | Creationism—History
of doctrines. | Evolution—Religious aspects—Christianity—History.

Classification: LCC BT695 (ebook) | LCC BT695 .C685 2017 (print) |
DDC 231.7/65—dc23

LC record available at https://lccn.loc.gov/2017030399

CONTENTS

ACKNOWLEDGMENTS

This volume represents the main findings of a research project jointly funded by our two universities, which devoted to these questions an intensive seminar at Keble College, Oxford, in July 2014, followed by a larger conference at the University of Notre Dame a year later.

We would like here to express our sincere thanks to the John Fell Fund at the University of Oxford as well as to the Faculty Research Support Program at the University of Notre Dame, whose generous support made possible the planning and implementation of both consultations and thereby facilitated the production of the volume here presented. Without this material support from both our universities, the conversations facilitated by this project could not have been brought to fruition.

Our thanks are due also to conference support teams at both universities for their impeccable hospitality.

We are most grateful, too, for the assistance received from three of our current or recent graduate students. Jeremiah Coogan, a graduate student first at Oxford and now at Notre Dame, helped with research assistance in preparation for the 2014 conference. Dr. Michael Francis supported the organization of the July 2015 conference at Notre Dame, of which he is a recent PhD graduate. Stephen Long, a current doctoral student at Notre Dame, assisted in the initial editing of the manuscripts and preparing them for submission to the press.

Stephen Little and the editorial team at University of Notre Dame Press have been exemplary in their support, and we wish to express our thanks to them as well as to the two anonymous reviewers of the volume proposal.

Gary Anderson, University of Notre Dame
Markus Bockmuehl, University of Oxford
Easter 2017

Introduction

MARKUS BOCKMUEHL

"In the beginning, [when] God created the heavens and the earth . . ."
To Jews and Christians, this has always seemed a foundational statement about who we are and how we got here. But debates of the last
two centuries richly illustrate the extent to which religion and science
have struggled even to maintain a common conversation about it—let
alone to agree on what, if anything, it might truthfully mean.

The last two centuries have seen vast and, for the ordinary observer,
often disorienting gains in scientific understanding—not just of the
fundamental cosmological and physical kind, but also in terms of empirical observation whether of astronomy or paleobiology. For a long
time the most obvious dissensions have concerned questions of *origins*:
How did life—including our own life—evolve on this planet? Does
the universe itself have a finite beginning or end? Do we perhaps inhabit just one of a vast number of parallel universes?

Christian theology, too, has traveled a long way from debates about
the supposedly "literal" meaning of Genesis that once occupied public concern in the nineteenth and early twentieth centuries, but which
would in fact have seemed incomprehensibly myopic not just to classical

1

authors[1] but equally to the leading Christian teachers of late antiquity.[2] Meanwhile, scientific ideas of quantum physics, general relativity, or indeed evolution have long been invoked with mixed success and per-suasiveness by theologians, apologists, and others as providing a way out of discourses mired in either scientific determinism or a God of ever-shrinking gaps.

All this has certainly assisted what in recent years has become a newly reinvigorated engagement with the Christian doctrine of creation "out of nothing"—and with the objections to it that have emerged from a variety of directions both scientific and ideological, and many of which are engaged in the pages that follow.[3] Are we, for all this effort, any nearer to understanding what that opening quotation might signify in the twenty-first century? In his 2016 Reith Lectures on the origins of the universe and the nature of black holes, the iconic British cosmolo-gist Stephen Hawking reiterated the famous dictum of Pierre-Simon Laplace (1749–1827) that science has no need for the "hypothesis" of God. The point, in other words, is not so much to deny God's existence as to insist that "he doesn't intervene" in scientific laws.[4]

In relation to that fundamental question of God's relation to the world, what might "creation" signify?

CREATION *EX NIHILO*? THE OXFORD–NOTRE DAME PROJECT

It was against the backdrop of questions like these that the editors of this volume called together a group of scholars from across a wide spectrum of expertise to investigate one ancient and seemingly obsoles-cent aspect of this debate. What, if anything, does the Judeo-Christian tradition now have to say about its ancient doctrine that the nature of God's relation to the world is always, both initially and continually, sovereign and unconditioned—in other words, creation "out of noth-ing," *ex nihilo*? What could that possibly mean? Why and how did this idea arise out of a biblical tradition that prima facie appears not to sup-port it? And what significance or relevance, if any, might this doctrine still have today, whether for theology or for the dialogue between reli-gion and science?

The preliminary fruits of our labors are here presented in the hope that they will help to energize the continuing rediscovery of this subject matter's importance for theology more broadly. We lay no claim to comprehensive coverage either historically, philosophically, or indeed cosmologically. Nevertheless the resulting volume offers a contribution that is greater than the eclectic sum of its parts, offering for perhaps the first time a reconsideration of the doctrine against such a broad historical sweep of exegetical, theological, philosophical, and scientific reflection.

The discussion below clearly illustrates that the questions thus resourced and articulated promise rich potential for continued research and interdisciplinary engagement, both between theology's own subdisciplines and also with those of scientific cosmology. And of course our work here is extensively indebted to a much larger forum of debate and publications on this subject, some of them authored by contributors and other participants in these conferences.

THE ARGUMENT OF THIS VOLUME

In keeping with the central research question for this project, the present volume is divided into five parts, progressing from the doctrine's biblical roots to its eclipse in modern theology—and on to the question of its interface with and relevance, if any, to scientific cosmology.

Biblical Roots

The first and most extensive part addresses the biblical origins of the doctrine of creation *ex nihilo*.

Gary A. Anderson's opening essay takes its starting point from the locus classicus of Genesis 1, showing that while the Hebrew text appears to show God creating the world out of preexisting matter, even the earliest Jewish translations and interpretations of this text already voice the understanding that this act of creation includes the materials from which God proceeds to make the world. Yet even the priestly creation account's emphatic elimination of polytheistic themes of conflict against chaos from the standard ancient Near Eastern cosmogonies already demonstrates that the divine act of creation is for Scripture constrained by no rival or contingency and is matched in Genesis 2:1–3 by a definitive and indeed eschatological rest. Anderson follows Ian McFarland, Janet Soskice, and Kathryn Tanner in noting that, far from being preoccupied with protological interpretations of Genesis 1, the Christian development of this doctrine is less concerned with how the world came to be than with how it is sustained and governed.[5] Unlike for Greco-Roman philosophy, matter does not limit what God can do: God's unconstrained sovereignty over the world does not exclude but includes his intimate involvement with his creatures, and indeed this sovereignty alone permits the interrelationship of human and divine agency.

Examining "why *creatio ex nihilo* for theology today?," Janet Soskice recovers what she finds to have been be a foundational but also a "recessive" doctrine, often unexamined in modern times. Instead of implying any preoccupation either with ecological matters or with "big bang"–type theories of the origins of the universe, this is above all part of the doctrine of God rather than a statement about the nature of the world. It concerns God's sovereign power, goodness, and freedom to create, to govern, and to sustain—involving a "scripturally driven" metaphysics, which means that, even if not itself "in the Bible," the doctrine is nevertheless "biblical." And far from asserting an aloof or oppressive deity as some like Catherine Keller imagine,[6] the development of creation *ex nihilo* from its biblical roots in Philo and the patristic authors foregrounds God's simultaneous transcendence and presence, immutability and mercy, intimately—and in the end christologically—sustaining the goodness of his creation, "all things visible and invisible."

Following these programmatic essays to set the stage, two further chapters sample particular cross sections of the biblical evidence. Richard J. Clifford reviews key Old Testament texts in comparison with other ancient Near Eastern material.[7] While Sumerian and especially Akkadian cosmogonies like *Enuma Elish* and *Atrahasis* clearly influenced the biblical accounts, Genesis 1 distinctively stresses the sovereign and complete transformation of chaos into order, and darkness into divine light, while Genesis 2–3 introduces "agricultural" and especially "anthropological" scenarios of creation. Chaos threatens to return in other ways, as Job implies; the Psalms implore God to rule as King again in the face of the apparent reintroduction of chaos in the destruction of the temple, while Deutero-Isaiah relates the restoration of Zion to a renewal of the exodus and of creation.

The New Testament has in the past also borne the burden of furnishing proof for a Christian doctrine of creation *ex nihilo*. In the wake of critiques by Gerhard May, Frances Young, and others, however, it has long been recognized that formerly "classic" proof texts like Romans 4:17 (cf. John 1:3; Col. 1:16; Heb. 11:3) fall some considerable way short of the doctrine of creation specifically "out of nothing" that they were once assumed to establish.[8] Importantly, several Pauline texts in particular demonstrate a vital link between creation and *resurrection* that is also, incidentally, familiar among rabbinic commentators.[9] But while all agree that the New Testament statements are *compatible* with God's sovereign creation *ex nihilo*, what they actually affirm is arguably rather less specific than this.

That said, however, many New Testament texts do in fact support precisely the "metaphysics" of creation to which we have already alluded—including in Paul, John, and Hebrews. An exciting and richly suggestive reading of this insight in a more unexpected location is the subject of Sean M. McDonough's interpretation of "being and nothingness in the book of Revelation."[10] Revelation's repeated, christologically articulated affirmation of God as the One "who is and who was and who is to come" (Rev. 1:4, 8; cf. 4:8) contrasts the One who sits on the throne against the transitory nature of all other power in earth and even in heaven. This contrast plays out particularly vis-à-vis the nothingness of the dragon and the two beasts who find their culminating shape in the political "countercreation" of Babylon. They are a kind of antitrinity that "was and is not" (17:8) and goes to destruction, flagging the real potential of a dismantling or "decreation" of earth and heaven *into* nothing.[11] This is a possibility that, like the "nothingness" of evil (familiar to Augustine but also developed by Karl Barth), is superseded in the end only by the revelation of the New Jerusalem and by God's concomitant resurrection of the flesh *ex nihilo*.

With his treatment of creation and matter in Philo of Alexandria (c. 20 BC–c. AD 50), Gregory E. Sterling enables the argument to transition from the biblical to the patristic discussion. Taking his cue from Philo's influential but much-debated and variant statements about the origin of matter and about the temporality or eternity of creation,

Sterling examines *De opificio mundi* (*On the Creation of the World*) as a test case. Standing within the extensive reception history of both Genesis 1 and Plato's *Timaeus*, Philo identifies God and matter as the two causes of creation, one active and one passive, with God introducing order into the chaos of matter. Both are apparently eternal in *De opificio* (in contrast to *De providentia* [*On Providence*], which may address a more elite audience in his own school). Philo's primary concern throughout, however, is the unique transcendence and eternal power of God as the one who constitutes order into the temporality and chaos of matter. Thus, although Philo never asserts creation *ex nihilo*, he insists on the uniquely transcendent role of God in creation, thereby constituting an important bridge between Hellenistic and early Christian thought and setting the stage for the explicit articulation of this doctrine.

Creation out of Nothing in the Ancient and Medieval Church

The three following contributions survey the Christian development of the doctrine in late antiquity and the Middle Ages.

Khaled Anatolios examines Athanasius (c. 293–373) in *Against the Greeks* and *On the Incarnation* as among the most definitive statements of creation *ex nihilo* in all of patristic literature. Most significantly, perhaps, this doctrine is seen to carry existential as well as metaphysical import: in terms of the latter, creation *ex nihilo* rests in the idea of God's goodness, which comes to sublime expression in all creatureliness wholly and exclusively subsisting as the gift of God. Creatures commune with God exclusively through ecstatic participation in God's life, which in the self-giving narrative of Christ makes good the shortcomings of creation. Existentially, however, that metaphysic also sustains the very fiber of human life. It does so not least by overcoming death, which demonstrates humanity's propensity to nothingness, *ad nihilum*, wherever the gift of communion in the divine life is either absent or rejected—a theme distinctly reminiscent of motifs encountered in Revelation, above. In this way, the cross and resurrection effect a creation *ex nihilo* afresh, a "therapy of death" whose appropriation Anatolios finds ideally encapsulated in the Eucharist.

Working in the western Mediterranean a little over half a century later, Augustine (354–430) takes this doctrine of creation out of nothing as a given—and yet, as John C. Cavadini shows, both creation and nothingness are not straightforward either as philosophical concepts or as derivatives of Scripture, but rather remain grounded in the primacy of revelation itself. The very possibility of being, potential itself, is already the creational gift of God. Far from being a "myth," Genesis expresses (and "compresses") the reality of God's works analogously through the language of human experience in just the same way as the remainder of the biblical history does: creation and salvation constitute the same narrative. Augustine's further reflection on this in the *Confessions* gives voice to his ultimate conviction that the unmerited goodness of creation, out of nothingness and formlessness, is most visibly recapitulated in redemption—and evokes our response of unreserved thanksgiving.

Joseph Wawrykow traces the further development of this doctrine in two great thirteenth-century doctors of the church, Aquinas (c. 1225–74) and Bonaventure (c. 1217–74). Both carry forward the fathers' doctrinal theme of finding in divine creation the continuity of beginning and redemptive end. For them both God creates freely and intentionally in a Trinitarian act, granting both potentiality and actuality *ex nihilo*. Divine creation is good, free, and unconstrained. For Aquinas in particular, this finds an important point of departure in scriptural commentary. Aquinas also considers that God *could* have created (though he did not) a world without temporal beginning or end: *ex nihilo* means simply that only by the divine gift does a creature come into being and flourishing, and without this gift it would cease to exist. Turning then from creation's beginning to its end, Aquinas asserts that created being attains its fulfillment in communion with God, a coming forth that is at the same time a return to its source. For Bonaventure the study of visible reality furnishes traces of the Word— that is, the uncreated and incarnate Christ—showing the world to be the Creator's handiwork. Aquinas finds creation and salvation to be furnishing joint proof of the Triune God's love, wisdom, and desire for communion with others.

Creation *ex nihilo* in Jewish Thought

One of the more intriguing twists in the history of the idea of creation *ex nihilo* is the extent to which the doctrine appears to have taken shape partly in parallel and partly in observable interaction with Jewish and indeed Muslim thought in late antiquity and the Middle Ages. Two chapters addressing its impact in Judaism must here suffice to document this development.

The first, by Tzvi Novick, highlights the extent to which rabbinic thought is concerned with this doctrine not only from the cosmological point of view of God's creation of matter but also, and with equal seriousness, with an eye to God's intimate providential involvement in the world's affairs. The doctrine in the former sense is classically articulated (though not without reticence or ambivalence) in the late antique commentary known as *Genesis Rabbah*. Novick here chooses to foreground the additional, hugely influential "mythic" theme of creation by means of the Torah as a kind of blueprint, which is widely attested in this and other rabbinic as well as liturgical literature, and which draws heavily on the role of Wisdom in Proverbs 8:22, 30. This primordial Torah is not only textual but its own person, God's Logos but also his daughter espoused to Moses at Sinai, and thus potentially distinguishable as a locus of authority apart from God. Thus the Torah is at once cosmically alongside God and yet in some sense independent from him.

Moving forward to the twelfth century, Daniel Davies examines the importance of this doctrine for the more philosophical work of Maimonides (1135–1204). What matters in the *Guide of the Perplexed* is above all divine creation as such, with the question of the world's temporal beginning left somewhat in abeyance as not subject to thorough philosophical scrutiny, since there are no logical analogies to creation either *de novo* or *ex nihilo*—and one therefore cannot rationally prove such creation to be either possible or impossible. Consideration of the Torah requires creation *de novo* and indeed the possibility of miracles: this implies God's particular rather than merely universal knowledge, which in turn suggests that some aspects of the world may not be scientifically explicable. A more careful distinction between creation *de novo* and *ex nihilo* was only developed by subsequent interpreters of Maimonides, here found to culminate in Isaac Abravanel (1437–1508). Davies finds it arguable that Maimonides in fact accepts an eternal creation, although this is unlikely to be rooted in a conflict sometimes supposed between divine will and divine wisdom: God is free to create or not to create, which both validates and limits the scope of philosophical reason.

Creation *ex nihilo* in Christian Systematic Theology

The philosophical and theological arc of this volume's argument reaches its preliminary conclusion in three chapters addressing the doctrine's function in the history of modern systematic theology.

Cyril O'Regan sets the context by tracing modern theology's eclipse of the doctrine to the work of Baruch Spinoza (1632–77), who sought to counter earlier arguments about God's creation *ex nihilo* with a strictly mathematical account of reality. Spinoza's intellectual genealogy, O'Regan believes, is to some extent indebted to the Renaissance revival of Christian Neoplatonism, culminating in the work of Giordano Bruno (1548–1600), who had developed an earlier polemic against traditional theistic accounts of the world's contingency. In his resulting naturalism and antisupernaturalism, Spinoza went on to influence certain antimetaphysical convictions characteristic of German Romanticism and Idealism (despite their supposed opposition to naturalistic reductionism). Drawing attention to the importance of this intellectual-heritage genealogy for more recent theology including the work of Jürgen Moltmann and Catherine Keller,[12] the chapter attempts to account here for the twentieth- and twenty-first-century strength of conviction against the very viability of creation *ex nihilo* and indeed of any classical theistic account of creation.

Ruth Jackson provides a case study in the work of the seminal early nineteenth-century Protestant theologian Friedrich Schleiermacher (1768–1834). Developing his critical stance in dependence on Kant's critique of reason, he regarded doctrine as not susceptible to rational proof but only to historical taxonomy. The substance of a traditional doctrine of creation as such, by contrast, is subverted by scientific inquiry and, like all doctrine, requires adaptation to the rational demands of the day. Jackson shows that Schleiermacher nevertheless develops such a doctrine as concerned not with questions of cosmogony but with the present divine purpose of sustaining and redeeming the world. Creation *ex nihilo* means simply that the world and its history are utterly contingent on God at every moment, creation and its preservation being a single act of divine will. Reality coheres as to both divine and natural causality, with scientific inquiry and faith's feeling of "absolute dependence" sharing the same world.

Our systematic section concludes with David Bentley Hart's programmatic, full-bodied account of the relationship between God, creation, and evil, articulated in a sustained dialogue with the engagement of hell and theodicy in Dostoyevsky's *The Brothers Karamazov*. He argues that, quite apart from its cosmological or metaphysical dimensions, the doctrine of creation is also a fundamentally eschatological claim about the way the world as a whole exists in relation to God and the way God exists in himself. Hart concludes that all theodicy is contingent on the doctrine of *creatio ex nihilo*, since all causes are reducible to their first—and their final—cause. This renders views of God as an agent of eternal retribution and pure sovereignty incompatible with God as loving and self-giving: such ideas are incompatible with the God who created the world good and whose nature will be disclosed in full at the last judgment.

Creation *ex nihilo* and Scientific Cosmology

But does all of this have any bearing on the physical world we actually inhabit and observe, and which is today so comprehensively described and codified by science and technology? This is, to be sure, no trivial question. The present project's labor on the interface of the doctrine of creation with scientific cosmology has taken a deliberately cautious, tentative, and inceptive approach. This obviously leaves at one level plenty of scope for further research and interaction. At the same time, however, this tentativeness rightly expresses our sense that the points of genuine intellectual intersection and synergy between the disciplines are far from obvious but remain in need of discovery and patient exploration.

That interface is here addressed in three chapters by colleagues formally trained both as scientists and as theologians.

Adam D. Hincks examines the notion of creation out of nothing from the perspective of physical cosmology. Setting to one side discussions about whether God is "necessary" for the "design" of the universe, Hincks offers a brief survey of modern scientific cosmology's account of the origin of the universe including the so-called Big Bang theory, before focusing respectively on recent debates about a "multiverse" (i.e., multiple parallel universes), cyclical conceptions of time, and finally quantum cosmology's efforts to articulate the possibility of a universe from nothing. The apparent fine-tuning of the physical conditions of the earliest universe has sometimes been addressed by recourse to multiple parallel universes. But even such intrinsically unverifiable theories suppose that there exists in the very fabric and matter of the universe a "landscape of possibility" whose presence creation *ex nihilo* explains in terms of the world's radical contingency of being. Scientifically, the idea that the universe could have come from nothing has attracted increasing interest even on the part of those who seek to eliminate any divine role in creation, although this penultimate "nothing" of space and time still assumes a contingent potentiality driven by preexisting laws of physics. In the end physical cosmology always presupposes and more concretely explicates the same explanatory metaphysic of contingency which impels creation *ex nihilo*.

Andrew Pinsent concedes that at first sight there appears to be very little meaningful interaction between the claims of cosmology and theology. Yet might it be the case that, conversely, the loss of theological narratives of creation from the "background" of our scientific thinking may in turn begin to erode the longer-term viability of our insights into cosmology? Part of the problem, Pinsent suggests, is due to misapprehensions about the very nature of scientific *insight* rather than merely quantitative analysis or deduction. True understanding is often a matter of I-you relatedness—and particularly so when the second person is divine rather than human.[13] One aspect of God's ways of relating to the cosmos in this way is expressed through *creatio ex nihilo*, which encourages the expectation of order in creation and has in turn shaped our understanding of the cosmos. The loss of this second-person-perspective dimension in the West is documentable not only in philosophy but also in the history of art. Theological discourse enables the cultivation of such I-you insight precisely because it engages a God who seeks to communicate understanding.

In the final chapter, Andrew Davison returns once more to the recurring theme of contingency in proposing that the "ex" in creation *ex nihilo* furnishes an important clue to the nature of natural science, which invariably proceeds *from* something actual to its consequences. This is true even for recent physical cosmologies involving the universe's sudden "inflation," or, for that matter, for accounts of "no boundary" quantum gravity in which there is no longer a beginning of time. Yet science looks upon the appearing of the world from the inside of creation. It is theology, by contrast, which distinctively articulates the property of God as creating out of nothing, the divine agent constituting not an initial cause among other causes, not just "the beginning," but every moment of reality, time, or space. God's creation is the appearing of the world, of being and of potential itself, against no background.

NOTES

1. See David N. Sedley, *Creationism and Its Critics in Antiquity* (Berkeley: University of California Press, 2007), 66.

2. See, e.g., Peter Bouteneff, *Beginnings: Ancient Christian Readings of the Biblical Creation Narratives* (Grand Rapids: Baker Academic, 2008).

3. In addition to Catherine Keller, Ian A. McFarland, Gerhard May, Janet M. Soskice, and others referenced below, among recent publications it is worth singling out David B. Burrell et al., eds., *Creation and the God of Abraham* (Cambridge: Cambridge University Press, 2010); David Fergusson, *Creation* (Grand Rapids: Eerdmans, 2014); David Vincent Meconi, *On Earth as It Is in Heaven: Cultivating a Contemporary Theology of Creation* (Grand Rapids: Eerdmans, 2016). For scientific as well as ideological objections see several of the contributors to Thomas Jay Oord, ed., *Theologies of Creation: Creatio ex Nihilo and Its New Rivals* (New York: Routledge, 2015).

4. Stephen W. Hawking, transcript of "Black Holes Ain't as Black as They Are Painted," lecture 2 in the Reith Lectures 2016, broadcast on BBC Radio 4 on February 2, 2016, https://is.gd/Hawkin2016.

5. See Ian A. McFarland, *From Nothing: A Theology of Creation* (Louisville: Westminster John Knox, 2014); Janet M. Soskice, "*Creatio ex nihilo*: Its Jewish and Christian Foundations," in Burrell et al., *Creation and the God of Abraham*, 24–39; Soskice, "Creation and the Glory of Creatures," *Modern Theology* 29 (2013): 172–85 (part of an entire journal issue edited by Soskice on this topic; also published as Soskice, ed., *Creation "ex Nihilo" and Modern Theology* [Chichester: Wiley Blackwell, 2013]); Kathryn Tanner, *God and Creation in Christian Theology: Tyranny or Empowerment?* (Oxford: Blackwell, 1988).

6. Cf., e.g., Catherine Keller, *Face of the Deep: A Theology of Becoming* (London: Routledge, 2003).

7. Cf. previously Richard J. Clifford, *Creation Accounts in the Ancient Near East and the Bible* (Washington, DC: Catholic Biblical Association, 1994).

8. See Gerhard May, *Creatio ex Nihilo: The Doctrine of "Creation out of Nothing" in Early Christian Thought*, trans. A. S. Worrall (Edinburgh: T&T

Clark, 1994); Frances M. Young, "'Creatio ex Nihilo': A Context for the Emergence of the Christian Doctrine of Creation," *Scottish Journal of Theology* 44 (1991): 139–51.

9. Cf. further Markus Bockmuehl, "The Idea of Creation out of Nothing: From Qumran to Genesis Rabbah," in *Visualising Jews through the Ages: Literary and Material Representations of Jewishness and Judaism*, ed. Hannah Ewence and Helen Spurling (New York: Routledge, 2015), 17–31, and literature cited there; see also my comments on Tzvi Novick's chapter in this volume (page 8).

10. Cf. further Sean M. McDonough, *Christ as Creator: Origins of a New Testament Doctrine* (Oxford: Oxford University Press, 2009); Jonathan T. Pennington and Sean M. McDonough, eds., *Cosmology and New Testament Theology*, Library of New Testament Studies 355 (London: T&T Clark, 2008).

11. This term is often associated with the anthropology of Simone Weil. See, e.g., J. P. Little, "Simone Weil's Concept of Decreation," in *Simone Weil's Philosophy of Culture: Readings Toward a Divine Humanity*, ed. Richard H. Bell (Cambridge: Cambridge University Press, 1993); Lissa McCullough, *The Religious Philosophy of Simone Weil: An Introduction* (London: Tauris / New York: Palgrave Macmillan, 2014), 171–212. An eschatological interpretation of the term is articulated by Paul J. Griffiths, *Decreation: The Last Things of All Creatures* (Waco, TX: Baylor University Press, 2014).

12. Jürgen Moltmann, *The Trinity and the Kingdom: The Doctrine of God* (San Francisco: Harper & Row, 1981); Moltmann, *God in Creation: A New Theology of Creation and the Spirit of God* (San Francisco: Harper & Row, 1985 [The Gifford Lectures 1984–85]); Keller, *Face of the Deep: A Theology of Becoming* (London / New York: Routledge, 2003).

13. Cf. further Andrew Pinsent, *The Second-Person Perspective in Aquinas's Ethics: Virtues and Gifts* (New York: Routledge, 2012).

CHAPTER 1

Creatio ex nihilo and the Bible

GARY A. ANDERSON

The relationship of the doctrine of *creatio ex nihilo* to the Bible has been a much-vexed issue since the rise of historical criticism. All of the standard prooftexts for the doctrine have been shown to lack the clarity and precision that they were once thought to possess. This essay will come at this challenge from three directions. First, I will examine Genesis 1:1–3, the standard point of departure for every student of the doctrine. Second, I will turn to the central theological concerns that the doctrine addresses. Here I will take up Janet Soskice's important claim that the theological center of *creatio ex nihilo* should not be restricted to the question of the origins of the universe.[1] Gerhard May's influential work on the origin of the doctrine is not the only account that can be given.[2] To fill this out I will consider Kathryn Tanner's brilliant study, *God and Creation in Christian Theology*, a book which goes a long way toward reorienting the terms of discussion.[3] For Tanner the doctrine explains how the Bible can speak of God's utter transcendence from and immanence to the world in a noncontradictory fashion. A different set of biblical prooftexts will need to be examined in order to test the viability of this approach. My final point concerns the affective character of the doctrine, something I have learned from the writings of John Webster and David Hart. "The Christian vision of the world," Hart has observed, "is not some rational deduction from empirical experience, but is . . . a moral and spiritual labor."[4]

BIBLICAL EVIDENCE

Let me begin with the Bible. The two most commented-upon texts are Genesis 1:1 and 2 Maccabees 7:28.[5] For many modern scholars, 2 Maccabees appears to be the better candidate of the two, for it seems to contain an explicit denial of the preexistence of matter: "Look at the heaven and the earth and see everything that is in them, and recognize that God did not make them out of things that existed." But, as scholars have shown, the assertion that God did not make the world out of things that existed could have merely implied that he fashioned the world from unformed matter. For we have contemporary Greek evidence for the use of an almost identical idiom to describe the engendering of children by their parents.[6] This does not mean that the author of 2 Maccabees understood the term this way; at the same time, that possibility cannot be ruled out. As a result this text fails as a decisive prooftext for the doctrine. The most we can say is that 2 Maccabees is patient of the doctrine of *creatio ex nihilo*.

The so-called priestly creation story, Genesis 1:1–2:4a, is also a contested text. The consensus among scholars (with which I agree) is that the first three verses depict God forming the world out of preexistent matter. On this view the first two verses constitute a set of subordinate clauses that set up the main clause in verse 3: [1] "When God set out to create the heavens and the earth, [2] and when the earth was a formless void and darkness covered the face of the deep, while a wind from God swept over the face of the waters, [3] then God said, 'Let there be light'; and there was light."[7] On this understanding, verse 2 is a description of the chaotic substrate that preceded God's first creative act. To this we can add the problem of the "darkness" that is mentioned in verse 4 ("And God saw that the light was good; and God separated the light from the darkness"). It precedes God's creative work of making light.

One way out of this impasse is to appeal to the Greek translation of the Hebrew original. The Septuagint renders Genesis 1:1 as an independent sentence and thus portrays the making of the heavens and the earth as the first act of creation and the subsequent description of the chaotic nature of the earth, heaven, and waters as a description of how they appeared after this first creative act.[8] Indeed, as Menahem Kister has shown, it is a short step from the LXX to an early Jewish exegetical tradition that understood all the items listed in Genesis 1:2 as items created by God.[9] The adoption of the LXX translation in the prologue to the Gospel of John lends considerable authority to this particular translation for the Christian reader of the Bible.[10] Although I am very sympathetic to using both the Septuagint and John to supplement what we learn from Genesis 1, I do not think we should abandon the Hebrew text as a lost cause. Let me explain why the first chapter of the Bible may still be of some value for *creatio ex nihilo*.

A crucial point to bear in mind is a distinction that Brevard Childs has made between a discrete textual witness and its underlying subject matter.[11] We have the discrete, literary witness of each biblical author, whose distinct, perspectival voice must be heard. But there is also an underlying subject matter that these various witnesses are grappling with, something that Childs identifies with the Latin word *res* or the German *Sache*. As an example let us consider the person of Jesus Christ. The biblical scholar is responsible for two things: first, hearing the distinctive voice of each of the various New Testament authors and allowing them to speak about Jesus in their own singular fashion and without harmonization. The Lukan Jesus, for example, must not be confused with the Johannine. But the scholar must also take an additional step and address the underlying reality of the Jesus who is confessed in the creeds. To limit the task of exegesis to that of uncovering different voices is to abandon the theological task proper to exegesis in the first place.

When biblical scholars address the literary shape of Genesis 1:1–3, one of the first things to be noted is the parallels with the Mesopotamian story of creation, the *Enuma Elish*. But just as significant are the differences between the two accounts. As biblical scholars have pointed out, the material that preexists creation is presented in vastly different ways in the two cosmogonies. The *Enuma Elish* presumes an epic battle between the God who will emerge as sovereign and the powers of chaos, while the Bible describes the creation of the world as taking place without any opposition.[12] As Jon Levenson succinctly puts the matter: "Genesis 1:1–2:3 *begins* near the point when the Babylonian poem *ends* its action!"[13]

To emphasize the dramatic turn that Genesis 1 takes, let us consider what happens to the figure of Leviathan or the sea dragons in the course of creation's six days. As is well known, a wide variety of biblical texts trace a path not dissimilar from what is found in Assyriological and Canaanite materials. In these texts the sea dragon (*tannin*, singular; *tanninim*, plural) appears as a primordial chaos monster who acts with purposes athwart those of God. Consider, for example, Psalm 74:13: "You divided the sea by your might; you broke the heads of the dragons [*tanninim*] in the waters." Or Isaiah 51:9: "Was it not you . . . who pierced the dragon [*tannin*]?" But also important is the way in which the term for the sea dragon can stand as a poetic variant for other terms for the primeval monsters: "On that day the LORD . . . will punish Leviathan the fleeing serpent, . . . and he will kill the dragon [*tannin*] that is in the sea" (Isa. 27:1).

In stark contrast to all of these examples stands the witness of Genesis 1:

> And God said, "Let the waters bring forth swarms of living creatures, and let birds fly above the earth across the dome of the sky." So God created the great sea monsters [*tanninim*] and every living creature that moves, of every kind, with which the waters swarm, and every winged bird of every kind. And God saw that it was good. God blessed them, saying, "Be fruitful and multiply and fill the waters in the seas, and let birds multiply on the earth." And there was evening and there was morning, the fifth day. (vv. 20–23)

Here the sea monster is created by God and wholly under his control. No longer an adversary of any stripe, he can be included within the formula of approbation: "And God saw that [what he had made] was good." Jon Levenson summarizes the novelty of Genesis 1 in this fashion: "In Genesis there is no active opposition to God's creative labor. He works on inert matter. In fact, rather than *creatio ex nihilo*, 'creation without opposition' is the more accurate nutshell statement of the theology underlying our passage."[14]

At one level there is nothing to dispute here. But at the same time, this evaluation is not completely satisfying. We must recall that *creatio ex nihilo* is a doctrine that arises in a Greco-Roman environment. That is, it arose in a world in which the eternity of matter implied that the gods were constrained by its limitations when they created the world. But this particular problem is not something that the biblical writer ever faced or could even imagine.

This is an important clarification to make because many commentators make the strong claim that Genesis 1 refutes the doctrine. But if we are pursuing this question strictly from the perspective of what our textual witnesses allow, it would be fairer to say that God does not face any opposition to his creative endeavors as is the rule in the ancient Near East. True, matter is preexistent, but one must concede that this datum means something quite different when we import it into a Greco-Roman environment. For there the issue of preexistent matter connotes a significant qualification of divine power.

Here is where the notion of the text's *res* or *Sache* comes into play. There can be no doubt that the author of Genesis 1 inherits an account of creation that presupposes the need to destroy the forces of chaos first. These so-called *Chaoskampf* texts have been well studied by biblical scholars. But the author of Genesis 1 has consciously and utterly rejected this idea. If we were to sit down with our priestly scribes and give them a brief introduction to Greek cosmology, emphasizing for them the fact that preexistent matter necessarily restricts what God can accomplish in the material world, can we imagine that they would accept such a notion? Though certainty obviously alludes us, I find it hard to imagine.

But let me return to the issue of the chaos substrate. As Levenson has noted, the materials listed in Genesis 1:2 form a primordial chaos. But, as he goes on to say, the same holds true for darkness. "Light, which is God's first creation, does not banish darkness. Rather it alternates with it: 'There was evening and there was morning' in each of the six days of creation. . . . The priority of 'evening' over 'day' reminds us of which is primordial and recalls again that chaos in the form of darkness has not been eliminated, but only confined to its place through alternation with light."[15] On this understanding, darkness is part of the primordial chaos substrate that confronts God as he sets out to create the world. Like the "matter" of Greek cosmogonies, it would appear to limit God.

Yet such a notion is overturned by a close reading of the entire narrative. For, as countless commentators have noted going all the way back to the rabbinic period, the seventh day does not append the formula that was standard for the previous six days: "There was evening and there was morning, the Xth day." On the seventh day, all trace of this primordial darkness disappears. Gerhard von Rad writes:

> The Sabbath at creation, as the last of the creative days, is not limited; the concluding formula ("and it was evening and it was morning...") is lacking, and that too, like everything else in this chapter, is intentional. Thus Gen 2.1 ff. speaks about the preparation of an exalted saving good for the world and man, of a rest "before which millennia pass away as a thunderstorm" (Novalis). It is tangibly "existent" protologically as it is expected eschatologically in Hebrews (Heb., ch. 4).[16]

And Jon Levenson adds:

> "No wonder the Mishnah can call the eschatological future, "a day that is entirely Sabbath and rest for eternal life" and designate Psalm 92, the song "for the Sabbath day," as the special hymn for that aeon. The reality that the Sabbath represents—God's unchallenged and uncompromised mastery, blessing, and hallowing—is consistently and irreversibly available only in the world-to-come. Until then, it is known only in the tantalizing experience of the Sabbath.[17]

But it is not simply the Mishnah that makes this move. As Yair Zakovitch points out, Isaiah 60 utilizes a tradition about the special light that was available for the first days of creation to describe the conditions that will define the city of Jerusalem at the eschaton.[18] The pertinent section reads:

> The sun shall no longer be
> your light by day,
> nor for brightness shall the moon
> give light to you by night;

but the LORD will be your everlasting light,
    and your God will be your glory.
Your sun shall no more go down,
    or your moon withdraw itself;
for the LORD will be your everlasting light,
    and your days of mourning shall be ended. (vv. 19–20)

What is striking about this text—indeed something it shares with the seventh day—is that darkness is not some sort of primordial chaos that God must work around. Rather, darkness is an element of the cosmos that not only is under God's providential power but can and will be eradicated at the close of the world's history.

Robert Wilken, in his book *The Christians as the Romans Saw Them*, noted that the Roman thinker Galen had intimated the doctrine of *creatio ex nihilo* prior to its appearance in the works of Theophilus and Irenaeus. What Galen observed was that the Bible describes the created order as arising from the power of the divine word alone and not limited by the physical characteristics of matter. Though Galen's remarks were based on some knowledge of Genesis 1, it is not hard to imagine that Isaiah 60 would have been just as bothersome to him. Light, in his mind, required the mediating agency of the sun and stars. Summarizing Galen's train of thought, Wilken writes:

> Certain things are impossible by nature and God does not—indeed cannot—do such things. He chooses the best possible way, the way according to reason. . . . The world of nature cannot be understood unless it is recognized that all things, including the creator, are governed by unalterable laws according to reason. The laws determine the way things are and always will be, not because God decided they should be this way, but because that is the best way for them to be. God is part of nature. He is, in the hymn of the Stoic Cleanthes, "leader of nature, governing all things by law."[19]

The only conclusion I think we can draw from the Bible's final canonical form is that the existence of darkness at creation must have been something God permits rather than confronts by necessity. Or, putting the matter differently, Genesis 2:1–3 (read in conjunction with

Isa. 60) provides the standard historical-critical interpretation with an aporia. As we have seen, reading Genesis 1:1 in light of *Enuma Elish* suggests that God is both confronted with and limited by the state of the universe prior to creation. Hence, the modern propensity to treat Genesis 1:1 as a subordinate, temporal clause. But by the time we get to the seventh day (or the eschaton), this assumption must be qualified. In other words, the close of the first creation story forces the reader to go back and rethink what is described at the beginning. But let me be clear. I am not suggesting that this changes how we view the grammar of 1:1. Grammar remains grammar. But the close of this story stands in some tension with the beginning. Though Genesis 1 does not teach *creatio ex nihilo* in the way early Christian theologians might have thought, it does not rule it out as decisively as many modern readers have assumed.

Central Concerns of the Doctrine

Let me turn from the first creation story to what systematic theologians have identified as the central theological concerns of the doctrine. The reason for doing so is that many biblical scholars have presumed that the doctrine stands or falls on the interpretation of Genesis 1. But if the doctrine is more than just an account of the world's origin, then Janet Soskice is certainly correct in exhorting us to widen our frame of reference as to what counts as biblical evidence. I will take, as my point of departure, Ian McFarland's recent book, *From Nothing: A Theology of Creation*.

He begins his account with the figure of Theophilus of Antioch, a bishop who around the year 180 wrote a treatise titled *To Autolycus*. Therein we find the claim that "God brought everything into being out of what does not exist, so that his greatness might be known and understood through his works."[20] Irenaeus of Lyons, of course, makes the very same claim. But the larger issue at stake here is not so much how the world came to be as how the world is governed. Theophilus and Irenaeus want to establish that God's transcendence over the world does not come at the cost of his intimate oversight of its affairs.

The concern of governance can be seen in the striking contrast between the way Justin Martyr on the one hand and Theophilus and Irenaeus on the other treat the relationship between divine transcendence and immanence. Because Justin is beholden to the Platonic notion of preexistent matter, "God is unable to act directly on or be immediately present to creation: God is and remains outside the phenomenal world."[21] For Irenaeus, on the other hand, God's transcendence does not connote remoteness from the material order. Quite the contrary, McFarland writes: "This divine fullness establishes the most profound intimacy between Creator and creature: the same God 'who fills the heavens and views the depths . . . is also present with everyone of us. . . . For his hand lays hold of all things . . . is present in our hidden and secret parts, and publicly nourishes and preserves us.' God's transcendence does not imply distance from creatures, but is rather the ground for God's engagement with them."[22] As R. A. Norris summarizes the matter: "What makes God different from every creature—his eternal and ingenerate simplicity—is thus, for Irenaeus, precisely what assures his direct and intimate involvement with every creature."[23] In a world in which matter stands over against God, God is necessarily limited by the constraints it imposes. Though divine transcendence is not at risk, the degree of intimacy that God can have with the world is severely qualified.

This distinctive feature of *creatio ex nihilo* is the subject of Kathryn Tanner's remarkable book *God and Creation in Christian Theology*. In this work, she shows how this doctrine enables one to affirm both divine immanence and transcendence without qualifying one in terms of the other. The blurb that Eugene Rogers provides on the back cover of the book is most illuminating: "Before I read *God and Creation*, I thought Christians had to choose between grace and free will. If they chose grace, so much the better. As I read, I found myself moved. Grace and free will were not rivals but companions."

Rogers's candid remarks reveal the deep philosophical assumptions that most readers bring to the Bible. Even two thousand years into the Christian project readers still think of divine grace as an external power that stands over against human free will. If an action, for example, requires 80 percent grace, then we contribute the other 20 percent. But Tanner would call such a worldview more Greek than biblical. In other words, because God's being is not distinct from the being of everything else that exists, he must establish his identity over against it. This is what the eternity of matter entails. *Creatio ex nihilo*, on the other hand, allows one to conceive this relationship quite differently: both God and the human agent can contribute 100 percent to any particular action. Tanner puts the matter thus: "Since divine agency is necessary for any action of the creature at all, it cannot be proper to say that God's activity is added on to the creature's." To which she adds this citation from Karl Barth: "In the rule of God we do not have to do first with a creaturely action and then—somewhere above or behind, but quite distinct from it . . . with an operation of God Himself. To describe *concursus divinis* we cannot use the mathematical picture of two parallel lines. But creaturely events take place as God Himself acts."[24]

One way to appreciate the importance of this teaching is to consider an exegetical example. A doctrine, after all, is useful only to the degree that it makes us better readers of the biblical text. In his recent work on divine and human agency in the writings of Saint Paul, John Barclay articulates a position that closely resembles what Kathryn Tanner has articulated.[25] And importantly he arrives at this view as a result of a close reading of several key passages in the Pauline correspondence. For my part, I will turn to two of the most important moments in Abraham's life and the challenge they have posed for biblical commentators. In Genesis 12:1–3 Abram is called by God "out of the blue": "Now the LORD said to Abram, 'Go from your country and your kindred and your father's house to the land that I will show you. I will make of you a great nation, and I will bless you, and make your name great, so that you will be a blessing. I will bless those who bless you, and the one who curses you I will curse; and in you all the families of the earth shall be blessed.'" At this point in the story, Abram has done nothing to merit the stupendous promise that he receives. This point was not lost on ancient exegetes, who proceeded to invent a myriad of stories to fill in this lacuna. In so doing, they simply accented the fact that there is no explanation for the choice. Gerhard von Rad saw, and innumerable other commentators have seen, this choice of God as an excellent example of divine grace.[26] Everything depends on the will of the electing deity.

When we come to Genesis 22, however, after Abraham's extraordinary act of obedience to God's command to sacrifice his beloved son, the terms of the covenant are now reformulated, but this time as a fitting reward for his obedience:

The angel of the LORD called to Abraham a second time from heaven, and said, "By myself I have sworn, says the LORD: Because you have done this, and have not withheld your son, your only son, I will indeed bless you, and I will make your offspring as numerous as the stars of heaven and as the sand that is on the seashore. And your offspring shall possess the gate of their enemies, and by your offspring shall all the nations of the earth gain blessing for themselves, because you have obeyed my voice."

Although the terms of the promise in both texts are similar, the grounds for the promise could not be more different. Whereas Genesis 12 places the matter wholly in God's hands, Genesis 22 ascribes the promise to the merits of Abraham's deed: "Because you have done this . . . I will indeed bless you." It is striking to observe that von Rad makes no mention of this repetition of the promise. Although one cannot be certain, it is likely that this silence has to do with the author's discomfort with meritorious human actions. If so, von Rad enacts in his commentary the position confessed by Rogers above prior to his grappling with the doctrine of *creatio ex nihilo*: divine grace and human merit are irreconcilable.

Tanner's work shows us that had von Rad digested Barth or Aquinas on this issue, he could have done justice to the text in question.[27] One need not see the Bible's emphasis on human merit in Genesis 22 as canceling out the grace that was given in Genesis 12. To adopt the vocabulary of Thomas Aquinas, we could understand the act of election in Genesis 12 as the moment of "justification" when grace is given by God apart from any human merit. But having received this grace, Abraham is then enabled by this divine power to effect meritorious deeds that mark his progress toward sanctification. Barclay's description of Paul's "participationist" soteriology could easily be transferred to the book of Genesis: "Grace does not just invite 'response' but itself effects the human participation in grace, such that 'every good work' can be viewed as the fruit of divine power as much as the product of believers themselves."[28]

It is striking that Barclay's amplification of what he learned from E. P. Sanders is already evident in the thinking of Athanasius. In a key passage he writes: "When we render a recompense to the Lord to the utmost of our power . . . we give nothing of our own but those things which we have before received from Him, this being especially true of His grace, that He should require, as from us, His own gifts." And Khaled Anatolios explains as follows:

> Our response to God's grace both is and is not our own. It is not our own insofar as even this response derives from God's grace and is "received." And yet it is our own precisely because we do actually receive it: "those things which you give Me are yours, as having received them from Me." Moreover, it is precisely their becoming "our own" through our having received them which makes it possible for us to "give" them back to God. If they do not become our own, we would not be able to give them back to God; neither would God be able to require them back of us. But the fact that they do become our own means that the reciprocity of human and divine continues in an ascending cycle: God gives us grace and requires it back of us; we receive it and offer it back to God. "Virtue" and "holiness" are thus conceived in terms of this ascending dialectic, as the "offering back" as gift, of what is already received as gift. Here we see how a perceived dichotomy between striving for virtue and the participation in grace is really quite far from the more complex conception of Athanasius.[29]

The last sentence speaks volumes for the theological problem we have been tracing. It is almost impossible not to think of striving for virtue and participation in grace as irreconcilable opposites. One of the principle functions of the doctrine of *creatio ex nihilo* is to allow the reader of the Bible to make sense of passages in which divine grace and human free will seem to be set against one another. And that, I would suggest, is the sine qua non of any Christian doctrine. *Creatio ex nihilo* provides a metaphysical account of the world that allows for a deeper engagement with the way the Bible characterizes the divine and human agency. As John Webster has put the matter, "Creation out of nothing served to spell out the ontological entailments of the distinction between the eternal creator and the temporal, contingent creatures who are the objects of his saving regard, resisting ideas of the creator as one who merely gave form to coeval matter, and so accentuating the limitless capacity and freedom of God."[30]

ONTOLOGICAL ENTAILMENTS

Let me dwell on the subject of these "ontological entailments" just a little longer. Robert Wilken, let us recall, showed us that Galen intuited the doctrine of *creatio ex nihilo* before the Christians themselves had come to broad agreement about it. In particular, Wilken argues that the Christian view of God's providential power offended Greek and Roman sensibilities:

> God, in the Greek view, dwelt in a realm above the earth, but he did not stand outside of the world, the *kosmos*. Earth and heaven are part of the same cosmos, which has existed eternally. The world is not the creation of a transcendent God. The cosmos has its own laws, and all that exists—the physical world, animals, man, and the gods—are subject to nature's laws. "Certain things are impossible to nature," said Galen, and "God does not even attempt such things at all." Rather, "he chooses the best out of the possibilities of becoming."[31]

We have already noted the challenges posed by Genesis 1:3 and Isaiah 60. Both of these texts claim that God can illumine the world without recourse to the means that nature has provided: the sun, moon, and stars. Another offense against reason can be found in the revolutionary way that wisdom texts (and eventually, the New Testament and early Christian thinkers) came to understand the charitable act. In these materials, showing kindness to the suffering was not just a good deed but an alignment of one's actions with the structure of the universe. One could argue that a discussion of the virtue of charity fits better within a theology of creation than a discussion of religious ethics.

Peter Brown's magnificent recent book, *Through the Eye of a Needle*, has highlighted the significance of the theological shaping of this distinctive practice. Greco-Roman citizens, he observes, were not miserly. Wealthy donors funded lavish public buildings all over the empire. But their generosity always included the expectation that honor and other public accolades would come their way. In a world ruled by what Brown calls the iron laws of reciprocity, "it was considered bad luck to dream that one gave money to a beggar." Such dreams portended death: "For Death is like a beggar," the saying went, "who takes and gives nothing in return."[32]

In the synagogue and church, however, a different construal of the charitable act was taking shape. The fact that the poor could not repay was a crucial ingredient for the value of the almsdeed. But not because of a concern for unadulterated altruism—that is more a modern than an ancient value—but because of the statement deeds of charity made about the way God governed the world.

This point is made well in a story that the rabbis told about an encounter between Rabbi Gamliel and an unnamed pagan philosopher.[33] The latter was bothered by the Torah's command that one should assist the poor and have no second thoughts while doing so. Acting so carelessly would bankrupt the man of means, and the result would be two indigent persons, not just one. In the response that R. Gamliel gives, it is important to make one point clear. In the Bible, a gift to the poor was often understood to be a no-interest loan.

> R. Gamliel said: "If a poor man sought a loan from you, would you consent?" He replied, "No!" "And if he brought a deposit?" He replied, "Yes!" "If he brought you someone not quite fitting to stand as surety?" He replied, "No." "And if he brought you the governor as surety?" He replied, "Yes."
>
> "Isn't it a matter of *a fortiori* logic: If you will issue a loan when a person of means goes surety, how much the more so when 'He who spoke and made the world' goes surety. For scripture says, '*He who is generous to the poor makes a loan to God, and God will surely repay.*' (Prov. 19:17)."[34]

The retort of R. Gamliel is astounding. Our Greco-Roman philosopher imagines the charitable act solely within the framework of intrahuman reciprocity. "Certain things are impossible to nature," Galen had claimed. "God does not even attempt such things at all." That neatly sums up why this pagan thinker rejected R. Gamliel's understanding of charitable action. But in the biblical understanding, charity is an action that God directly oversees. The ways of providence conform with the intentions of the creator when he made the world.

Creatio ex nihilo—recalling the words of John Webster—rejects the idea that the creator simply gave form to coeval matter. If that was

the case, then the rules of reciprocity ought to govern charitable behavior. Matter, we must assume, restricts what God can do. The fact
that the world does not operate within the ambit of these expectations
gives eloquent testimony to "the limitless capacity and freedom of
God" in creating and governing the world.

It may be worth recalling that Christian charitable practices were
envied by many in the Roman world. Julian the Apostate famously attempted to import them into a non-Christian setting. Yet his ambitions
failed. Rodney Stark explains: "For all that [Julian] urged pagan priests
to match these Christian practices, there was little or no response because *there were no doctrinal bases or traditional practices* for them to
build upon."[35] The doctrine that was conspicuously lacking was *creatio
ex nihilo*, a doctrine that allowed Christian thinkers to see that the gra-
cious intentions of the creator were not limited by the materials at his
disposal. Rather, it was through those very materials that those intentions were granted expression. Inserting Christian charitable practices
into a pagan context was something like transplanting an organ into a
new body. Without powerful drugs in place, the recipient will not recognize the new organ and will reject it. For Christian charity to flourish, a radical new way of thinking about God's relationship to the
world had to take root.

CREATIO EX NIHILO AS A SPIRITUAL LABOR

And this leads to my final point, which I will make more in the way of a
suggestion than a detailed argument. Affirming *creatio ex nihilo* is, as
David Hart asserts, "not some rational deduction from empirical experience, but . . . a moral and spiritual labor."[36] Nowhere is the truth of this
better reflected than in the way the virtue of charity is enacted with the
life of Tobit. Tobit is something of a Joban figure—his heroism in assisting the poor is not rewarded; instead, it leads to blindness and what
threatens to be a premature and tragic death. And yet, in spite of these
challenges, Tobit holds fast to the commandment. With characteristic
insight, Saint Augustine captures nicely the irony of the moment:

> Tobit was blind, yet he taught his son the way of God. You know
> this is true, because Tobit advised his son, *Give alms, my son, for*

almsdeeds save you from departing into darkness (Tob 4:7, 11); yet
the speaker was in darkness himself. . . . He had no fear that his son
might say in his heart, "Did you not give alms yourself? Why,
then, are you talking to me out of your blindness? Darkness is
where almsgiving has evidently led you, so how can you advise me
that *almsdeeds save you from departing into darkness?*" (*Enarratio
in Psalmum* 96.18)[37]

The confidence of Tobit is altogether puzzling. "How could Tobit
give that advice to his son with such confidence?" Augustine goes on
to ask. And this is the answer he provides: "Only because he habitu-
ally saw another light. The son held his father's hand to help him walk,
but the father taught his son the way, that he might live.—And the
'other light' that Tobit saw, of course, is the light of *faith*!" (*Enarratio
in Psalmum* 96.18).[38]

The notion that Tobit saw another light recalls an important passage from the *Confessions*. At the end of this work, when Augustine is
commenting upon the story of creation, he makes an astute observation
about the literary structure of that narrative. During the first six days of
creation—which describe the world that we live in—God concludes his
successive efforts with an affirmation of the goodness of what he has
made. This judgment is given special emphasis at the close of the sixth
day, in which God declares that all that he has made is "*very* good."[39]

But this raises an important question. Can we, as readers of the biblical text, affirm what God declares to be the case? The only way to do
so, Augustine argues, is through divine grace (*Confessions* 13.31, 46):[40]

But as to those who do by Your Spirit see these things, it is You
who see in them. Thus when they see that these works are good, it
is You who see that they are good; when anything pleases us because of You, You are what pleases us in that thing, and when by
Your Spirit something pleases us, it pleases You in us. "*For what
man knows the things of a man, but the spirit of a man, which is in
him? So the things also that are of God, no man knows, but the spirit
of God. Now we have received not the spirit of this world, but the
spirit that is of God, that we may know the things that are given us
from God*" (I Cor 2:11).

In this text we see the two themes we have been following tightly stitched together. On the one hand there is the ability to discern the goodness with which God not only made the world but continues to uphold and guide it. As that pagan philosopher with whom R. Gamliel spoke knew so well, the world does not present itself as a place directed by divine mercy. The Greeks were not unwise to presume that one would be better off relying on the principle of reciprocity. Even the gods are constrained by the ways of nature. For R. Gamliel (and Saint Basil) only divine revelation (in this case, Prov. 19:17) could enable one to see the astonishing manner in which God is related to the world. But revelation on its own is not sufficient. One also needs the assistance of the Holy Spirit to act in accordance with the commandments God has given. In his stupendous obedience to the command to offer his only son, Abraham was not earning his salvation—period. Rather, he was enabled to complete this meritorious deed in a way that honored both divine and human agency. "In crowning our merits," Augustine had said, "you are crowning your own gifts."[41] And so for the affirmation of the goodness of the created order. The world, as it is presently constituted, does not present itself as good to the sensitive observer. We can only speak of it as such when we are graced to see it as God sees it. Affirming the doctrine of *creatio ex nihilo* is not simply an exegetical task; it requires the supernatural gift of faith.

The relationship between doctrine and biblical exegesis is both complex and fraught with controversy. A hallmark of modern approaches to the Bible is the independence of the exegete from the disputes that have arisen in interconfessional contexts. Given the fact that many presentations of the doctrine ground the concept on a faulty reading of Genesis 1:1–3, a consensus has arisen that the doctrine has little to do with the Bible itself. But in the early Christian sources themselves, Genesis 1:1 is not the most important piece of the puzzle. As Anatolios, for example, has shown, the doctrine is more interested in the dependence of the created order on God than in clarifying the conditions of its initial origin. As we saw in the second part of this essay, a major concern of the doctrine is to clarify how human and divine agency interrelate. I suggested that one way of testing the doctrine's biblical character would be to ask whether the doctrine can help us exegete biblical texts where the question of divine and human agency is at issue.

In addition to this, because the doctrine puts such a premium on dependence, the practice of charity also confirms the doctrine. As I have argued at great length elsewhere, early Christian charity has more to do with metaphysics than morals. That is, the teaching about charitable actions and the rewards they generate is meant to reveal the (wondrous) type of world God has created and—on the basis of this information— how one might flourish in it. Roman thinkers greatly esteemed Christian charity, and some like Julian tried to import these patterns of living into the pagan realm. Yet those efforts were unsuccessful because they lacked the requisite theological underpinning. Behind the practice of charity as taught in the Bible is the presumption that God superintends such acts and that those who give in this sacrificial fashion will ultimately be rewarded. The reward is not so much a motivator of the behavior in question, but an indicator of the type of world God has fashioned. To pagan thinkers, this was an irrational assertion. Matter restricts what the gods can do. Better to conduct one's affairs in accord with the "iron-clad laws of reciprocity" than cherish notions about divine sovereignty that do not hold water.

In both these instances (charity and grace/merit) certain metaphysical assumptions are presumed. God governs the natural order in a way that respects human autonomy and rewards sacrificial generosity. God does not operate within the rules of intrahuman (and so, this-worldly) reciprocity. Though we did not claim that Genesis 1:1–3 establishes this, we did show that Genesis 2:1–3 profoundly qualifies the independence of matter that we might have inferred from the first three verses of the Bible. This, plus the evidence of Second and Third Isaiah, strongly push the reader of the Bible toward the doctrine itself. It is a trajectory internal to the larger canonical witness. The fact that as early as the book of Jubilees we have texts claiming that God created the primordial matter of Genesis 1:2 confirms this. It is on these grounds that the doctrine has deep biblical roots.

NOTES

1. J. Soskice, "Creation and the Glory of Creatures," *Modern Theology* 29 (2013): 172–85.

2. Gerhard May, *Creatio ex Nihilo: The Doctrine of "Creation out of Nothing" in Early Christian Thought*, trans. A. S. Worrall (Edinburgh: University of Edinburgh Press, 1994).

3. Kathryn Tanner, *God and Creation in Christian Theology: Tyranny or Empowerment?* (Minneapolis: Fortress Press, 1988).

4. David Bentley Hart, *The Doors of the Sea: Where Was God in the Tsunami?* (Grand Rapids: Eerdmans, 2005), 58.

5. For an example of this, see the recent discussion in Paul Copan and William L. Craig, *Creation out of Nothing: A Biblical, Philosophical, and Scientific Exploration* (Grand Rapids: Baker Academic, 2004), and the literature cited therein.

6. May, *Creatio ex Nihilo*, 8.

7. The text of the NRSV has been slightly adjusted.

8. See chapter 7 in this volume, by John Cavadini, for an excellent explanation of how Augustine reads the first few verses of Genesis.

9. Menahem Kister, "*Tohu wa-Bohu*, Primordial Elements and *Creatio ex Nihilo*," *Jewish Studies Quarterly* 14 (2007): 229–56.

10. This is the tack that Ian McFarland takes in his recent book *From Nothing: A Theology of Creation* (Louisville: Westminster John Knox Press, 2014). For him, the significance of the Gospel of John is twofold. First, no mention is made whatsoever of the formless waste of Gen. 1:2, and second, "the sole precondition . . . for creation is God." And not a solitary God, McFarland is quick to add, but a God who is defined by his relationship to his Word: "In this way, at the same time that John 1 stands as the most explicit biblical statement of the unconditional character of God's creating work, it also signals that creation from nothing is not merely a claim about God's relation to the world, but also a statement about God's own identity" (McFarland, *From Nothing*, 23).

11. Brevard Childs, *Biblical Theology of the Old and New Testaments: Theological Reflection on the Christian Bible* (Minneapolis: Fortress Press, 1992), 80–90.

12. In the world of Gen. 1, the only grounds for explaining the emergence of evil is human sin. So Ronald Hendel (from a typescript of his forthcoming *Anchor Bible* commentary): "God's perception of the goodness of things in Genesis 1 is reversed at the beginning of the P flood story, when God sees that the earth and all flesh have become corrupt (6:12). In the intertextual relations between Gen. 1 and 6:12, the initial goodness of things turns out to be a somewhat fragile quality, capable of being disrupted and corrupted by violent deeds. The goodness of things seems to be God's intention, but it is an ideal condition which living things can spoil, and which then requires a (cleansing) destruction and re-creation."

13. Jon Levenson, *Creation and the Persistence of Evil: The Jewish Drama of Divine Omnipotence*, 2nd ed. (Princeton: Princeton University Press, 1994), 122 (emphasis original).

14. Ibid., 122.

15. Ibid., 123.

16. Gerhard von Rad, *Genesis: A Commentary*, rev. ed. (Philadelphia: Westminster Press, 1972), 62–63.

17. Levenson, *Creation and the Persistence of Evil*, 123.

18. Yair Zakovitch, *Mashmiʿa shalom mevasser ṭov* (Haifa: Haifa University Press, 2004).

19. Robert Wilken, *The Christians as the Romans Saw Them* (New Haven: Yale University Press, 2003), 87.

20. *To Autolycus* 1.4 as quoted in McFarland, *From Nothing*, 1.

21. McFarland, *From Nothing*, 11. In support of this position, McFarland cites this passage from Justin Martyr's *Dialogue with Trypho*: "He who has but the smallest intelligence will not venture to assert that the Creator and Father of all things would leave behind everything above heaven and appear on a little portion of the earth."

22. McFarland, *From Nothing*, 12.

23. R. A. Norris, *God and World in Early Christian Theology* (New York: Seabury Press, 1965), 86.

24. Tanner, *God and Creation*, 94. The citation from Barth is taken from *Church Dogmatics*, 3:1.

25. John Barclay, "Grace and Transformation of Agency in Christ," in *Redefining First-Century Jewish and Christian Identities: Essays in Honor of E. P. Sanders*, ed. Fabian E. Udoh (Notre Dame, IN: University of Notre Dame Press, 2008), 372–89.

26. Von Rad, *Genesis*, 159.

27. But the point I want to make is more Websterian—the doctrine depends on the spiritual affection of human wonder. We should not reduce it to a piece of objective knowledge. As Tanner's work shows: the modern world has demonstrated a massive forgetfulness about what the doctrine teaches even by those who affirm it!

28. Barclay, "Grace and Transformation," 385.

29. Both the citation from Athanasius and the commentary of Anatolios come from Khaled Anatolios, *Athanasius: The Coherence of His Thought* (New York: Routledge, 1998), 174–75.

30. John Webster, "Creation from Nothing," in *Christian Dogmatics: Reformed Theology for the Church Catholic*, ed. Michael Allen and Scott R. Swain (Grand Rapids: Baker Academic, 2016), 126–47.

31. Wilken, *Christians as the Romans Saw Them*, 91.

32. Peter Brown, *Through the Eye of a Needle: Wealth, the Fall of Rome and the Making of Christianity in the West, 350–550 AD* (Princeton: Princeton University Press, 2012), 76.

33. For a strikingly similar Christian version of this story, see the passage from Saint Basil that I discuss in *Charity: The Place of the Poor in the Biblical Tradition* (New Haven: Yale University Press, 2013), 30–32.

34. The translation is mine. The original text is from *Midrash Tannaim zum Deuteronomium*, ed. D. Hoffmann (Berlin: Itzkowski, 1908), 84.

35. Rodney Stark, *The Rise of Christianity* (Princeton: Princeton University Press, 1996), 88 (emphasis original).

36. Hart, *Doors of the Sea*, 58.

37. *The Works of St. Augustine: Exposition of the Psalms 73–98*, trans. M. Boulding (Hyde Park, NY: New City Press, 2002), 456.

38. Ibid.

39. But Augustine also knows that the world which God fashioned on the first six days is not "the best of all possible worlds," to quote Leibniz. That awaits the seventh day, that is, the eschaton. The *Catechism of the Catholic Church* (§310) puts it this way: "But why did God not create a world so perfect that no evil could exist in it? With infinite power God could always create something better (*STh* I, 25, 6). But with infinite wisdom and goodness God freely willed to create a world 'in a state of journeying' towards its ultimate perfection. In God's plan this process of becoming involves the appearance of certain beings and the disappearance of others, the existence of the more perfect alongside the less perfect, both constructive and destructive forces of nature. With physical good there exists also physical evil as long as creation has not reached perfection (*SCG* III, 71)."

40. Augustine, *Confessions*, trans. F. J. Sheed (Indianapolis: Hackett, 1993), 317.

41. As found in *Catechism of the Catholic Church* (Vatican City: Libreria Editrice Vaticana, 2000), §2006. The original is from *Enarratio in Psalmum* 102.7.

CHAPTER 2

Why *Creatio ex nihilo* for Theology Today?

JANET SOSKICE

Creatio ex nihilo is both a foundational and a recessive Christian teaching. There are some doctrines most Christians have heard about, even if they don't claim to fully understand—the doctrine of the incarnation, the doctrine of the Trinity, and teachings about grace, providence, and free will. Other teachings—for that is all the word "doctrine" means— sit quietly undergirding the whole without much being questioned or contested and rarely come to the attention of anyone but the doctoral student or professional theologian and philosopher of religion: that God is good, that God is One. *Creatio ex nihilo* is one such recessive Christian doctrine, but it is a particularly important one, for it underlies much Christian thought and practice, devotional as well as systematic and apologetic, on the problem of evil, the possibility of miracles, the nature of religious language, grace, the efficacy of intercessory prayer, and God's loving presence to the created order.

   Creatio ex nihilo is an emergent Christian teaching like the doctrine of the Trinity and, like that teaching, once established as a mainstream teaching (by the early fourth century at the latest), was rarely, in itself, a matter for debate.

It is a teaching enshrined in the creeds: "I believe in God the Father almighty, maker of heaven and earth."[1] Major Reformation disputes involved grace, ecclesiology, sacraments, redemption, and eschatology but not the doctrine of creation. From the time of the Cappadocians onwards *creatio ex nihilo* has been, East and West, for better or (some now say) for worse, a foundational teaching of Christian thought.

However, no doctrinal formulation should be exempt from critical scrutiny, and in recent years *creatio ex nihilo* has come under fire as antiquated and destructive, especially from thinkers influenced by process philosophy and the work of Alfred North Whitehead and Charles Hartshorne. Process positions have been energetically reworked alongside postmodern and feminist critical theory and some strands of evangelical philosophical theology.

I will take as my working definition this: *creatio ex nihilo* affirms that God, from no compulsion or necessity, created the world out of nothing—really nothing—no preexistent matter, space, or time.

Should you idly use the term with churchgoers or even most academic philosophers or scientists, my bet is that they will assume, should they have any view at all, that "*creatio ex nihilo*" just means the big bang theory. They will understand it to be a thesis of cosmic origins at the beginning of time. But *creatio ex nihilo* is not, or not predominantly, a cosmogonic theory happily coincident with the big bang theory as long as that theory of the origins of the universe holds scientific sway. To put it bluntly—perhaps a little too bluntly—*creatio ex nihilo* is not a teaching about the cosmos but about God. Thomas Aquinas, for instance, thought that God *could* have created, *ex nihilo*, an everlasting world— that is, a world without beginning or end—although Aquinas believed, on the basis of scripture, that the world in fact had a beginning.[2]

The teaching centrally concerns the power, goodness, and freedom of God, and the dependence of "all that is" (for convenience' sake I will say "the world") on God or, more specifically, on God's free choice to create and to sustain, which comes to the same thing. It is thus, profoundly, a teaching about grace and gift, though it has many other positive ramifications. Christian teaching is that, were God to cease holding the world in being for a moment, it would not be.

Creatio ex nihilo is an emergent teaching in the period of Second Temple Judaism and passes from there into early Christianity. It is not, to my mind, stated straight out in scripture, but nor is it an arbitrary "add-on" from Greek philosophy. On the contrary, *creatio ex nihilo* is not a teaching of Hellenistic philosophy at all, if by that one means the classical sources. David Sedley points out in his *Creationism and Its Critics in Antiquity*, "That even a divine creator would, like any crafts-man, have to use pre-existing materials is an assumption that the an-cient Greeks apparently never questioned." Sedley mentions *creatio ex nihilo* in order to distinguish it from the topic he is addressing in his book, *creationism*, which *was* prevalent and contested amongst ancient philosophers and which he defines as "the thesis that the world's struc-ture and contents can be adequately explained only by postulating at least one intelligent designer, a creator god."[3] It is well to remember the contrast. While the Greek philosophers had "creationisms" in abun-dance, they did not have the radically transcendent deity of Christian orthodoxy.

Neither Plato nor Aristotle had a creator God in the Jewish or Christian sense. Aristotle's god is the source of motion but not of being itself, and Plato's famously mythic *Timaeus*, which remains poetically unclear enough to allow for many construals (many of them subse-quently Christian), has a demiurge that molds preexisting matter. We can find movements toward the Jewish and Christian notion of a creator God in Middle Platonism (first and second centuries CE), and, by the time of Neoplatonists like Plotinus, you have something like a doctrine of creation. But the Neoplatonists were already, as is well documented, influenced by Jewish and Christian writings. To my mind, we should follow Robert Wilken and cease speaking so much of the Hellenistic influences on Christianity and start talking more about the Christian (and Jewish) influences on Hellenism. It seems evident that when *cre-atio ex nihilo*, in some variant, appears in the pagan philosophy of late antiquity, it is not least because of the influence of Jewish ideas about God. Aristotle could understand the concept of *creatio ex nihilo* but thought it absurd, for if there were ever truly nothing—no space, no time, no anything—then there would be nothing now. His view was that the cosmos must be everlasting, a view that I think is held in ever-more-cunning variants by most secular astrophysicists today.

I would suggest we say that *creatio ex nihilo*, if not "in the Bible," is certainly biblical. It is a scripturally driven piece of Christian metaphysics. That is why any adequate reappraisal for today needs expertise in biblical studies, Second Temple Judaism, reception history, patristics, rabbinics, late antique studies, and medieval and modern theology and philosophy (including now philosophy of science), as in this volume. It is all too rare to find a topic which brings all these disciplines together and in addition has real traction in the world of faith and religious apologetics. *Creatio ex nihilo* prompts questions of theological method that cut across our specialist areas and bring the expertise of the professional theologian into the concerns of the faithful—what does it mean to say a teaching is "biblical"? Why and on what basis does a Christian doctrine, accepted since antiquity, become outdated or misleading? How should we "receive" reception history? How does modern biblical criticism engage with a scientific and materialistic culture?

As mentioned, within the panoply of Christian teachings—Christology, anthropology, Trinity, pneumatology—*creatio ex nihilo* is an aspect of the doctrine of God. It is hammered out sometime between the third century BCE and the second century CE as a response, by Jews and Christians, to a fundamental question: Who is the God we worship? *Creatio ex nihilo* is not to be conflated with the "theologies of nature" which have, rightly, developed so much in the past thirty years. It is not, at root, a teaching which bears directly on environmental concerns, our obligation to future generations, our relation to non-human animals, global warming, or migration and population, though it has things to say to all of these. These are all truly important questions, many of them as yet insufficiently addressed by theologians and philosophers of religion, about the created order and the place of the human creature within it. *Creatio ex nihilo* is rather a first-order teaching (fundamental in that sense) which grounds Christian address to these topics *across the board*, as it does Christology, eschatology, and political theology.

The doctrine is not, as mentioned, principally a cosmogonic thesis; it is not primarily about the "beginnings" of the world—that is, if we mean by this temporal beginnings—as are many cosmogonic creation narratives of the ancient Near East and maybe the early chapters of Genesis, although certainly *creatio ex nihilo* has a bearing on to how

Genesis 1–3, as a cosmogonic narrative, has been interpreted and received. The question to which *creatio ex nihilo* is a response is not
"Where did the world come from?" so much as "Who is this God to
whom we pray?" or, more acutely, "Who is the God who will come to
our aid in time of need?" The biblical texts persistently referenced in
early formulations of *creatio ex nihilo* are not from Genesis but from
the Psalms and Isaiah, both full of references to the Creator God but
also to the Redeemer. Indeed the two are often wed. At the heart of the
doctrine are God's power and loving-kindness, qualities which are to
the fore during persecution and oppression, as for Jews during the period of Second Temple Judaism.

If *creatio ex nihilo* is not a rival empirical thesis or scientific contention parallel to the big bang theory but a statement of the dependence of all that is, including space and time, on God, then, as such,
creatio ex nihilo is not incompatible with multiverses or any other
astrophysical theories of world origin, as C. S. Lewis and the Ink-
lings canvassed in their fictional writings many years ago. It does,
however, have a point of impact with scientistic, reductive modern
materialism and thus remains important for contemporary Christian
apologetics.

Having thus laid out my wares, I would like to proceed by first
looking at some of what David Burrell calls "neuralgic points." These
are instances when, as a theologically informed Christian, you become
aware something is wrong. These are just a few instances, to which I
am sure readers can add their own.

First, a conversation reported to me by a theologian friend who
found himself sitting on a plane next to a graduate student in astrophysics. As they discussed their respective vocations, the young astro-
physicist said he used to believe in God but could not do so now because the world was too complex. Question: What kind of a God had
he believed in?

Second, a discussion of my own during a radio broadcast where I
was paired, in a discussion on the doctrine of creation, with a social activist Anglican priest who is also an active media presence. His conviction was that Christians today do not care about the doctrine of creation, and rightly so, he thought, because it does not affect anything
that matters. Question: what "doctrine of creation" is he thinking of?

Third, after church and informally, a parishioner, an educated Catholic but not a theologian, asked me by way of conversation, "What are theologians today saying about creationism?" It was quickly apparent he was not asking my critical view about what scholars and sociologists of religion today call "biblical creationism"—the belief that the world with all its creatures is made by an act of God in six days, thus excluding evolutionary theory (there are many definitions of "biblical creationism"). On the contrary, he was asking what the current teaching on creation was and assuming, as probably many if not most Catholics and other Christians in the pews do, that *the Christian teaching on creation* was, until relatively recently, that the world had been made in six days and this had now been toppled by Darwin, leaving theologians with . . . what? Nothing, or nothing plausible to say. That my questioner should believe this to be the case is not at all surprising since this is the version of the theology of creation pulped out endlessly by campaigning atheists like Richard Dawkins on all the media outlets. Presuming such goes some way to explain the position of my radio vicar, whose apologetic strategy was simply to leap into the "Christians do not care about the doctrine of creation" mode.

Part of the reply to the six-day creationists must be that neither Augustine, Philo, nor a number of theologians of the early church read the early chapters of Genesis in this way. Many of these early readers noted that the sun and the moon were only made on the fourth day, so the Bible could not be describing days in our sense, and so on. The animals, Augustine surmised, might have been created in some seminal form and taken many years to develop as we know them. He did not thus doubt divine design, but he did not shoehorn it into six units of twenty-four hours.

We are not yet at *creatio ex nihilo*, but we can see why its current reticence, or eclipse, is to be regretted. So much public air time has been given in the past thirty years and possibly longer to debates about evolution and the book of Genesis that the person in the street, and even in the pews, just thinks this "is" the heartland of the traditional Christian doctrine of creation. This is not to say debates about cosmogony and evolution are unimportant and uninteresting, but they are not as the foci of the classical theology of creation. The nature of the six days was not, I suggest, foremost in the minds of those formulating the

Nicene and Apostles' Creeds, but rather the conviction that all that is, in heaven and on earth, comes from God, and as in Genesis, *is good*.

I first became concerned about the lack of knowledge regarding the doctrine of *creatio ex nihilo* at a conference on divine action held at the Vatican Observatory in the 1990s. It was the last in a series of such gatherings which involved astrophysicists and theologians. In conversation with George Ellis, a distinguished cosmologist and a Christian, I realized previous discussions had not involved *creatio ex nihilo* as a topic and that the scientists present had not been introduced to the idea. Yet this teaching has been at the core of defense of the possibility of miracles, revelation, and divine activity more broadly for over sixteen hundred years. There had been little or no discussion, for instance, of Aquinas's views (grounded in his commitment to *creatio ex nihilo*) of the ways in which actions can be fully and freely those of natural causation (and by extension human freedom) and also those of God. It was not that *creatio ex nihilo* had been discussed and dismissed; it had not been raised. But if *creatio ex nihilo*, historically so central to Jewish, Christian, and Muslim apologetics on divine action, could not be used apologetically in the face of modern science, then we should at least have a good discussion why not.[4]

In another strand, my own research into the naming and knowing of God had made me aware of the increasing, and increasingly sharp, criticism of what is variously called the "God of classical theism" or the "God of the classical attributes"—particularly, but not solely, from feminist theologians. Whether or not I can be counted as a feminist theologian, I certainly consider myself as a feminist and a theologian, and I do not want to ingest a God who is pure poison—authoritarian, controlling, dominating, homophobic because omnipotent and impassible, and therefore heedless of the stumblings of creation and, by association if nothing else, "male." That there are serious grounds for grievance in the way women have "heard" Christian teaching about the transcendent God I do not doubt. But this reasonable discontent with an anthropomorphic deity has been overlaid with criticism of the "God of the attributes" taken from process theologians and modern Hegelians, and has emerged in an energetic critique which deserves a response.

According to Charles Hartshorne the Christian fathers crippled theology with Hellenistic assumptions.[5] Early Hellenistic encroachment deformed the purity of the Galilean message, leaving us with a sterile, distant, and hostile God who had no means of relating to a changing, suffering world—or, worse, an imperious tyrant, a dominating and crushing power. What Catherine Keller has called a *dominology* thus emerged.

It is, however, difficult actually to read the theologians of the early church and find this loathsome God. Augustine in the *Confessions* praises a God who is utterly transcendent and wholly present—immutable and infinite yet merciful, intimately present, and just. Or we might better say that for Augustine God is merciful and intimately present *because* this God is at the same time eternal, immutable, and infinite. That Augustine was able to bring these two sets of seemingly antagonistic predicates together is precisely a consequence of his to understanding of *creatio ex nihilo*.

It is no longer intellectually credible to oppose biblical and "Hellenistic" assumptions. The findings of biblical scholars and historians of Second Temple Judaism make it evident that Christianity emerges from Hellenistic Judaism and is, in many ways, a form of it. The literate world of Roman antiquity had been "hellenized" to a greater or lesser extent since the time of Alexander's conquests. Writings in Syriac and Samaritan Hebrew bear the influence of Greek thought, as do the letters of Saint Paul and John's Gospel. The theologians of the early church made use of surrounding philosophy—which was already quite a mix of Aristotelian, Stoic, and Platonic thought—and were happy to admit this was so, but their doctrine of God was not taken straight off the shelf from the philosophers. Nor was their teaching of *creatio ex nihilo*. If anything the evidence is just as strong, as I have already suggested, that the indebtedness was the other way around: Christians—and before them Jews—initiated the development of Western metaphysics in the matter of radical divine transcendence.

Here Philo, a Jew of the early first century, is an important witness. I share the view of Jean Daniélou that Philo was the first theologian to treat fully of divine transcendence. John Dillon, too, speaks of Philo's "extreme transcendentalizing" of God and credits this to his Judaism. Philo writes as one happily proud of his Greek philosophical training but faithful, as he sees it, to the God of Abraham. He is happy to reject the philosophers' teaching when it conflicts with that of Moses, and he does so on creation. He explicitly rejects Aristotle's view that the universe is ungenerated and eternal.[6] Philo believes that God has created all things. God has created the world out of nonbeing, molding formless matter. All things are dependent on God, but God is sufficient to himself, and was so before the creation of the world.[7] God "created space and place coincidentally with the material world" (*De confusione linguarum* 136). God created time itself, "for there was no time before the cosmos, but rather it either came into existence together with the cosmos or after it" (*De opificio mundi* 26).[8] The cosmos is totally dependent on God, and God in no sense dependent on the cosmos. And finally, "God, being One, is alone and unique, and like God there is nothing" (*Legum allegoriae* 2.1).[9]

If Philo does not have the doctrine of *creatio ex nihilo* fully formed, then we find in him all the essential building blocks. It is the centrality to Philo of radical divine transcendence that drives his treatment of religious language. Since God cannot strictly be like any created being, we cannot class God or insert God into any category appropriate to our created kind. Thus, strictly speaking, God cannot be named. Philo is our earliest surviving source for certain Greek alpha-privatives which bear directly on naming and knowing God. No name can properly name the Existent (*to on*), but God through his courtesy gives us names in scripture which we may use—for instance "I am the God of Abraham, and the God of Isaac, and the God of Jacob." This unnameability becomes, in Philo, not the point at which philosophy separates us from revelation but the means for demonstrating how much we are in need of revelation.

Maimonides, many centuries later and as far as we can tell with no knowledge of Philo, says remarkably similar things about creation, divine transcendence, and religious language:

> Those who follow the Law of Moses, our Teacher, hold that the whole Universe, i.e., everything except God, has been brought by Him into existence out of non-existence. In the beginning God alone existed and nothing else. . . . He produced from nothing all existing things such as they are, by His will and desire. Even time itself is among the things created; for time depends on motion, i.e., on an accident in things which move, and the things upon whose

motion time depends are themselves created beings, which have passed from non-existence into existence. We say that God *existed* before the creation of the Universe, although the verb *existed* appears to imply the notion of time; we also believe that He existed in infinite space of time before the Universe was created; but in these cases we do not mean time in its true sense. We only use the term to signify something analogous or similar to time. For time is undoubtedly an accident, and, according to our opinion, one of the created accidents.[10]

When discussing Philo in his landmark book on the subject, John Dillon says his stated concern is with Middle Platonism broadly, and he openly admits that he will not go into what is Jewish or might be original philosophizing in Philo's thought.[11] In a footnote Dillon observes the oddity that Philo will often vary the Platonic title "That Which Is" (*to on*) with a more personal form derived from the Septuagint, "He Who Is" (*ho on*). "This may be taken as influence from Judaism," Dillon adds, "and so is of no concern to us."[12] This is perhaps fair enough given his stated concerns, but for anyone interested in Judaism, Christianity, and the subsequent history of Western metaphysics this is surely an interesting and important fusion of readings. Dillon does note Philo's "extreme transcendentalizing" of God and his "greater personal reverence for God" (by contrast to pagan Middle Platonists); both, he thinks, are driven by his Judaism. He adds that this greater reverence is responsible, in Philo's writings, for the occasional "downgrading of the ability of the human intellect (unaided by God's grace) to comprehend truth." But this is a tendentious way of expressing matters. We might just as well speak of Philo's *regrading* of the ability of the human intellect—if God is creator of all that is, and even of time itself, it is no "downgrading" of human capacity to say that we cannot grasp the divine essence! Indeed, as Philo insists, God alone cannot be classed among "things," or creatures—no onto-theological story which folds God into such a sequence can obtain.

When we turn to the contemporary criticism of *creatio ex nihilo*, let us keep in mind Philo's insistence that there was no "time" before the created cosmos but rather time came into existence either together with the cosmos or after it (*De opific.* 26),[13] and remember Augustine's remarks along similar lines as he chides those who ask what God was doing "before" God created the world. Process philosophers did not characteristically aim their guns at *creatio ex nihilo* but at the idea of a God who was somehow independent of and apart from the temporal order. The God of classical theism—immutable, impassible, eternal (in certain senses)—was not, these philosophers argued, the God of the Bible but rather a Hellenistic ghoul to whom no one could relate. They proposed an eternal, or we might better say, an everlasting God inserted within the unfolding of the created order. This approach has proved attractive in recent decades to feminist theologians and some in the science-and-religion debate.

An impressive and influential book which draws on process thought but which is constructed specifically as a critique of *creatio ex nihilo* is Catherine Keller's *The Face of the Deep: A Theology of Becoming*.[14] Themes of Keller's book have been taken further in a book of collected essays, *Theologies of Creation:* Creatio Ex Nihilo *and Its New Rivals*, which contains essays by Keller and Philip Clayton.[15] In her elegiac and passionately written *The Face of the Deep*, Keller attacks the "dominology" of classical theism—a God of unconditioned omnipotence is, in Keller's eyes, a God of unconditioned and oppressive dominance. *Creatio ex nihilo* is implicated throughout, for a God who creates all dominates all. By contrast Keller wants theological openness, freedom, divine gifts, and grace.

From contemporary French feminist theory and especially Luce Irigaray, Keller has embraced the grammar of chaos, fluidity, and uncharted depths. Classical theology and *creatio ex nihilo* are, on her reading, by contrast, concerned with control, division, barriers, fearful of the feminine primal chaos—"tehomophobic," in Keller's coinage.[16] The fathers elided, or effaced, Genesis 1:2 with its primal, feminine chaos in favor of a lineal, managed salvation history.

Hers is thus a campaigning text, richly mixing process thought, postmodern feminism, and biblical studies, and I am full of admiration for it—not least because it is written with real vigor and addresses real needs. Keller lambasts patristic reliance on rhetoric and polemic, while being rhetorical and polemical herself . . . just the strategy they themselves use. I disagree not with her wider ambitions but with her conviction that it is *creatio ex nihilo* which underwrites the evils she wishes to purge from theological practice—misogyny, homophobia, totalitarianism, racism, disdain for the environment. Indeed I want to suggest that the doctrine, when classically deployed, frees us from the Tin-Pot-Despot God she so rightly despises.

Here are a few of her points and some responses.

Keller argues that *creatio ex nihilo* is not scriptural but rather novel and postbiblical. Closer attention to the Bible would show us that Genesis nowhere mandates *creatio ex nihilo*.

To this I would say—"Agreed!," but point out that while Keller draws most of her reflection and criticisms out of the handling by theologians of Genesis 1–3, the grounding biblical texts for the classical elaboration of *creatio ex nihilo* are characteristically, as I have mentioned already, not the Genesis cosmogony but passages, many passages, from the Psalms, Isaiah, and deuterocanonical texts like Judith and 1 and 2 Maccabees, not to mention John's Gospel and the Pauline epistles.

> Our help is in the name of the LORD,
> who made heaven and earth. (Ps. 124:8)

> For he spoke, and it come to be;
> he commanded, and it stood firm. (Ps. 33:9)

> Let all your creatures serve you,
> For you spoke, and they were made. (Jth. 16:14)

While Keller sees that *creatio ex nihilo* is a *possible* paraphrase of Genesis 1, she argues that by adopting it the church fathers closed other hermeneutic options, including more enterprising and embracing forms of Platonism. Instead *creatio ex nihilo* "locked dogma into *'the pure dualism of originating* Logos *and prevenient Nothing.'*"[17] This, she later elaborates, was a "simple form of Hellenistic dualism . . . between the changeless, impassionable eternity of God and the dissolute mutability of the material world. . . . According to the logic of *ex nihilo*," Keller continues, "one is either good or evil, corporeal or incorporeal, eternal or temporal, almighty or powerless, propertied or inferior."[18] This sounds very unpleasant, but it also sounds like the dualistic schemes prevalent in late antiquity which early Christianity was at pains to avoid. We need only look to Augustine and the Manichees. Christianity, unlike Manichaeism, embraced the goodness of creation and of the body. It flew in the face of a world which divided into spiritual (good) and material (bad), and how could a religion whose central teachings were the incarnation—where Godself becomes flesh—and the resurrection of the body do any other?

The best way to address Keller's criticisms, while at the same time not dismissing their existential force, is to say that for Athanasius, the Cappadocians, John Damascene, and Augustine it was precisely *creatio ex nihilo* which slipped the chains of the destructive dualism prevalent in late antiquity where matter was bad and spirit was good. All of the created order, as biblically expressed in the text of Genesis, is good— all of it made by God. The fundamental contrast is not that of corporeal and incorporeal, or material and immaterial, but the contrast between God and creatures—and this is not a "binary" at all.

We may detect here the influence of Gerhard May, on whom Keller and many others, including me, rely. While not himself hostile to *creatio ex nihilo*, May, in his otherwise helpful treatment, puts too much emphasis on the creation of matter. But that "God creates matter" is only one plank, albeit a finalizing and important one, in the raft of teachings which make up *creatio ex nihilo*. Keller and, to a degree, Jon Levenson are false steers in seeing *creatio ex nihilo* as about an immaterial God and a material created order.[19] If we proceed this way, we easily get into binaries—how can an immaterial God relate to a material creation? If God is powerful, we must be diminished. But this, I suggest, is a decidedly *modern* take on the matter. The contrast we see in the church fathers and in the New Testament itself could not possibly be between a material creation and an immaterial God. Philo, Paul, and the Jesus of the Gospels believed in numerous creatures which were not material in our sense—angels, powers, dominions, the soul. The binary, if it is one, in *creatio ex nihilo* is not between the material world and an immaterial God, but between the Creator and *everything else*—space, time, angels, souls, and so on. That, I suggest, is what the Nicene and Apostles' Creeds are at pains to express in insisting that God is the Maker of heaven and earth, of things visible and invisible. The soul, as Athanasius presses home in *De incarnatione*, is just as much a creature as the body. God and creatures are not simply two different kinds of things to be compared and contrasted, with one much bigger—and stronger—than the other. The contrast, to twist Wittgenstein, is too big to be a binary.

This takes us to dominology and hierarchy. If all that is has its being from God, and would not exist even for a microsecond without being held in being by God, then there just cannot be a relation of hierarchy with God at the top and the dust mite, or something much smaller, at the bottom and us in between. God, holding all that is in being, is equally present at all times, to every creaturely reality. This God cannot be the God of Heidegger's "onto-theology," the biggest being amongst beings.

This goes a good deal of the way to addressing a further criticism of Keller's, that *creatio ex nihilo* "closes the border between an immaterial Creator and material creation," truly a disastrous move were it so.[20] But in fact the teaching leads us in quite the opposite direction. *Creatio ex nihilo* allows us to grasp, if not fully comprehend, that God is always already there—nearer and more intimate to us than our own breath. The web of teachings that constitute *creatio ex nihilo* are never far away in medieval spiritual authors—for instance, as Julian of Norwich observes the world as a hazelnut held in her hand: tiny and vulnerable and yet, as she says, suffused with grace. It exists because God loves it.[21]

It is this intimacy of God to creation which I think allows for exciting reworkings for *creatio ex nihilo* in the contemporary science-and-religion debate, while not moving away from classical teaching as do, to my mind, various new forms of panentheism such as Philip Clayton's "open kenotic panentheism." *Creatio ex nihilo* rules out panentheism, for the world is in no sense part of God's body. The world is entirely dependent on God, but God is not dependent on the world. The world exists as continually gift and grace, and God's moment of creation is not some time long past but now. It is such insights that are behind modern retrievals of the theology of participation.

Rowan Williams's Gifford Lectures, *The Edge of Words*, play with this idea. He asks what we may deduce about God from the fact that we are speaking beings, that our universe is such that it generates, through whatever processes natural to it, creatures not only of intelligence but of speech.[22] Intelligence cannot be alien or an add-on to the natural world, or it would never—at least in secular terms—have arisen. But plainly it has.

Although Williams does not draw on it, there are interesting parallels with Galen Strawson's defense of panpsychism—the view that consciousness in some sense goes all the way down. Strawson, an analytic philosopher and an atheist, pitches against the modern binary of matter/spirit, especially in the form of the "mind/body problem." His argument is that the mind/body problem dissolves if we admit that the physical world just does give rise to consciousness. We cannot rest in the dualism he ascribes to Daniel Dennett, "where the experiential and the physical are utterly and irreconcilably different."[23] Williams is on similar grounds when he says we need to move beyond the lazy Cartesianism which sees the world as a crude dualism of "pure structure versus mindless stuff."[24]

Contemporary science, indeed science for the last one hundred years, has been unable to consider the world as Newton's collision of inert billiard balls. Instead all that is, materially, speaking, is energy. And indeed it appears that the universe is a network of energy and of communication, suffused and held in being by the Word who became flesh.

We have come, almost without noticing, to Christology, and here need to mark a central tenet of the traditional doctrine of creation which is submerged to the point of eclipse if our focus is a debate on the six days of Genesis and evolution. It is the Christian teaching that the world is made by God's Word, that same Word who became flesh and lived among us. To be biblical, any doctrine of creation must be christological. Far from being distant from us, the God through whom all things are made is the one through whom we exist; thus Saint Paul in 1 Corinthians: "For us there is one God, the Father, from whom are all things and for whom we exist, and one Lord, Jesus Christ, through whom are all things and through whom we exist" (1 Cor. 8:6). And in the deutero-Pauline Letter to the Colossians, "He is the image of the invisible God, the firstborn of all creation; for in him all things in heaven and on earth were created, things visible and invisible, whether thrones or dominions or rulers or powers—all things have been created through him and for him" (Col. 1:15–16).

This deserves more than space allows, as do Keller's arguments, but by summary I would suggest that the energy behind contemporary critics of *creatio ex nihilo* comes not as a new disquiet but an old one—one found in Hume but repristinated across the nineteenth-century critics of religion: Feuerbach, Freud, and Marx. It is that if God is elevated, then man is denigrated. It is curious, since so much postmodern and feminist thought has been at pains to expose binaries, that this one appears again and again. It must be one that Christianity addresses, and

I suggest it can do so by recovering the part of the doctrine of God unfolded through *creatio ex nihilo*. In this our creatureliness cannot be subordination but comes as gift. Julian of Norwich puts this "littleness" (which cannot be contrastive) in perspective:

> And he showed me more, a little thing, the size of a hazelnut, on the palm of my hand, round like a ball. I looked at it thoughtfully and wondered, "What is this?" And the answer came, "It is all that is made." I marvelled that it continued to exist and did not suddenly disintegrate; it was so small. And again my mind supplied the answer, "It exists, both now and for ever, because God loves it."[25]

Everything lives, moves, and has its being in God. Everything is grace, everything gift. The world is not random chaos but good. God is not nowhere but everywhere. This may be a hard teaching in times of pain, but the alternative is far worse.

NOTES

1. The Apostles' Creed. I will return later to say why it is *creatio ex nihilo* and not some other creational teaching invoked by that creedal clause.

2. Thomas Aquinas, *Summa Theologiae* I.46.2.

3. Sedley, David, *Creationism and Its Critics in Antiquity* (Berkeley: University of California Press, 2009), xvii. Paul Blowers's excellent *Drama of the Divine Economy* (New York: Oxford University Press, 2012) makes good use of Sedley and provides an extremely helpful guide to early creation theology.

4. This led to the further Vatican Observatory conference devoted to *creatio ex nihilo*, organized by Bill Stoeger, David Burrell, and me, with Jewish, Muslim, and Christian contributors—philosophers, scientists, and theologians. This became C. Cogliati, D. Burrell, J. Soskice, and W. Stoeger, *Creation and the God of Abraham* (Cambridge: Cambridge University Press, 2010).

5. See Philip Clayton, "Creation *ex nihilo* and Intensifying the Vulnerability of God," in *Theologies of Creation: Creatio ex Nihilo and Its New Rivals*, ed. Thomas Jay Oord (New York: Routledge, 2015).

6. Philo, *On the Creation of the Cosmos according to Moses*, introduction, translation, and commentary by David T. Runia (Atlanta: Society of Biblical Literature, 2001), §171. Hereafter *De opific.* All other references to Philo are from the Loeb edition, trans. F. H. Coulson.

7. "How must it not be impossible to recompense or to praise as He deserves Him who brought the universe out of non-existence?" (*Legum allegoriae* 3.10). "He is full of Himself and sufficient for Himself. It was so before the creation of the world, and is equally so after the creation of all that is. He cannot change nor alter and needs nothing else at all, so that all things are His but He Himself in the proper sense belongs to none" (*De mutatione nominum* 4.27). "Through His goodness He begat all that is, through His sovereignty He rules what he has begotten" (*De cherubim* 27–28). See also *De fuga et inventione* 46, *De vita Mosis* 2.267.

8. See Runia's comment on this in *On the Creation of the Cosmos*, 157.

9. Debates concerning whether we find in Philo a consistent teaching of *creatio ex nihilo* rumble on and depend, often, on what elements of this "raft" of teachings are taken as definitive. Frequently debate revolves around the question of whether Philo sees God as creating from some primal matter, after the manner of the *Timaeus*, or by divine fiat. The two are not strictly incompatible, however, since it is possible to hold that God created the primal matter from which the world is fashioned. This seems to be Philo's position. Later thinkers would argue that this *could* be an eternal matter, without violating its total dependence on God.

10. Moses Maimonides, *The Guide for the Perplexed*, trans. M. Friedlander (New York: Dover Publications, 1956), pt. 2, ch. 13, p. 171.

11. John Dillon, *The Middle Platonists* (London: Duckworth, 1977). He writes, "Our concern in this work is not with Philo as a whole, . . . but simply with the evidence he provides for contemporary Platonism. We cannot, therefore, go into the Jewish side of his thought, such as that was, or into any aspect of his philosophizing which may possibly be original to himself" (144). Philo, he believes, had little influence on the course of Middle Platonism, "though he certainly influenced the Christian Platonists of Alexandria, Clement and Origen." Why these should not be called "Middle Platonists" is another dispute.

12. Remarkably, the context is God's relation to the world and the question whether, given that Philo is our first extant source for certain negative names of God, Philo is responsible for introducing the notion of the "unknowable" God into Greek thought. Dillon, *Middle Platonists*, 155.

13. See Runia's comment on this in Philo, *On the Creation of the Cosmos*, 157.

14. Catherine Keller, *The Face of the Deep: A Theology of Becoming* (London: Routledge, 2003).

15. See note 5. The first footnote of Oord's introduction to his edited volume cites both *Creation and the God of Abraham* and *Modern Theology* 29, no. 2 (April 2013), "Creation 'ex Nihilo' and Modern Theology," as places where one may read the views of the advocates of the teaching. This is a lively current debate.

16. Keller, *Face of the Deep*, 26.

17. Ibid., 10.

18. Ibid., 46, 49.

19. See Jon Levenson, *Creation and the Persistence of Evil: The Jewish Drama of Divine Omnipotence* (Princeton: Princeton University Press, 1994).

20. Keller, *Face of the Deep*, 60.

21. Note that she sees "the whole world" not held in God's hand as the Sunday school hymn goes and which could suggest dominology to the infant mind, but in *her own* hand.

22. Rowan Williams, *The Edge of Words: God and the Habits of Language* (London: Bloomsbury, 2014).

23. Galen Strawson, "Realistic Monism: Why Physicalism Entails Panpsychism," in *Consciousness and Its Place in Nature: Does Physicalism Entail Panpsychism?*, ed. Anthony Freeman (Exeter: Imprint Academic, 2006), 5.

24. Williams, *Edge of Words*, xi.

25. Julian of Norwich, *Revelations of Divine Love*, trans. Clifton Wolters (London: Penguin Books, 1966), 68.

CHAPTER 3

Creatio ex nihilo in the Old Testament/Hebrew Bible

RICHARD J. CLIFFORD, S.J.

Most contemporary biblical scholars recognize that the formulation of the Christian doctrine of *creatio ex nihilo* was largely the result of second- and third-century debates with Gnosticism and related intellectual currents, but would nonetheless argue that the doctrine has a good biblical basis, especially in Old Testament texts. The Bible speaks many times of the Lord's powerful creative act that brought the world from chaos into being, and of the goodness and worth of the material world. Given the focus of this volume on creation from nothing, I will concentrate my attention on the movement from chaos to cosmos. The perspective is a natural one, for ancient Near Eastern poets frequently gave attention to the precreation state reversed by the creative act. A consistent interest of the Notre Dame conference that generated this volume was precisely what is revealed in the transition from precreation to the created state, and it is worthwhile to see whether some ancient texts had similar perspectives and what conclusions might be drawn from those texts.

In this essay I will first note the differences between ancient and modern cosmogonies, then briefly survey relevant cosmogonies of Israel's neighbors, and, finally, examine major biblical cosmogonies, limiting myself to their transitions from "nothing" to "something." The examination of biblical cosmogonies will be partial rather than complete.

ANCIENT VERSUS MODERN VIEWS OF CREATION

Important differences between ancient and modern Western conceptions of creation are often not sufficiently appreciated. Modern conceptions, especially those formed under the under the well-nigh-universal assumption of evolution, tend to underestimate how important the first instance of a created reality was to ancient thinkers.

There are four major differences between ancient and modern assumptions about creation.[1] The first is the process. Ancient Near Eastern peoples generally imagined cosmogonies on the model of human activity (building, begetting, a king's powerful utterance, defeating an enemy) or a natural process such as an egg hatching or a fertile hillock left behind by the receding Nile flood. Sometimes a cosmogony involved wills in conflict in which the victor imposed his own arrangement of the universe. Moderns, on the other hand, see creation as the impersonal interaction of physical forces extending over eons and reject any psychologizing of the process.

The most significant difference, however, is the result or product of the act of creation. Ancients did not make the dichotomous modern distinction between "nature" and human beings. For them the terminus of creation was human society organized for the service of the gods, often including kingship, language, the arts of agriculture—in short, culture and crafts. Moderns, on the other hand, usually see the terminus of creation as the physical world, typically our planet within its solar and stellar systems, which is one reason modern cosmology often includes astronomy. Human community and culture do not usually come into consideration. If life is discussed, it is life in its simplest biological sense.

Other differences between ancient and modern conceptions follow from the two mentioned above. Ancients tended to tell stories to describe creation, whereas moderns customarily make use of scientific reports. Scientific reports assume an evolutionary perspective (primitive to developed, simple to complex) and are impersonal. Scientists offer fresh hypotheses to take account of new data, whereas ancients devised stories, or varied existing ones, when they wished to explain a particular aspect of their world. It is not always easy for modern people, who typically regard a story as either entertainment or illustration, to take the story itself as a carrier of serious meaning. But for the ancients, who often saw creation as involving wills, story was a natural way of reporting. Nuances and perspective were conveyed by the selection and omission of narrative detail and plot variations. The ancients' acceptance of different versions of creation is traceable to this understanding. Furthermore, moderns expect an account of creation to explain *all* the data and be compatible with established theories. The criterion of truth for ancient Near Eastern cosmogonies, on the other hand, was compatibility with tradition and dramatic plausibility. Drama selects, omits, concentrates; it need not render a complete account. An ancient cosmogony can be about a single reality and leave others out of consideration.

A final clarification regarding terminology is necessary. The English word "chaos," used to describe the state preceding the creative act, can be misleading when used of ancient accounts. Chaos in modern speech ordinarily implies disorder and random motion. Yet precreation in many ancient texts was a state of inertia, nonmotion, absence of key elements of society, nonsolidity, and total darkness.

THE COSMOGONIES OF ISRAEL'S NEIGHBORS

Sumerian cosmogonies (third and early second millennia BCE), written in a non-Semitic language, influenced the Akkadian (Semitic language) cosmogonies, some of which influenced the Bible. Despite their only indirect influence on the Bible, they are worth a brief review, because of their special interest in the precreation period. According to the authoritative synthesis of Jan van Dijk, Sumerian literature had two creation systems: "cosmic," based in the city of Nippur, which involved earth and sky, and "chthonic," based in the city of Eridu, which involved only earth. In "cosmic" creation, the gods An (heaven, the sky god) and Ki (earth) create by their marriage act, and their firstborn, Enlil, separates them. Humans emerge plant-like from the earth. An embryonic universe, where the gods of inchoate culture lived, preexisted creation; it was conceived as a "primeval city," *uru* (*uru-ul-la*), ruled over by a lord, *en* (*en-uru-ul-la*).

In the "chthonic" system, Enki, personified underground water, creates by impregnating the rivers and fertilizing earth. The chthonic system presupposed the existence of earth and focused on the moment when abundant waters made life bloom upon it—vegetative, animate, and human. After the earth bloomed, culture was introduced.[2] In both cosmic and chthonic systems (and in later Akkadian cosmogonies) the gods at creation assigned each person or thing a "destiny" or essence (*namtar* = Akkadian *šimtu*), and they determined the course of the universe, *gišḫur*. The origin was the defining moment; that is why people took cosmogonies so seriously. One can readily see how "non-evolutionary" is an outlook that privileges an entity's moment of origin, rather than its later development.

The concreteness of precreation nothingness is clear in the opening lines of a 276-line composition in the chthonic tradition, *Enki and Ninhursag*.[3]

> At Dilmun, no crow cries "ka'gu,"
> no francolin [type of partridge] goes "dardar,"
> [15]no lion kills,
> no wolf takes a lamb.
> Unknown is the dog herding the goats,
> unknown is the pig, eater of grain.
> The widow does not spread malt on the roof,
> [20]no bird in the sky forages for it.
> No dove goes with head held high.
> No one with eye disease says, "I have an eye disease,"
> no one with a head disease says, "I have a head disease."
> No old woman says, "I am an old woman,
> [25]no old man says, "I am an old man."
> No young woman, not yet bathed, makes her ablutions in the city.
> No man crossing the river cries, ". . ."
> No herald tours the frontiers in his charge.
> No singer utters a *joyous song*,
> [30]a lamentation at the end of the city. [And so on.]

Precreation here is the absence of particular elements of society rather than abstract nothingness. Society is a system with distinctions, for example, between animals in contact with human beings and those not in contact (the herding dog in line 17 is the transition between the two). Life is portrayed as action, and nonlife as nonaction.

Akkadian cosmogonies demonstrably influenced biblical accounts. The clearest influences are that of the flood account in *Gilgamesh* XI on Genesis 6–8 and that of the plot of *Atrahasis*—creation, fault, flood, and renewal of creation—on Genesis 1–11.[4]

Most Akkadian cosmogonies are short and function bound, that is, part of an operation or ritual. The wide variety of verbs of creation in such accounts suggests there was no single underlying concept of creating, for example, "to make appear," "to give a name," and by far the most common verb, *banû*, "to build; to beget, generate." As in Sumerian, destinies or characterizations were fixed on the day of creation, which is exemplified by the "Incantation against Toothache."[5]

[1]After Anu [had created heaven],
Heaven had created [*banû*] [the earth],
The earth had created the rivers,
The rivers had created the canals,
The canals had created the marsh,
(And) the marsh had created the worm—
The worm went, weeping, before Shamash [the sun god],
His tears flowing before Ea:
"What wilt thou give me for my food?
What will thou give me for my sucking?"
"I shall give thee the ripe fig
(And) the apricot."
"Of what use are they to me, the ripe fig,
and the apricot?
[10]Lift me up among the teeth
And the gums cause me to dwell!
The blood of the tooth I will suck,
And of the gum I will gnaw
Its *roots*!"
Fix the pin and seize its foot.
Because thou hast said this, O worm,

May Ea smite thee with the might
Of his hand.

The sufferer reminds the gods that the worm should not be eating his gums, for the gods originally designed the worm to eat rotten fruit. The toothache violates the gods' original intent.

Function-bound cosmogonies often center on the temple, a reminder that the gods created the human race to serve them in temples, where they collected what was due them. For the same reason the king is important as the organizer of the gods' human servants. In all Akkadian texts, humans are created to be slaves of the gods.

Cosmogonies also occur in the prefaces of the long-popular genre of disputation in which two creatures debate which of the two is more noble and more useful to the human race. The creatures often begin by describing their moment of origin.[6] The introduction to the disputation *Palm and Tamarisk* tells of the creation of the two plant contestants. Wilcke has reconstructed the Emar version.[7]

[1-5]In light-filled days, in dark n[ights], in [far-off] years, when the gods had founded (*kunnu*) the land, had built (*epēšu*) cities for far-off humans, when they had heaped up the mountains and dug the canals that give life to the land, the gods of the land met in assembly. Anu, Enlil, (and) Ea deliberated together; among them sat Shamash, and in their midst sat the great Mistress of the gods.
[6-11]Formerly kingship did not exist in the land, and rule was given to the gods. But the gods grew fond of the black-headed people and g[ave?] them a king. The people] of the land of Kish assembled around him so that he might protect (? them). The king planted a date palm in his palace, the space around it he filled with tamarisk(s). In the shadow of the tamarisks, meals were served; in the shadow of the date palm, the crafts were grouped, the drum was beaten—the people rejoiced, the palace exulted.

The cosmogony culminates in the king's planting the date palm and tamarisk on his palace grounds.

A second group of Akkadian creation accounts are lengthy and are not function bound. They explore and explain existential themes and then deal with postcreation reality; in this they somewhat resemble the

Sumerian chthonic Enki traditions, which talk about human culture and civilization. Two are especially relevant for the Bible. The first is called *Atrahasis*, composed in the eighteenth century BCE; it assumes the existence of the earth and explains why humans were created and why are they mortal. The second is *Enuma Elish*, eleventh century or, according to some, the eighteenth century, which explains how Marduk achieved the first place in the Babylonian pantheon.

Atrahasis begins with the striking line, "When gods were men," that is, a subordinate class of gods known as the Igigi, who were slaves of an upper class of gods, the Anunnaki. Eventually the Igigi rebel. At the urging of Ea the god of wisdom and the mother goddess, the gods permit substitute workers to be created from the blood of the chief rebel god and clay. The solution works well at first, but the noise of an ever-expanding race angers the sleepless gods, who send an annihilating flood to wipe out the race. But Ea, unwilling to destroy his handiwork, tells his favorite, Atrahasis, to build an ark. Initially angry at Ea's stratagem, the gods soon relent when they realize how much they depend on human workers. Ea creates a revised human race, this time building in population controls, among which the most striking is mortality; humans will have a life span and will no longer propagate without limit. If one uses the criteria I outlined in the beginning of this essay, *Atrahasis* must be classed as a creation account. W. G. Lambert regards it as " 'a Babylonian history of mankind,' for it begins with the universe in essentially its present form and takes up the circumstances which led up to the creation of man, with subsequent history up to the flood";[8] but several ancient cosmogonies begin in the same way, presuming the existence of the world and explaining how certain features became part of human life.

Atrahasis has another claim on our attention, its plot: creation, fault, flood, and new creation. Though the plot of Genesis 1–11 cannot be proven to be directly dependent on *Atrahasis*, the plots of both (and other models as well) attest to a genre used to explore "philosophical" and "theological" issues of the era.[9]

Another lengthy cosmogony, *Enuma Elish*, is sometimes called "*the* creation epic." In his long-awaited *Babylonian Creation Myths* (2013), W. G. Lambert asserts (in my opinion too sweepingly) that "other than *Enuma Elish* there is no systematic treatment of cosmology in Sumero-Babylonian Literature."[10] *Enuma Elish* begins with two beings, Apsû and Tiāmat; neither name bears the dingir sign signifying divinity. It is possible to take a political interpretation: Tiāmat is the personified doublet of Apsû, created for the sake of setting up rival kingships. The poet is perhaps more interested in politics—rival lines of kingship—than in natural phenomena. The gods are created within them (line 9), and the theogony funnels down to the god Ea, who slays Apsû by an incantation. Apsû and Tiāmat became hostile to the gods born within them. After Apsû's death, power is exercised by Tiāmat and his general Kingu. The latter royal line is contrasted throughout the epic with another line, that of Lahmu and Lahamu, Anshar and Kishar, Anu, Ea, and Marduk. In a battle of rival dynasties, Ea vanquishes Apsû and builds a palace to commemorate his victory. Ea's victory and the palace built to commemorate it foreshadow the greater conflict to come between Marduk and Tiāmat.

When Tiāmat eventually arises in anger, the assembly of gods commission Marduk to do what they are not able to do—go forth to battle Tiāmat. The assembly proclaims Marduk's destiny to be supreme for the duration of the emergency, and after he gains victory, they grant him permanent supremacy. He constructs the universe from Tiāmat's body, splitting it in two and making the upper part the heavens and the lower part earth. His city of Babylon became central, replacing Nippur, the city of Enlil, as the gods' meeting place. The gods build Esagil as his temple. Empowered by his tremendous victory, Marduk creates humankind from the blood of the rebel god, "on whom he imposed the service of the gods, and set the gods free" (VI.34, Lambert). The epic ends after Marduk is given fifty names glorifying him.

Enuma Elish is not interested in providing information about how the world began, but in showing how Marduk, even before his birth, was destined to contain the chaotic forces represented by Tiāmat and Kingu and to take over the power of the gods (Ea and Enlil) who preceded him. Marduk attained undisputed kingship by defeating the rival claimant, Tiāmat, and fashioning the universe from her corpse, including humans as slaves to maintain the universe. This interpretation views chaos in political terms—arbitrary and irrational political rule, exercised without the permission of the assembly of the gods, and sometimes associated with primordial powers. Creation, on the other hand, consists of political stability and peace.

Egyptian cosmogonies generally have not been regarded as influencing the Bible, with the possible exception of the *Memphite Theology* (a thirteenth-century text), which some scholars see as an inspiration for creation by word in Genesis 1. The composition celebrates the god Ptah of Memphis, the most important Egyptian city during the Old and Middle Kingdoms. Ptah was an artisan who was thought to "in-form" or imprint material with his mental image. As an artisan, by his actions he made an immaterial image into something material. For that reason, some scholars have suggested a parallel to Genesis 1.

Ugaritic cosmogonies, all mythological texts originating before 1200 BCE, in a Northwest Semitic language and poetic style akin to classical biblical Hebrew poetry, depict the struggles for royal power between the storm god Baal Haddu and his adversaries Mot (Death) and Yammu (Sea). The senior god El, though weak, nonetheless has the power to declare winners in the struggle. There are no creation-from-nothing accounts of the kind found in Mesopotamia or the Bible; the world already exists, and the concern is maintaining the universe against disturbances by the destructive Sea and infertile Mot (Death). Conflict takes place within an agricultural framework. Dominance by Mot results in famine; dominance by Baal brings rain and fertility. It is possible that the Ugaritic stories reflect the alternation of agricultural seasons of the Levant—wet and fertile cool seasons (winter) and the hot and arid summers.

There are remarkably close parallels between scenes in these texts and biblical passages, for example, conflict with sea in Exodus 15, Psalm 89, and Psalm 93, and conflict with death / wilderness sterility as in Deuteronomy 32 and Isaiah 43:16–21. But there is nothing like the major biblical cosmogonies of Genesis 1–3 and Proverbs 8:22–31, which are concerned with creation from chaos.

BIBLICAL CREATION ACCOUNTS

The major biblical accounts occur in five groups: (1) Genesis 1–11; (2) communal laments: Psalms 44, 74, 77, 80, 83, 89; (3) hymns, such as Psalm 93; (4) Isaiah 40–55; and (5) wisdom literature: Proverbs 8 and Job.[11] Instead of extended exegeses, I will offer observations on the movement from chaos to order in these accounts.

Genesis 1

One of the text's functions may be unappreciated by modern audiences: it is introductory, like many ancient cosmogonies, especially the Akkadian disputations discussed above. In a thought world unmarked by evolutionary assumptions, the first moment of the universe, its instant of origin, said volumes about the divine purpose in directing subsequent history. Genesis 1 lifts up themes that readers were meant to notice as they read Genesis, and indeed the entire Pentateuch, which was edited for an exilic audience: God's easy mastery over unpromising matter, life on earth as self-renewing and ineradicable, the dignity of all humans as bearers of the image of God and rulers of the universe, and humans' mandate to continue in existence through having children ("be fruitful and multiply") and acquiring their own territory ("fill the earth and subdue it"). It is perhaps because the Pentateuch's original readers were so anxious about their future existence and returning to their own land that Genesis 1 emphasizes so strongly the enormous gap that once existed between inert chaos and the life-filled universe that God drew from it.

I will concentrate on how that enormous gap between opening chaos and orderly end was overcome. The description of chaos in verse 2 is exceptionally detailed. I will try to make the case that verse 2 influences the entire cosmogony. Step by step, chaos—dark, unseen, motionless, dead—is transformed into a cosmos, shining with light, teeming with life, and ruled over by God's earthly servants, depicted with royal traits (the image of God).

The pace of the transformation of chaos (v. 2) into beauty ("good," or "very good," seven times across the narrative) is unhurried and majestic. Chaotic elements mentioned in 1:2 reappear in later verses as tamed and harmonious, for example, the depiction of the earth as formless and dark and the waters as wind-swept is reversed in the summary verse in 2:1, "Thus the heavens and the earth were finished, and all their host" (NRSV "multitude"). Though word studies of the vocabulary in 1:2 are of value, the best clue to understanding the transformation is the divine actions required to undo chaos.

Fortunately, the recent retranslation of verses 1–3 by the New Jewish Publication Society Translation (NJPS) and the New American

Bible Revised (NABR), based on excellent evidence, enables us to see an important point obscured by the traditional translation of verse 1 in isolation, "In the beginning, God created heaven and earth." The new translation: "In the beginning *when* God created the heavens and the earth, the earth was a formless void and darkness covered the face of the deep, while a wind from God swept over the face of the waters. *Then* God said, 'Let there be light'; and there was light" (emphasis added). This translation tells us something genuinely new and important, that is, the very first act of creation is the divine luminescence lighting up impenetrable darkness and hiddenness, separating thick darkness into night and allowing light to be day. It is a separation rather than a destruction, which is a mark of effortless divine action. Divine light as transformative radiance is attested also in Psalm 104:1–2: "You are clothed with honor and majesty, wrapped in light as with a garment." The next step taken by God continues to dismantle the chaotic mass, separating the unconfined, smothering waters into waters above (providing rain) and waters below (providing springs and wells). Into the untamed waters God thrusts an inverted dome, bringing earth into visibility and fertility from the water of rain and springs. The onomatopoetic Hebrew phrase *tōhû wābōhû*, "formless void," describes the encompassing waters. Freed from the waters, earth begins to bloom, able to enliven itself through the seeds of plants and the animals described in the verses that follow. No longer inert, it becomes the home of countless life forms.

A final and climactic reversal of inactive chaos becomes clear when the whole text is surveyed. We understand at the end what Genesis 1 considers to be the very essence of life—motion, in particular *self-motion*, the antithesis of the inertia of chaos. The very structure of Genesis makes it clear. The six days of creation form matching panels; for example, Day 1 matches Day 4, Day 2 matches Day 5, and so forth. The two panels are balanced, the first describing the *making* of the three domains of earth, skies, seas, and the second, the *populating* of those domains with mobile inhabitants, each classified by their mode of locomotion through their environment—animals crawling or walking on all fours upon land, birds flying through the air by flapping their wings, fish moving through the waters by their fins. The definitive defeat of chaotic inertia is a universe filled with mobile creatures moving under their own power. Life is conceived as a kind of "vitalism," self-movement. One thinks of the Hebrew idiom for running water, *mayyîm ḥayyîm,* "living water."

Another point should be made about the forward thrust of the text. Readers cannot fail to notice the idyllic quality of the scenario: strikingly unlike Genesis 2–11, chapter 1 makes no mention of sin. Instead, the created world, including the human race, is declared "good," even "very good," seven times! Why? Let me speculate: this is the world that God intends, and therefore this is the world that will, at the consummation of human history, exist. To alter slightly the ancient Christian prayer, the Gloria: "as it was in the beginning, is *not* now, but will be forever." Genesis 1 is eschatological as well as protological.

To summarize, the easy and total transformation of chaos in Genesis 1 communicated to exiled and defeated Israel the good news that God had the capacity to create them once again to be a fruitful and great people dwelling in their own land.[12] Moreover, the transformed earth was destined to be permanent.

Genesis 2–3

Like the chthonic tradition in Sumerian and *Atrahasis,* the story opens with the world already in existence, though it differs, as in those antecedents, from the world of today. Startlingly different from Genesis 1, it cannot be harmonized with the earlier passage through any amount of exegetical ingenuity: in Genesis 2–3 creation takes longer than six days, the man is created before the animals, and the man and the woman are created separately. Unbothered by what modern readers might consider contradictions, an ancient editor placed here a cosmogony that was evidently less interested in the origin of the world than in explaining how the first man and the woman became the creatures they are today.[13]

Since our interest is in the movement from chaos to order, from "before" to "after," I point out two significant before-and-after scenarios in Genesis 2–3, one "agricultural" and the other "anthropological." The two scenarios deal with what is most defining in humans, one mainly affecting the male in that culture (farming), and the other affecting mainly the female (bearing and raising children). Before the couple sinned, agriculture consisted in tending the garden of God, which was irrigated by an ever-flowing stream from the Deep branching into four rivers fertilizing the earth. After the sin, the couple was expelled into a new agricultural system in which the man laboriously tilled soil that was dependent on rain. The soil had been there from the beginning, of course, but it was dormant, for "there was no one to till the ground" (Gen. 2:5).

In the "anthropological" scenario, the man and the woman before they sinned enjoyed fullness of life and knowledge simply by being in the presence of the living and wise God. (The garden was considered to be an extension of the house of God.) To be sure, they were not inherently immortal like heavenly beings, formed as they were from earth, nor did they have the wisdom of heavenly beings. But such limits did not matter as long as they were in *God's* garden. After the sin, "death" in the sense of living outside Eden, the sphere of life, was imposed on humans. Humans now had a life span.

Genesis 2–3 is not about the origin of the universe but only one part of it—human beings. It explains how two defining elements, one affecting males and the other, females, came to be, for they were not there originally. The man is seen in his role as a farmer, and the woman as a wife and mother. Just as mortality was not in the earliest divine design according to *Atrahasis*, Genesis 2–3 makes clear that laborious rain-dependent farming and hazardous childbearing were not what God first had in mind for the human race; the change in design came about through humans' fault. (In *Atrahasis*, the fault was the gods'.) Because of the couple's own limitations and proclivity to sin, humans now have to live in a more circumscribed and limited world than the one God originally intended.

Genesis 2–3 accounts for the gap between God's intent for humans and their actual state. God intended them to live in right relationship with him in his own dwelling, but the reality is that they must eke out a laborious and sometimes perilous existence outside the garden. The reason for the gap was the couple's decision to go outside their relationship with God to acquire knowledge proper to another order of beings. Their act of eating forbidden fruit was both an act of disobedience and an act of idolatry.

Their disobedience is obvious, their idolatry less so. The couple went for the gift and bypassed the giver, vividly illustrating Hosea 2:8:

"[Israel] did not know that it was I who gave her the grain, the wine, and the oil, and who lavished upon her silver and gold that they used for Baal." The prophet Hosea indicted the people for seeking from other gods the benefits that were in reality gifts of the Lord. The man and woman in Eden sought to be wise with stolen heavenly knowledge instead of living on earth with God.

They did not lose everything, however. Though the pair missed out on the fullness of life and wisdom intended for them, they came away with a lesser version of each. They continued to live, but not in the garden of Eden. And as for wisdom, they learned the essential human knowledge of how to farm the soil and beget the next generation. Their descendants could access the garden and the tree of life by visiting God's dwelling, seeking wisdom, and living according to God's word. Expulsion from the garden of Eden may have pushed the man and the woman into a harder existence, but it gave the human race an indelible image of a future life with God.

Communal Lament (Petition) Psalms

The psalms recite before God and the community the glorious founding events whose long-term effect has been called into question by the present disaster. The prayer is that God will "remember" the ancient deed and renew it so as to shame Israel's enemies who rejoice in their downfall. Of the many such laments (44; 74; 77; 80; 83; 89), Psalm 74 complains of the destruction of the temple. As this psalm tells it, the temple memorialized the Lord's slaying of the chaos monster; it symbolized the secure and safe world established by that victory over chaos. Psalm 74 devotes six of its twenty-three verses (vv. 12–17) to describing that act of creation.

> [12]Yet God my King is from of old,
>> working salvation in the earth.
> [13]You divided the sea by your might;
>> you broke the heads of the dragons in the waters.
> [14]You crushed the heads of Leviathan;
>> you gave him as food for the creatures of the wilderness.
> [15]You cut openings for springs and torrents;
>> you dried up ever-flowing streams.

[16]Yours is the day, yours also the night;
   you established the luminaries and the sun.
[17]You have fixed all the bound of the earth;
   you made summer and winter.
[18]Remember this, O LORD, how the enemy scoffs,
   and an impious people reviles your name.

The psalmist presumes chaos has reemerged and asks God to act as king once again by conquering chaotic forces represented by the enemies of Israel and by rebuilding the temple. Verses 13–14 list the chaotic forces to be vanquished, and verses 15–17 describe creation as paired (orderly) elements—organizing the cosmic waters to fertilize the earth (v. 15; cf. Gen. 1:6–10; Ps. 104:5–9; Prov. 3:19–20; 8:27–29), arranging darkness into a beneficial night-day sequence (Ps. 74:16; cf. Gen. 1:3–4), and demarcating the agricultural year (Ps. 74:17; cf. Ps. 104:19–23). The destruction of the temple signaled the destabilizing of creation and diminishment of the creator's glory.

The psalmist acknowledges that creation did not eliminate evil once and for all, but that chaos threatens and can reappear. One can pray, as this psalm does, that God will reassert his kingship and reestablish cosmic order.[14]

Enthronement Hymn: Psalm 93

The most accurate translation of the opening phrase of the psalm, *Yhwh mālāk*, is "The LORD has become king." It is generally avoided by translators, however, in favor of the more bland "The LORD is king," on the grounds that "The LORD has become king" might suggest that Lord was once not king. The hymn clearly celebrates a moment when the Lord is recognized as having defeated the chaotic forces of flood / mighty waters / sea, establishing his palace, and issuing his decrees. Creation is a past event that can be annually celebrated, probably in the New Year Festival.[15]

Isaiah 40–55

Like the communal laments and enthronement psalms, Isaiah 40–55 views God's creation victory as a past event capable of being reactivated and recelebrated. Differently from the psalms, however, Isaiah explicitly places in parallel primordial creation and Israel's creation in the exodus; for example:

> Awake, awake, put on strength, O arm of the LORD! Awake, as in days of old, the generations of long ago! Was it not you who cut Rahab in pieces, who pierced the dragon? Was it not you who dried up the sea, the waters of the great deep; who made the depths of the sea a way for the redeemed to cross over? So the ransomed of the LORD shall return, and come to Zion with singing; everlasting joy shall be upon their heads. (51:9–11)

His prayer is not a psalmic plea for reenactment, but a call to participate in the reenactment that the prophet discerns is taking place now. In the highly dramatic perspective of the prophet, Israel had ceased to exist after 586 BCE, since the Lord's house lay in ruins and Israel no longer dwelt in Zion. Only one thing could restore Israel to life—redoing the act that made them into a people in the first place, this time not from Egypt but from Babylon. "Crossing the Reed Sea" or "passing through the wilderness" ultimately meant the same thing—defeating the primordial enemy of human community, Sea, Wilderness/Sterility. Hence the prophet used the language of exodus and of creation in parallel, as in Isaiah 43:16–21: verses 16–18, "the former things," and verses 19–21, "the new thing."

> Thus says the LORD,
> who makes *a way* in the Sea,
> *a path* in the mighty waters,
> who brings out chariot and horse,
> army and warrior;
> they lie down, they cannot rise,
> they are extinguished, quenched like a wick:
> Do not remember the former things,
> or consider the things of old.
> I am about to do a new thing;
> now it springs forth, do you not perceive it?
> I will make *a way* in the wilderness

and *path*[16] in the desert.
The wild animals will honor me,
the jackals and the ostriches;
for I give water in the wilderness,
rivers in the desert,
to give drink to my chosen people,
the people whom I formed for myself
so that they might declare my praise.

The "historical" language of the exodus is combined with the "mythic" language of creation to show the worldwide dimensions of the act. The ancient deed that brought Israel into being must be reenacted.[17] When Israel returns to Zion, the nations of the world will acknowledge the power of the Lord, who has become supreme over all deities. Second Isaiah speaks three times of Israel as a witness (43:10, 12; 44:8) so that the nations will look at them embarking on a new exodus and recognize that the Lord has brought a people back to life.

As in the psalms, the prophet regards the desperate situation of Israel as an eclipse of creation order. But unlike the psalms that pray that the Lord will enact again his creation victory in the future, the prophet has discerned that the Lord is doing that act of creation/exodus at the present time. He therefore urges Israel to take part in that new act— embark boldly in a new exodus that would display the Lord's glory to the nations.

Proverbs 8:22–31

Proverbs 1–9 personifies wisdom as a woman urging humans to accept her as a guide to life. In Proverbs 8, Woman Wisdom establishes her authority by asserting she was there when God created the cosmos. She is the most senior creature, and in that culture of reverence toward the old she is the most honorable being in the world and the surest guide to a happy life.

22 Yahweh begot me as the first of his work,
   the first of his acts of long ago.
23 Ages ago I was set up,
   at the first, before the beginning of the earth.

24   When there were no depths, I was brought forth,
    when there were no springs abounding with water.
25   Before the mountains were shaped,
    before the hills, I was brought forth—
26   when he had not yet made earth and fields,
    or the world's first bits of soil.
27   When he established the heavens, I was there,
    when he drew a circle on the face of the deep.
28   When he made firm the skies above,
    when he established the fountains of the deep,
29   when he assigned to the sea its limit,
    so that the waters might not transgress his command,
    when he marked out the foundations of the earth,
30   then I was beside him, like a sage
      ['āmôn, NRSV "master worker"];
    and I was daily his delight,
    rejoicing before him always,
31   rejoicing in his inhabited world
    and delighting in the human race.

The cosmogony proceeds in a parallel movement, verses 22–26 and 27–31. The first describes precreation as the absence of features essential to life and culture (as in the Sumerian *Enki and Ninhursag*, discussed above, and Gen. 2:5), and the second cosmogony unfolds in a positive fashion.

The aim of the dual cosmogony is not to give information about creation but to establish Woman Wisdom's authority to impart wisdom to human beings. She witnessed the creation of the universe and was herself the first person created, enjoying from her birth the honor of an intimate association with God.[18] Why was it necessary to ground her authority and not, say, the authority of the father who also speaks authoritatively in Proverbs 1–9? The answer, I suggest, is because in that culture the authority of a father to teach his son was simply taken for granted. The novelty of Proverbs is the analogy it sets up between the father (on two occasions with the mother) imparting wisdom to his son and Woman Wisdom imparting wisdom to every human being. Proverbs' personification is a novelty and so must be demonstrated.

The Book of Job

Creation is an integral part of a story about Job the just man who protests against disasters in his life. After suffering patiently divinely permitted assaults on his family and his person, Job explodes with anger in chapter 3, cursing the day of his creation; he rejects his friends' defense of God's ways and accuses God of governing the world unwisely and unjustly.

The content and purpose of the creation accounts differ according to the speaker. To Job, creation of the universe is so closely linked to his own creation that God's randomness and injustice toward him is simply one more instance of God's randomness and injustice toward the world (9:5–13; 10:8–13; 12:13–25). The pious Bildad sees only order and majesty in God's work (25:1–6; 26:5–24), and Elihu sees in the workings of nature a basis for unquestioning awe (36:24–37:24). God asserts the wisdom and justice of his own creation without apology (38:1–40:5; 40:6–42:6).

Job accused God of (1) lack of wisdom and (2) lack of justice in creating. God responds to the first charge in 38:1–40:2 (I created for myself, not for you), and to the second charge of injustice in 40:6–41:34. Regarding the second speech, it is important to recognize that justice means *the ability to operate a just universe*, that is, uphold the righteous and punish the wicked. Job 40:12 expresses the meaning of justice concisely: "Look on all who are proud, and bring them low; tread down the wicked where they stand." The second speech explains the meaning of justice by describing two beasts, the land animal Behemoth and the sea animal Leviathan. They exemplify fearsome power beyond human knowledge or control, yet they have a place in God's universe. They fulfill no function useful to humans, they cannot be domesticated and do not serve human beings. Though they are ultimately under divine control (40:15, 24; 41:2–4), God for reasons not stated allows them to exist despite their potential for harming humans. In the literary structure, the beasts at the end of the book echo "Satan" (the rendering of NRSV; Heb. *haśśāṭān*, but best rendered "the adversary"), whom God allowed to "incite" him (2:3). Why should there be an enemy of the human race within the heavenly court itself? No answer is given to this problem of evil, beyond the assurance that the adversary, like the beasts, is somehow under the control of God. God retains ultimate control over the beasts as well as over the adversary: "All that [Job] has is in your power; only do not stretch out your hand against him" (1:12); "Very well, he is in your power; only spare his life" (2:6). There is no guarantee, however, that evil will not ravage human beings.

Thus creation in Job is an utterly transcendent act of God done with a wisdom and justice beyond the assessment of humans. It cannot be searched out (chap. 28) or summed up by traditional wisdom, as is shown by the three friends' inability to speak rightly for God (42:7–8). God creates for God; the divine purpose is inscrutable; human beings should not assume that they are the center of the universe. Traditional cosmogonies often began with the gods vanquishing evil, often personified as a monster. But in the book of Job creation concludes with the monsters unvanquished, and God admiring them in eloquent poetry! They are, to be sure, on God's leash, but move in ways that terrify the human race. And this is how God wants it to be. But, equally important, God also prizes and honors Job, and finally restores what he has lost.

Conclusions

1. Many ancient cosmogonies describe or presuppose a precreation state, which can cast light on the nature and purpose of the creation account. Precreation is sometimes imagined concretely, as *an absence* of defining features of society and civilization rather than blank nothingness.

2. In some biblical passages, chaos has not been definitively eliminated but can return and become dominant. In Genesis 1, chaos is brought under control or "separated" rather than annihilated. Definitive Sabbath rest is therefore possible only in the world to come. Present Sabbath observance celebrates God's control of a still potentially dangerous universe. One can therefore speak of "the drama of divine omnipotence" (Levenson).[19]

3. Some cosmogonies describe a primordial event that can be remembered, that is, recited or reenacted in liturgy in the hope that the original power will become active in the present. The Mesopotamian creation account *Enuma Elish* was read in the presence of a statue of Marduk on the fourth day of the twelve-day New Year Festival in

Babylon. There is good evidence for a New Year festival in Israel at which time enthronement psalms such as 93 may have been recited. The translation of *Yhwh mālāk* as "Yahweh has become king" seems to reflect an enthronement of the Lord and of his earthly representative, the king, at the turn of the agricultural year.

4. Ancient cosmogonies were composed for a purpose other than to give an exact "historical" description of how the world came to be. Some were written to introduce material (the long-lived genre of debate, Genesis 1), others to exalt a deity (*Enuma Elish*, Ps. 93), or explain a current reality by describing its first occurrence when the imprint of the god or gods was clearest (Gen. 2–3), or to ground an element considered essential to a society in the moment of creation (wisdom in Prov. 8; temple and divine decrees in Ps. 93).

5. To underline the worldwide significance of Israel and its history, the Bible at times blends the "mythic" language of the creating of the world and the "historical" language of the creating of Israel, the exodus (Ps. 74; 89:1–31; Isa. 43:16–21).

6. In the Old Testament, creation was considered a past act affecting the present. Communal laments and Isaiah 40–55 express the belief that its original power could be activated.

Notes

1. I draw from my *Creation Accounts in the Ancient Near East and in the Bible*, Catholic Biblical Quarterly Monograph Series 26 (Washington: Catholic Biblical Association, 1994), 7–10.

2. *Enki and the World Order* deals with culture, and *Enki and Ninmah* deals with social order. *The Sumerian Flood Story* has a preflood phase of human existence, as does the *Sumerian King List* and *Ewe and Wheat*.

3. My rendering of Pascal Attinger, "Enki et Ninursaĝa," updated version, University of Bern, 2015, http://www.unibe.ch/unibe/portal/fak_historisch/dga /iaw/content/e39448/e99428/e122665/e122821/pane122850/e122895/1_1_1.pdf; an earlier version was published in *Zeitschrift für Assyriologie* 74 (1984): 7–9.

4. For reliable translations and notes of *Enuma Elish* and *Atrahasis*, see Stephanie Dalley, *Myths from Mesopotamia: Creation, the Flood, Gilgamesh, and Others*, rev. ed., Oxford World's Classics (Oxford: Oxford University Press, 2009).

5. Translation of E. A. Speiser in *Ancient Near Eastern Texts Relating to the Old Testament*, ed. James B. Pritchard, 3rd ed. (Princeton: Princeton University Press, 1969), 100–101.

6. H. J. L. Vanstiphout, "The Mesopotamian Debate Poems: A General Presentation (Part I)," *Acta Sumerologica* 12 (1990): 276–78.

7. Claus Wilcke, "Die Emar-Version von 'Dattel-palme und Tamariske'—ein Rekonstructionsversuch," *Zeitschrift für Assyriologie* 79 (1989): 161–90. My rendering of Wilcke.

8. W. G. Lambert, ed. and trans., *Atrahasis* (Winona Lake, IN: Eisenbrauns, 2013), 169.

9. For two early and diverse treatments of the relationship, see A. R. Millard, "A New Babylonian Story," *Tyndale Bulletin* 18 (1967): 3–18; W. L. Moran, "The Babylonian Story of the Flood," *Biblica* 52 (1972): 51–61.

10. W. G. Lambert, *Babylonian Creation Myths*, Mesopotamian Civilizations (Winona Lake, IN: Eisenbrauns, 2013), 169.

11. All translations are from the NSRV except as noted.

12. Making this subtle point does not diminish God's commitment also to bless the nations with increase and with territory.

13. For a fuller version of these remarks, see my article "Learning from Our First Parents: Can We See Adam and Eve Anew?," *America: The Jesuit Review*, October 24, 2014, http://americamagazine.org/learning-our-first-parents.

14. For an authoritative discussion of the possibility of chaos returning, see Jon D. Levenson, *Creation and the Persistence of Evil: The Jewish Drama of Divine Omnipotence* (Princeton: Princeton University Press, 1994).

15. For a clear discussion of the often-proposed New Year Festival and the translation of *Yhwh mālāk*, see John Day, *The Psalms*, Old Testament Guides (Sheffield: JSOT Press, 1990), 67–87.

16. With several commentators, I emend MT *nhrwtt*, "rivers," to *ntybwt*, "paths," on the basis of the Qumran manuscript 1QIsaᵃ and in accord with Hebrew parallelism. Emphasis added to show the parallelism.

17. Even a small number of returnees were enough for the exodus to take place.

18. The ultimate origin of personified wisdom in Prov. 8 is debated. In the opinion of many scholars, Heb. *'āmôn* is an Akkadian loanword *ummānu*, "scribe, sage, heavenly sage." For discussion, see Richard J. Clifford, *Proverbs*, Old Testament Library (Louisville: Westminster John Knox, 1999), 99–101; Alan C. Lenzi, "Proverbs 8: Three Perspectives on Its Composition," *Journal of Biblical Literature* 125 (2006): 687–714.

19. Levenson, *Creation and the Persistence of Evil*.

CHAPTER 4

Being and Nothingness in the Book of Revelation

Sean M. McDonough

They don't gather grapes from thorn-bushes, or figs from thistles (Matt. 7:16)—nor would one expect to gather musings on ontology from the Apocalypse. But the book of Revelation devotes considerable space to the matter of Being and Non-Being, and may thus prove surprisingly useful in exploring the doctrine of *creatio ex nihilo*.[1] If nothing else, the book contains more about *creatio* than is sometimes recognized, and it offers a wealth of stimulating material for thinking about the *nihil*.

CREATION IN REVELATION

The Apocalypse regularly affirms that God created the universe, though it must be admitted that the precise notion of creation *ex nihilo* is not immediately evident. The praise of God in chapter 4 culminates in the acclamation, "Worthy are you, our Lord and God, to receive glory and honor and power, for you created all things, and by your will they were and were created."[2] The verse might perhaps accommodate *creatio ex nihilo*—God's will, and nothing else, is the cause of all that is—and well-meaning scribes were happy to nudge it in that direction by inserting a "not" into the penultimate clause ("they were not and were created") or by more brazenly substituting "they came into being" for "they were."[3] But these emendations only indicate that the presumed original reading could equally have been read by the unwary as implying that the world had always been around in some fashion: "They were [always there, in some way] and [then] they were created [i.e., into a proper cosmos]." Less textually problematic for John's theology of creation is the summary of the "eternal gospel" in 14:6: "Fear God and give him glory, for the hour of his judgment has come, and worship him who made the heaven and earth, the sea and the springs of water." At the close of the book, God's declaration "Behold I make all thing new" is realized in the Paradise Regained that is the New Jerusalem; one can hardly miss the Edenic imagery of the tree of life and the river of life flowing through its midst.

God's act of creation is affirmed throughout Revelation. But what of the *ex nihilo*? John, of course, hardly comes out and asserts: "God did not use preexisting matter in his fabrication of the universe." Nonetheless, his portrait of God does invite development in that direction. The most critical element in this regard is John's description of God as "the One who is and who was and who is to come" (1:4, 8; 4:8; cf. 11:17; 16:5), an adaptation of the Septuagint's description of God in Exodus 3:14, *egō eimi ho ōn*. It is clearly an important name for John, and germane to our purposes for at least two reasons. First, the "was" part of the formula likely points to God's role as creator.[4] Second, the central confession that God is "the one who is" already carried considerable philosophical freight in early Judaism. A writer like Philo could hardly miss the connection between the Platonic ideas that "really are" (*to ontōs on*) and the Septuagint's assertion that God is "the one who is," and the designation became a central part of his philosophical project of reconciling Torah and Greek philosophy.[5] While John is not working in the philosophical mode,[6] he is keenly aware of the stark distinction between the world and the One Who Sits on the Throne, before whom heaven and earth will flee away (Rev. 20:11). In contrast to the transient world below, God just is. This does not in and of itself constitute a demonstration that John believed in creation *ex nihilo*, but it is surely consonant with such a belief, and may indeed be thought to logically entail such a belief.

"Countercreation": The Nothingness of Babylon

We descry creation *ex nihilo* in Revelation only with considerable effort. By contrast, the fundamental nullity of those in opposition to God is exposed throughout the book. While God just *is*, created entities have a far more troubled relationship with being. John starts in on the theme by carefully distinguishing the signs of his vision from what they signify. Note the parallelism in his commission in 1:19–20:

> γράψον οὖν ἃ **εἶδες** καὶ ἃ **εἰσὶν** καὶ ἃ μέλλει γενέσθαι μετὰ ταῦτα. **20** τὸ μυστήριον τῶν ἑπτὰ ἀστέρων οὓς **εἶδες** ἐπὶ τῆς δεξιᾶς μου καὶ τὰς ἑπτὰ λυχνίας τὰς χρυσᾶς· οἱ ἑπτὰ ἀστέρες ἄγγελοι τῶν ἑπτὰ ἐκκλησιῶν **εἰσιν** καὶ αἱ λυχνίαι αἱ ἑπτὰ ἑπτὰ ἐκκλησίαι **εἰσίν**.

> ---

> Now write what you have **seen**, what *is*, and what is to take place after this. As for the mystery of the seven stars that you **saw** in my right hand, and the seven golden lampstands: the seven stars *are* the angels of the seven churches, and the seven lampstands *are* the seven churches.

While the precise meaning of the verses is much disputed,[7] the disjunction of *seeing* and *being* should be evident.

But the distinction between the signifier and the signified in 1:19–20 is only the introduction to a far more portentous deployment of the verb "to be" later in Revelation. In the fractured world of the Apocalypse, appearance is regularly divorced from reality. Thus the church at Smyrna experiences tribulation and apparent poverty, but the Spirit affirms, "You are rich." By contrast, their opponents "claim to be Jews" but "are not"; they are instead a "synagogue of Satan" (2:9; cf. 3:9).[8] The congregation at Sardis is exposed in a similar way in 3:1: "I know your works; you have a name of being alive, but you are dead." The excoriation of Laodicea is even more thorough: "For you say,

'I am rich, I have prospered, and I need nothing.' You do not realize that you are wretched, pitiable, poor, blind, and naked" (3:17).

Through all this, John indicates that those who turn against God are accruing a kind of ontological deficit. The connection between what they are and what they appear to be has been shattered, and their being begins, as it were, to hemorrhage from the wound. One might argue that such a lack of integrity hardly constitutes genuine nothingness. But as we venture farther into Revelation, we find that the "merely" hypocritical characters in chapters 2 and 3 bear a disturbing resemblance to the cosmos-threatening forces which dominate the action in the later chapters of the book. Again the verb "to be" plays a critical role.[9]

We may begin by noting that the structure of chapters 12–20 points toward the disjunction of being and seeming. As numerous scholars have observed, this section is dominated by a chiasm involving the "Satanic trinity" of the dragon, the first beast, and the second beast, whose plans find civilizational expression in Babylon.[10] They are marched onto the stage in chapters 12–14, then summarily marched off in reverse order in chapters 15–20. On the surface, the kingdom of evil seems to enjoy a plenitude of existence. Babylon appears to hold absolute sway in the world, a virtual fulfillment of the creation mandate to "fill the earth and subdue it." "All the world," we are told, follows after the beast and worships the dragon who gave him power (13:3–4). The expression of admiration for the beast, "Who is like the beast, and who can fight against it?," is particularly galling to John, since it represents a blasphemous appropriation of the Psalmist's praise for YHWH (see, e.g., Ps. 89:7). In *The Meaning of the City*, Jacques Ellul aptly terms this Satanic enterprise a "countercreation." Ellul's vivid description of Cain's motives for city building apply equally well to Babylon in the Apocalypse:

> Now he is going to make the world over again. This unsatisfying world, this world from which perfection is excluded, where Cain introduced all possible pain, Cain is now going to reconstruct. In fact, the word should not be "reconstruct," but "construct." For in Cain's eyes it is not a beginning again, but a beginning. God's creation is seen as nothing. God did nothing, and in no case did he finish anything. Now a start is made, and it is no longer God beginning, but man. And thus Cain, with everything he does, digs a little deeper the abyss between himself and God.[11]

But despite the apparent splendor of the dragon, the beasts, and Babylon, it is evident to John that they are a mere counterfeit of the Holy Trinity and the New Jerusalem. As such they have only a suspect, shadowy existence. The bankruptcy of Babylon and the Satanic trinity is made evident with particular clarity in chapters 17–19. The Beast is described in the following way in 17:8: "The beast that you saw was, and is not, and is about to ascend from the bottomless pit and go to destruction." This is an obvious parody of the aforementioned divine designation "the one who was and is and is to come" (1:4 and elsewhere). The contrast between the present participles is particularly instructive. To the extent that the career of the beast in Revelation 17 may be an adaptation of the myth of Nero redivivus,[12] the "is not" component may address precisely his temporary absence from the stage of world history. But it is hard to miss the direct contrast with the description of God as "the One who is."[13] Coupled with the prediction that the beast "is going to destruction," the "is not" seems to stress that the beast, who has set himself up as a surrogate god, has succeeded only in revealing his essential nothingness.

The same may be said for the depiction of Babylon in chapters 17–18. Babylon exults in its position atop the world: "I rule as a queen; I am no widow, and I will never see grief" (18:7). But it has no foundation in the enduring reality of God, and thus it will perish "in a single day" when God sweeps it away (18:8). Far from being the epicenter of the cosmos, it will become a howling wasteland, a haunt of demons, a prison house of every unclean spirit (18:2). Babylon, the one-time lair of the beast, like the beast returns to nothing, because in its willed estrangement from God, it fundamentally *is* nothing. Its splendid adornments of gold and jewels are stolen goods, looted from the nations it has exploited; and in any case they are ultimately God's property, as evidenced by their (re-?)appearance in the New Jerusalem.[14]

The Apocalypse, in its typically idiosyncratic fashion, thus illustrates the theological trope that evil has no proper existence but is instead only parasitical upon the good. Amongst many examples, the most pertinent development of the theme may be Athanasius's discussion in *On the Incarnation*. As Khaled Anatolios notes in the present volume, Athanasius believes that the creation of humanity from nothing raises the troubling possibility that they might willfully return to the nothingness whence they came. Athanasius writes:

For the transgression of the commandment was making them turn
back again according to their nature; and as they had at the beginning come into being out of non-existence, so were they now on
the way to returning, through corruption, to non-existence again
[ὥσπερ οὐκ ὄντες γεγόνασιν, οὕτως καὶ τὴν εἰς τὸ μὴ εἶναι φθορὰν
ὑπομείνωσι τῷ χρόνῳ εἰκότως]. The presence and love of the Word
had called them into being; inevitably, therefore, when they lost
the knowledge of God, they lost existence with it; for it is God
alone Who exists, evil is non-being, the negation and antithesis of
good [εἰς τὰ οὐκ ὄντα ἀποστραφέντας, οὐκ ὄντα γάρ ἐστι τὰ κακά,
ὄντα δὲ τὰ καλά, ἐπειδήπερ ἀπὸ τοῦ ὄντος Θεοῦ γεγόνασι, κενωθῆναι
καὶ τοῦ εἶναι ἀεί]. (*De incarnatione* 1.4)[15]

John fleshes out the narrative of this "return to nothingness" throughout the Apocalypse.

DECREATIO . . .

God's response to Babylon's blasphemous attempt at countercreation
is (to borrow another phrase of Ellul's) "decreation."[16] Throughout
Revelation, God oversees the systematic dismantling of the world. One
might equally regard this as the destruction of the idolatrous countercreation or as the exposure of the essential nothingness of the Satanic
enterprise. In either case, this decreation is set in antithetical parallelism
with the creation accounts elsewhere in scripture. God in a sense brings
the world to *nothing*, both as a sign of judgment against the forces of
evil and as a prelude to re-creation.

Before we proceed further, it is important to clarify what we mean
when we say that God takes apart what he has made. Naming him as
the agent of decreation raises the specter of a God who seemingly can't
decide whether he wants to create the world or destroy it. The central
chapters of Revelation prove especially helpful in addressing this problem, since John provides a very nuanced account of agency throughout
the drama. God is assuredly portrayed throughout the Apocalypse as
the One Seated on the Throne, in full command of the cosmos. But the
scenes of cosmic dissolution are regularly prefaced with the Greek

word *edóthe*, "it was given."[17] This is not simply a circumlocution for "God gave." The destruction which follows is often ascribed to malevolent actors: this is particularly clear in the case of the demonic warriors who ascend from the Abyss in chapter 9, or the frog spirits emanating from the mouths of the Satanic trinity in chapter 16. In Revelation 17, the self-destructive nature of evil is laid bare when the beast and the kings of the earth devour the harlot, Babylon. God does not, we might say, actively enjoy what they are doing. This becomes particularly evident in the narrative of the beast. We read in 13:5–7 that the beast "was given a mouth uttering haughty and blasphemous words . . . [and] to make war on the saints and to conquer them." Assuming this is another "divine passive,"[18] we can hardly assert that God endorses blasphemy against his own name or the unjust slaughter of his people. It may be granted that the final shaking of heaven and earth can only be the work of God. But the details of decreation are a complex mesh of what God does directly and what others do that works toward the fulfillment of his purposes. Thus the direct responsibility for much of the mayhem in the vision is laid at the door of human and superhuman agents. It is not simply a question of God tearing things up in a fit of pique.

The theme of decreation is elaborated with particular care in these same chapters of Revelation, which are structured by the sevenfold sequences of the seals, the trumpets, and the bowls in chapters 6–16. The plagues in these chapters are as often as not direct blows against the created order: in the sixth seal alone, we see the sky roll back like a scroll, the heavenly luminaries grow dark, and the stars fall. In the trumpet judgments the waters turn to blood, and trees and grass are consumed; similar things transpire in the bowl judgments. At times the catastrophes even appear to map the sequence of the Genesis accounts. As David Aune notes with respect to 8:12: "It is perhaps not mere coincidence that on the *fourth* creative day, God is reported to have created the sun, moon, and stars (Gen. 1:14–19), so that the cosmic destruction that occurs here can be understood against the background of the creation account."[19]

The dis-ordering of the world is equally evident in a phenomenon like the locust-demons issuing from the Abyss in Revelation 8: they are a monstrous composite of creatures who ought rightly to remain separate, and they transgress the boundaries of their abysmal home to wreak havoc on earth. To the extent that the good order of creation includes proper human dominion over the earth, the calamities attending warfare in the first four seals can be subsumed under decreation, as can the power exercised over humanity by the beast. As the analogue in Daniel 7 makes clear, this is an inversion of the Edenic order, where the Son of Man is meant to rule over the beasts.

One might object that at the literary level many of these catastrophes stem directly from the plagues on Egypt at the Exodus. One can hardly dispute this—indeed, the central thread of Revelation is precisely the end-times exodus of God's people moving out from their oppressive rulers and into the glorious kingdom of God. The plagues play a central role in the proceedings. But it is crucial to recognize that the Exodus narrative is itself steeped in creation and decreation imagery.[20] Israel was "fruitful" and "multiplying," "filling the land/earth" (Exod. 1:6) before Pharaoh's assaults; Moses' mother looked and "saw that he was good [*tov*]" (2:2; my translation); the Spirit from God moves over the waters and dry land appears for the deliverance of Israel (14:21–2). The plagues correspondingly take away Egypt's living space: the sun is smote, the waters are bloodied, the swarming things of Genesis 1 swarm where they ought not to swarm, until in the end Pharaoh is swallowed up in the microcosmic abyss of the Red Sea.[21]

By appropriating Exodus in the way he does, John in effect appropriates the creation narratives, even if they are playing in reverse. This also fits with John's other prophetic forebears, such as Jeremiah, who could describe the looming destruction of Jerusalem as an anticreation (4:23–26):

> I looked on the earth, and lo, it was waste and void;
> and to the heavens, and they had no light.
> I looked on the mountains, and lo, they were quaking,
> and all the hills moved to and fro.
>
> I looked, and lo, there was no one at all,
> and all the birds of the air had fled.
> I looked, and lo, the fruitful land was a desert,
> and all its cities were laid in ruins
> before the LORD, before his fierce anger.[22]

The structure of the sevenfold sequences in Revelation also points to a connection with the creation week.[23] The number seven is an obvious clue. It is true that seven is a significant number in many cultures, and it is just possible that the sevenfold scheme stems from the trumpet-blowing narrative of Joshua before Jericho. It is hard to deny the effect of the latter on the trumpet judgments of Revelation, which culminate in the fall of a city and the advent of God's kingdom; this may have in turn formed the template for the other sequences. It is also true that a sevenfold sequence is likely in view in the summary of the Egyptian plagues in, for example, Psalm 105:28–36.[24] But in light of the abundant evidence in the text that the entire created order is being dismantled, Genesis 1 has at the very least made an important contribution to the schema.[25]

This is confirmed when we look more closely at the rhythm of the plague sequences. While there is a clear progression in severity as we proceed from the seals to the trumpets to the bowls—we move from judgments that affect a quarter of the earth to a third of the earth to the whole earth—the septets share a common pattern: the sixth item in each septet brings us to the very brink of final judgment, while the seventh item represents the consummation of this judgment. We thus have a six-plus-one scheme in place, in clear parallel to the creation week. Thus the sixth seal presents a quaking earth, a blackened sun and bloody moon, an unfurled sky, and the lament, "Fall on us and hide us from the face of the one seated on the throne and from the wrath of the Lamb; for the great day of their wrath has come, and who is able to stand?" This certainly looks like the end of all things. While the opening of the seventh seal in 8:1 initially offers us only a half-hour's silence, this silence ought to be linked with the prophetic motif of silence before the divine judge (Zeph. 1:7; Zech. 2:13; Hab. 2:20). In addition, it is probable that the eschatological "thunders, sounds, lightning, and earthquake" of 8:5 are connected with the seventh seal.

The sixth trumpet, meanwhile, is strikingly similar to the final battle against evil more fully depicted in the famous Armageddon of the sixth bowl: four angels by the River Euphrates (9:14; cf. 16:12) are released, resulting in cataclysmic warfare (9:15–16; cf. 16:14). While the better part of two chapters intervenes between the blowing of the sixth and seventh trumpets, it is possible we are meant to view the fall of the city in 11:13 in association with the sixth trumpet.[26] The seventh trumpet begins with the definitive announcement, "The kingdom of the world has become the kingdom of our Lord and of his Messiah." We also find the prior description of God as "the one who is and who was and who is to come" transformed into "the one who is and who was" (11:17); the obvious implication is that he has now *come* in final judgment. The consummation is equally in view in the seventh bowl: a voice declared, "It is done!," and "every island fled away, no mountains were to be found" (16:17, 20).

In the seals, trumpets, and bowls, the world is dismantled in six narrative units, after which we have what we might call a Sabbath of final judgment. John certainly develops the theological significance of the pattern beyond what we find in Genesis. The interludes between the sixth and seventh items, for instance, are no mere lacunae, but instead serve as encouragements for repentance and perseverance. In these spaces we have an answer provided to the question from 6:17: "The great day of their wrath has come, and who is able to stand?" Those who are sealed by God (7:2) or measured by him (11:1; cf. Zech. 2:1–5; Ezek. 40:5–16.) or "keep their clothes on" (16:15) may indeed stand before God in final judgment.[27] Nonetheless, John's enhancements should not obscure the fact that the sevenfold catastrophes are at least in part modeled on the creation week.

The decreation culminates in chapter 20, where heaven and earth flee away from the face of the one seated on the great white throne (20:11). The dead are then judged in this in-between space between the fleeing of the first heaven and earth and the introduction of new heaven and earth in 21:1. The distinction between the now world and the new world is here portrayed in the sharpest terms. The old cosmos is nowhere to be found.

. . . *AD NIHILUM*?

We have argued that John consciously portrays God decreating the world in a counterpoint to his creation of the world in the beginning. We must now ask the further question: Does this decreation amount to *nothing*? Does God annihilate the world in order to make way for a completely new one? A prima facie reading of Revelation 20–21 augurs for an affirmative answer: the disappearance of the first heaven and first earth is about as definitive a sign of annihilation as one could imagine.[28]

But things are not so simple. We must first recognize that John is reporting a vision, and thus we must mind the aforementioned distinction between the things he *sees* and what they *are* (or perhaps in this case what they *are not*). Such a cautious approach is rewarded when we look more carefully at the details of Revelation 20–21. Note, for instance, that the New Jerusalem—which descends from heaven in 21:2—bears the names of the tribes of Israel on its gates, and the names of the twelve apostles on its foundation stones. This indicates that the New Jerusalem serves at one level as a symbol of the people of God.[29] For our purposes, however, it demonstrates that God's city does not in fact fall full-formed from heaven into nothingness: it is rather the culmination of the work and witness of (at least) the patriarchs and apostles in history. We must likewise recognize that the "nations" and the "kings of the earth" streaming into the city have not suddenly sprouted into being in the eschaton—they are the same characters who have been playing a far more sinister role in the proceedings of the Apocalypse up to this point. How this radical transformation is effected lies outside our purview; we only emphasize again the strong element of continuity with previous parts of the vision and the eschatological denouement in the New Jerusalem.

John, then, sees continuity between the current world order and the coming world order, and he hardly commits to the literal obliteration of all matter. Does this imply that the language of nothingness has then lost all utility for explicating the Apocalypse? Not at all. We have seen that John has woven subtle meditations on being and nothingness throughout his text, all the while surrounding it with hardly subtle portraits of the world as we know it falling to ruins. Even if a strict obliteration of matter is not in view, we may rightly speak of an *effective nothingness* in the Apocalypse. The narrative disappearance of the first heaven and first earth in Revelation 20 maintains its force as a depiction of *one aspect* of eschatological reality: the ultimate collapse of the current corrupt world system when confronted with the unveiled God. Athanasius in the passage above said that creatures are "on the way to returning, through corruption, to non-existence again"; John suggests that under the leadership of the dragon the cosmos in some sense reaches that unhappy destination.

In this John sits very much in the mainstream of the biblical tradition. Like virtually all the writers of the New Testament, John felt particularly attracted to the latter chapters of Isaiah, and thus the use there of "nothingness" is of special interest.[30] Consider Isaiah 40:17: "All the nations are as nothing [*kĕ'ayin*] before him; they are accounted by him as less than nothing and emptiness [*tohû*]." Throughout the latter chapters of Isaiah the nothingness of the nations and their idols is regularly contrasted with affirmations of God's creative power (cf. v. 28: "The LORD is the everlasting God, the Creator of the ends of the earth"), so the use of *tohû* here catches the eye. Perhaps even more interesting is Isaiah 45:6–7: "I am the LORD, and there is no other ['*êyin 'od*]. I form light and create darkness, I make weal and create woe; I the LORD do all these things."

Other writings in the New Testament could equally use the language of "not-being" to describe states of affairs other than the absolute absence of matter. The language of nonexistence, for example, is critical in two pertinent Pauline texts. Toward the end of 1 Corinthians 1, Paul reminds his puffed-up Corinthian congregation of their lowly place in the social hierarchy: "Not many of you were wise by human standards, not many were powerful, not many were of noble birth"; nonetheless, "God chose what is foolish in the world to shame the wise; God chose what is weak in the world to shame the strong; God chose what is low and despised in the world, *things that are not, to reduce to nothing things that are*, so that no one might boast in the presence of God" (vv. 26–29; emphasis added). God's ability to overturn societal expectations in his saving work is likened to his work in primal creation. "Nothingness" provides God with fresh opportunities to exercise his creativity. The same may be said of Romans 4:17, where Paul speaks of Abraham's faith in God, "who gives life to the dead and calls into existence the things that do not exist." Ernst Käsemann goes so far as to speak of this in terms of *creatio ex nihilo*, such that the plight of Abraham is a *redigi ad nihilum*.[31] Even if one takes exception to this point, the fact remains that Paul believes that contrasting a state of nonexistence with God's creative call is a fitting way to speak to Abraham's problem and its solution.

John's pervasive use of the verb "to be" suggests that he is operating in a similar way. While from one angle we may say that God redeems what he has already made, it is equally true that the world as such in the Apocalypse holds no intrinsic hope for renewal. It is not simply a question of God fanning into flame the embers of a quiescent cosmos. Things have well and truly fallen apart, such that only the God who called all things into being can set them on their proper course again.

Theological Analysis of "Nothing"

This tour of Revelation should be sufficient to show that being and nothingness matter to John. It appears, however, that we are left with two distinct aspects of not-being. On the one hand, we have Babylon and its spiritual underwriters, whose apparent superbeing is *revealed* to be an illusion. On the other hand, we have the good created order, which is caught up in the rebellion of wicked agents and through no fault of its own is effectively *reduced* to nothing as a preparation for the glories of the world to come. The latter makes tolerable sense within a theology of creation. The natural cycles of life and death, integration and dis-integration, serve as signposts of God's willingness to take things apart in order to build them up again. Revelation simply extends this logic to the cosmos as a whole. But what of the former? Is it helpful to assert that Babylon both *is* and in a more fundamental way *is not*? One approach, moving in the direction set by Athanasius above, is to examine the parlous ontological state of all that defies the advance of God's kingdom. We may briefly consider two modern travelers on this route, Karl Barth and Wolfhart Pannenberg.

Barth's discussion of nothingness, *das Nichtige*, in *Church Dogmatics* III/3 is one of the most challenging passages in his corpus.[32] Barth begins by recognizing an "innocent" not-being which is nothing more than a recognition that the creature is not-God, and that a given creature x is not creature y. (This is close to Plato's supposition that things in the world of flux share both in being and not-being.) No created entity enjoys the fullness of being enjoyed by the eternal God: "The diversities and frontiers of the creaturely world contain many 'nots.' No single creature is all-inclusive. None is or resembles another. To each belongs its own place and time, and in these its own manner, nature and existence."[33]

True "nothingness," by contrast, is virtually a synonym for evil in Barth's account. It is thus not surprising that Barth's description of nothingness, for all its uniqueness, matches up with the paradoxical descriptions of evil in the theological tradition: *das Nichtige* cannot be said to exist in the proper sense of the word, as do God and his creatures, but it is nonetheless somehow *there*. Part of Barth's address to the problem (the word "solution" in this regard hardly seems fitting) consists in saying that nothingness only comes to be as a result of God's rejecting it. It can thus only be known by creatures as that which God has rejected—we might say that it cannot claim being "in its own right" since it is so thoroughly wrong. *Das Nichtige*

> "is" problematically because it is only on the left hand of God, under His No, the object of his jealousy, wrath, and judgment. It "is" not as God and His creation are, but only in its own improper way, as inherent contradiction, as impossible possibility. . . . That which God renounces and abandons in virtue of His decision is not merely nothing. It is nothingness, and has as such its own being, albeit malignant and perverse. A real dimension is disclosed, and existence and form are given to a reality *sui generis*, in the fact that God is wholly and utterly not the Creator in this respect. Nothingness is that which God does not will. It lives only by the fact that it is that which God does not will. But it does live by this fact.[34]

Barth may assist us, then, not by uncovering some new way of "making sense" of the fact that Babylon can both be there in the world and ultimately be revealed as a nullity. Instead, he affirms that this paradox lies at the heart of the mystery of evil and is constitutionally inexplicable.

Wolfhart Pannenberg offers a somewhat different approach to the problem with his notion of "retroactive ontology."[35] For Pannenberg, the future determines not only the knowledge of the past, but the very being of things: "For thought that does not proceed from the essence of a thing is not what persists in the succession of change, for which, rather, the future is open in the sense that it will bring unpredictably new things that nothing can resist as absolutely unchangeable—for such thought only the future decides what something is."[36] This lack of ultimate reality is particularly clear in the case of evil. Mark Hocknull summarizes: "The ontological nullity of evil arises from the future of evil. It is sealed only by the victory of God in the event of the reconciliation on the cross and in the eschatological consummation of creation. According to Pannenberg's ontology, the future determines reality and therefore evil has no reality, because in eternity it will not exist. It has no future."[37] No less than Barth, Pannenberg must acknowledge that evil does make itself known as some kind of "reality" in the world.[38] But as the idiom goes, at the end of the day it proves to be nothing.

The straightest way forward, however, may be via Revelation's own image of Babylon as a counterfeit city. As we have seen above, John portrays the Satanic enterprise as a vain attempt to establish an independent civilization. But Babylon can only be built with created goods purloined from God: the gold and pearls and people belong to him and can only properly adorn his city. Thus, all that "Babylon" names is the illusion of radical autonomy; it is a mere label affixed to someone else's property. Its claims to genuine existence ring hollow. When these unjustly acquired accouterments are stripped away, there is nothing left. To put it in fabular terms, the spell of genuine being lasts only as long as that being is affirmed as a gift from God. Once it is snatched away as one's own property . . . the spell is broken.

RECREATIO

Whether we are treating of the nothing that the world becomes, or the nothing that the kingdom of evil "is," Revelation's final word is this: "See, I am making all things new" (21:5). God is able to dispel the deceptiveness of Satan and his minions with their shadow kingdom, and he is able to raise up again a world that has fallen into ruins. He thus proves himself to be the one whose creative word retains its power in all circumstances. As we have seen above, the word of absolute new creation in Revelation 21:5 must be balanced with aspects of continuity between the first heaven and the first earth and their successors. One might imagine, for instance, that Paradise has simply been on leave for a while, and is now returning to its proper place as the abode of redeemed humanity.[39] But as we have indicated above, there is an absoluteness to this declaration of God which makes it at least a close parallel to creation *ex nihilo*, and perhaps its functional equivalent. One might even be so bold as to say that this word in 21:5 outstrips the declarations of

Genesis 1: the depredations of the Satanic trinity and rebellious humanity have defiled the old creation, such that God must first with great effort erase the *tabula* before he can write the story of the new creation.

What insight, then, does the Apocalypse shed on the doctrine of creation *ex nihilo*? If the doctrine is taken in a narrow sense, we might regretfully answer: next to nothing. One can make a strong argument from the theological tradition that creation *ex nihilo* serves a very precise, protological purpose—to guard against the idea that God was confronted with anything but himself in his primal act of creation. Everything that follows may be subsumed under providence, or *creatio continua*, or judgment, or something else again. Nothing means nothing, and once anything is there, the doctrine ceases to be relevant. On this view of things, the doctrine is a highly specialized tool in the dogmatic kit. The Apocalypse's designation of God as "the One who is" might hint at this construal of creation *ex nihilo*, but that would be the extent of its contribution.

Revelation, however, invites us to consider taking a more expansive and dynamic view of creation *ex nihilo*. If one grants that "effective nothingness" accurately captures John's portrayal of the nullity of evil, and the subsequent decreation of the cosmos, then the primal act of creation *ex nihilo* may now be seen as the overture of a cosmic symphony which will continue to develop the themes of coming-to-be and passing-away, all orchestrated by the God "who puts to death and gives life" (Deut. 32:39). The God of the Apocalypse alone truly *is*, and he calls into being everything that exists. But it appears that genuine, enduring existence is not simply a given for the creature. As Athanasius indicates, nothingness proves to have a strange allure: the prospect of "freeing" the world from God leads to the vain attempt at countercreation. God's response is the systematic dismantling of the hijacked cosmos; what God had brought together, he now puts asunder. Babylon's story ends up being the consummate cautionary tale of what *might have been*.

Such a view of things balances the world-affirming nature of most modern creation theology with the sobering note of judgment that sounds through much ancient teaching. Rather than ignoring the evident death and decay in the world, one can face it head on, seeing it both as the inevitable result of catastrophically bad decisions by willful creatures and as the strange decreative path upon which God is leading the cosmos. Things do fall apart, and return to primal chaos: "The earth shall be utterly laid waste and utterly despoiled; for the LORD has spoken this word. The earth dries up and withers, the world languishes and withers; the heavens languish together with the earth. The earth lies polluted under its inhabitants; for they have transgressed the laws, violated the statutes, broken the everlasting covenant" (Isa. 24:3–5). The pollution of the earth triggers the purgation of divine judgment. But this is not by way of denying the promise of creation, but of fulfilling it: if God brings the world to nothing, it is only so that he might finally say, "See, I am making all things new."

We may conclude by citing a few pertinent passages from Tertullian, who did as much as anyone to strengthen the doctrine of *creatio ex nihilo* in the ancient church. In his treatise *Against Hermogenes* (34), he makes a crucial allusion to Revelation 20–21:

> Besides, the belief that everything was made from nothing will be impressed upon us by that ultimate dispensation of God which will bring back all things to nothing. For "the very heaven shall be rolled together as a scroll"; nay, it shall come to nothing along with the earth itself, with which it was made in the beginning. "Heaven and earth shall pass away," says He. "The first heaven and the first earth passed away," "and there was found no place for them," because, of course, that which comes to an end loses locality.[40]

Tertullian's support for *"decreatio ad nihilum"* is matched by his affirmation of the ongoing relevance of *creatio ex nihilo* in *On the Resurrection of the Flesh*.

> Firmly believe, therefore, that He produced it wholly out of nothing, and then you have found the knowledge of God, by believing that He possesses such mighty power. But some persons are too weak to believe all this at first, owing to their views about Matter. They will rather have it, after the philosophers, that the universe was in the beginning made by God out of underlying matter. . . .

[In either case] both alternatives support my position. For if God produced all things whatever out of nothing, He will be able to draw forth from nothing even the flesh which had fallen into nothing; or if He moulded other things out of matter, He will be able to call forth the flesh too from somewhere else, into whatever *abyss* it may have been engulfed. And surely He is most competent to re-create who created, inasmuch as it is a far greater work to have produced than to have reproduced, to have imparted a beginning, than to have maintained a continuance. On this principle, you may be quite sure that the restoration of the flesh is easier than its first formation.[41]

Since Tertullian much prefers the explanation that God did in fact create everything out of nothing, the most salient part of the quotation becomes, "For if God produced all things whatever out of nothing, He will be able to draw forth from nothing even the flesh which had fallen into nothing." Substitute "cosmos" for "flesh," and we have a distillation of the Apocalypse's distinctive contribution to *creatio ex nihilo*.

NOTES

1. Paul Minear's study "Ontology and Ecclesiology in the Apocalypse" (*New Testament Studies* 12 [1966]: 89–105) is of obvious interest, but he looks primarily at the intersection of ontology and ecclesiology, and does not directly address the question of being and nonbeing as we do here.

2. All Bible quotations are from the NRSV unless otherwise indicated.

3. The verse is something of a hornet's nest of variants, though the evidence is pretty squarely in favor of the Nestle-Aland text. The tenth-century 046 is the best witness for the insertion of the "not" (and even that may have stemmed from a reduplication of the previous word), and the tenth-century 2329 champions the shift to "came into being." A smattering of decent witnesses (1854, 2050, some versions of the Majority text, and the Sahidic) solves the "problem" by employing the present-tense "they are," though this could have arisen by way of itacism. Alexandrinus omits the final clause "and were created" altogether.

4. See, e.g., Exod. 3:14 in Targum Ps-Jonathan: "He who spoke and the world was, who spoke and all things were . . . *I am he who is and who will be*

has sent me to you." *Targums Neofiti 1 and Pseudo-Jonathan: Exodus*, trans. Michael Maher, The Aramaic Bible (Collegeville, MN: Liturgical Press, 1994); emphasis added. Cf. Exod. 3:14 Targum Neofiti and Fragmentary Targum (G). Cf. Philo, *De vita Mosis* 2.100: "For, as He alone really is, He is undoubtedly also the Maker, since He brought into being what was not."

5. See, e.g., *Det.* 160, where Philo explains that Exod. 3:14 shows "that others lesser than He have not being, as being indeed is, but exist in semblance only, and are conventionally said to exist." Cf. *Mut.* 7; *Fug.* 165; *Post.* 15.

6. Though we should not forget the numerous occurrences of "apocalyptic" motifs in Plato himself. See, e.g., the famous image of the soul winging its way toward heaven only to be thwarted by Desire in the *Phaedrus*, or the vision of the underworld in the *Republic*. Sergius Bulgakov remarks with great perception: "The mythopoetic character of philosophy finds open expression in Plato who passes from the heights of dialectic investigation to myth with an indifference that is seductive for philosophers and with an apparently premeditated disorderliness. . . . His most intense philosophical speculation makes room for myth, which in no way occupies an accidental place in his thought—sometimes the most fundamental assertions having the significance of a necessary argument are stated in the form of myth." *Unfading Light*, trans. Thomas A. Smith (Grand Rapids: Eerdmans, 2012), 83.

7. See the comprehensive discussion in G. K. Beale, *The Book of Revelation* (Grand Rapids: Eerdmans, 1999), 152–70.

8. The language is jarring to modern ears, though it fits securely in the inner-Jewish polemics of the first century. The likely historical setting involves a situation where some Jewish authorities were denouncing Jewish and Gentile Christians to the Romans as "non-Jews," thus depriving them of legal protection and functioning in the role of the Accuser, Satan. See Richard Bauckham, *The Theology of the Book of Revelation* (Cambridge: Cambridge University Press, 1993), 124–25.

9. Cf. Michael Gilbertson, *God and History in the Book of Revelation: New Testament Studies in Dialogue with Pannenberg and Moltmann* (Cambridge: Cambridge University Press, 2003), 194: "But the regular glimpses of ultimate reality on both the temporal and spatial planes underline the provisionality of 'what appears to be.' God's ultimate victory is assured. The apparent victories of his enemies are illusory."

10. See, e.g., Bauckham, *Theology of the Book of Revelation*, 89.

11. Jacques Ellul, *The Meaning of the City*, trans. Dennis Pardee (Grand Rapids: Eerdmans, 1970), 6. Ellul will make the connections with Babylon explicit later in the book, and it is a key theme running through his commentary on the Apocalypse.

12. A cluster of legends that suggested either that Nero only *appeared* to die and was in fact hiding out in the East ready to wreak his vengeance on Rome, or that Nero had died but would return from the dead. For brief summaries see Beale, *Book of Revelation*, 17–18, 689–93.

13. See Philo and the patristic tradition.

14. John frames chapters 17–22 as a "tale of two cities": he uses the same introductory formula for the visions of Babylon and the New Jerusalem ("Then one of the seven angels who had the seven bowls came and said to me, 'Come, I will show you . . .'" [17:1]; almost verbatim in 21:9) and highlights the shared adornments of gold, pearls, precious stones, and people (cf., e.g., 17:4 and 21:11–27).

15. Translated by A Religious of C. S. M. V. (Community of St. Mary the Virgin) (New York: Macmillan, 1946).

16. See Jacques Ellul, *L'Apocalypse: Architecture en Mouvement* (Paris: Desclée, 1975), 72–74; Beale (*Book of Revelation*, 486–87) shows sympathy with Ellul's view. Note also Joseph Blenkinsopp's recent book on Genesis 1–11: *Creation, Un-Creation, Re-Creation* (London: T&T Clark, 2011).

17. See, e.g., 6:1, 8, where the horsemen are "given" to take peace from the earth, and smite a fourth of the earth with death and famine; 9:1–5, where an apparently wicked angel is "given" the key to the Abyss, and the demon hordes that pour forth from it are "given" the power of scorpions to torment the earth dwellers.

18. It is barely possible that the "given" here refers to the dragon acting in imitation of God, but this seems very unlikely in light of the use of *edóthe* elsewhere in Revelation. See Beale, *Book of Revelation*, 695.

19. D. E. Aune, *Revelation 6–16*, Word Bible Commentary 52B (Dallas: Word, 1998), 523 (emphasis original).

20. See Beale, *Book of Revelation*, 486.

21. We may also note the repeated command for Moses to go to Pharaoh *in the morning* (7:15; 8:16; 9:13), which gives an implicit evening/morning structure to the plague narrative. Cf. also the division between *light* for the Hebrews and *darkness* for the Egyptians in 10:22–23.

22. Cf. the opening of the prophecy of Zephaniah: "'I will utterly sweep away everything from the face of the earth, says the LORD. I will sweep away humans and animals; I will sweep away the birds of the air and the fish of the sea. I will make the wicked stumble. I will cut off humanity from the face of the earth,' says the LORD" (Zeph. 1:2–3).

23. We might compare the "Apocalypse of Weeks" in 1 En. 93, which subsumes all of world history into a ten-week schema. But in addition to the numerical difference, the specifically decreative imagery of the dissolution of the natural order is not as evident in the Apocalypse of Weeks as it is in Reve-

lation. One does wonder whether one of the editors of Enoch might have seen the seven-week schema as a self-contained unit (note the dislocation of weeks 8–10 in chap. 91, whereas the first seven weeks are in chap. 93).

24. See also Aune's discussion, *Revelation 6–16*, 2:499–507.

25. Austin Farrer makes considerable use of the creation week / Sabbath motif in his catalytic study *A Rebirth of Images* (Boston: Beacon, 1963). Indeed, he wishes to see the influence of the creation story not only in the overt cycles of seven, but also in the appearance of the beasts of chap. 13, whom he connects with the sea and land beasts of creation days five and six (see esp. pp. 36–42). Like much in the book, Farrer's imagination may outrun the evidence; but he has in my view lit upon a crucial theological theme in Revelation, and even his more inventive suggestions cannot be dismissed out of hand.

26. Beale (*Book of Revelation*, 601) suggests it may be associated with the seventh trumpet, which is also a possibility. This would of course fit well with the Jericho story, though the problem remains that in the Apocalypse's narrative the city falls before the seventh trumpet is blown.

27. This protection of the faithful from consummate judgment bears obvious likeness to the Passover, which is of course instituted just prior to the final plague in the exodus.

28. For a recent, thorough treatment of the problem of continuity and discontinuity in Revelation's portrait of the new heavens and new earth, see Mark B. Stephens, *Annihilation or Renewal?* (Tübingen: Mohr Siebeck, 2011).

29. As Bauckham argues, this clear evocation of *people* does not preclude the New Jerusalem from also representing the renewed *place* of God's people, which is characterized above all by the *presence* of God in its midst. See Bauckham, *Theology of the Book of Revelation*, 132.

30. See esp. Jan Fekkes, *Isaiah and Prophetic Traditions in the Book of Revelation* (Sheffield: JSOT Press, 1994).

31. Käsemann, *Perspectives on Paul* (London: SCM, 1971), 90–93; see also John Barclay, *Paul and the Gift* (Grand Rapids: Eerdmans, 2015), 140–41.

32. Matthew Rose provides a helpful, if critical, summary of Barth and nothingness in *Ethics with Barth: God, Metaphysics and Morals* (Farnham: Ashgate, 2010), 175–81.

33. Karl Barth, *Church Dogmatics*, ed. G. W. Bromiley and T. F. Torrance, trans. R. J. Ehrlich (Edinburgh: T&T Clark, 1960), III/3:349–50.

34. Ibid., 352. With respect to the knowledge of nothingness Barth writes:

> Since real nothingness is real in this third fashion peculiar to itself, not resembling either God or the creature but taken seriously by God Himself, and since it is not identical either with the distinction and frontier between God and creation or with those within the creaturely world, its revelation

and knowledge cannot be a matter of the insight which is accessible to the creature itself and is therefore set under its own choice and control. Standing before God in its own characteristic way which is very different from that of the creature, the object of his concern and action, His problem and adversary and the negative goal of his victory, nothingness does not possess a nature which can be assessed nor an existence which can be discovered by the creature. There is no accessible relationship between the creature and nothingness. (*CD* III/3:350)

35. For a helpful discussion of this aspect of Pannenberg's theology in direct dialogue with the Apocalypse, see Gilbertson, *God and History in the Book of Revelation*, 171–76.

36. Pannenberg, *Jesus, God and Man* (London: SCM, 1968), 136. See quotation and further discussion in Gilbertson, *God and History in the Book of Revelation*, 172. God himself is not excluded from this truth: "Only in the future will the statement 'God exists' prove to be definitely true. . . . What turns out to be true in the future will then be evident as having been true all along."

37. Mark Hocknull, *Pannenberg on Evil, Love and God* (Farnham: Ashgate, 2014), 61–62.

38. Hocknull, *Pannenberg on Evil*, 62.

39. Note, e.g., Enoch's journey to Paradise in the remote east or northeast, in 1 En. 17–19; for discussion, see Kelley C. Bautch, *A Study of the Geography of 1 Enoch 17–19* (Leiden: Brill, 2003), 64–66.

40. Peter Holmes's translation in *The Ante-Nicene Fathers* 3:496–97.

41. *On the Resurrection of the Flesh* 11; Holmes's translation, *Ante-Nicene Fathers* 3:553.

CHAPTER 5

"The Most Perfect Work"

The Role of Matter in Philo of Alexandria

GREGORY E. STERLING

As Augustine thought about creation he wrote: "Have you, O Lord, not taught me that before you gave form and specific shapes to that shapeless matter [istam informem materiam], there was nothing, no color, no figure, no body, no spirit?" He immediately added: "However, there was not nothing at all; there was a certain lack of form without any specific shape."[1] The bishop went on to identify this *informitas* with the language of Genesis 1:2: "Therefore may I not think that the shapelessness of matter [informitatem materiae]—that you made without specific shape and from which you made this beautiful world—was properly made known to humans, so that it is called *the invisible and formless earth* [terra invisibilis et incomposita]."[2] In spite of the connection with scripture, he felt compelled to acknowledge: "I, in truth, O Lord, if I may confess to you all, both with my mouth and with my reed, whatever you taught me about that matter [de ista materia] . . . I thought of it with numberless and varied shapes, but in fact did not understand it."[3]

I have often thought of these statements of Augustine when thinking about Philo of Alexandria's statements about matter (ὕλη). David
Runia characterized Philo's understanding of primordial matter as "the
least satisfactorily developed and most obscure area of Philo's thought."[4]
The accuracy of his judgment is reflected in the divergent assessments
of it: some think that Philo anticipated the later Christian understanding of *creatio ex nihilo*,[5] others argue that in keeping with Hellenistic
philosophical thought he held that matter was eternal,[6] and still others
throw their hands up in the air and state that Philo is too inconsistent
for us to make a firm judgment.[7] Nor can we leave the classification of
answers to this simple schema. There is another issue that touches directly on the concept of matter. There has been a debate about the nature of creation in Philo: did it take place in time or was the creative act
eternal in the sense that as God thinks the Ideas there is a reflex that
brings temporal reality into existence?[8] What is the impact of this debate on our understanding of matter in Philo?[9]

We should acknowledge at the outset that there is no simple way to
unravel the concept in Philo. It is unsatisfactory to focus on a single set
of statements[10] or to line one set of statements up against another.[11] Nor
can we simply appeal to the Hellenistic philosophical tradition or to the
Jewish tradition as determinative. Philo knew and used both. I propose
to work through the issues by examining the statements on matter in *De
opificio mundi*. I have selected the first treatise in the Exposition of the
Law as a test case because it explicitly works with both Genesis and
Plato's *Timaeus*. The Jewish exegete mentioned ὕλη in three contexts. We
will examine each context by summarizing Philo's statements, exploring
potential sources, considering parallel treatments in other parts of the
Philonic corpus, and reflecting on the impact of Philo's views on later
authors. By situating his statements in the tradition that he received, his
other comments on the same concepts, and the tradition that he influenced, I hope that we will be able to bring some clarity to his view(s).

Two Principles

It is worth reminding ourselves that *De opificio mundi* is the first treatise
in the Exposition of the Law. Philo may have written a *hexameron* on
Genesis 1 in the Allegorical Commentary, but it has been lost if he did.[12]

Philo did not use lemmata in the Exposition as he did in the Allegorical Commentary; rather he paraphrased the biblical text and then commented on his paraphrase. In the case of *De opificio mundi*, he typically selected key terms in the biblical text and wove them into the fabric of his exegesis.[13] This means that we will use much the same methodology to determine allusions to the biblical text as we will use to determine references to Plato's *Timaeus*. There are echoes but few citations.

Philo's Proemium

Philo wrote a preface that set out the basic orientation of his understanding of creation (§§7–12). He opened with a brief doxography in which he challenged those who admire the world rather than the maker of the world, arguing that they "claim that it is without origin and eternal" and "falsely and impurely malign God with extended inactivity."[14] Philo did not identify his opponents, but if we compare the description here with the doxography that opens *De aeternitate mundi*, it appears that Aristotle and Platonists influenced by him are the primary targets.[15] The basis for his opposition is theological or metaphysical: Philo rejected the eternity of the world based on the implications this position had for an understanding of God and God's actions. By contrast, Philo argued that Moses recognized "that it was absolutely essential that among what exists there is an active cause and a passive [τὸ μὲν εἶναι δραστήριον αἴτιον, τὸ δὲ παθητόν]." He identified the active cause with the Mind of the universe. He then described the passive: "The passive is lifeless, immovable on its own, but when moved, shaped, and given life by the Mind, it turns into the most perfect work, this cosmos."[16] Philo did not repeat the noun "cause" after the adjective "passive." The omission sets up a degree of ambiguity about his understanding of the passive: is it a cause or an object?[17] We will find the same ambiguity in a later text.

Sources

There appear to be two primary sources behind Philo's exposition: Genesis 1 and Plato, *Timaeus* 29E–30A. Philo was not, however, working directly from either text: he was working from the interpretations that sprang from them. More specifically, he appears to be drawing from a tradition that posited two causes or principles. There have been three explanations of these two principles. Some have thought that Philo had Stoics in mind since they are said to hold two principles: the active understood as God and the passive understood as matter.[18] However, the Stoics were materialists who believed that only bodies could act or be acted upon; the incorporeal could neither act nor be acted upon.[19] It is difficult to believe that Philo would have supported such a metaphysical system here. Even more problematic is the fact that Philo held that God was distinct from creation; God cannot be identified with the cosmos as the Stoa suggested. It appears that while Philo used Stoic language, his thought was distinct.[20]

Others have thought that Philo might have Aristotle in mind since he distinguished between an active and a passive principle.[21] However, Philo has just dismissed the views of Aristotle as one who held that the cosmos was "without origin and eternal"; it is hard to believe that he is now turning to them.

The final option is that Philo may have drawn from a Platonic tradition. John Dillon has called our attention to two texts that align neatly with Philo's comments.[22] The first is a doxographical text in Cicero that preserves the thought of Antiochus of Ascalon.[23] According to Cicero, Antiochus "divided it [nature] into two principles: the one was active and the other submitting itself to this one from which something was made. In the one that acted they thought resided power; in the one that was acted on a certain matter [materia]."[24] Theophrastus attributed the same view to the Old Academy. Aristotle's successor wrote: "Here he [Plato] wished to make the principles two in number." He then named them: "one underlying things as matter, which he calls the 'all-receptive,' the other being the cause and source of movement, and this he attaches to the power of God and of the Good."[25] It may be that Antiochus revived a view of the Old Academy using Stoic language. The broad similarities between the statements of Antiochus and Theophrastus on the one hand and the position articulated by Philo on the other suggest that he was drawing on the Platonic tradition for the two causes that he identified with God and matter, even if he did not explicitly identify the causes with the Receptacle of the *Timaeus* or the Good of the *Republic*.

The specification of two causes among these Platonists was not, however, left to stand untouched. Mauro Bonazzi has shown that Eudorus held that there were two levels of principles: the ἀρχή or God and the στοιχεῖα or Monad and Dyad. More importantly, Eudorus, working under the influence of Pythagorean thought, subordinated the lower level under the higher, namely the "One" or the "God above" (ὑπεράνω θεός).[26] Philo not only shared the two levels, but—as we will see—the crucial concern to elevate the "God above" over the cosmos.

Parallel Texts in Philo

Philo also used the two principles found in *Opif.* 8–9 in another text. In an explanation of the *Aqedah* (Gen. 22), he said: "Note the active cause [τὸ δρῶν αἴτιον], the fire. Note also the passive [τὸ πάσχον], the matter [ἡ ὕλη], the wood. Where is the third, the finished product?"[27] It is interesting that Philo used the same distinction between the active cause and the passive here as in *De opificio mundi*. In both cases he referred to "the active cause" and "the passive" without supplying the noun "cause" for the passive. Should we avoid using "cause" with respect to the passive? The point made by Bonazzi is apposite: Philo has two principles or causes, but in reality, there is only one "because *to patheton* should be understood not so much as a real principle as the passive element on which the active principle intervenes."[28]

While the point is not explicit in this text, it is in other Philonic texts. In the dialogue *De providentia*, Philo wrote: "Plato recognized that these things are constructed by God, and that unadorned matter has been turned into the cosmos with its adornment. For these were the first causes, from which also the cosmos came into being."[29] The statement is—as we have seen—a standard Platonic interpretation of two causes: God and matter. Philo continued: "Since also the lawgiver of the Jews Moses depicted water, darkness and the abyss as being present before the cosmos came into being. But Plato spoke of matter."[30] This equation of water, darkness, and the abyss with matter suggests that Philo could speak of matter as a cause. He, at least, recognized that it was acceptable within the Platonic tradition.

One of the ways that we can understand how Philo could refer to matter as a cause is through his use of prepositional metaphysics. As is well known, Platonists and Stoics applied prepositions to Aristotle's theory of causes[31] to offer metaphysical explanations of the cosmos.[32] Philo is an important witness to the Platonic position.[33] He understood Adam's statement that he had "gained possession of a person through God [διὰ τοῦ θεοῦ]" to be a mistake since God was a cause, not an instrument.[34] He explained: "For many things must come together for the generation of something: the by which [τὸ ὑφ' οὗ], the from which [τὸ ἐξ οὗ], the through which [τὸ δι' οὗ], and the for which [τὸ δι' ὅ]." Philo explained: "The by which [τὸ ὑφ' οὗ] is the cause [αἴτιον], the from which [τὸ ἐξ οὗ] is matter [ἡ ὕλη], the through which [τὸ δι' οὗ] is the tool [τὸ ἐργαλεῖον], the for which [τὸ δι' ὅ] is the purpose." Finally, he applied this scheme to the construction of the cosmos: "The cause [αἴτιον] is God, by which [ὑφ' οὗ] it came into existence, its material [ἡ ὕλη] is the four elements out of which [ἐξ οὗ] it has been composed, its instrument [ὄργανον] is the Logos of God through whom [δι' οὗ] it was constructed, the purpose [αἰτία] of its construction is the goodness of the Demiurge."[35] It is thus entirely possible to refer to God and matter as causes, as long as we understand that they are not identical or equal causes, but causes in distinct ways.

Later Tradition

This, however, raises a tension that lies at the heart of understanding Philo's concept of primordial matter. If we call matter a cause or a principle, have we given it a status alongside of God? Philo is not ambiguous in expressing the need to honor God above matter or the Creator above the created. But doesn't his language suggest that God created the cosmos out of matter? Basil expressed the theological objection clearly in his *Hexameron*: "If matter were uncreated, then it would from the very first be of a rank equal to that of God and would deserve some veneration."[36] Did Philo address this? Within this text he has expressed a concern, but has left the status of matter ambiguous. He has affirmed the superiority of God,[37] but has left the Platonic view of matter as a cause in place—although he qualified it.

A DESCRIPTION OF MATTER

Day One

The second occasion in which Philo referred to matter in *De opificio mundi* was in his account of day one.[38] We need to consider two statements in his exposition of "day one." The first appears in the context of asking why God created the cosmos. Philo wrote: "If someone wanted to look for the cause why the universe was created, it seems to me that he would not err from the mark if he said what one of the ancients said." The ancient that he has in mind is Plato, who wrote: "Let us now state for what reason the one who constructed creation and the universe constructed it. He was good and no envy ever occurs in the good concerning anything. Since he was devoid of envy, he wished that everything should be like him as much as possible."[39] Philo paraphrased Plato in the following: "The Father and Creator is good, for which reason he did not begrudge matter [οὐσία] a share in his excellent nature, although it has nothing good in itself, yet it is capable of becoming all things."[40]

This led him to a description of matter. He gave a list of seven contrasting pairs between matter in its original state and in its potential state. Here is the list:

Natural State	Potential State
ἄτακος	τάξις
ἄποιος	ποιότης
ἄψυχος	ἐμψυχία
<ἀνόμοιος>	ὁμοιότης
ἑτεροιότητος μεστή	ταυότης
ἀναρμοστίας μεστή	τὸ εὐάρμοστον
ἀσυμφωνίας μεστή	τὸ σύμφωνον

Natural State	Potential State
Without order	Ordered
Without quality	Having quality
Without likeness	Having likeness
Without soul	Ensouled
Full of inconsistency	Consistent
Full of incongruities	Congruous
Full of a lack of harmony	Harmonious

Note the negativity of matter signaled by the alpha-privative adjectives and nouns (I have translated the alpha-privatives by "without"). Yet this matter has potential when God transformed it.

Sources

One of the most perplexing features of Philo's account of creation is that he used two different schemas to indicate the line of demarcation between the intelligible world and the sense-perceptible world. He began by calling attention to the distinction between the cardinal number "one" and the ordinal numbers used for the "second" through the "sixth" days. He suggested that "day one" referred to the creation of the intelligible world and the second through the sixth days to the creation of the sense-perceptible world.[41] When he came to the second creation account in Genesis 2, he switched the line of demarcation between the intelligible world and the sense-perceptible world and argued that the first creation account in Genesis 1 referred to the creation of the intelligible world and the second creation account in Genesis 2 referred to the creation of the sense-perceptible world.[42]

Several attempts have been made to explain how he could have shifted the line of demarcation between the intelligible world to the sense-perceptible world from "day one" to the first creation account. Some think that there is no real shift. Valentin Nikiprowetzky suggested that the second account was a recapitulation of the first account, except the second dropped the seven-day schema.[43] David Runia thought that the second account was a fuller exposition of the intelligible world because Philo recognized the limits of the arithmological and didactic functions of the first account.[44] Thomas Tobin, on the other hand, recognized the shift and suggested that Philo incorporated different exegetical traditions without resolving the tension.[45] I agree with Tobin that Philo knew more than one Platonizing interpretation of the creation accounts. There is evidence for a distinct exegetical tradition that understood "day one" to refer to the intelligible or invisible world.[46] Philo included this tradition as well as the interpretation that considered the two creation accounts as referring to the intelligible and sense-perceptible worlds, respectively. I differ from Tobin by suggesting that Philo was less concerned about where the line between the intelligible world and the sense-perceptible world was drawn in the text than he was about making sure that the line was brightly drawn and demonstrated the metaphysical dependence of the sense-perceptible world on the intelligible world.

The recognition of these traditions has two major implications for our enquiry: Philo understood Genesis 1:1–5 to refer to the intelligible world. This means that he did not read Genesis 1:1–2 to refer to a primordial state of the sense-perceptible world.[47] It is not possible to argue that matter was eternal for Philo simply by appealing to Genesis 1:1–2.[48] Similarly, we should realize that his description of matter reflects a tradition that underscored matter's negativity and potentiality.

Parallel Texts in Philo

Philo gives other descriptions of matter in its original state and of God's transformative work, introducing order into a disordered state. The most impressive is in his discussion of Deuteronomy 23:2–3, which lists those who are excluded from the assembly.[49] One group consists of individuals who have crushed genitals. Philo offered an allegorical interpretation in which he suggested that the crushed are those who deny the reality of the Ideas. He wrote: "Some claim that the incorporeal ideas are an empty name without a share in true reality, removing the most essential substance of their own existence, namely the archetypal pattern of all that has qualities of substance."[50] He went on to explain why this was so serious: "The view that removes the Ideas confuses everything and leads to the earliest state of the elements without form and without quality."[51] He exclaimed: "What could be more out of place than this?" And then explained: "For God produced everything from that substance—although he did not deal with it himself since it was not acceptable for the happy and blessed to handle limitless and chaotic matter, but he made use of the incorporeal powers whose true name is the Ideas."[52] Philo can be fuller in his description of primordial matter in other texts,[53] but this makes it clear that God created the cosmos out of primordial matter—although it does not postulate the origin or eternity of that primordial matter.

There is a second text that we should also consider, although it does not mention matter explicitly. Philo offers an interpretation of Genesis 1:1–3 in *De opificio mundi* 29–32. He interprets the basic items mentioned in the biblical text as Platonic Ideas: "First then the Creator made an incorporeal heaven, an invisible earth [γῆν ἀόρατον], the Idea of air and the void. He named the one darkness since the air is black by nature and the other the abyss because the void is of immense depth and cavernous." Philo continues: "Then he made the incorporeal substance of water and of spirit and last of all, the seventh, light, which again was incorporeal and the intelligible model of the sun and of all the light-bearing stars that he was about to set in the heavens."[54] The text describes the creation of the seven incorporeal Ideas in Genesis 1:1–3 and says nothing about matter.

Harry Wolfson argued that since God created the Ideas of the elements and the void, it must also be the case that God created the sense-perceptible void and elements.[55] It was on this basis that Wolfson argued that Philo held a view of *creatio ex nihilo*. The problem is that Wolfson must assume a great deal: the text does not mention the four elements (fire is never mentioned) and does not make the critical connection between the intelligible world and the sense-perceptible world; that is, it does not indicate whether the Ideas were imposed on existing matter or created matter. There is more imagination than text in this reconstruction.

Does Philo ever connect the two in a treatise? He does in his dialogue *De providentia.* The section is reminiscent of the opening doxography in *De opificio mundi:* it begins with a critique of those who hold that the cosmos is eternal, having no beginning and not capable of being destroyed. It repeats the concern for divine inactivity, only this time the charge appears to be the same that Aristotle leveled against members of the Old Academy who argued for creation. The Stagirite wanted to know what God was doing prior to creation.[56] Those who argue for the eternity of the cosmos avoid this; however, they level a greater accusation against God. Philo specified the greater charge that he had in mind: they held that God ordered preexisting matter.[57] This however, raises the question: "Did matter take the place of a basic principle for God?"[58] The question is the same that Basil raised in his *Hexameron* that we cited above. For Philo as well as the later Christian the answer was no. The Alexandrian went on to give his own position: "God is continuously ordering matter by this thought. His thinking was not anterior to his creating and there never was a time when he did not create, the ideas themselves having been with him from the beginning." This is because "God's will is not posterior to him, but is always with him, for natural motions never give out." So, Philo concluded: "Thus ever thinking he creates, and furnishes to sensible things the principle of their existence, so that both should exist together: the ever-creating Divine Mind and the sense-perceptible things to which beginning of being is given."[59]

The statements in *De providentia* appear to be a working out of the basic problem that Philo raised in *De opificio mundi,* namely the eternity of matter and the need to subordinate matter to God. Philo might have given a different answer and argued that matter was so negative that it did not pose a threat to God.[60] However, he appears to refuse to recognize matter as a second principle in this text. He does not, however, simply argue that God created matter and then created the cosmos. Rather Philo suggests that God has always created. Since the ideas are God's thoughts,[61] as God thinks, the Ideas come into existence. At the same time, matter takes shape. It is all one simultaneous process. Since the process is eternal, matter was eternal and—at the same time—subordinated fully to God.[62] This is a considerable advance beyond the statements in *De opificio mundi.*

FIVE PRESUPPOSITIONS

A Summary and Its Sources

This leads us to our final text. At the end of *De opificio mundi,* Philo listed five tenets that he considered to be essential.[63] Erwin R. Goodenough called it "the first creed in history";[64] however, this is reading the text anachronistically. They represent tenets that Philo believed were essential to reading the Exposition of the Law and hence the Pentateuch correctly.[65] The five are as follows: God is eternal, God is one, the world was created, the world is one not many, and finally, God exercises providence over the cosmos. Two of these five are relevant for our consideration.

Philo's third presupposition is that the cosmos is created. He explained: "This is because of those who think that it is uncreated and eternal, who attribute to God nothing more."[66] The exegete has returned to the exordium of *De opificio mundi.* While Philo does not address the issue of matter in this statement, he emphasizes that God must be understood as being superior to the cosmos. He rejects the eternity of the cosmos on theological or metaphysical grounds since God must always be placed above all.

The fourth tenet is also relevant. Philo wrote that God "used all matter for the creation of the universe, since it would not have been whole if it had not been formed from all of it and consisted of the parts."[67] Philo's basic point about the perfection of the cosmos is drawn from Plato's argument that the cosmos is perfect because it used all of the four elements.[68] It is possible that he also had the biblical refrain, "God saw that it was good," in mind, although the connection is tenuous. It is more likely that he was influenced by the philosophical tradition, especially the Middle Platonic tradition that emphasized God's use of all matter in creation.[69] Philo was emphatic about God's use of all four elements and repeated it in other texts.[70] It was on this basis that he called the cosmos "the most perfect work" of God.[71]

Parallel Texts in Philo

The force of the argument is clear from one of these texts. In a section of *De providentia* that is preserved in Eusebius, Philo wrote: "Concerning the extent of matter [οὐσία], if it was in fact created, this should be said. For the creation of the cosmos God estimated the right amount of matter [ὕλη] so that there was neither too little nor too much." Philo explained: "For it would be out of place to hold that particular craftpersons when they make something—especially something expensive—estimate the right amount of material but that the One who invented numbers, measures, and the equalities in them did not pay sufficient attention."[72]

The point of Philo's statement is to defend God: God was a skilled Creator who took sufficient care with the creation of the world. This works particularly well with the view that we have argued for above that creation is part of a process in which God thinks the Ideas and creation follows from them. It is also in keeping with the basic concern that has been evident in all three texts that we have examined: Philo was first and foremost concerned with the priority of God. He bent other concepts to protect the uniqueness of God.

We may now return to our initial question: how did Philo understand matter? Our summary of some of the key texts indicates the challenges and complexities of dealing with Philo's statements. If we privilege one statement or one set of statements over others, we may claim that Philo held a consistent view. If we start with *De opificio mundi*, I am inclined to think that he considered matter eternal. At least the argument that God introduced order into chaotic matter appears to recognize the principle ἐκ τοῦ μὴ ὄντος οὐδὲν γίνεται (ex nihilo nihil fit).[73] If, on the other hand, we begin with *De providentia*, I think that he held a view of *creatio aeterna*. However, cutting the Gordian knot by opting for one text over against another does not solve the problem of how a single thinker could write both sets of texts.

It might be possible to explain some of the differences by the shift in audience. If the Exposition represents the work that Philo wrote for the widest possible audience, the dialogues represent works addressed to students within his own school. He could leave some things unexplained at a broad level that he could not when he addressed those who had greater expertise.

Another possible explanation for the distinction between the view in *De opificio mundi* and *De providentia* is to suggest that Philo's thought developed. This would work particularly well if *De opificio mundi* preceded *De providentia*. It would suggest that Philo began with the standard Middle Platonic position and then advanced it. Unfortunately, we cannot date the texts with any degree of certainty. The Exposition of the Law and the philosophical dialogues may both have come late in Philo's life.

Whatever the best explanation might be for the differences, we should not overlook the common point that appears in all of these texts. The constant is that Philo privileged the place of God. He registered this concern explicitly at the beginning and end of *De opificio mundi* (7–12 and 171) and again in *De providentia* 1.7–9. In his exposition of "day one" he made it clear that God introduced order into the disorder. His description of matter is negative until God works with it. Philo left no doubt about the relative place of God and matter. At the conclusion of the treatise, the Alexandrian returned to the importance of creation, arguing that to view the cosmos as uncreated and eternal undercuts the superiority of God over the cosmos. In his philosophical dialogue, Philo once again raised the issue of how our understanding of matter impacts our understanding of God. In all three cases, Philo reached a position that protected the uniqueness and transcendence of God.

I suggest that this theological concern led Philo to modify the Platonic tradition that he inherited. He was aware of the challenge that eternal matter posed for his understanding of God and attempted to address it. Yet he never affirmed that matter was created. At the same time, his basic concern to protect the sovereignty of God helped Christians who inherited his views to take that step, and a step beyond to *creatio ex nihilo*. This was not a step that Philo took; at least he never articulated it clearly.

Another way of thinking of his position is to realize that he is a bridge between Hellenistic philosophers who held to the eternity of matter and early Christians who believed that God created all.[74] Philo knew the debates of the former and anticipated the basic concerns of the latter, yet he represented neither fully. He was closer in some ways to Plotinus than he was to either Aristotle or the Fourth Lateran Council. For some of us, it is his struggle with the philosophical issues of his day and the questions that he posed in those struggles that continue to make him worth reading.

NOTES

1. Augustine, *Conf.* 12.3. All translations are my own unless otherwise noted.

2. Augustine, *Conf.* 12.4. The last, italicized phrase is a literal translation of the LXX of Gen. 1:2 (ἡ δὲ γῆ ἦν ἀόρατος καὶ ἀκατασκεύαστος), which appeared in the Old Latin (terra autem erat invisibilis et incomposita) but not the Vulgate (terra autem erat inanis et vacua).

3. Augustine, *Conf.* 12.6.

4. David T. Runia, *Philo of Alexandria and the "Timaeus" of Plato*, Philosophia Antiqua 44 (Leiden: Brill, 1986), 455. Compare the assessment of David Winston, *Logos and Mystical Theology in Philo of Alexandria* (Cincinnati: Hebrew Union College Press, 1985), 47: "His conception of primordial matter out of which God created the world is so vague that it is virtually impossible to ascertain his understanding of this concept with any degree of certainty."

5. Major Philonists who have held this position include Harry Austryn Wolfson, *Philo: Foundations of Religious Philosophy in Judaism, Christianity,*

and Islam, 2 vols. (Cambridge, MA: Harvard University Press, 1947), 1:295–324, esp. 300–310; Wolfson, "Plato's Pre-Existent Matter in Patristic Philosophy," in *The Classical Tradition: Literary and Historical Studies in Honor of Harry Chaplan*, ed. Luitpold Wallach (Ithaca, NY: Cornell University Press, 1966), 409–20; and Roberto Radice, *Platonismo e Creazionismo in Filone di Alessandria*, Metafisica del Platonismo nel suo Sviluppo Storico e nella Filosofia Patristica 7 (Milan: Università Cattolica del Sacro Cuore, 1989), 153–58, 378–82. Many others have explored the texts carefully and argued for this position. J. C. O'Neill, "How Early Is the Doctrine of *Creatio ex nihilo?*" *Journal of Theological Studies* 53 (2002): 449–65, is a recent example.

6. Among the major figures who have argued for this position are Hans-Friedrich Weiss, *Untersuchungen zur Kosmologie des hellenistischen und palästinischen Judentums*, Texte und Untersuchungen 97 (Berlin: Akademie Verlag, 1966), 18–74, esp. 59–74; Georgias D. Farandos, *Kosmos und Logos nach Philon von Alexandria* (Amsterdam: Rodopi, 1976), 279–90; Runia, *Philo of Alexandria and the "Timaeus" of Plato*, 155–57, 451–56; and Gerhard May, *Creatio ex Nihilo: The Doctrine of "Creation out of Nothing" in Early Christian Thought*, trans. A. S. Worrell (Edinburgh: T&T Clark, 1994), 9–21.

7. Many have qualified their views (e.g., Weiss and Runia above), but the best representatives of this view are Richard Sorabji, *Time, Creation, and the Continuum: Theories in Antiquity and the Early Middle Ages* (Ithaca, NY: Cornell University Press, 1983), 203–9, and Al Wolters, "*Creatio ex Nihilo* in Philo," in *Hellenization Revisited: Shaping a Christian Response within the Greco-Roman World*, ed. Wendy E. Helleman (Lanham, MD: University Press of America, 1994), 107–24.

8. The most important advocate of this view is David Winston, "Philo's Theory of Cosmogony," in *Religious Syncretism in Antiquity: Essays in Conversation with Geo Widengren*, ed. Birger A. Pearson, Series on Formative Contemporary Thinkers 1 (Missoula, MT: Scholars Press, 1975), 157–71; Winston, "Philo's Theory of Eternal Creation," *Proceedings of the American Academy of Jewish Research* 46–47 (1980): 593–606; Winston, *Philo of Alexandria: "The Contemplative Life," "The Giants," and Selections*, The Classics of Western Spirituality (Ramsey, NJ: Paulist Press, 1985), 23–25, 47–49; Winston, *Logos and Mystical Theology in Philo of Alexandria*, 47–49.

9. On this debate see Gregory E. Sterling, "*Creatio temporalis, aeterna, vel continua?* An Analysis of the Thought of Philo of Alexandria," *The Studia Philonica Annual* 4 (1992): 15–41.

10. E.g., Philo uses the expression of bringing into existence out of non-being, as in *Leg.* 3.10, ἐκ μὴ ὄντων, or *Mos.* 2.267, ἐκ τοῦ μὴ ὄντος. These expressions only indicate that something that did not previously exist came into existence. Cf. Attticus in Eusebius, *Praep. ev.* 15.6.7, οὐκ ὄντα πρότερον ἐποίησε

τὸν κόσμον. It is a mistake to cite these texts as evidence that Philo held a view of *creatio ex nihilo*.

11. Philo used ὕλη 177 times, most frequently without a reference to primordial matter. He often simply means the material or substance of something, e.g., a tree (*Opif.* 40, 142; *Leg.* 1.49; *Cher.* 100 [stones or wood]; *Det.* 105, 111; *Agr.* 19; *Plant.* 97; *Sobr.* 36 [wood]; *Conf.* 107 [stones or trees]; *Mos.* 1.19; *Spec.* 1.74; 4.209; *Contempl.* 69; *Aet.* 64, 96) or fire (*Sobr.* 43; *Migr.* 120; *Her.* 307; *Congr.* 55; *Somn.* 2.93, 181; *Mos.* 1.65; 2.58, 214, 220; *Decal.* 173; *Spec.* 1.254; 4.2, 83, 118, 125; *Virt.* 162; *Praem.* 71; *Legat.* 129, 130, 132; *Prov.* 2.40; *QG* 4.172; *QE* 2.15, 47, 50). A word study would not resolve the issue that we are addressing.

12. Thomas H. Tobin, "The Beginning of Philo's *Legum Allegoriae*," *The Studia Philonica Annual* 12 (2000): 29–43.

13. David T. Runia, *Philo of Alexandria, "On the Creation of the Cosmos": Introduction, Translation, and Commentary*, Philo of Alexandria Commentary Series 1 (Leiden: Brill, 2001), 10–17.

14. Philo, *Opif.* 7.

15. Runia, *Philo of Alexandria, "On the Creation of the Cosmos,"* 112–13, 121–23, and Abraham P. Bos, "Philo of Alexandria: A Platonist in the Image and Likeness of Aristotle," *The Studia Philonica Annual* 10 (1998): 66–86, argue that Philo had the Chaldeans in mind. For a critique of this view see Franco Trabattoni, "Philo *De opificio mundi 7–12*," in *The Origins of the Platonic System: Platonisms of the Early Empire and Their Philosophical Contexts*, ed. Mauro Bonazzi and Jan Opsomer, Collection d'études classique 23 (Leuven: Peeters, 2009), 113–22, whose criticisms are better than his own reconstruction of a biblical Platonism that ignores the evidence of Middle Platonism.

16. Philo, *Opif.* 9.

17. There is a dispute whether Philo intends to draw a parallel between τὸ δραστήριον αἴτιον and τὸ παθητόν. F. H. Colson, *Philo*, 12 vols., LCL (Cambridge, MA: Harvard University Press, 1929–153), 1:9, 11, renders: "one part active Cause and the other passive object." He is followed by Runia, *Philo of Alexandria, "On the Creation of the Cosmos,"* 115–16. On the other hand, Roger Arnaldez, *"De opificio mundi": Introduction, Traduction et Notes*, Les Oeuvres de Philon d'Alexandrie 1 (Paris: Éditions du Cerf, 1961), 147, rendered it "une cause active et une cause passive." Cf. also Weiss, *Untersuchungen zur Kosmologie*, 42. See the following section of the essay for my analysis.

18. E.g., Diogenes Laertius 7.134: "They think that there are two principles [ἀρχαί] in the universe, the active and the passive [τὸ ποιοῦν καὶ τὸ πάσχον]: the passive is the substance without quality, matter; the active is the Reason in it, God."

19. E.g., Cicero, *Acad.* 1.39; Sextus Empiricus, *Math.* 8.263.

20. Philo's use of Stoic language, but with a different framework, was recognized in a series of essays in a recent collection: Anthony A. Long, "Philo on Stoic Physics," in *Philo of Alexandria and Post-Aristotelian Philosophy*, ed. Francesca Alesse, Studies in Philo of Alexandria 5 (Leiden: Brill, 2008), 121–40, esp. 139; John Dillon, "Philo and Hellenistic Platonism," in ibid., 223–32, esp. 224, 229–30; and Mauro Bonazzi, "Towards Transcendence: Philo and the Renewal of Platonism in the Early Imperial Age," in ibid., 233–51, esp. 234–36.

21. E.g., Aristotle, *De an.* 3.4.430a; *De gen.* 1.7 323b; 2.9.335b; *Mot. An.* 8.702a; *Phys.* 8.4.255a.

22. John Dillon, "Cosmic Gods and Primordial Chaos in Hellenistic and Roman Philosophy: The Context of Philo's Interpretation of Plato's *Timaeus* and the Book of Genesis," in *The Creation of Heaven and Earth: Re-Interpretations of Genesis 1 in the Context of Judaism, Ancient Philosophy, Christianity, and Modern Physics*, ed. George H. van Kooten, Themes in Biblical Narrative: Jewish and Christians Traditions 8 (Leiden: Brill, 2005), 97–108. See also his "Philo and Hellenistic Platonism," 229–30, where he emphasizes the place of Antiochus as the source for the two principles in the Platonic tradition.

23. David Sedley, "The Origins of the Stoic God," in *Tradition of Theology: Studies in Hellenistic Theology*, ed. Dorothea Frede and André Laks (Leiden: Brill, 2002), 41–83, argued that this goes back to the Old Academy, specifically to Polemo or his school, but the evidence for this is thin.

24. Cicero, *Acad.* 1.24.

25. Theophrastus, frg. 230 (W. W. Fortenbaugh); trans. Dillon.

26. Mauro Bonazzi, "Towards Transcendence: Philo and the Renewal of Platonism in the Early Imperial Age," in Alesse, *Philo of Alexandria and Post-Aristotelian Philosophy*, 233–51; Bonazzi, "Pythagoreanizing Aristotle: Eudorus and the Systematization of Platonism," in *Aristotle, Plato and Pythagoreanism in the First Century BC*, ed. Malcolm Schofield (Cambridge: Cambridge University Press, 2013), 160–86, esp. 171–72. The key text is Simplicius, *In Phys.* 181.7–30.

27. Philo, *Fug.* 133–34.

28. Bonazzi, "Towards Transcendence," 235.

29. Philo, *Prov.* 1.22.

30. Philo, *Prov.* 1.22. Trans. Runia in *Philo of Alexandria and the "Timaeus" of Plato*, 119.

31. Aristotle, *Phys.* 2.3–9.194b–200b.

32. Seneca, *Ep.* 65, provides an overview of the positions.

33. See Gregory E. Sterling, "Prepositional Metaphysics in Jewish Wisdom Speculation and Early Christian Liturgical Texts," *The Studia Philonica Annual* 9 (1997): 219–38, esp. 227–28.

34. Philo, *Cher.* 124–27.

35. Philo has similar presentations in *QG* 1.58 (three causes) and *Prov.* 1.23 (four causes, although the last cause appears to have been πρὸς ὅ).

36. Basil, *Hex.* 2.4 (PG 29:32A).

37. Cf. also Philo, *Fug.* 198, where he is emphatic about God's superiority over matter: "For matter is dead, but God is something more than life, an always flowing spring of living, as he himself says."

38. Philo, *Opif.* 15–35.

39. Plato, *Tim.* 29E.

40. Philo, *Opif.* 21.

41. Philo, *Opif.* 15–16, 35.

42. Philo, *Opif.* 129–30.

43. Valentin Nikiprowetzky, "Problèmes du 'récit de la création' chez Philon d'Alexandrie," *Revue des études juives* 124 (1965): 271–306. For a critique see Runia, *Philo of Alexandria and the "Timaeus" of Plato*, 553–54.

44. Runia, *Philo of Alexandria, "On the Creation of the Cosmos,"* 19–20, 309–11.

45. Thomas H. Tobin, *The Creation of Man: Philo and the History of Interpretation*, Catholic Biblical Quarterly Monograph Series 14 (Washington, DC: Catholic Biblical Association of America, 1983), 20–35, 59–60.

46. Gregory E. Sterling, "'Day One': Platonizing Exegetical Traditions of Genesis 1:1–5 in John and Jewish Authors," *The Studia Philonica Annual* 17 (2005): 118–40. The other key texts that suggest that this interpretation of "day one" had wide circulation are John 1:1–5 and 2 En. 24:2–26:3.

47. For a treatment of the interpretation of Gen. 1:2 in Judaism during this period see Menahem Kister, "*Tohu wa-Bohu*, Primordial Elements and Creatio ex Nihilo," *Jewish Studies Quarterly* 14 (2009): 229–56.

48. Cf. Augustine, *Conf.* 12.5–9, who thought that the earth of Gen. 1:1 referred to unformed matter.

49. Philo, *Spec.* 1.324–29.

50. Philo, *Spec.* 1.327.

51. Philo, *Spec.* 1.328.

52. Philo, *Spec.* 1.329.

53. E.g., Philo, *Her.* 157–60, esp. 160: "God did not praise the matter with which he had worked: lifeless, faulty, and dissolvable, even by itself perishable, irregular, unequal, but he praised the things he made." Cf. also *Contempl.* 3–4, esp. 4: "Their names [the names of the elements] are the inventions of sophists, but the elements are lifeless matter [ἄψυχος ὕλη] and immovable by their own power but placed as a foundation by the Creator of all for every kind of shape and quality."

54. Philo, *Opif.* 29. Kister, *"Tohu wa-Bohu,"* 242–43, pointed out that Jub. 2:2–3 also knows that seven things were created on day one and thinks that Philo and the author of Jubilees drew on a common tradition. This is possible; however, I am inclined to think that both drew the seven from the biblical text: heaven, earth, waters, spirit, the abyss, darkness, and light. Their presuppositions are different. Cf. also Gen. Rab. 1:9 and the discussion of Maren Niehoff, *"Creatio ex nihilo:* Theology in *Genesis Rabbah* in Light of Christian Exegesis," *Harvard Theological Review* 99 (2005): 37–64; Kister, *"Tohu wa-Bohu,"* 247–56.

55. Wolfson, *Philo,* 1:300–310, esp. 306–10.

56. Ps-Plutarch, *Mor.* 881B–C.

57. Here I disagree with Sorabji, *Time, Creation, and the Continuum,* 204, who thought that the maximum charge was that creation implied God was finished with his work.

58. Philo, *Prov.* 1.7.

59. Philo, *Prov.* 1.7.

60. So Runia, *Philo of Alexandria and the "Timaeus" of Plato,* 451–55.

61. On this concept in Philo see Roberto Radice, "Observations on the Theory of Ideas as the Thoughts of God in Philo of Alexandria," *The Studia Philonica Annual* 3 (1991): 126–34.

62. Compare the statement of Alcinous, *Did.* 169.32–37: "When he says that the cosmos is created [γενητόν], one must not understand him to say that there was ever a time when the cosmos did not exist; rather, it is always in a state of becoming [ἐν γενέσει] and discloses a more ancient cause [ἀρχικώτερόν τι αἴτιον] of its existence."

63. Philo, *Opif.* 170–72.

64. Erwin R. Goodenough, *An Introduction to Philo Judaeus,* 2nd ed. (Oxford: Blackwell, 1962), 37.

65. Runia, *Philo of Alexandria, "On the Creation of the Cosmos,"* 391–94, provides an overview of the assessments and offers a helpful perspective.

66. Philo, *Opif.* 171.

67. Philo, *Opif.* 171.

68. Plato, *Tim.* 32c–33a.

69. E.g., Plutarch, *Quaest. conv.* 720b–c.

70. Philo, *Plant.* 5; *De Deo* 7.

71. E.g., *Plant.* 6, 131; *Conf.* 97; *Mos.* 2.267; *Spec.* 2.59. Cf. also *Aet.* 15 and *Prov.* frg. 1.

72. Philo, *Prov.* frg. 1 (Eusebius, *Praep. ev.* 7.21.1–4).

73. Philo cited this at *Aet.* 5. Cf. Aristotle, *Metaph.* 11.6.1026b.

74. See Janet M. Soskice, *"Creatio ex nihilo:* Its Jewish and Christian Foundations," in *Creation and the God of Abraham,* ed. David B. Burrell et al.

(Cambridge: Cambridge University Press, 2010), 24–39, esp. 33–34, where she correctly points out that Philo is not consistent but provides the basic foundation for *creatio ex nihilo* through his metaphysics by grounding them in Exod. 3:14; Soskice, "Creation and the Glory of Creatures," *Modern Theology* 29 (2013): 172–85, esp. 177–81, where she again points out that Philo lays the metaphysical foundations of *creatio ex nihilo* by his understanding of God.

CHAPTER 6

Creatio ex nihilo in Athanasius of Alexandria's Against the Greeks– On the Incarnation

KHALED ANATOLIOS

An analysis of Athanasius's doctrine of creation *ex nihilo* as articulated in his classic double treatise, *Against the Greeks–On the Incarnation*, can make a distinctive contribution to our understanding of this fundamental Christian teaching in at least three ways. First, it is arguably one of the most systematically emphatic treatments of this aspect of the doctrine of creation in patristic literature. This emphasis is all the more fascinating and instructive for being unevenly distributed. The first chapters of the first part of the Alexandrian's double treatise, *Against the Greeks*, treat of divine creative activity and the original state of creation without any mention of the "*ex nihilo*," while its latter chapters begin to stress this motif in a way that will be even further intensified in the second part of the treatise, *On the Incarnation*. It seems that Athanasius himself discovered the significance of this aspect of the doctrine of creation in the course of composing his double treatise.[1] An attentiveness to his treatment of creation's origin *ex nihilo* in this work thus not only provides us with an opportunity to ponder his explicit rationale for emphasizing this teaching but also provides a dramatic demonstration of the specific difference this teaching makes to the presentation of the Christian understanding of creation, a difference manifest in the development of the text itself.

Second, this work deals with the doctrine of creation in a thematic way and yet its overarching aim is not to provide a description of creation itself, as we find, for example, in patristic commentaries on the Hexaemeron, but rather to offer a rationally plausible account of the Christian proclamation as a whole, encompassing "knowledge of religion and the truth about the universe [ἤ μὲν περὶ τῆς θεοσεβείας καὶ τῆς τῶν ὅλων ἀληθείας γνῶσις]."[2] An analysis of Athanasius's doctrine of creation *ex nihilo* in this treatise can thus provide us with an exemplary, if not uniquely normative, demonstration of the location and role of this doctrine within the theological enterprise considered as a whole. As we shall see, Athanasius's theological procedure especially highlights the continuity between the orders of creation and salvation, and the doctrine of creation *ex nihilo* plays a foundational role in informing this continuity.[3]

Third, as a consequence of this integration of the doctrine of creation *ex nihilo* within the entirety of the Christian proclamation, Athanasius provides us with a distinctively "existential" account of this doctrine. Recalling Heidegger's dismissal of classical metaphysics as the reifying occlusion of the self-disclosure of Being and his advocacy for its replacement by an "existential analytic" that probes into the fundamental structures of "being-in-the-world," we can say that Athanasius's treatment of *creatio ex nihilo* decisively transcends this dichotomy. The Alexandrian's presentation of this doctrine makes metaphysical truth claims about divine and created beings and their interrelation, but it is even more preoccupied with showing how these metaphysical truths are manifest in the existence of human beings in this world, once this world is interpreted in light of the Christian proclamation. His "existential" analysis of the doctrine of creation *ex nihilo* can still speak to our postmodern world.

In service of a reading of Athanasius's *Against the Greeks–On the Incarnation* that is attentive to the distinctive contributions that I have claimed for it, my analysis will proceed in three movements. I will first present my understanding of Athanasius's construal of the necessary mutual correlation of the doctrines of creation and redemption in the Christian proclamation, since this construal structures the work as a whole. I will then analyze Athanasius's ontology of creation *ex nihilo*, tracing its development from *Against the Greeks* to *On the Incarnation*, with reference to three key features: divine goodness, the dialectic of creaturely being, and the ontological status of evil and death. Third, I will attempt to show how the doctrine of *creatio ex nihilo* determines Athanasius's soteriology. In my conclusion, I suggest that Athanasius's existential analysis of the doctrine of creation *ex nihilo* could be extended further by a consideration of the Eucharist as the event in which the human creature can experience its being-from-nothing in its most salutary form, as thanksgiving and praise for divine goodness.

THE DOCTRINE OF CREATION WITHIN
THE CHRISTIAN PROCLAMATION

The function and significance of Athanasius's doctrine of creation, in relation to his theological vision as a whole, have been subjected to two prevalent distortions.[4] First, and most pervasively, his later anti-Arian emphases on the radical otherness between God and the world and the inherent instability of creatures are abstracted from their native context of Athanasius's more fully articulated theology of creation in the earlier *Against the Greeks–On the Incarnation*. Second, the latter half of that double treatise is usually read in isolation from the first. The result of the latter fragmentation is that *On the Incarnation* is read as a self-contained *Cur Deus Homo* argument, while *Against the Greeks*, if considered at all, appears to be a refutation of idolatry in the mode of apologetic triumphalism. When Athanasius himself declares at the very beginning of this treatise that "all idolatry has been overcome" by the cross of Christ,[5] one can wonder if this amounts to an unwitting confession that he is in fact engaged in the erudite beating of a dead horse. However, a close reading of the introductory remarks of both parts of this double treatise reveals that Athanasius is implementing a well-considered strategy based on a particular conception of how the theology of creation is related to the proclamation of the crucified and risen Christ within the Christian account of truth.

As noted above, Athanasius declares in the opening words of *Against the Greeks* that his subject matter is "knowledge of religion and the truth about the universe." He further asserts that this knowledge is available in the teaching of Christ and is self-validating: "Knowledge of piety and the truth about all things does not so much require human teaching as it is knowable of itself . . . and manifests itself more clearly than the sun through the teaching of Christ."[6] While the scriptures are sufficient witness to Christ's teaching, Athanasius justifies his own theological exposition as a response to those who consider faith in Christ to be "irrational [ἄλογον]." He further contends that this refusal of Christ's teaching is motivated by the rejection in particular of the message of the cross, whereas it is actually the cross which is the key to true knowledge: "When they slander the cross, they fail to see that its power has filled the whole world, and that through it the works of the knowledge of God have been manifested to all."[7] The cross is not a blight on creation, argues the Alexandrian bishop, but rather heals it; it is the "therapy of creation."[8] It is because of the cross that idolatry has been overthrown and the whole world has been filled with the knowledge of God. Consequently, it is reasonable to conclude that "the one who ascended the cross is the Word of God and the Saviour of all."[9]

After his extended "refutation of idolatry" through the course of *Against the Greeks*, Athanasius's introduction to *On the Incarnation* returns to the same theme of the cross of Christ as the key to the plausibility of the Christian proclamation. The cross is slandered by Jews and mocked by Greeks, but through it Jesus Christ provides persuasive witness to his divinity, demonstrates the fittingness of what human beings consider to be impossible and unsuitable, and overthrows the illusion of idols.[10] Immediately after this reprise of the introduction to *Against the Greeks*, Athanasius explains that the first task in the exposition of the message of the incarnation and the cross is to recall the Christian conception of creation: "We must first speak about the creation of the universe and of God as its Creator, so that one may accordingly consider it fitting that its renewal was accomplished by the Word who created it in the beginning."[11] Athanasius then proceeds to outline various philosophical and heretical accounts of creation before reiterating the Christian teaching on creation *ex nihilo*. He follows that reiteration by returning to the question of "why, when we set out to speak about the incarnation of the Word, we are now expounding on the beginning of humanity."[12] His response is that the correct account of human origins is necessary for understanding the rationale of the incarnation, "in order that you may know that our own cause was the motive for his descent."[13]

What do these two introductions to the two parts of Athanasius's double treatise tell us about the function of the doctrine of creation in his presentation of the Christian proclamation as "rational" and self-evident? Given the parameters of his project, he is understandably not concerned with providing a description of the genesis of the cosmos. Rather, he is supposing that the "rationality" and "fittingness" of Christian discourse consists, at least partially, in proposing a coherent and mutually referential account of Christ and creation. In proclaiming Christ to be the Savior of the world, one of the constituent tasks of Christian theology is to provide an account of this world which is saved by Christ. But Athanasius does not resort to any prolegomenon by way of an account of creation that arises from a reasoned apprehension of the world apart from faith and which then grounds faith. Rather, he begins with an exposé of idolatry which demonstrates humanity's propensity to misunderstand creation and to confuse the creature with the Creator. Even though "creation itself cries out and indicates its Maker and Creator, who rules over all, the Father of our Lord Jesus Christ,"[14] this cry has been both muffled and systematically distorted by humanity's propensity to idolatry. In his preoccupation with the theme of idolatry and its overcoming by Christ, Athanasius is not merely indulging in triumphalistic gloating but rather demonstrating his claim that the truth about creation is knowable only through Christ. This world which is saved by Christ is in fact not knowable on its own terms apart from its being saved by Christ. The crucified and risen Christ *makes sense* of creation and renders it luminous and transparent again to the activity and presence of "the Father of our Lord Jesus Christ," and is thus both ontologically and epistemologically "the therapy of creation." At the same time, an account of creation which is itself derived from the proclamation of Christ "makes sense" of the crucified and risen Christ. Thus, it is only the mutual reference of creation and

Christ that saves the Christian proclamation from being dismissible by its detractors as "irrational [ἄλογον]," and which positively demonstrates the self-evidence of the Christian proclamation as "shining more brightly than the sun."[15] This seems to be the underlying formal structure that binds together the material contents of the two parts of this double treatise. *Against the Greeks* outlines the basic elements of a Christian ontology in contrast to the misunderstanding of both God and creation which is represented by idolatry, while *On the Incarnation* demonstrates the "rationality" of the proclamation of Jesus Christ as the incarnated, crucified, and risen Lord by showing its consistency with the ontology which this proclamation itself prescribes. An account of Athanasius's doctrine of creation *ex nihilo* cannot abstract from this foundational design and simply extract various affirmations of this doctrine in order to count Athanasius as one of those who considered it a fact that creation came to be from nothing. Rather, it must show how Athanasius understood this doctrine to be integral to the "rationality" of the Christian proclamation, as indicating the consistency of the mutual referencing of ontology and soteriology within that proclamation. In pursuit of this task, we can now proceed to an account of how the doctrine of creation *ex nihilo* informs Athanasius's account of a Christian ontology.

ATHANASIUS'S ONTOLOGY OF CREATION *EX NIHILO*

Creation *ex nihilo* and Divine Goodness

Throughout *Against the Greeks–On the Incarnation*, Athanasius consistently introduces statements about the origin of creation with an affirmation of divine goodness. Though he does not advert to particular biblical passages to support this characterization, it is obviously consistent with the scriptural presentation of the God of Israel and the Father of Jesus Christ as a God of unbounded mercy and love. At the same time, Athanasius was writing within a context in which questions regarding the characterization of divine goodness in relation to divine involvement in the world were vigorously debated and were significant markers of distinct philosophical movements. A foundational text for both Greek philosophy and Christian theology on this issue, and on the subject of the genesis of creation generally, was Plato's *Timaeus*. In a key passage within this dialogue, Plato reiterates his fundamental contrast between the realms of being and becoming (27D). The world of sensible things clearly belongs to the realm of becoming and not to that of being, which is "always in existence and without beginning" (28B). Therefore, it came into being, says Plato, "by a cause" (28B). This cause is styled "the Artificer" or "Demiurge" (28C), whose activity consists in bringing disorder into order according to the archetypes that constitute the realm of unchanging being. Plato does not speak of a creation "from nothing" but of the imposition of the intelligible, true, and beautiful upon disorderly matter. The motive for this activity was the goodness of the Creator, who desired that his own perfections be reflected in the realm of becoming:

> Let me tell you then why the creator made this world of generation. He was good, and the good can never have any jealousy of anything [ἀγαθῷ δὲ οὐδεὶς περὶ οὐδενὸς οὐδέποτε ἐγγίγνεται φθόνος]. And being free from jealousy, he desired that all things should be as like himself as they could be. This is in the truest sense the origin of creation and of the world. . . . God desired that all things should be good and nothing bad, so far as this was attainable. Wherefore also finding the whole visible sphere not at rest, but moving in an irregular and disorderly fashion, out of disorder he brought order, considering that this was in every way better than the other.[16]

The question of whether Plato was positing a punctiliar beginning of a created cosmos was controverted among his ancient commentators.[17] However, his affirmation of divine goodness and beneficence toward creation became standard and was further intensified in Stoic denunciations of the Epicurean denial of divine providence. At the same time, there was a notable tendency in the progress of Platonic thought which posited the highest divine principle, who is named "the Good" by Plotinus, as increasingly distant and removed from less transcendent divine entities who communicated order and intelligibility to matter.[18] In his characterization of God as Creator, Athanasius presumes Plato's conception of divine goodness but subverts the increasing contemporary emphasis on separating divine transcendence and immanence, insisting that the fullness of divine transcendence coincides with God's direct interaction with and care for a creation which he brought into being from nothing.[19] There are four passages in *Against the Greeks–On the Incarnation* which reiterate the same logical structure whereby an affirmation of divine greatness and goodness is immediately followed by an account of creation. A brief survey of these passages will demonstrate how the doctrine of *creatio ex nihilo* progressively informed and enhanced Athanasius's characterization of divine goodness.

The first of these passages occurs near the beginning of *Against the Greeks* and does not contain an explicit doctrine of *creatio ex nihilo*. It implicitly refutes the Platonic logic of attributing the highest divine transcendence and the creative "demiurgic" function to two separate beings within an ontological hierarchy. Rather, God's "beyondness" and his beneficence toward creation are coordinate characterizations of the one God, who creates through his Word (Logos). Divine beneficence toward the human creation is depicted in an incipiently Trinitarian manner. The Logos is the true Image of the Father, while humanity was made "according to the Image" of the Word, in order to participate in the Word's imaging of the Father. Notwithstanding these significant points of contrast with the Platonic tradition, this passage contains clear Platonic overtones. Particularly noteworthy for our purposes is the fact that, in the absence of a consideration of *creatio ex nihilo*, the fundamental dialectic of creaturely being is characterized in terms of the Platonic contrast between the intelligible and the sensible:

> God, the Creator of the universe and King of all, is beyond all being and human conception. Since he is good and exceedingly gracious, he has made human beings in his own image through his own Word, our Savior Jesus Christ, and he also made the human race perceptive and cognizant of existent things through its similarity to him. He granted it also a conception and knowledge of its own eternity, so that as long as it maintained this likeness, it would never depart from the manifestation of God or leave the company of the saints, but holding on to the grace of him who granted it, and also the special power given it by the Father's Word, it would rejoice and converse with God, living a secure and truly blessed

and immortal life. Without any impediment to the knowledge of the divine, human beings contemplate, by virtue of their purity, the image of the Father, God the Word, in whose image they were made. They are astounded when they contemplate his providence toward all things and are superior to sensual things and all bodily impressions and, by the power of their mind, cling to the divine and intelligible things in heaven.[20]

As we advance toward the last third of *Against the Greeks*, we encounter a passage manifesting the same logical sequence of the affirmations of divine goodness and the coordinance of divine transcendence and immanence, followed by an account of God's original creative act. In this passage, however, there is the insertion of an explicit doctrine of creation's coming to be from nothing. This development brings about further adjustments in Athanasius's doctrine of creation. Whereas in the passage quoted above it is asserted that in the original creation humanity had no "impediment to the knowledge of the divine" and could enjoy knowledge of God so long as it maintained its abstraction from material realities, here the fact that humanity was created *ex nihilo* is considered as preempting its knowledge of God. The incommensurability between Creator and created beings is depicted in absolute terms, and these terms impose themselves even on rational creatures who, in the Platonic tradition, have a natural kinship with the intelligible realm. However, God's creative act includes a compensation for the ontological gap between humanity's origin from nothingness and God's uncreated being. Moreover, God orders and designs the entire creation so as to communicate knowledge of himself. Thus, the overcoming of the gap between the uncreated God and the creation that comes to be from nothing is both a divine act and a constitutive aspect of the creation itself:

> God is good and loves humanity and cares for the souls which he has brought into being. Since he is by nature invisible and incomprehensible, being above all originated being, the human race would not have been capable of attaining knowledge of him, inasmuch as they were made from nothing while he was uncreated. Therefore, God ordered creation through his Word in such a way that although he was invisible by nature, yet he might be known to

human beings through his works. . . . For God did not misuse his invisible nature—let no one assume that pretext—and leave himself completely unknowable to people.[21]

In this passage, we see Athanasius's distinctive and recurring preoccupation that God does not "misuse" his own transcendence. Such a "misuse" would consist in God's letting the difference between his own nature and that of the originated creation supervene over the positive relation between God and the world. Rather, God makes benevolent use of his own transcendence in the very act of creation, constituting it so that its intrinsic being may render God recognizable. Athanasius finds scriptural warrant for this understanding in Romans 1:20, "Ever since the creation of the world his eternal power and divine nature, invisible though they are, have been understood and seen through the things he has made," and Acts 14:15–17, which not only asserts that God "made the heaven and the earth and the sea and all that is in them," but, more significantly for Athanasius's purpose, declares that in all this creative activity, God did not leave himself without "a witness in doing good" (οὐκ ἀμάρτυρον αὐτὸν ἀφῆκεν ἀγαθουργῶν). This understanding of the benevolent divine compensation for creation's inherent nothingness is further elaborated in *Against the Greeks* 41, which articulates a doctrine of creation from nothing both in terms of the philosophical notion of "participation" and the biblical conception of creation's being "in Christ." Creation's being from nothing is simultaneously its being in God:

> The reason why the Word of God entirely pervaded the things that came into existence is truly wonderful, and it shows that things should not have occurred otherwise than just as they are. For the nature of created things, having come into being from nothing, is fleeting and mortal when considered on its own terms. But the God of all is good and exceedingly gracious by nature; therefore, he is also a lover of humanity. For the good is not jealous of any one, so he envies nobody being but rather wills for everyone to be, in order that he may love humanity. Seeing that all created nature, according to its own definitions, is fleeting and susceptible to dissolution, in order to prevent this from happening and the universe

dissolving back into nonbeing, after making everything by his own eternal Word and granting being to creation, he did not abandon it to be carried away and suffer through its own nature, to the point of being in danger of returning to nothing. Rather, being good, he governs and establishes everything through his own Word who is himself God, so that creation may be illuminated by the leadership, providence, and ordering of the Word and enabled to remain secure, since it participates in the Word who is truly from the Father and is thus aided by him to exist, lest it suffer what would happen, I mean a reversion to nonexistence, if the Word did not protect it: "For he is the image of the invisible God, the firstborn of all creation, because through him and in him subsist all things, visible and invisible, and he is the head of the church" [Col. 1.15], as the servants of the truth teach in the holy writings.[22]

I have quoted this passage at length because it gathers together a number of important aspects of Athanasius's fully developed understanding of the ontology of creation *ex nihilo*. Yet again, we encounter the recurring affirmation of divine goodness. But this time the Alexandrian insinuates a subtle but significant contrast between the Platonic conception of divine creative goodness and the one indicated by the doctrine of creation *ex nihilo*. As we have seen, Plato's *Timaeus* identifies the motive for the creative ordering of formless matter by saying that the Demiurge is good and "the good can never have any jealousy of anything [ἀγαθῷ δὲ οὐδεὶς περὶ οὐδενὸς οὐδέποτε ἐγγίγνεται φθόνος]." Athanasius pointedly echoes this explanation when he says that "the good would not be jealous of anyone" (ἀγαθῷ γὰρ περὶ οὐδενὸς ἂν γένοιτο φθόνος). But after recalling this Platonic association of creative activity with beneficent liberality, as contrasted with the jealous withholding of one's gifts, Athanasius indicates that the doctrine of creation *ex nihilo* extends the divine liberality beyond the imposition of order to the bestowal of being itself; the Christian God "envies nobody *being* but rather wills for everyone to be [ὅθεν οὐδὲ τὸ εἶναί τινι φθονεῖ, ἀλλὰ πάντας εἶναι βούλεται]." This liberality of the divine granting of being includes within it the divine subsidizing of creation's intrinsic ontological poverty. God does not only bring creation into being from nothing but also maintains it from relapsing into nothingness. For Athanasius, this maintenance is not something separate from the act of creation, but integral to it. In this passage, we see Athanasius using the terminology of "securing" (βεβαιοόω), "protecting" (τηρέω), and "remaining" (μένω) to speak of the divine ontological subsidizing of creation. The use of the last term in Athanasius's ontology is analogous to its Johannine use with reference to Christian discipleship, though the Alexandrian does not make this connection explicit. Just as Christ's disciples can "do nothing" unless they "remain" in him (cf. John 15:4–5), so creation escapes its own "nothingness" only by "remaining" in God.[23] Athanasius speaks of this remaining in the technical philosophical language of "participation": creation can "remain secure" because it "participates in the Word" (Λόγου μεταλαμβάνουσα). But he also associates it with scriptural language of God's "establishing" creation and enabling it to "remain," as in Psalm 118:90–91 (LXX): "You have established the earth and it remains. By your command it remains today."[24] Thus, created being, from its very inception, is a dynamic movement from nothingness to a *remaining* and a being established in God, and it is this entire movement and not merely its point of departure that constitutes *creatio ex nihilo*. For Athanasius, this movement, while being external to the divine substance, inasmuch as it is not constitutive of divine being, nevertheless takes place "in God." In the passage quoted above, he uses Colossians 1:17 to make this point, which is further insisted upon in the succeeding chapter, where Athanasius speaks of the Word as "present in all things . . . containing and enclosing them in himself."[25]

A final example of Athanasius's understanding of the doctrine of creation from nothing as a teaching about divine goodness can be found in *On the Incarnation* 3. In this second part of his double treatise, Athanasius is largely concerned with soteriology, the message of the incarnation, life, death, and resurrection of Christ as the remedy to the human predicament. But we have already noted Athanasius's strategy of presenting the "rationality" of this proclamation by demonstrating its consistency with an ontology, an account of the creation that is saved by the crucified and risen Christ. At the beginning of *On the Incarnation*, Athanasius regathers the elements of his theology of creation which had been introduced in the first part of the treatise, *Against the Greeks*. He also now explicitly confronts competing philosophical and heretical accounts of creation and contrasts them with the

Christian teaching of creation from nothing. The Epicureans contend that the world came into being on its own (αὐτομάτως) and by chance, but the ordered variety of created phenomena belies this conception and indicates a cause which precedes creation. The Platonists believe that God made the world from preexistent and unoriginated matter, but this imputes weakness to God, for "how could he be called Maker and Creator if his creative ability had come from something else, that is, from matter?"[26] Then, there are the gnostic "heretics" who assert that the Creator of this world is other than the Father of our Lord Jesus Christ. Athanasius refutes their beliefs by recalling Jesus's references to God as the Creator of men and women (cf. Matt. 19:4) and the Johannine statement that all things were made by the Word "and without him not one thing came into being" (John 1:3). The Alexandrian dismisses all these alternative conceptions of creation as "mythologies."[27] The true Christian conception is that the world was brought into being from nonexistence, as evidenced by a maximal interpretation of Genesis 1:1, "In the beginning God made heaven and earth," and Hebrews 11:3, "By faith we understand that the worlds were prepared by the word of God, so that what is seen was made from things that are not visible." This Christian teaching is once again introduced by an affirmation of divine goodness:

> God is good—or rather, he is the source of goodness. But the good is not jealous of anything. Because he does not jealously begrudge being to anything, he made all things from nonbeing through his own Word, our Lord Jesus Christ. Among all the things upon the earth, he was especially merciful toward the human race. Seeing that by the logic of its own origin it would not be capable of always remaining, he granted it a further gift. He did not create human beings merely like all the irrational animals upon the earth, but made them according to his own Image, and granted them participation in the power of his own Word, so that having a kind of reflection of the Word and thus becoming worded, they may be enabled to remain in blessedness and live the true life of the saints in paradise.[28]

This passage, which occurs near the beginning of *On the Incarnation*, echoes the first passage we cited in evidence of Athanasius's linkage of the doctrine of creation with divine goodness, culled from the open-ing of *Against the Greeks*. In both passages, we have an affirmation of divine goodness followed by the characterization of human beings as enjoying the "grace" (χάρις) of a special participation in the Word. In both passages, also, "paradise" is interpreted as consisting of humanity's enjoyment of communion with God. But in the latter passage, Athana-sius's clearer grasp of the implications of the doctrine of creation *ex ni-hilo* has transformed all three notions. Whereas the earlier passage spoke of the creative manifestation of divine goodness in largely noetic terms, as God's making humanity "perceptive and understanding of re-ality," this passage pointedly alludes to the Platonic notion of divine goodness only to trump it with the designation of God as making all things from nonbeing. The same ontological maximalism applies to the notion of the "grace" of humanity's participation in the Word. In the earlier passage, this "grace" was also depicted in epistemological terms; it is the power to rise above sensible things and contemplate intelligible realities and thus "converse with God." But in the later passage, the special grace granted to human beings is a capacity to assent to the di-vine preservation from nothingness. Indeed, the stress on creation's origination from nothing underscores the conception that creaturely being is wholly and without remainder gift. To be a creature is nothing other than to-be-gifted! Paradise, then, the positive fulfillment of the divine-human relation, is not simply the contemplation of God and the admiration of divine "providence towards the universe," as it was in the earlier passage, but is now depicted in terms of humanity's con-scious participation in its gifted "remaining" in being, its exodus from nothing. In the condition of paradise, the human creature enjoys its own groundless existence as wholly gift, or "grace, χάρις."

The Dialectic of Creaturely Ontology:
Natural Nothingness, the Grace of "Remaining," and Divine Law

In the passages we quoted above, we can see that the doctrine of cre-ation from nothing indicates for Athanasius a dialectic in God's rela-tion to creation. God is other than creation, transcending all creaturely being, and yet by his goodness and love brings about the being of cre-ation, maintains it in being, and protects it from relapsing into nothingness. Athanasius also conceives of creaturely being in dialectical terms, though these terms also undergo a development in tandem with an increasingly explicit emphasis on creation *ex nihilo*. We have seen that in the opening chapters of *Against the Greeks* Athanasius is still conceiving of the fundamental dialectic of human existence in terms of the Platonic polarity of the sensible and the intelligible. But after the insertion of the doctrine of creation *ex nihilo*, the Alexandrian presents the creaturely dialectic in terms of its origination from nothing and its maintenance in the gift of being. Athanasius formulates this dialectic in the language of *physis* ("nature") and *charis* ("grace").[29] However, this language must be not overlaid with later understandings of nature and grace. Athanasius's usage of these terms in this context delineates inseparable aspects of the constitution of created being as such, with *physis* referring to the terminus a quo of creaturely being-*from-nothing* and *charis* designating the terminus ad quem of the same creature's *being*-from-nothing. Practically every aspect of Athanasius's theology in this treatise depends on a correct appreciation of the mutual reference of these inseparable aspects of human existence which together identify the character of human existence as wholly gifted. There would be no human existence if there were not the "gift, *charis*," of a divinely endowed establishment in being, and this existence would not be wholly gift if its "nature, *physis*," did not consists in an origination from nothing.

A failure to grasp the simultaneity and correlativity of this dialectic has led to serious misinterpretations of both Athanasius's theology of creation and soteriology. One such regnant misreading is to suggest that, for Athanasius, the most radical predicament for human existence is precisely the ontological indigence which he designates as creation's "*physis*." It would be consistent then to interpret the Alexandrian's soteriology as concerned with the healing of this ontological instability rather than with the redemption of sin.[30] However, this interpretation is not only reductive of Athanasius's more complex dialectical understanding of human ontology; from the perspective of the Alexandrian's own understanding, the interpretation itself reproduces the fundamental logic of human sin. Athanasius is clear that creation's origin from nothingness is not a threat to its being as long as it maintains its participation in the divine power that sustains it. When Athanasius speaks of creation's inherent weakness, he clarifies that this is not a global characterization of the condition of created being as such but rather a perspectival focus on the aspect of creation's "from-nothingness" when that aspect is isolated in abstraction from its participation in the divine gift of being: "For the nature of created things, having come into being from nothing, is fleeting and mortal *when considered on its own terms.*"[31]

But, as we shall see, it is the very structure of sin to consider creation "by itself," "on its own terms," and apart from its radical relatedness to its Creator. To complain of creation's radical weakness, as if that were the problem, is thus to make calculations based on the presupposition of creaturely autonomy, which is already to depart from the wholesome dialectic of creaturely being-from-nothingness. For Athanasius, however, creation's origination from nothing, which ineluctably conditions the creature's being as radically dependent, is not a problem. Or, if we must speak that way, we can say that it is a "problem" that is preemptively solved by divine goodness, inasmuch as God is dependable and faithful to the initial "exodus" of creation from nothing. From the creaturely side, however, the dialectic of creaturely ontology is, if not a problem, at least a provocation for human freedom. Humanity, along with being gifted with a supereminent participation in the divine Word, relative to other creatures, is also gifted with responsibility for its own being. Its freedom, however, unlike its being, is not *ex nihilo* but conditioned by this very ontological dialectic. Humanity's most fundamental option, granted to it at the very inception of its being, is either to willfully "remain" in participation in God or to decline from such participation and thus slide back toward nothingness.[32]

A distinctive contribution of Athanasius's theology of creation *ex nihilo* is the way in which this doctrine informs his understanding of human freedom. The key move which enables this integration is his inclusion of the divine appeal to human freedom, in the form of divine law, within his understanding of the original creation and not merely as an event subsequent to it. It is easy to overlook both the fact that Athanasius executes this maneuver and its theological significance. We have already quoted above a passage from *On the Incarnation* 3, wherein Athanasius speaks of the divine goodness as bringing everything from nothing into existence and granting to humanity the "added grace" of an eminent participation in the Word. When he immediately proceeds to refer to the divine commandment to refrain from eating of the tree of the knowledge of good and evil, it seems that he is simply following the general order of the narrative of Genesis, from chapters 1 to 3. In fact, Athanasius is not only recounting the scriptural sequence but also condensing it into a single event in which God makes the original human being, like the rest of creation, *ex nihilo*, and establishes it in being. The granting of "the law" is conceived as intrinsic to the act of the human creature's being established in being and being protected from its nothingness. The law thus "secures" the gift of the human creature's originating movement from nothing into being:

> And knowing again that the free choice of human beings could turn either way, he preemptively secured the gift that he gave by a law and a fixed place. When he brought them into his own paradise, he gave them a law, so that if they guarded the gift and remained good, they would retain the life of paradise . . . but if they transgressed . . . they would suffer the corruption of death in accordance with their nature, and would no longer live in paradise. From then on, they would die outside of it, and would remain in death and corruption."[33]

Athanasius's conflation of the divine acts of creation and law-giving raises large questions about the scope and dimensions of our conception of the "initial" act of creation from nothing. Athanasius attends to this act not merely as the fact of the eruption itself from nothing, leaving out of consideration the being of what so erupts. Rather, creation from nothing is God's act of establishing new being, and the created termini of this divine act thus include the various modes by which distinct beings are established.[34] For Athanasius, the beings of the nonrational world are established as conveying knowledge of the divine presence and activity, and that feature is intrinsic to their creation from nothing.[35] The being of human beings is distinctly established as ordained to freely assent to its own being-from-nothing and to preserve its own immunity to nothingness through its free participation in divine life. Athanasius sees the divine law-giving as constitutive of this divine establishment of distinctly human being and thus as integral to humanity's being-from-nothing. Far from bearing a heteronymous relation to created being, the divine law secures the gift of *creatio ex nihilo* by revealing and commending to humanity the ineluctable terms by which the gift of being is to be received, namely, through an enduring participation in divine life which is existentially performed as obedience. Thus the law not only enacts the same divine goodness which brought about creation and manifests the radical and ineluctable giftedness of created being; it also adds the further gift of protecting or "securing" the original gift of creation from its forfeiture by human beings.[36] The divine solicitude for "securing the gift" of creation thus even includes the threat of death which the law poses, since the purpose of this threat is precisely to avert death and thus to enable humanity's "remaining" in its exodus from nothing, even unto deification. Quoting the book of Wisdom, Athanasius maintains that the intent of the law is to provide the "assurance of incorruptibility" (Wis. 6:18). With this understanding of the role of the law in the original creation, the paradisiacal contemplation that was interpreted in the early chapters of *Against the Greeks* in the Platonic terms of abstraction from the sensible and adhering to the intelligible is now reconceived in terms of keeping the divine law which orients humanity's union with God:

> For if, having the nature of what once did not exist [Εἰ γὰρ φύσιν ἔχοντες τὸ μὴ εἶναί ποτε], they were called into existence by the approach of the Word and his love for humanity, it followed that once human beings were deprived of the understanding of God and had turned towards nonbeings . . . then they were also deprived of eternal existence. Such a dissolution entails a remaining in death and corruption. For the human being is by nature mortal in that he was created from nothing. But because of the likeness to the one who is, if he had guarded this through contemplating God, he would have mitigated his natural corruption and would have remained incorruptible, as the book of Wisdom says, "The keeping of the law is the assurance of immortality."[37]

Creation *ex nihilo*, Evil, and Death

With the recognition of the significance of Athanasius's inclusion of the divine law-giving within the act of humanity's creation from nothing, we are now on the verge of seeing how his soteriology is configured by his ontology of creaturely being. But one intervening agendum is to clarify how this ontology conceives of the evil and death which is overcome through Christ's salvific work. One of the most important functions of the doctrine of *creatio ex nihilo* in early Christian theology was to counteract gnostic and Manichaean notions that evil is partially constitutive of created reality. Indeed, the provenance of evil is Athanasius's first concern immediately after his introductory remarks in the first chapter of *Against the Greeks*. He opens the second chapter with the assertion that "evil was not from the beginning" but was contrived "later" by human beings.[38] The Alexandrian objects to the doctrines of "some Greeks," probably referring to the Manichees, who declared that "evil existed in reality and by itself" and "had existence and being of itself."[39] He also rebukes the gnostics who invent another God besides the Father of Christ, whom they consider to be "the maker and author of evil and the artificer of creation."[40] In tracing Athanasius's response to these notions, we can again see a development running from the early chapters of *Against the Greeks*, which seem to be more influenced by Platonic ontology and from which the doctrine of *creatio ex nihilo* is absent, to the second part of the treatise, *On the Incarnation*, in which that doctrine is determinative.

In the early chapters of *Against the Greeks*, Athanasius uses three standard Platonic approaches to the question of evil, though he aligns each of them to a distinct aspect of Christian teaching. First, he takes over the Platonic notion of the nonsubstantiality of evil to make the point that all created substances are the work of the one God, "Lord of heaven and earth" (Matt. 11:25), "who fills everything contained in heaven and earth."[41] The notion of the nonsubstantiality of evil is really an affirmation of the absolute goodness and inculpability of God, who makes nothing that is not good: "Evil neither came from God nor was in God. . . . It did not exist in the beginning, nor does it have any being."[42] Second, the Alexandrian adopts the Platonic conception of evil as phantasmal, the mind's contrivance of the unreal. Athanasius assimilates this notion to the practice of idolatry: "Evil was not from the beginning. . . . But it was human beings who later began to conceive and contrive it on their own. In this way they invented for themselves the notion of idols, considering nonexistent things as real."[43] Third, in the early chapters of *Against the Greeks*, Athanasius tends to associate evil with the movement from the intelligible to the sensible. Humanity was originally created to be "superior to sensual things and all bodily impressions."[44] But human beings "turned their minds away from intelligible things" and "went after what was closer to themselves—and what was closer to them was the body and its sensations. . . . Expending themselves in this way and being unwilling to turn away from things nearby, they imprisoned their souls in the pleasures of the body."[45] The reality of death is also subsumed into this scheme, as if it were merely a phenomenon that pertained to the body and the soul's disordered attachment to the body:

> For turning away from the one true being, namely God, they henceforth devoted themselves to the various and fragmented desires of the body. Then, as usually happens, since they were devoting themselves to each and every desire, they began to adopt such an attachment towards them that they were afraid of losing them. In this way the soul has become vulnerable to fears and cowardice and pleasures and thoughts of mortality. Since the soul is unwilling to turn away from these desires, it has become fearful of death and separation from the body.[46]

When we come to the second part of the treatise, *On the Incarnation*, Athanasius's conception of evil seems to have undergone a subtle but dramatic transformation that is very much bound up with a heightened emphasis on *creatio ex nihilo*. We can identify three features of that transformation. First, instead of the understanding of evil as a descent from the intelligible to the sensible, here we have its depiction as essentially a decline toward the nothingness from which creation originated. The intensified focus on *creatio ex nihilo* makes the teleology of evil much more radical. The ultimate intentionality of evil is not merely the dalliance of the soul with inferior corporeality but the creature's repudiation of its own being-from-nothing by a willful being-towards-nothing. Evil is now seen as the exact reversal of the dynamic movement of *creatio ex nihilo*; we can properly characterize it as *creatio ad nihilum*, even if this is not the Alexandrian's exact terminology. Second, there is a corresponding transformation in Athanasius's conception of death. Whereas, as we have seen, in the early chapters of *Against the Greeks*, death is presented only as a corporeal phenomenon which threatens the soul when the soul becomes overly attached to the body, here death is seen as the enforcement of the "*ex nihilo*" aspect of creation's being (*physis*) once that is separated from the "gift" (*charis*) of participation in divine life. The third, and perhaps most significant, transformation in Athanasius's conception of evil in the course of this treatise is a consequence of his understanding of divine law as integral to the original establishment of divine being. In the early chapters of *Against the Greeks*, evil is simply a human enterprise in which God has no dramatic role. In *On the Incarnation*, the responsibility for evil is no less attributed to human agency. But now the positing of the possibility of evil, which is intrinsic to the divine law-giving, is attributed to God and is thus depicted as constitutive of the act of creation.

Athanasius's ingenious fidelity to the Genesis narrative sequence with regard to locating divine law, with its promise and threat, as integral to the constitutive movement of humanity's creation from nothing opens up suggestive horizons for broaching questions about the origin and persistence of evil and the conflictual character of creation.[47] In Athanasius's treatment, evil is clearly not something substantive or independent of God's purview and mastery. It is not something that is already there to confront God when God sets out to create. But, true to the account of Genesis itself, it is something that God himself posits as a possibility in the very act of creation, when he entrusts creation's constitutive movement from nothingness into being to the freedom of the human creature so constituted. We can say that in the case of rational and free creatures, *creatio ex nihilo* ineluctably posits the possibility of *creatio ad nihilum.*

Moreover, when the biblical God presents the human being with the choice either to be obedient to the law of participation in divine life or to disobey that law and decline toward nothingness, he not only posits the possibility of conflict as intrinsic to the act of creation but also preemptively enters into that conflict. While Athanasius depicts the divine law-giving as setting out the terms of the ontological structure of the divine-human relation, the divine proclamation of these terms is not simply an objective and impartial relaying of information on God's part. Rather, as we indicated earlier, these terms are proclaimed in order to safeguard humanity from the corruption of its decline from participation in God back to its autonomous nothingness.

God thus takes the side of creation in the very act of creating, with a view to the possibility of an impending combat for the preservation of creation. The prevalence of the language of "securing" and "protecting" in Athanasius's depiction of the original act of creation reinforces this interpretation. Indeed, the logic of this usage encourages us to see the scriptural paradigm of the narration of the divine creative act not merely in the Genesis account of the divine "making" of heaven and earth but also in the Exodus account of God leading his people away from destruction and into a land where they can dwell with him. It would be faithful to this logic to say that, for Athanasius, the act of creation is a divinely led "exodus" from nothing. The Alexandrian's emphasis on the divine "protection" of creation from its inception is misconstrued when it is seen as positing an originally unstable and corruptible creation that will be "fixed" by the incarnation. It is rather an indication of Athanasius's highly condensed biblical theology in which God's covenantal protection is read back into the very act of creation. But protection implies threat. And if the protection is original to the act of creation, then so, in some sense, is the threat. In Athanasius's inclusion of divine law-giving within the act of creation from nothing, he presents God as taking responsibility from the outset for the threat that accompanies the very inception of creation and preemptively acting to overcome it. Thus, the divine stance that grounds the economy of salvation which culminates in Christ is seen to be already fully present in the original act of creation *ex nihilo*. We may now turn to a fuller consideration of how Athanasius's theology of creation *ex nihilo* determines his account of Christian salvation.

CREATIO EX NIHILO AND CHRISTIAN SALVATION

I noted at the beginning of this essay that Athanasius sets for himself the task in this double treatise of establishing the "rationality" of Christian faith on the basis of a consistent account of creation and salvation. The Christian proclamation posits an ontology of the terms of the God-world relation as well as an account of how these terms persist and are fulfilled in the Christian account of salvation in Christ. The first part of this dialectic is laid out largely in the first part of the treatise, *Against the Greeks*, though we have seen that it is also recapitulated in the early chapters of the second part, *On the Incarnation*, with a more pervasive emphasis on the doctrine of *creatio ex nihilo*. The second part of the treatise, *On the Incarnation*, is preoccupied with showing how Christ's salvific work "makes sense" of creation by bringing it to fulfillment, despite the prevalence of sin and evil. We have seen that a predominant theme in Athanasius's elaboration of the ontology of *creatio ex nihilo* is the divine goodness which brings creation into being from nothingness. When the Alexandrian turns to an account of the "rationality" of the incarnation as consistent with the ontology of creation, he again consistently appeals to the criterion of divine goodness. Just as God brought creation into being because it was not fitting for divine goodness to begrudge the granting of existence to others, so it would not be fitting for divine goodness to allow this gifted existence to be destroyed. Since sin and evil essentially consist in the reversal of God's creative act, a creaturely decreation, Athanasius seems to see them as a direct challenge to the Creator himself:

> Moreover, it would have been unfitting for what had once been created rational and had participated in the Word to perish and revert again to nonbeing through corruption. For it would not have been worthy of the goodness of God that what had been brought into being by him should be corrupted because of the deceit which the devil had practiced on human beings. . . . Therefore, since rational beings were undergoing corruption . . . what should God, who is good, have done? Let corruption prevail over them and death capture them? Then what would have been the point of their having been created in the first place? For it would have been more fitting if they had not been created than that, having come into being, they should be neglected and perish. For the neglect of them would have indicated the weakness of God rather than his goodness.[48]

Athanasius's assertion that if God had not intervened to preserve his creation from reverting to nothingness, he would have been shown to be weak echoes his earlier statement that the Platonic doctrine of creation as the imposition of form on preexistent matter posits divine weakness. In both cases, the power of God is explicitly related to the doctrine of *creatio ex nihilo*. Divine strength is manifest in God's bringing creation into being out of nothing and, equally and consistently, in God's preserving creation from relapsing into nothingness. In both cases, divine power is explicitly related to divine goodness. God's power is manifest in his capacity to realize his own goodness. But it is precisely this divine power of goodness that is challenged by sin. Athanasius dramatizes this challenge in the form of a "divine dilemma" whose resolution is the incarnation, death, and resurrection of Christ. One side of this dilemma, as we have seen, is that God's goodness cannot permit the utter destruction of the creation which is the product of that goodness. The other side of the dilemma is that humanity, having sinned, was subject to the punishment of sin. This punishment could not be averted since "it was impossible to flee the law" established by God.[49] It would not have been appropriate even for God to simply annul this law: "For it would have been absurd that, after having spoken, God should lie, and that after he had established a law that humanity would die by death if it transgressed the commandment, humanity would not in fact have died after it transgressed, but God's word was made void instead. For God would not have been truthful, if after he said that humanity would die, it did not die."[50] The resolution of this dilemma came about only with the appearance and sacrificial death of Christ, who accomplished the salvation demanded by divine goodness by taking upon himself the sentence of death:

> He was merciful to our race and compassionate in regard to our weakness. He submitted to our corruption but did not capitulate to the dominion of death. In order that what had come into being should not perish and the work of the Father among humanity may not be rendered futile, he took to himself a body which was not foreign to our own. . . . And thus taking a body like ours, since all were subject to the corruption of death, he surrendered it to death on behalf of all and offered it to the Father. He did this through his love for humanity in order that, as all die in him, the law of corruption in humanity might be abrogated—since its power was spent in the Lord's body and it would never again claim ground over human beings who are like him—and in order that, as human beings turned to corruption, he might turn them back again

to incorruption and might give them life instead of death, because he made the body his own, and by the grace of the resurrection banished death from them like straw before the fire.[51]

It is clear from this passage and others like it that the widespread opinion that Athanasius is exemplary of a putative "Greek patristic model of salvation" in which human salvation is accomplished through the incarnation, rather than the death of Christ, is utterly unfounded. Moreover, we find in Athanasius an entirely coherent synthesis of two soteriological models that are often pitted against one another and aligned with East and West, respectively—an "ontological" model, in which salvation is conceived as the communication of divine life to humanity through the incarnation, and a "juridical" or "moral" or "functional" model, in which human sin is forgiven through Christ's suffering, which pays the "penalty" or "debt" of human sin. The foundation for this synthesis in the Alexandrian's theology is his understanding of law and sin as not only "juridical" and "moral" categories but also as ontological events. The law, as we have seen, accomplishes the securing of humanity's movement from nothing into existence. Sin, however, reverses that movement and thus effectively realizes humanity's self-perpetuated decreation. For Athanasius, Christ's salvific work cannot merely bypass the ontological effects of sin, and thus, Christ must die as a "fulfillment" of the divine sentence that sin leads to death.[52] Christ's death is a fulfillment of divine justice, precisely as a vindication of the truth that humanity can live only through participation in divine life. God cannot negate this truth without negating his own being as the source of creaturely being. But Christ's death also fulfills God's solidarity with humanity's decreation and reverses it through his own self-offering, his indestructible being-unto-the Father which is ineluctably native to his being, as the Word and Image of the Father. For Athanasius, the "rationality" of the Christian proclamation finally consists in this synthesis of an ontology of creation with the proclamation of Christ's salvation: creaturely being is a radically gifted being-from-nothing; sin consists in the reversal of this being-from-nothing into a being-towards-nothing; Christ enters into the extremity of our being-towards-nothing through his human death and reverses it by his own being-unto-the Father which brings about his and our resurrection.

CONCLUSION: THE EXISTENTIAL MEANING OF
CREATIO EX NIHILO IN ATHANASIUS

At the outset of this paper, I suggested that Athanasius's theology of creation *ex nihilo* is both metaphysical, in the classical sense, and existential, in a way that is not foreign to modern sensibilities. His exposition of this doctrine includes truth claims about divine and created beings and their interrelations, while also indicating how these truths are operative in human existence, so that "they shine more brightly than the sun" when they are disclosed by Christian faith.[53] The metaphysical foundation of Athanasius's doctrine of *creatio ex nihilo* is his conception of divine goodness. In the context of competing construals of how divine goodness is manifest in the relation between divinity and the world, Athanasius presents Christian faith as positing a maximal and unsurpassable account of divine goodness as the bestowal of created being as entirely and without remainder gifted. All that is which is not God is a gift of God. Quite to the contrary of Heidegger's complaint that classical metaphysics reifies being, the metaphysical claims of Athanasius's theology of *creatio ex nihilo* evoke a conception of the absolute groundlessness of gifted created being, such that the creature can never enclose Divine Being but can only have access to this Being through ecstatic participation in the divine life. For Athanasius, these metaphysical claims about the goodness of God and the groundlessness of created being are given coherent and persuasive expression in the Christian narrative which presents the entire story of reality as that of the compensation of divine goodness for creation's deficiency, whether that deficiency be creation's nonparticipation in the absolute gratuity of its initial bestowal of being or its subsequent willful rejection of its own gifted being.

But Athanasius also has his own "existential analytic" insofar as he depicts the metaphysical truths posited by the doctrine of creation *ex nihilo* as inscribed into the fundamental structure of human existence. One trajectory of this existential analysis is his theology of death, which we can briefly contrast with Heidegger's understanding of death as a fundamental "*existentiale*."[54] Heidegger, of course, has no account of the origin of death; death is simply a manifestation of Being-in-the-world, *Dasein*, as ineluctably temporal and finite.[55] For Heidegger, existential authenticity, the openness to Being's self-disclosure, demands that the human being live his life in anticipation of death. Authentic human existence must therefore take the form of being-unto-death, a courageous embrace of "the nullity that determines *Dasein* in its ground."[56] For Athanasius, too, the current human condition is that of being-unto-death, and his theology of creation *ex nihilo* is preoccupied with the interpretation of human death. However, the Alexandrian sees this being-unto-death not as something radical to the constitution of Being, but rather as the negative consequence of creation's groundlessness once rational beings decline the gift of participation in divine life. Death is thus a recurring demonstration of creation's being from nothing, in the negative mode of its sinful being-towards-nothing, *creatio ad nihilum*. However, the Christian proclamation proposes that there is an omnipotent divine goodness that consistently overcomes nothingness, whether it be the benign nothingness of creation's groundlessness or the vicious nothingness of human sin. The Christian message of salvation presents the cross as the manifestation of humanity's being-unto-death but also declares that the unique being-unto-death of the Creator who brought creation into being from nothing represents a new and final exodus from the nothingness which haunts creation. The proclamation of Christ's salvific death on the cross thus contains the promise of a new *creatio ex nihilo*, a return to the original gratuity of its full participation in divine life.

   If we ask, finally, what would constitute an authentic experiential appropriation of this positive renewal of *creatio ex nihilo*, Athanasius can also provide some aid toward an appropriate response. Such an appropriation would not essentially consist in some scientifically aided discovery of the "first moments" of creation, nor in an existential awareness of nothingness and death as dialectical components of human existence. Just as nothingness cannot be experienced as something separate from creation, so creation's being *from-nothing* (what Athanasius calls its *"physis"*) cannot be experienced apart from its *in-God-ness* (what Athanasius calls its *"charis"*). Indeed, the former can only be a function of the latter. So, *creatio ex nihilo* can only be experienced on the part of creatures as an awareness of their entire being as gifted by God and directed toward God. This experience of ecstatic and redeemed and deified groundlessness is what Christians ideally experience in the

Eucharist. It is, at any rate, the reality which the Eucharist objectively performs. Athanasius does not say as much, but, once again, his language of Christ's salvific death, which he calls the "therapy of creation," as an "offering" and "sacrifice" is suggestive of eucharistic connotations. It would be entirely consistent with the essential logic of his understanding of the doctrine of creation *ex nihilo* to see it as ultimately undergirding a eucharistic account of human existence, as articulated in the anaphora of the Liturgy of St. John Chrysostom:

> It is fitting and right to sing to you, to bless You, to praise You, to give thanks to You, to worship You in every place of your dominion: for You are God, beyond description, beyond understanding, invisible, incomprehensible, always existing, always the same; You and your only-begotten Son and your Holy Spirit. Out of nothing, You brought us into being, and when we had fallen, raised us up again; and You have not ceased doing everything until You brought us to heaven and graciously gave us your future kingdom. For all these things, we thank You and your only-begotten Son and your Holy Spirit.

Notes

1. The first explicit mention of *creatio ex nihilo* in *Against the Greeks* (hereafter, *C. Gent.*) is in ch. 35, though there is nothing to contradict that teaching in the earlier material of this treatise. On a different subject, the nature of the human soul, Andrew Louth has previously noted "a very sharp contrast between the two parts of the treatise, the *Contra Gentes* and the *De Incarnatione.*" See his "The Concept of the Soul in Athanasius's *Contra Gentes–De Incarnatione,*" *Studia Patristica* 13, ed. E. A. Livingstone, Texte und Untersuchungen 116 (Berlin: Akademie Verlag, 1975), 227. On the dating of this double treatise, see K. Anatolios, *Athanasius: The Coherence of His Thought* (London: Routledge, 1998), 26–30.

2. *C. Gent.* 1.

3. For this reason, Athanasius confirms and exemplifies the function of the doctrine of creation in early Christian theology in informing the whole "drama of the divine economy," to use the felicitous description of Paul Blowers in his magisterial recent work, *Drama of the Divine Economy: Creator and*

Creation in Early Christian Theology and Piety (Oxford: Oxford University Press, 2012). For his discussion of Athanasius's understanding of *creation ex nihilo*, see pages 173–76.

4. For a more extended treatment of this theme, see my "Creation and Salvation in St. Athanasius of Alexandria," in *On the Tree of the Cross: Georges Florovsky and the Patristic Doctrine of Atonement*, ed. Matthew Baker et al. (Jordanville, NY: Holy Trinity Seminary Press, 2016), 59–72.

5. *C. Gent.* 1. All translations of Athanasius's texts are my own.

6. *C. Gent.* 1.

7. *C. Gent.* 1.

8. *C. Gent.* 1.

9. *C. Gent.* 1.

10. *Inc.* 1.

11. *Inc.* 1.

12. *Inc.* 4.

13. *Inc.* 4.

14. *C. Gent.* 27.

15. *C. Gent.* 1.

16. Plato, *Timaeus* 29E–30A. English translation: *The Collected Dialogues of Plato, Including the Letters*, ed. Edith Hamilton and Huntington Cairns, Bollingen Series 71 (Princeton: Princeton University Press, 1961), 1162.

17. See Richard Sorabji, *Time, Creation, and the Continuum: Theories in Antiquity and the Early Middle Ages* (Chicago: University of Chicago Press, 1983), esp. 268–72.

18. See Rowan Williams, *Arius: Heresy and Tradition*, 2nd ed. (Grand Rapids: Eerdmans, 2002), 215–29.

19. On the centrality of the coincidence of divine transcendence and immanence in Athanasius's theology, see Anatolios, *Athanasius: The Coherence of His Thought*.

20. *C. Gent.* 2.

21. *C. Gent.* 35.

22. *C. Gent.* 41.

23. On this important motif in Athanasius, see K. Anatolios, *Athanasius*, Early Church Fathers (New York: Routledge, 2004), 61–63.

24. My translation. Cf. Ps. 119:90–91 NRSV: "You have established the earth, and it stands fast. By your appointment they stand today." Athanasius quotes the Septuagint: "ἐθεμελίωσας τὴν γῆν καὶ διαμένει. Τῇ διατάξει σου διαμένει ἡ ἡμέρα" (*C. Gent.* 46).

25. *C. Gent.* 42. On the divine containment of creation as a patristic motif, see William R. Schoedel, "Enclosing Not Enclosed: The Early Christian

Doctrine of God," in *Early Christian Literature and the Classical Intellectual Tradition: In Honorem Robert M. Grant*, ed. William Schoedel and Robert Wilken, Théologie Historique 53 (Paris: Éditions Beauchesne, 1979), 75–86.

26. *Inc.* 2.

27. *Inc.* 3.

28. *Inc.* 3.

29. For a fuller account of this terminology, see Anatolios, *Athanasius: The Coherence of His Thought*, 53–67.

30. Cf. R. P. C. Hanson, *The Search for the Christian Doctrine of God: The Arian Controversy, 318–381 AD* (New York: T&T Clark, 1988), 430: "For Athanasius in fact our sinfulness is bound up with our changeable, corrupt state. What we must be redeemed from is not *primarily* sin or disobedience but corruptibility, from which sin and disobedience flow." Hanson does not say as much, but his logic really amounts to saying that what we are saved from is primarily the original constitution of creation!

31. *C. Gent.* 41 (emphasis added).

32. *Inc.* 3.

33. *Inc.* 3.

34. Athanasius's perspective in this regard is consistent with the biblical understanding of creation as bringing about not merely the appearance of entities but the establishment of order and well-being. See Richard Clifford's article, ch. 3 in this collection.

35. Cf. *C. Gent.* 35.

36. See my "Creation and Salvation," esp. 67–71.

37. *Inc.* 4.

38. *C. Gent.* 2.

39. *C. Gent.* 6.

40. *C. Gent.* 6.

41. *C. Gent.* 6.

42. *C. Gent.* 7.

43. *C. Gent.* 2.

44. *C. Gent.* 2.

45. *C. Gent.* 3.

46. *C. Gent.* 3.

47. Cf. Jon Levenson, *Creation and the Persistence of Evil: The Jewish Drama of Divine Omnipotence* (Princeton: Princeton University Press, 1988); John Webster, "Creation from Nothing," in *Christian Dogmatics: Reformed Theology for the Church Catholic*, ed. Michael Allen and Scott R. Swain (Grand Rapids: Baker Academic, 2016), 126–47.

48. *Inc.* 6.

49. *Inc.* 6.

50. *Inc.* 6.

51. *Inc.* 8.

52. *Inc.* 10.

53. *C. Gent.* 1.

54. For further comments contrasting Athanasius and Heidegger, see my "The Witness of Athanasius at the (Hoped-for) Nicene Council of 2025," *Pro Ecclesia: A Journal of Catholic and Evangelical Theology* 25, no. 2 (2016): 220–36.

55. For a trenchant critique of Heidegger's immanentist conception of Being as "Dasein," see David Bentley Hart, *The Beauty of the Infinite: The Aesthetics of Christian Truth* (Grand Rapids: Eerdmans, 2004), esp. 217–29.

56. M. Heidegger, *Being and Time*, 62.

CHAPTER 7

Creatio ex nihilo in the
Thought of Saint Augustine

JOHN C. CAVADINI

That the world was created "out of nothing" is, for Augustine, settled teaching very early in his writing.[1] Yet it is interesting that he does not treat this idea as a concept whose meaning is self-evident, as though it were a "clear and distinct" philosophical idea, independently existing among philosophical choices that scripture teaches as such. Instead, I would argue, his use of this idea is to evoke "creation" as a mystery that must remain, essentially, a mystery, one that (in other words) refuses to resolve itself into a clear and distinct philosophical idea, though it certainly has philosophical implications.[2]

But far from using the concept as a philosophical idea, intelligible in its own right and which scripture "teaches," he uses it instead, I would like to argue, as a formal marker of revelation itself. This is not to say that the concept cannot have intelligibility in philosophical terms. For Augustine, it clearly does—for example, it involves the difference between the immutable nature of the Creator and the mutable nature of something created out of nothing. But Augustine does not use the idea as though its content and meaning were not fully and constitutively determined by revelation, so fully and completely that a proper explanation of it requires reference not only to what God has revealed but to the fact *that* God has revealed anything at all, and in what manner.

DE GENESI CONTRA MANICHAEOS

The *De Genesi contra Manichaeos* (hereafter *DGCM*) is Augustine's earliest exegetical work.[3] It is intended to defend ("defendere," 1.4.7) the "scriptures of the Old Testament" (1.1.2) against Manichaean critique. A more or less standard contemporary evaluation of this work would give it, I think, notoriously low grades as an exercise in exegesis.[4] This is partly because it has seemed to recent interpreters as so constitutively Platonizing that it almost ends up replacing biblical teaching with a Platonic conception of incorporeal reality. This Platonizing teaching, in turn, is what offers the actual antidote to Manichaean dualism, as though the dispute were simply between two philosophical schools, one espousing dualism and one espousing monism.

And yet Augustine says explicitly that he is writing especially with the less educated or even the uneducated in mind, since they are just as likely to be convinced by Manichaean critique of the scriptures as the learned. The refutation will not be by ornate and elegant phrasing that only the educated can tolerate, but by the clarity of the realities themselves ("rebus manifestis") when they are expressed in "ordinary and simple language" (1.1.1). This probably means that Augustine is going to present his defense of the text in a way that could be used by a teacher to explain it to uneducated catechumens or perhaps even by priests who might have used it to preach.[5]

At any rate, Augustine does not bring up the idea of creation out of nothing as though it were a doctrine taught directly by scripture. There is no scriptural text whose "meaning" is that God created everything from nothing.[6] A modern interpreter might consider that the doctrine of *creatio ex nihilo* is a kind of philosophical transposition of an idea originally expressed in nonphilosophical images, that in Hebrew antiquity the abstract notion of "nothing" would not have meant anything, and that the picture of the earth offered as without form, a dark, watery abyss, is what the philosophical concept of "nothing" comes to "translate."

But Augustine is a better exegete than that, even though the text he is reading could tempt one toward such a strategy: "Terra autem erat invisibilis et incomposita, et tenebrae erant super abyssum" (Now the earth was invisible and shapeless, and darkness hovered over the abyss; Gen. 1:2). Though it is invisible and shapeless, as nearly "nothing" as we can imagine, scripture still says it is something, and that even this is created. Augustine calls this stuff "unformed matter" (informis materia; 1.7.11, following Wis. 11:18) and explains that this is what the Greeks mean by "chaos," and, while we can recognize the philosophical language, Augustine does not insist on it.[7]

The point is that "unformed matter" is something of which we have no experience, a "res ignota" (1.7.12). The words used to describe it—"invisible," "shapeless," "dark"—are used so that everyone, including the uneducated, can understand that this is not something we have "perceived or handled" or ever could "perceive or handle," that is, experience in any way, though the word "water" indicates that it is completely malleable to God, and the words "heaven" and "earth" indicate not what it already was, but what it could be ("non quia iam hoc erat, sed quia hoc esse poterat"; 1.7.11). In other words, it is not nothing, but almost nothing more, namely, pure potential or possibility.

Augustine wants us to understand that *the possibility to be something, the potential to be something, itself comes from God.* This too is created, for potential or possibility is not nothing: there is no potential in nothing. "And this is why we are absolutely right to believe that God made all things from nothing, because even though everything that has form was made from this material, this material itself all the same was made from absolutely nothing" (de omnino nihilo; 1.6.10), the "omnino" emphasizing the difference between nothing and the invisible, shapeless, dark matter, which could seem to be hardly anything at all, since we cannot experience it.

These comments are offered in rebuttal to the Manichaean criticism, which Augustine recounts as, "How did God make heaven and earth in the beginning, if the earth was already there, invisible and shapeless?" (1.3.5). Augustine had begun his answer by pointing out one of the "most obvious things" (res apertissimas), one of the "manifestly clear points" (cf. "manifestius" here at 1.3.5) he had promised to address, namely, that the text says that God made that very heaven and earth that is invisible and shapeless, namely, the thing which is not nothing, but yet not anything specific. This was made "before God distributed the forms of all things in their proper places and settings, with their duly arranged differences; before he said, *Let light be made*, and *Let the firmament be made*, and *Let the waters be collected together*, and *Let the dry land appear* (Gen. 1.3, 6, 9), and the rest of it which is set out in the same book in such a simple order that even little children can grasp it. Yet it all contains such great mysteries" (magna mysteria; 1.3.5).

What mysteries are these? We get a good idea of what they are if we pay attention to the Manichaean critique of the seven-day structure of the creation account, and to Augustine's response. The Manichaean critique of the seven-day structure is recurrent, but it is most pointed and focused regarding the accounts of the fourth and seventh days. With regard to the fourth day: "How, after all, could the three previous days have been without the sun, since now we see that it takes the rising and the setting of the sun to complete a day, while the night is made for us by the absence of the sun, during its return from the other part of the world to the east?" (1.14.20).

Augustine at first answers that we could assume, perhaps, that the amount of time that a normal day requires would be signified in the case of each of the first three days, regardless of the absence of the sun, but he changes his mind because he notices that in each case it says, "and there was made evening and there was made morning," which cannot happen without the sun. The sun is what makes evening and morning. Therefore in all of the cases we are to understand "that in that particular passage of time the actual changes from one work to the next [ipsas distinctiones operum] were given these names: 'evening' on account of the completion of the finished work [propter transactionem consummati operis] and 'morning' on account of the next work to come [propter inchoationem futuri operis], from the similarity [similitudine] with human work, which for the most part begins in the morning and ends in the evening."

Augustine remarks on this use of language by adding that "the transference [transferre] of words from human things to express divine things is customary in the divine scriptures" (1.14.20). They are expressed this way so that even children can understand them, and yet what is expressed is something that could not be fully expressed in any words, a great mystery, which is that God actually does things, "works," in time, after time has been created, and yet there is no myth.

The Manichaean problem, Augustine had earlier remarked when he was considering the creation of light and the separation of light from darkness, is that "they are deceived by their own myths [fabulis]" when they come to read scripture, because in their myths God is depicted as embattled, with the forces of darkness fighting against him. When they read the book of Genesis, they are deceived because they make a genre mistake, reading it as though it were a myth, meaning a story where God exists in a larger world and has debts and liabilities in it. To the Manichees, Genesis presents a laughable myth, a poor competitor to their own mythology, one that is internally inconsistent and altogether childish, and so they mock it. In other words, they fail to distinguish between a "myth" and an account of "mysteries."

The Manichees assume that the language is used directly, not in a transferred way. They do not "know" the scriptures (1.1.2). Augustine advises them that the best solution is to get to know them better. After all, "the deeper we plunge into the scriptures and get used to them, the more familiar we become with their style and manner of speaking" (1.9.15), and we realize that, while "nothing can be said about God that is at all worthy of him," still scripture's way of speaking does not indicate that God is weak, but rather defers to our weakness so that we can be nourished and arrive at that to which no human speech can attain (1.8.14).

It is easy at just this point to jump the philosophical gun and say that what Augustine means is that we are nourished by scripture until we are able to grasp the incorporeal, spiritual reality of God the way the Platonists can.[8] But that doesn't seem to capture precisely what Augustine is trying to say here. Doubtless a grasp of spiritual reality can help here, and yet it could also be problematic if you think that the purely timeless, unchangeable spiritual essence that is God could not get involved and actually (as it were) punch the clock and *do* something in this universe.[9] To regard the Bible as, in effect, a philosophical myth to be allegorized to suit philosophical taste would also be a genre mistake, because it would dissolve away the "mystery" just as effectively as the Manichaean reading does.

We can see this most clearly if we move on to Augustine's recounting of Manichaean objections to the biblical account of the seventh day. "What they say is, 'What need did God have for resting? Was he perhaps worn out and tired by the works of the six days?' And they also point to the Lord's own evidence, where he says, *My Father is working up until now* (Jn. 5.17), and on the strength of this they take in many unlearned people, whom they are trying to convince that the New Testament contradicts the Old" (1.22.33). Augustine responds that this text uses a figure of speech common in the scripture (so common as to be a "rule," "regula"),[10] namely, that what God is said to do, he is actually causing to be done in us. In this case, God's resting on the seventh day indicates "the rest he is going to give us from all our works, if we too have done good works" (1.22.34). In this case too, the rule applies with even more force than usual, because "our good works themselves are to be attributed to him who calls us, who instructs us, who shows us the way of truth, who entices us also to choose it for ourselves, and furnishes us with the strength to fulfill his commands" (1.22.24)—so that our works are in some way his works too.

Still, Augustine realizes that it is hard to get this just from the text in Genesis. So he explains how "throughout the whole text [textum] of divine scriptures" one can see, as it were, six working ages, differentiated by textual markers, as it were from infancy to old age, and these match the six days of creation. For example, the first age of a human being is infancy, when we first begin to enjoy light, which is like the first day of creation, on which God made light. Augustine comments that the seven days of creation are like a "kind of miniature image" (brevis aliqua imago; 2.1.1) which serves as a figure of the whole of the "saeculum" from its beginning to its end.

On the sixth day, in the senectitude of the world, "man is made *to the image and likeness of God* (Gen. 1:26–27), just as in this sixth age our Lord is born in the flesh. . . . And just as on that day *male and female* (Gen. 1.27), so also in this age Christ and the Church" (1.23.40). In this age "Christ rules the souls that defer to him," and in the Sabbath age yet to come, "they will take their rest with Christ from all their works" (1.23.40).

We have been taught by modern higher criticism of the Bible to regard exegesis such as this as completely fanciful, as having no claim on our attention beyond its historical interest, and certainly not on the meaning of the Hexaemeron, but Augustine's point is that the Hexae-meron "means" the same way in which the rest of the story "means." It is not as though there is a special work called "creation" which is finished once and for all, to be followed by the story for which it pre-pared, but that the mysteries of God's actions in creation are seen best in the history of all of God's actions in the world, and in a sense they are the same actions.

There was never a time when creation "ended" and after which sal-vation history "began," but in some ways what we are tempted to call "creation" and leave it at that is still happening, or the "work" of God that issued in creation is still going on.[11] If the creation account can "image" the rest of the story, then the rest of the story can reveal more fully what "creation" was in the first place. "There are no words, there-fore, that can possibly describe how God made and established heaven and earth and every creature which he set in place there," Augustine comments when he has finished his typology, and then continues, "but this exposition through an order of days presents them as an account of things done, in such a way as to concentrate on them chiefly as pre-dicting things to come in the future" (1.23.41). The acts of creation were truly "acts" or "works" of God, "compressed," as it were, beyond words as far as being able to say "how," but their compression does not make the account of them either a myth or a philosophy in mythic dis-guise. They point back, not to a primordial state, but to the ultimate mystery of God's will. The same will that was revealed when the Word of God "emptied himself" in relationship with the people of Israel (most fully revealed in the incarnation as Augustine will recount in book 2, at 2.24.37), this very same will is operative most fully in the cre-ation of the human being at the apex of the Hexaemeron. It is the same self-emptying, as it were, in advance; a commitment; a dedication; where can one find the words?

They are not found by recourse backward in time. Going back-ward is the instinct of myth, but in this case going backward only sends you all the more inexorably forward! If you are reading correctly, you find in the very text itself, in its very manner of speaking, only the same, self-accommodating, self-emptying will you find reading forward. You do not find another beginning, a narrative leverage point beyond or before God's will. To get to know God's will, on the other hand, does not mean to try to locate it in a narrative framework that preexists the narrative of biblical revelation, but to accept the story revealed as itself an invitation to get to know God's will by becoming friends with God instead of trying to find something "that does not exist," something greater than God's will (1.2.4) as revealed. The doctrine of creation out of nothing involves at very least the claim that there is no counternarrative to the whole of biblical revelation, nor even a supplementary narrative that would add anything essential, because there is nothing from which such narratives could begin or to which they could appeal. The doctrine of creation out of nothing makes the claim that God genuinely acts in creating, but that what this means, the character and nature of God's acts in creation, can only be ascertained by looking forward to the whole of the story of revelation. The doctrine of creation from nothing is, among other things, the doctrine that creation is irreducibly a revealed mystery. The doctrine points powerfully to the primacy of revelation itself.

Incidentally, becoming friends with God means acquiring charity, as it says in 1 Timothy 1:5, which Augustine cites: "'Now the end of the commandment is love coming from a pure heart and a good conscience and a faith unfeigned'" (1.2.4). This is good to know for anyone trying to ascend *above* revelation by philosophical allegory of the narrative. There is no ascending above the acts of God or the text that reveals them. Both the "little ones" and the spiritual people "have the same food," that is, "the scriptures and divine law" (1.25.43), and if the spiritual people understand scripture more fully, there is no understanding that rises above charity, the "fullness of knowledge," love for the will of God as revealed in the text.[12] The doctrine of creation from nothing is the doctrine that there is not only nothing "before" what is revealed, but nothing "above" it, either. Inspect the narrative of creation as closely as you like, and you will find only the will of God as operative in the rest of scripture, which speaks irreducibly of God's acts and the love from which they arise and which they reveal.

THE CONFESSIONS

In the *DGCM*, Augustine pays substantial attention to what Origen would call the moral or "soul" sense of the text, in addition to the literal or historical and the spiritual or prophetic. So all three of the senses that Origen finds in scripture are treated, though they are not named as such. The same is true if we fast-forward now to the *Confessions*, though the "soul" sense is to the fore, with one very special soul as the locus of the interpretation, while the literal and the prophetic or spiritual are operative as well.

The genius of the *Confessions* is to specify the soul's sense autobiographically. The results of the *DGCM* are not dropped or left behind, but consolidated and better integrated across the three senses. Along the way we see Augustine's careful, precise exegesis reaffirmed, namely, that the Bible says virtually nothing about nothing. The doctrine of *creatio ex nihilo* is not so much an extrabiblical doctrine about "nothing," but the doctrine that creation is God's sovereign act, the meaning of which cannot be grasped or specified apart from the whole of revelation. It points to the fact that the meaning of God's act of creation, and therefore the meaning of everything created, is irreducibly specified by revelation, and thus that revelation is primary, whether you are looking backward, forward, or within.

Surprisingly, the first full citation of Genesis 1:1–2 does not come until book 12 of the *Confessions*. We encounter the same translation as in the *DGCM*: "'In principio fecit deus caelum et terram: terra autem erat invisibilis et incomposita et tenebrae erant super abyssum'" (Gen. 1:1–2, cited at *Conf.* 12.13.16).[13] Though this is the first full citation, Genesis 1:2 receives an advance partial quote at the beginning of book 12—still surprisingly late (first time at 12.1.3: "Et nimirum haec *terra erat invisibilis et incomposita et* nescio qua profunditas *abyssi*, super quam non erat lux, quia nulla species erat illi: unde iussisti, ut scriberetur, quod *tenebrae erant super abyssum*; quod aliud quam lucis absentia?" [This earth was, moreover, neither visible nor organized; it was an abyss of inconceivable depth over which no light dawned, because it had no form. This is why you commanded your writer to record that *darkness loured over the abyss*, for what does that mean, except complete absence of light?]).[14]

And yet, without what one could call a citation, the imagery from these verses first appears much earlier in the *Confessions*, in book 2: "Cui narro haec? Neque enim tibi, deus meus. . . . Et ut quid hoc? Ut videlicet ego et quisquis haec legit cogitemus, de quam *profundo* clamandum sit ad te" (But to whom am I telling this story? Not to you, my God. . . . And why? So that whoever reads it may reflect with me on the depths from which we must cry to you; 2.3.5; cf. Ps. 130:1—*profundo* is a word joined in Augustine's mind to the "abyss" of Gen. 1:2, as at 12.1.3, cited above).[15]

Shortly afterward, "Ecce cor meum, deus, ecce cor meum, quod miseratus es in imo *abyssi*" (Look upon my heart, O God, look upon this heart of mine, on which you took pity in its abysmal depths; 2.3.5). What "abyss"? It is specified in the next sentence, in the soul sense: "Dicat tibi nunc ecce cor meum, quid ibi quaerebat, ut essem gratis malus et malitiae meae causa nulla esset nisi malitia. Foeda erat, et amavi eam; amavi perire, amavi defectum meum" (Enable my heart to tell you now what it was seeking in this action which made me bad for no reason, in which there was no motive for my malice except malice. The malice was loathsome, and I loved it. I was in love with my own ruin, in love with decay; 2.4.9).[16] What abyss? The abyss of being in love with one's own destruction, of loving one's own "decay," of loving it "gratuitously," for nothing other than itself. This is the abyss of not being able to give an account of one's actions, of having no story, no narrative, because love of decay for the sake of itself is irrational, and cannot give an account of itself (for if it could, it would be rational).

And yet, wait a minute, it is in fact being narrated! The book of Genesis supplies the point of view from which this incoherence, *as* an incoherence, can be identified, formed as a narrative quantity, as part of a story larger than itself. It is an "indication of" or a making known of or a "pointing out" of a You who is *Creator* of every nature. It is just one example of a perverse imitation of the You who is Creator (indicant [persons such as Augustine was] creatorem te esse omnis naturae; 2.6.14).[17] It is an imitation by wandering far away and setting oneself up against this You who is Creator and who is being addressed in the narration. The perverse imitation is, specifically, a "shadowy likeness of omnipotence" (*tenebrosa* omnipotentiae similitudine)[18] and is, as such, the "maimed freedom" (mancam libertatem) of someone who has not exactly lived up to the "likeness" he was originally intended to be— "Ecce est ille servus fugiens dominum suum et consecutus umbram!" (How like that servant of yours who fled from his Lord and hid in the shadows![19] Cf. *Sermons* 88.6)—Adam, whose deformed liberty forces him into the shadows (see Gen. 3:8), into a monstrously deformed life, the pit of death (mortis *profunditas*, line 55).

From this point of view, what one discovers in the incoherent love of one's own destruction is the love of "nothing," for, from the perspective of the narrative of creation and fall, what Augustine loved by loving the theft he committed in book 2 was "nothing." The theft was "nothing" and the fellowship he loved in committing the theft was emphatically "nothing":

> Quem fructum habui miser aliquando in his, quae nunc recolens erubesco, maxime in illo furto, in quo ipsum furtum amavi, nihil aliud, cum et ipsum esset nihil et eo ipso ego miserior? Et tamen solus id non fecissem—sic recordo animum tunc meum—solus omnino id non fecissem. Ergo amavi ibi etiam consortium eorum, cum quibus id feci. Non ergo nihil aliud quam furtum amavi; immo vero nihil aliud, quia et illud nihil est. (2.7.16)[20]

In other words, from the perspective which now informs his "memoria" (2.7.15),[21] enabling it to "recall" these events, he can see that, though he loved "nothing," and thereby loved his own destruction, he was not, despite his best efforts, able to erase himself into nothing, though, through love of nothing, he descended into the formlessness of the shadowy abyss, a depth which cannot narrate itself but which nevertheless, in spite of itself, still signifies the Creator.[22]

From this abyss, Augustine has been delivered by God's grace and mercy, which forgave Augustine's sins, melting them away, he says, like ice (2.7.15),[23] and gave him the perspective from which he could see that he had loved nothing in loving his theft. "Nothing" does not appear apart from the perspective of delivery from loving it, and the mention of it serves only to direct attention to God's act of mercy in deliverance, in giving Augustine a story to tell. The Psalms give Augustine words to voice his gratitude for having a memory that is more than a memory of nothing and that can tell its story without fear: "*Quid retribuam domino* [Ps. 116:12], quod recolit haec memoria mea et anima mea non metuit inde? Diligam te, domine, et gratias agam et *confitear nomini tuo* [Ps. 54:6]" (How can I repay the Lord for my ability to recall these things without fear? Let me love you, Lord, and give thanks to you and confess to your name).

In these texts from book 2, "nothing" appears as the absolute privation of narratability, something, in other words, which cannot be experienced, and yet one can choose to love "nothing" and thereby come as close to nothing as one can—in the words used to describe the *abyss* of Genesis 1:1–2, "almost nothing," "nearly nothing" ("prope nihil," "paene nullam rem," made "de nulla re"; so "from nothing" is not always "ex nihilo"; *Conf.* 12.8.8).[24] The "abyss" of formless matter has no story, no identity—*except* that it was created. Formless matter is the primal "earth" which God made "in the beginning," and it exists at the limit of narrative, *as* the limit of narrative; it is in fact the boundary of narrative, dependent upon the rest of the story to have a place in narrative at all (see 12.4.4–5.5).

"Nothing" cannot be experienced, but by God's grace and mercy, its close neighbor, the abyss of formlessness, can be experienced and narrated, because one can experience being recalled from this abyss, and thereby see it as an "abyss." One can descend into non-narrative-ability and live to *tell* it and, because of revelation, have language with which to tell it. Intelligibility cannot be erased, because the world was created in God's Word, and beyond this Word, which is the Beginning, there is nothing. Even grace forms, or re-forms, *something*,[25] and in the telling of one's rescue from a self-induced unintelligibility, one ends up realizing that even this unintelligibility is intelligible and can be distinguished from "nothing." "Invoco te, deus meus, misericorida mea, qui fecisti me et oblitum tui non oblitus es" (Upon you I call, O God, my mercy, who made me and did not forget me when I forgot you; *Conf.* 13.1.1).[26]

That is the work of the Creator, who does not "forget," who "remembers" and who forms remembering: there is no ultimate unintelligibility—that would just be nothing. So in praising God for returning one to the land of stories, one praises God as Creator as well, because one sees that there is no depth of formlessness that can be experienced that is actually "nothing." Creation "from nothing" is, in a way, the restriction of unintelligibility to "nothing," so that there is no ultimate unintelligibility anywhere, and one sees this when God's grace re-forms one from self-induced formlessness. One sees creation most fully as it is recapitulated by redemption.

We can see in this recapitulatory approach to creation the carrying forward of the hermeneutic of the *DGCM*, which placed the Hexaemeron in prophetic correspondence to the rest of the biblical narrative.

Here, using the soul sense to integrate the whole, Augustine reverses the dynamic. It is entirely a biblical approach.

In the opening lines of book 9 we read, "But where had my power of free will been throughout all those long years, and from what depth, what hidden profundity, was it called forth in one moment?" (Sed ubi erat tam annoso tempore et de quo *imo altoque* secreto evocatum est in momento liberum arbitrium meum; 9.1.1) Long before we get to the explicit exegesis of the Hexaemeron in books 11–13, we are familiar with the *deep, formless, invisible and dark* from Genesis 1:2, because the related imagery from the Psalms of redemption (and from Exodus and elsewhere), which in the Bible serves to interpret this image from Genesis, is used to interpret Augustine's rescue from his self-imposed descent into the loss of story, of coherence, of the integrated meaning, the form, that comes from freedom.

Augustine, always a careful exegete, here as in the *DGCM* pre-serves the biblical account of creation as *formation* of something form-less that already existed and preceded formation. He does not interpret the "abyss" as "nothing," and in *Confessions* 12.3.3 cites Wisdom 11:17 (as he did in *DGCM*), picturing God creating the world out of formless matter (materia informi).[27] Augustine talks about how he used to try to picture this "materia," picturing "disgusting, hideous forms, distortions of the natural order . . . something weird and grotesque" (12.6.6), that is to say, something out of mythology, probably Manichaean, something that could resist God.

The Bible presents something which is not nothing, but not yet anything in particular, a "nothing-something" (nihil aliquid) or "an-is-that-is-not" (est non est), to use Sr. Boulding's clever translations (12.6.6; cf. 12.3.3: "non tamen omnino nihil").[28] In other words, what is "formed" is not nothing. Nothing cannot be formed. Formability, the possibility of meaning, does not come from nothing. It comes from God—not just the form, but the possibility of form: "Et unde utcum-que erat, nisi esset abs te, *a quo sunt omnia* [Rom. 11:36; 1 Cor. 8:6], in quantumcumque sunt?" (And whence would it [formless matter, ca-pable of being formed] have any kind of being, if not from you, *from whom are all things* which to any degree have being? 12.7.7).[29] This does not mean that "heaven and earth" were created from God as some part of God ("Fecisti enim caelum et terram non de te"),[30] but rather in God's

Wisdom, which is in fact "de te"[31] the "Beginning" (which is the same as God's Word, as we already know from book 11 and the *DGCM*).

Wisdom or Word or Intelligibility is "God from God," but the very possibility of meaning that is *not* God also comes from God, meaning not from anything else, including itself as mere possibility. That is what it means to say that God creates from nothing: "fecisti aliquid et de nihilo" (12.7.7).[32] In other words, "creation from nothing" means precisely that the world did *not* come from "nothing," as though "nothing" had any potentiality for meaning, as though it contained any possibility, and so were secretly something "more" than nothing even while being nothing. "Nothing" is not "possibility." That is the formless matter, and *that* comes from God, without being from God's substance. "Et aliud praeter te non erat, unde faceres ea, deus, una trinitas et trina unitas: et ideo de nihilo fecisti caelum et terram" (Apart from yourself nothing existed from which you might make them, O God, undivided Trinity and threefold Unity, and therefore you made heaven and earth out of nothing; 12.7.7),[33] or, even more forcefully, "Tu eras et aliud nihil, unde fecisti caelum et terram" (You were, but nothing else was, from which you might make heaven and earth). Or again, "For you, Lord, made the world from formless matter [Wis. 11:18], and that formless matter that was almost nothing at all you made from nothing at all, whence you would make all the things which fill the sons of men with wonder" (Tu enim, domine, fecisti mundum de materia informi, quam fecisti de nulla re paene nullam rem, unde faceres magna, quae miramur filii hominum; 12.8.8).[34]

As Maria von Trapp, in the film *The Sound of Music*, along with many ancient philosophers, put it, "Nothing comes from nothing, nothing ever could." Augustine imposes nothing on the biblical text— or rather, he does not impose "nothing"; he does not say the text says that God created any thing from nothing, but that the text presents us with the thing closest to nothing that there is, "the earth formless and void, ... the dark ... the deep"—the potentiality for meaning, form, narrative ... and says that *that* comes from God, who is "Wisdom" and "Account–Word–Reason–Intelligibility" and, as such, "Beginning." There is no other "beginning" of the story. "Nothing" is not part of the story. That's the point. Augustine shows that the biblical text brings us to the very border of intelligibility, the very possibility of history and meaning, and says, beyond that, is nothing. We are summarily referred away from "nothing," and back to the narrative. The doctrine of creation from nothing represents the primacy of revelation.

The "recapitulatory" dynamic of the Bible is what ultimately shows us that there is no other "beginning" of the story, by reading the "beginning" from the "end" of the story. In the end, or at least in the climax of the story, we see where all meaning comes from, and thus where the "Beginning" of the story is. It is this recapitulatory dynamic of the Bible in which Augustine has been "forming" his reader from book 2 of the *Confessions* onward, as he uses the Psalm texts referring to salvation in the language and imagery also associated with creation.

The climax of Augustine's use of this recapitulatory biblical dynamic, of seeing creation from the perspective of redemption, is in book 13, where the creation story is read "allegorically"—as an allegory of redemption. But really the word "allegory" does not help us much, even though Augustine himself uses it (though sparingly; see 13.24.37), because we fill in our own meaning for "allegory," when in fact what Augustine performs here is the "recapitulatory" view of creation that he learned from the Bible itself and that he has been teaching us all along with the help of biblical texts.

Without reproducing it in whole, I can illustrate what Augustine is doing in the allegory by discussing the beginning of it, which is, strictly speaking, at 13.12.13. It starts with baptism, which in the ancient church was associated with enlightenment:

> Holy, holy, holy, Lord my God, in your name, Father, Son and Spirit, were we baptized, and in your name, Father, Son and Holy Spirit, we administer baptism, for among us too has God in his Christ created a heaven and an earth: the spiritual and carnal members of his Church. Before our earth was formed by his teaching it was invisible and unorganized, and we were shrouded in the darkness of ignorance [terra . . . invisibilis erat et incomposita . . . et tenebris] because you castigated humankind for its sin and your judgments are deep as a chasmic abyss [abyssus]. But your mercy did not forsake us in our misery, for your Spirit hovered over the water [spiritus tuus superferebatur super aquam]; and you said, *Let there be light; repent, for the kingdom of heaven is near, repent,*

and let there be light [Gen. 1:3; Matt. 3:2; 4:17]. And because our souls were deeply disquieted within themselves, we remembered you, O Lord, from our muddy Jordan; we called you to mind in that mountain which, though lofty as yourself, was brought low for us [Ps. 42:5–6, sung by catechumens in procession to the baptistry; see Boulding, 351n56]. Disgusted with our darkness, we were converted to you, and light dawned. See now, we who once were darkness are now light in the Lord [see Eph. 5:8].

Being "light in the Lord" means seeing our previous state as dark and unformed, as lacking all form, as having no story to tell, as having descended through sin to a formlessness out of which we had been called, and we can see that this call was operative "from the Beginning." We receive all light in Christ, everything, all meaning, all identity, all freedom to be ourselves, that is, to have a story with a true beginning, and so we can see the beginning of the story more clearly, and we, who are studying the issue of *creatio ex nihilo*, can see what is at stake in the doctrine as Augustine introduces his recapitulatory allegory, at 13.2.2:

> What advance claim did heaven and earth have upon you, when you made them in the Beginning? Let your spiritual and corporeal creation speak up and tell us what rights they had. In your Wisdom you made them, so that on your Wisdom might depend even those inchoate, formless beings, whether of the spiritual or the corporeal order. . . . What prior entitlement had they to exist even as formless things, when they could not exist at all except by your creation?

This includes spiritual creatures, both in their unformed state and in the formed state of conversion to the Light and to the Lord, so that they are "indebted to your free grace [*gratiae*][35] both for [their] initial life and for [their] life in the beatitude which [they] won by changing for the better in being converted to you" (13.3.4).

The beginning of the story is God's gratuitous good will, his grace, which needs nothing (13.4.5) and upon which nothing has a claim. Not only is the story given (form), but the possibility of a story is given (unformed matter and spirit). That is the point of *creatio ex nihilo*, namely, the complete opposite of what it sounds like: that "nothing" holds not even the possibility of meaning—even that comes from God, who, as Intelligibility in himself (as Trinity), has no *need* for any other intelligibility. In other words, God is free, and thus the cosmos is free, that is to say, free to have a real story, with a true beginning and a true end. The "goodness" of creation, a theme that preoccupies Augustine in *Confessions* because of his polemic against Manichaeism, is precisely that it had no antecedent merit to restrict God's freedom, and so is truly good and truly free. One can really say "Thank You!" for that! In fact, *creatio ex nihilo* simply means that the meaning of life is learning to say "Thank you" ever more repeatedly, ever more intimately, ever more deeply, for this "Thank you" is eternal and has no end. Isn't that biblical enough?

NOTES

I would like to thank Gary Anderson for inviting me to deliver a paper at the conference he organized on *creatio ex nihilo*, and for then inviting me to submit a paper to this volume. I owe a debt of gratitude to Thomas Clemmons for his help in completing some of the notes and in editing the text, and to Stephen Long for his editorial assistance throughout, and for helping me to think through some of the issues in the paper. I also would like to acknowledge helpful advice from Cyril O'Regan. Of course any deficiencies that remain are solely my own.

　　1. This point, as well as the centrality of the idea of *creatio ex nihilo*, is made very forcefully by the best monograph on this topic that I know of, N. Joseph Torchia, O.P., *Creatio ex nihilo and the Theology of St. Augustine: The Anti-Manichaean Polemic and Beyond* (New York: Peter Lang, 1999); see especially ix–xvi, 231–56. The earliest mention in Augustine's writing is *Soliloquia* 1.1.2: "Deus qui de nihilo mundum istum creasti, quem omnium oculi sentiunt pulcherrimum."

　　2. In this regard, it is interesting that Rowan Williams can write a whole article which is, in effect, on the idea of creation from nothing, but which never mentions it, except in the hint given in the title: Rowan Williams, " 'Good for Nothing'? Augustine on Creation," *Augustinian Studies* 25 (1994): 9–24; see esp. 19: "Either God has the resource within the divine life for fullness of bliss, in which case no divine act changes or enlarges this in its essence; or God does

not have such resource, and this divine lack can only be supplied by another agent—and to postulate another agent would be to abandon any commitment to the notion of a coherent universe. . . . Thus creation really is 'good for nothing': its point is not to serve a divine need."

3. For the critical Latin text of *De Genesi contra Manichaeos*, see the edition in Corpus Scriptorum Ecclesiasticorum Latinorum (CSEL), vol. 91, ed. Dorothea Weber (Vienna: Österreichischen Akademie der Wissenschaften, 1998). For citations in English translation, I have used that included in the volume *On Genesis*, trans. Edmund Hill, ed. John E. Rotelle (Hyde Park: New City Press, 2002), while providing occasional emendation based on the original Latin.

4. See Dorothea Weber, "*Communis Loquendi Consuetudo*: Zur Struktur von Augustinus, *De Genesi contra Manichaeos*," *Studia Patristica* 33 (1997): 274–79. Also, Robert J. O'Connell writes, "Augustine's 'spiritual exegesis' permits him to take extraordinary liberties with what is often the most obvious meaning of the Scriptural text, something of which he seems at times uncomfortably aware." *St. Augustine's Early Theory of Man* (Cambridge, MA: Belknap Press, 1968), 156.

5. This is witnessed perhaps in Augustine's reading other exegetical works that likely had a similar audience. Martine Dulaey, "L'apprentissage de l'exégèse biblique par Augustin: Première partie Dans les années 386–389," *Revue des Études Augustiniennes* 48 (2002): 277–95. Dulaey cites numerous parallels between Augustine's exegesis in *DGCM* and Ambrosiaster, Tertullian, Cyprian—and she even posits Origen, Novatien, and Victorinus of Poetovio, as well as an unknown *Onomasticon* that Jerome and Augustine may have used (287–94). Dulaey writes, "Quand Augustin s'est pour la première fois affronté aux manichéens dans le champ de l'exégèse biblique, il ne l'a pas fait armé de sa seule bonne volonté et de ses lectures néoplatoniciennes" (294).

6. If there were such a passage, the best candidate is 2 Macc. 7:28, but Augustine does not cite this passage in the *DGCM*, nor in the *Confessions* (the edition in Corpus Christianorum: Series Latina (hereafter CCSL), vol. 27, notes an allusion at *Conf.* 12.17.25, p. 228 at line 27, but Augustine does not draw attention to it as a Scriptural text), nor in *City of God*.

7. For an excellent brief summary of Augustine's understanding of unformed matter and for philosophical antecedents, see the valuable comments of Martine Dulaey at *Bibliothèque Augustinienne* 50 (Paris: Institut d'Études Augustiniennes, 2004), 50–52, note complémentaire 2, as well as the commentary of Madeleine Scopello in the introduction of the same volume, pp. 118–21, with regard to the controversy with the Manichaeans. See also Torchia, *Creatio ex nihilo and the Theology of St. Augustine*, 35–38, for the background in Chris-

tian biblical exegesis for the two-step creation theory, that is, creation of unformed matter and then its formation (though the two steps are actually simultaneous), and for the Hexaemeron exegetical tradition before Augustine.

8. "Spiritual exegesis" and "spiritual understanding" of the text cannot
be limited simply to an ability to conceive incorporeal substance as Plotinus or
other Neoplatonic philosophers might conceive it. If for no other reason, in
this text it certainly includes exegesis of the text as prophetic, that is, as referring to external events in time and space even if in the future. Thus for Roland
Teske, the "homo spiritualis" of *Confessions* 13 is the Christian who has mas-
tered a Neoplatonic way of thinking, which would, among other things, imply
that the uneducated Monica, with whom Augustine had ascended to touch
idipsum itself, was not a "spiritual," and it would also imply that someone
whose will was fixed in charity but was philosophically ignorant could not be
a *homo spiritualis*. See Roland J. Teske, " 'Homo Spiritualis' in the *Confessions*
of St. Augustine," in *Augustine: From Rhetor to Theologian*, edited by JoAnne
McWilliams (Waterloo, ON: Wilfrid Laurier University Press, 1992), 67–76.

9. This idea is thoroughly and fruitfully explored in a recent dissertation
completed at the University of Notre Dame by Monica Mata: "Myth and
Mystery: Augustine's First Commentary on Genesis 1–2:3" (2013), 164–70,
197–219. Mata also shows how "spiritual exegesis" and "spiritual understanding" cannot be limited to, or even include as a sine qua non, the philosophical
ability to conceive an incorporeal substance.

10. This rule is an example of metonymy. Michael Cameron, *Christ Meets
Me Everywhere: Augustine's Early Figurative Exegesis* (Oxford: Oxford University Press, 2012), 48–61.

11. The idea of the whole of human life as a continuation of one's creation
is eloquently and compellingly argued by Marie-Anne Vannier in her book
"Creatio," "Conversio," "Formatio," chez S. Augustin (Fribourg, Switzerland:
Éditions universitaires, 1991). She discusses "creatio de nihilo" on pages 106–9,
but the idea is implied in the whole of the book. *Creatio* is the original creation
from nothing; *conversio* is the turning of the created human being (in this case)
toward God in the Word, and this means a life of continuing configuration to
the Word made flesh; and *formatio* is the end result provided by eschatological
repose in God through perfect configuration to Christ (see esp. 149, 156). But in
another sense, the whole process is *creatio* (see, e.g., 135), the idea being that in
calling us to *conversio*, God calls us to participate in our own creation, and thus
truly be created. This also explains why the literal and allegorical exegesis in
book 13 of *Confessions* coincide at the point of the creation of the human
being—see John C. Cavadini, "Eucharistic Exegesis in Augustine's *Confessions*," *Augustinian Studies* 41 (2010): 106–7.

12. Martine Dulaey makes, not the same, but a related point on the finality of charity, *Bibliothèque Augustinienne* 50, p. 55.

13. CCSL 27, p. 223, lines 2–3.

14. Ibid., p. 217, lines 1–4 (trans. Boulding). The English translation used throughout the rest of this paper (occasionally emended) is that found in *The Confessions*, trans. Maria Boulding (Hyde Park: New City Press, 1997).

15. CCSL 27, pp. 19–20, lines 6–7, 8–10.

16. Ibid., p. 22, lines 14–18.

17. Ibid., p. 24, lines 47–48; see Boulding, p. 71.

18. Ibid., lines 52–53.

19. Ibid., lines 53–54.

20. Ibid., p. 25, lines 1–7. "What fruit did I ever reap from those things which I now blush to remember, and especially from that theft in which I found nothing to love save the theft itself, wretch that I was? It was nothing, and by the very act of committing it I became more wretched still. And yet, as I recall my state of mind at the time, I would not have done it alone; I most certainly would not have done it alone. It follows, then, that I also loved the camaraderie with my fellow-thieves. So it is not true to say that I loved nothing other than the theft? Ah, but it is true, because that gang-mentality too was a nothing."

21. Ibid., p. 24, line 1.

22. The shadowy abyss in itself, that is, unformed matter, is not evil but good. But, as Augustine makes clear, it never actually exists in itself, apart from some form which God gives it. To love it as though it ever existed on its own is to hate the work of creation itself, which both brings unformed matter into existence and forms it simultaneously. There is no love of unformed matter— something that is just as inaccessible to our experience as nothing—that is not a preference of formlessness to form as a gift given. It is a rejection of form precisely insofar as form is (and must ultimately be) a gift, and thus necessarily also a rejection of the potential for form, itself a gift created from nothing. Thus the love of nothing is not a love of any thing, not a turning toward something, but irreducibly a turning away. That is why those who turn toward themselves in preference to God, and thus forsake God and "exist in oneself," though it "is not immediately to lose all being," is to "come closer to nothingness" (*City of God* 14.13: "Nec sic defecit homo, ut omnino nihil esset, sed ut inclinatus ad se ipsum minus esset, quam erat, cum ei qui summe est inhaerebat. Relicto itaque Deo esse in semet ipso, hoc est sibi placere, non iam nihil esse est, sed nihilo propinquare"; CCSL 48, pp. 434–35). The original evil will is a defection, a falling away of the will from God, and, though it can only be seen in evil works, is not itself a work: "Mala vero voluntas prima, quoniam omnia opera mala praecessit in homine, defectus potius fuit quidam ab opere Dei ad sua opera

quam opus ullum." *City of God* 14.11, CCSL 48, p. 431. On the dynamic of "turning away" or "aversio" as a degradation of oneself as a creature, a refusal of cocreation, see Vannier, "*Creatio*," 134, 177, etc.

23. CCSL 27, p. 25, lines 4–5.

24. Ibid., p. 220, lines 8 and 11.

25. In *City of God* 14.11. As Augustine comments in this same section, although the evil is a defect in a nature that remains good, one does not eliminate the evil by destroying the defective nature, but by healing the nature. This section in *City of God* recalls the comments made in *Conf.* 7.11.17–12.18 to the effect that a given nature, insofar as it exists, remains good, and that unless it were good, it could not be corrupted, though the fact that it can be corrupted is due to its not being God, that is, to its not being immutable, and that in turn points to the fact that it was made from nothing.

26. CCSL 27, p. 242, lines 1–2.

27. Ibid., p. 220, lines 10–11.

28. 12.6.6 in ibid., p. 219, line 29; 12.3.3 in ibid., p. 218, lines 12–13.

29. Ibid., p. 219, lines 1–2.

30. Ibid., line 7.

31. Ibid., line 6.

32. Ibid., lines 6–7.

33. Ibid., lines 9–11.

34. Ibid., p. 220, lines 10–12.

35. Ibid., p. 243, line 8.

CHAPTER 8

Aquinas and Bonaventure on Creation

Joseph Wawrykow

Bonaventure and Aquinas, two great thirteenth-century scholastic theologians, offer robust treatments of creation, and the teaching of each about creation exhibits the characteristics that are customarily associated with medieval scholastic theology in the West: learned, thoughtful, insightful, methodical, invigorating. And integrated. That is, while creation in itself is subjected to searching inquiry—here, the reference is to the treatment of creation *ex professo*, as a discrete topic of theological inquiry—and in the process the main aspects of a Christian affirmation of the Creator and of the world as created are enumerated, the doctrine of creation in fact weaves its way throughout the entire theology, as informing the account of God and God's self-manifestation and God's call of humans to community and ultimately union with God, made possible by the engagement in God's world of the transcendent God who loves. There is, by way of anticipation of what follows, a deep conviction in both Aquinas and Bonaventure of the intimate link between creation and salvation; in this, the two theologians are simply reflecting the medieval Western Christian consensus. Accordingly, this presentation falls into two main parts. After sketching their basic teachings about creation (teachings which agree in most, but not all, details), I will focus on the link that each author makes between creation and salvation, the human flourishing that culminates in full and final communion with God. For Bonaventure and Aquinas alike, God is both beginning and end, and their insistence on, and appreciation of, God's creative activity informs their account of the attainment by human beings to the beatifying God.

On Creation

Aquinas reflects on creation, on God's creating, in the full range of his writings, and the account of creation is consistent throughout. To indicate that range of writing: a teaching on creation is found in his *systematic* writings (e.g., his *Scriptum* on the *Sentences* of Peter Lombard, and, his *Summa Theologiae* [*ST*]); in his commentaries on such works as the *liber de causis*, Pseudo-Dionysius's *Divine Names*, and various writings of Aristotle; in his disputed questions *de potentia* (the third of which is devoted in nineteen articles to creation as effect of the divine power); in a brief, but pointed, treatise on the eternity of the world from his final years; and of course in the biblical commentaries, which form a substantial portion of the Thomistic corpus (as a reminder, as a university master, Aquinas was a master of, precisely, the "sacred page," and his university lectures were devoted exclusively to the interpretation of scripture). Of the biblical commentaries, especially pertinent for our topic are those on the New Testament books in which Christ's creative activity is alleged (we have Aquinas's commentaries on John, on Hebrews, on Colossians).[1]

Creation figures prominently in the full range of Bonaventure's writings as well—in such systematic writings as his own "commentary" on the *Sentences* of Peter Lombard, the *Breviloquium*, the disputed questions on the Trinity,[2] and in writings of a more overtly spiritual bent. Of these last, I will be turning later in this chapter to Bonaventure's *Itinerarium mentis in Deum* (the *Journey of the Mind to God*) and even more to his *Collations* on the Hexaemeron,[3] an enormous exercise in spiritual theology from his final years.

The teachings of Aquinas and Bonaventure on creation are avowedly "Christian," rooted in scripture as mediated by the Christian theological and dogmatic traditions. Both theologians attend to the ancient creeds—viewed as apt summaries of the scriptural witness—which affirm God's creation of heaven and earth (that is, of all that there is) and the role of the Word in that creative activity. The two theologians had access to a more recent ecclesial proclamation of faith that also highlighted the principal aspects of the Christian belief in the creator God, in the statement issued by Lateran IV (in 1215).[4] Framed as a positive expression of Christian faith, but with an eye as well on the resurgent dualism that had emerged in parts of Western Europe, Lateran IV proclaims that the one God who is three persons is the

> *one principle* of all things, creator of *all things* invisible and visible, *spiritual and corporeal*; who by *his almighty power* at the *beginning of time* created *from nothing* both spiritual and corporeal creatures, that is to say angelic and earthly, and then created human beings composed as it were of both spirit and body in common. The devil and other demons were created by God naturally *good*, but they became evil by their own doing. Man, however, sinned at the prompting of the devil.

For scholastic theologians, access to early Christian theologizing on creation was available in various forms, not least through the *Sentences* of Peter Lombard.[5] The *Sentences* were a mid-twelfth-century composition that by the end of the first third of the thirteenth century had become integral to the training of scholastic theologians, including Bonaventure and Aquinas. The budding thirteenth-century scholastic offered lectures on all four books of the *Sentences*, which reviewed the main topics in theology along with the positions on those topics held by significant early writers, especially Augustine. In his second book, the Lombard discusses creation, and his organization and treatment set the tone for later scholastic treatments. Thus, in the first distinction of book 2, the Lombard discusses what creation is (and what it is not—it is not a "making out" of preexistent material; it is creation *ex nihilo*) and denies an eternity of the world. And in later distinctions (12 and following), he discusses the six days of creation in the Genesis account. In these later distinctions in book 2, Peter notes the disagreement among the fathers on how to take the six days. God creates; God distinguishes; God embellishes. In the distinguishing and embellishing (the six days), is there an actual discursiveness, an actual unfolding of created reality with one "day" following another? So thought the majority of the fathers. Or were the six days simultaneous, with the distinction of days to be taken figuratively? For their part, in their later systematic writings, Bonaventure and Aquinas retain a discussion *ex professo* of creation (what it is), followed by a discrete exposition of the six days. In Bonaventure's case, for example in the *Breviloquium*, he sides with the Lombard and with the majority of the fathers: the work of the six days is an actual unfolding (distinguishing, embellishing) over time;[6] Aquinas, on the other hand, for example in the questions in the prima pars of the *ST* devoted to the six days (qq. 65–74), is inclined to side with the minority position, that creation, in the coming to be and distinguishing, was simultaneous (although certain species would emerge only subsequently).[7]

While their teachings on creation are scriptural and Christian-traditional, in their presentations on creation Bonaventure and Aquinas also benefited from the recovery of Aristotle, that is, the translation into Latin, whether from Greek or from Arabic, of works by Aristotle that had been unavailable to the Latin West, along with commentaries and positions adjacent to the Aristotle.[8] Even apart from this recovery, medieval Christians knew of positions that differ markedly from the Christian teaching about creation. Their patristic sources knew of teachings that, for example, affirmed the eternity of the world (given the eternity of the cause of the world *or* the eternity of matter that is not due to that cause of the world) or viewed nondivine reality as a necessary emanation from the divine.[9] Yet the recovery of Aristotle and of other writings transmitted along with his still had its value, giving fresh impetus to considering what is involved in the Christian proclamation and what is at stake in that proclamation, and for refinement of expression of the creator God and the way in which what isn't God stands in relation to God.[10]

For Bonaventure and Aquinas, creating is free, volitional, and intentional and purposeful; and creating speaks to God's power, goodness, and wisdom. In creating, God grants being; by God's will, things come to be and receive all that they have—their actuality as well as their potential—from God. This creating is *ex nihilo*; God is not working on existing matter, as if giving some existing stuff shape or form or realizing some potential. As the cause of all, including potential, God gives rise to all, form and matter, in creatures. Thus, creatures stand in a relation of utter dependence on God, and they are, and are what they are, and continue to be, due to God's creative will. Creating is a free act: God stands under no necessity to create; God need not create to be God.

And yet it is quite in keeping with God's character to create. God is good, utter goodness; and in the words of the Pseudo-Dionysius (echoed by both Aquinas and Bonaventure), it pertains to goodness to diffuse itself.[11] God loves God's own goodness and wishes, freely, to share that with what is not God. And so the free act of creation is the expression of God's love, by which God conveys God's goodness to creatures and allows what is not God to share in, participate in, God, in the ways appropriate to creatures. This loving communication by God of being and goodness is at the same time a wise communication. God brings to be what is and is good, as made by God, in a sapiential way; God's sharing is according to God's wise plan. This sapiential communication accounts for the multiplicity and variety of creatures, each of which has its own being and goodness, as patterned on God.

Aquinas secures the point by asking whether God loves the better more, that is, loves the more what is possessed of more good.[12] There is a crucial difference between God's loving and the love that humans have. Human love is evoked by a good, by something that is truly or apparently good. A human will love more what is more good. God's love, in distinction, is causal, not evoked; and so God loves the better more in the sense of willing to some more good than to others. The human, endowed with rationality, is loved more than a nonrational being. God's causal love is thus an important feature of Aquinas's account of creation; he will, not incidentally, invoke it as well in talking about providence and predestination (by which creatures are ordered to their appropriate ends and brought to those ends) and incarnation and grace.

Both Aquinas and Bonaventure can summarize God's creating in terms of three of the four causes.[13] God is the *efficient* cause, the sole agent in creating. God creates directly, and not through intermediaries. God's goodness is the *final* cause of creating, for God loves God's goodness and wishes to share that. And there is an *exemplarity* in creating, inasmuch as creatures (who are not God) can by God's plan look like, resemble God, while falling short of the being and goodness (and wisdom) that is God. Only of the material cause is there no place in the Christian account of creation; creation is *ex nihilo*.

Although it may appear so to the understanding, there is no change or movement in the coming to be of what God creates, of what is created by God.[14] We can observe various changes in the world. For example, locomotion is a change, by which someone changes location. A seed developing into a plant is a change, by which something changes into something else (with which, however, there is continuity between the terminus a quo and terminus ad quem). And paper being burned and so becoming ashes is a change. In each of these changes, there is a subject, a someone or something that does or undergoes. The paper has the potential to become ashes when subjected to burning; a seed has the potential to be the plant; it is an individual who changes places. To none of these can creation be assimilated. "Nothing" is not a thing, a some-thing that is subject to change or that changes. Rather, that there is anything outside of God is due to the divine power, to God's creative activity. God wills, and things come to be. Nothing is presupposed to God's activity; there is nothing on which God might be acting. Whatever there is is because of the Creator.[15]

A brief foray into prepositional theology may be helpful here.[16] What is the force of the "*ex*" in the phrase *creatio ex nihilo*? For Aquinas, the import of the *ex* is twofold. First, the *ex* underscores sequence: something that had not been is by God's creating. And second, the *ex nihilo* is denying a material cause. There is nothing on which God is working in the coming to be of the creature. It is by the divine power that something exists. There is no movement from one term to another; there is simply the term of God's creative act, of conveying of being (*esse*).

There is a Trinitarian cast to the teachings of both theologians about creation. The First Principle is the triune God, and the persons exercise their proper causality in creating. For Aquinas, as he puts it in his commentary on the first book of the Lombard's *Sentences*, "The procession of the persons is the cause, the reason, for the procession of creatures."[17] The procession of creatures is due to and reflects the eternal relations constitutive of the divine persons, the Father eternally speaking the Word, the Spirit eternally proceeding from Father and Word.

As Gilles Emery has confirmed in his many publications, Aquinas remains faithful to this insight throughout his writing career.[18] Thus, in a passage that has become iconic for students of Aquinas (who doubt the more recent claim that Aquinas had severed the immanent from the economic Trinity), Aquinas states the importance of God's revelation of God's triune character, for both an account of creation and of salvation.[19] As he writes in *ST* I.32.1 ad 3:

> There are two reasons why the knowledge of the divine persons was necessary for us. [First] It was necessary for the right idea of *creation*. The fact of saying that God made all things by His Word excludes the error of those who say that God produced all things by necessity. When we say that in Him there is a procession of love, we show that God produced creatures not because He needed them, nor because of any other extrinsic reasons, but on account of the love of His own goodness. So Moses, when he had said, "In the beginning God created heaven and earth," subjoined, "God said, 'Let there be light,'" to manifest the divine Word; and then said, "God saw the light that it was good," to show the proof of the divine love. The same is also found in the other works of creation. In another way, and chiefly, [= the second reason] that we may think rightly concerning the salvation of the human race, accomplished by the Incarnate Son, and by the gift of the Holy Ghost.

In sum, the God who creates is manifested in the creation; the triune God who creates is manifested in the creation; and creating reflects the inner life of the triune God.

Bonaventure, too, links intimately the immanent and the economic Trinity and asserts the triune God as Creator.[20] When he is thinking of Augustine and Anselm, the account is close to that of Aquinas: the second person is the Word eternally spoken by the Father, the Holy Spirit the love of Father and Word. And so, as in Aquinas, the Father, to whom power is appropriated, creates through the Word, to whom wisdom is appropriated, and in the love that is the Holy Spirit; and the world as created is a work of wisdom and love, by which creation looks like God. Bonaventure has as well a second way of limning Trinitarian relations, here working off of Richard of St. Victor's meditations in *De Trinitate* on the fecundity of goodness, and applying the Pseudo-Dionysian adage mentioned earlier, about the good as diffusive of itself, to the inner life of God. In his fontal plenitude, the Father eternally gives rise to, loves, the Son; and in their mutual love Father and Son give rise to, love a third. On that account of the triune God, the coming to be of creatures—that diffusion of good—will be patterned on the eternal diffusions of good that are the triune God.

Patterning, however, is not identity, and both Bonaventure and Aquinas insist on the differences between the creation and the triune God. For one thing, creating is free and unnecessitated. That there is a world is due to God's willing/decision, which is free (God does not need to create, although creating is in keeping with God's goodness and triune character). The Trinity of persons, in contrast, eternally is, and the being of one person is not due to a "decision" of another. And, for a second thing, the Word who is eternally spoken by the Father is one in being and nature with the Father, eternally receiving from the Father divine being and nature. No creature, no matter how exalted, is identical in being or essence with the God who is its cause. There is an infinite, ontological distance between the Creator and what God has freely made.

An Eternal Creation?

The agreement between the teachings on creation of Aquinas and of Bonaventure is considerable, but not total. For Bonaventure, that the world has a temporal beginning is implied by the affirmation of creation *ex nihilo*.[21] Any arguments that the world is eternal can be rebutted; numerous convincing arguments that the creation has to have a temporal beginning can be advanced. For Bonaventure, to hold a creation *ex nihilo* and a world eternal in duration, lacking temporal beginning, is impossible. Underlying Bonaventure's equation (or at least close association) of *ex nihilo* and the non-eternity of the world is a concern to maintain the difference between God and world; would not the ascription of eternity to the world grant an equality with the eternal God?

For his part, Aquinas prefers to distinguish more clearly between *ex nihilo* and a temporal beginning of the creation. To say the one is not to say the other. They are distinct claims. It is not that Aquinas thinks that the world is eternal. He doesn't. He holds as a matter of Christian faith that the created realm has a temporal beginning, as attested in the opening line of Genesis (according to one plausible interpretation of "principium").[22] But he thinks that God could (have) create(d) a world that is eternal in duration; to affirm *ex nihilo* is not thereby to say that the world has a temporal beginning.

In his late *De aeternitate mundi*, Aquinas begins his analysis by asking whether the notions "to be created according to entire substance" and "to have no beginning in duration" are compatible. They would be mutually irreconcilable if one or both of the following could be established: that an efficient cause must precede its effect *in duration* and/or that *nonbeing* must precede being in duration. But (to look at the first): an efficient cause need not precede *in duration* its effect. Such is not the case in the observable realm of causes whose effect is instantaneous (e.g., fire heating, sun illuminating); so much the more of the God who causes, instantaneously, the whole substance of creatures. Nor does it matter, in terms of the putative duration preceding an effect, that God is volitional; for God does not deliberate (think things through, ponder options), but simply/eternally wills. What does matter is not a precedence in duration but a precedence *in nature*; and God is cause and is Creator; and it lies within God's power to will an eternal effect.

As for nonbeing "preceding" being (the other point that needs examining): the "nothing" of the *ex nihilo* is tricky, and it may be that despite the best intentions, there has been a smuggling in (by Thomas's opponents) of a notion of change here, in which, in creation, nonbeing gives way to being, such that the creature in its nonbeing comes to have being. First there would be nonbeing, nothing; and then, something (and that would militate against the creation of an effect without temporal beginning). But, Aquinas clarifies, that is not what is entailed by the affirmation of creation *ex nihilo*. *Ex nihilo* is asserting that all that a creature is and has comes from God, from God's willing, and that if God did not grant being, there would be no creature. And, to complete the point, if God were to withdraw being, the creature would cease to be, would not be, would revert in that sense to nonbeing.

A world that lacks a temporal beginning is, then, possible. And such a created effect would not be equal to God. The effect is derived from another, from its cause; God has no cause of God's being. And "eternity" as affirmed of such a world would differ from the eternity of God. For it is one thing, as Boethius has observed, to be led through endless life, which Plato attributed to the (eternal) world, and another to enjoy the presence of endless life wholly and equally embraced, which manifestly is proper to God. The world is marked by change, which is measured by time; but as Augustine has said (here also quoted), there is no change in God, and for God there is no past or future, but all is present. There is then no eternity of God and of the world, so imagined, in a univocal sense; an eternal world would neither denigrate God nor exalt the world.

CREATION AND SALVATION: BONAVENTURE

For both Aquinas and Bonaventure, creation is about the beginning, about the origin of things in God and God's sustaining of what God has brought into being. But for both, creation also has to do with the end, with the attainment by human beings of the end offered them by God, full communion with God. In their theologies, *exitus* is paired with *reditus*, creation with human flourishing and salvation; and the soteriologies of Bonaventure and Aquinas make much of creation, as both possibility and means, in portraying the movement of humans, by operations of knowing and loving, to their God-appointed end. The journey of humans to God as end is, as Augustine puts it in the first book of his *De doctrina christiana* (a text well known to both Aquinas and Bonaventure), a movement of *creatures*, rational creatures, and in that movement rational creatures are, as Augustine puts it, in effect "returning to their homeland,"[23] to their Maker who is their end. In what follows, I will offer some examples (illustrative, not exhaustive) of how *exitus* can figure in the *reditus* in these two medieval theologies, beginning with two treatises by Bonaventure.

The *Soul's Journey into God* (the *Itinerarium mentis in Deum*) is a masterpiece of spiritual theology.[24] Spiritual theology in the Middle Ages is concerned with purgation (especially the removal of sin and the remedying of its effects), illumination (by which someone comes to know what is important and existentially appropriates that), and perfection (which has to do with union with God and coming to rest in God). A given writing may play up one or another aspect of the spiritual life. The *Itinerarium* in the main presupposes purgation and concentrates on illumination, with a gesture at the end, in discussing a seventh step, at perfection.

Bonaventure exhibits great skill in the organization of this work. The first six steps of the journey of this writing, on illumination, describe and advocate a *mediated* encounter with God via the human's purposeful knowing; the seventh step, which here is affirmed as utter gift, which may be given by God to those who are prepared by the first six steps, gestures at the *unmediated* knowing and loving of God that is the goal of human existence. In these six steps, there are three main objects of contemplation: the world; the self; and the names of God found in scripture, Being (in the Old Testament) and Good (in the New). The three main objects of contemplation are doubled, to indicate the modes of mediation. Thus, in the first two steps, God is manifested *through* and *in* the world. Here, the doctrine of creation receives its full due. What exists, individually and collectively, by God's wise creating, manifests God, reflects God, in terms of both essential attributes and distinction of persons. God then is manifested through the world as made by God. God is also active *in* the world as creator and sustainer and as providential governor, and meditation on the world will also attend to that divine activity in the world. Knowing the world and assessing it correctly, then, can and should provide a knowing of God.

So too in the third and fourth steps: God is known *through* the self—seen as *image* of God—and through its powers, testifying to divine unity and trinity; God is known *in* God's redemptive work in Christ, by which the soul is freed of sin and reformed, to be and to function as God intends. As for meditation on the names of God: God is Being itself; and all beings receive their being from God, and creaturely (participated) being reflects that of God. And, in the sixth step, on Good, God is said to be Good, Goodness itself, and Bonaventure trades on the diffusiveness theme as expressed by Pseudo-Dionysius— with regard to God's inner life, as well as God's works ad extra, including in the incarnation—as described in the first main section of the chapter. Much has been made of Bonaventure's sacramentality, in this writing and elsewhere: creaturely things are indeed signs, made and ordained by God and able to point beyond themselves, to God.[25] Presence, too, is crucial. God is present to what God has made, as patterned on God, and in God's activities in the world and in the self. In apprehending things, in reflecting on the world and on the self, God too is to be apprehended in God's presence, con-tuited, as Bonaventure puts it, in the knowing of self and world.

The *Collations on the Hexaemeron*, too, is an exercise in spiritual theology, and again the focus is on illumination. There is some overlap with the *Itinerarium*, not least in terms of sacramentality and presence, but the *Collations*, even though unfinished, is much, much longer and is governed by a different principle of organization.[26] The opening three collations provide an overture in spiritual theology, describing the importance of understanding and wisdom and the conditions for their attainment. Subsequent collations take the six days of Genesis (actually, the seven days) as their point of departure, as their structuring principle. For Bonaventure, each day has to do with understanding, a kind or way of understanding, and several collations are devoted to each understanding, to tease out its nature, scope, and purpose.

Thus, the first day, on which light was made, has to do with the understanding to which human intelligence might reach by its own power; and human intelligence, he adds, is the basis for the understandings associated with the other days. The second understanding is that of the second day, when a firmament was made in the midst; this firmament is faith, which is the origin of wisdom and the origin of knowledge, whether of eternal or temporal things. The understanding that is the third day, when the waters were gathered together and dry land appeared, is the scriptures, in which God teaches saving truth and which contain several senses, levels of meaning, to be uncovered through close, faithful reading. The fourth day, when God said, "Let there be lights," has to do with meditation on the heavenly hierarchies, as suggested by the sun, the moon, and the stars. The fifth and sixth days have to do with prophecy and rapture, respectively, and the seventh day, that of rest, has to do with heavenly repose, with the direct knowing and loving of God.

As it turned out, Bonaventure did not reach in the *Collations* to the fifth and following days; the collations break off at the twenty third, and only the first four days receive their due, or rather the understanding that each of those days suggests in *Bonaventure*'s reckoning. Even from this brief summary, it will be apparent that the approach in the *Collations* to the opening of Genesis is rather different than that found in his commentary on the *Sentences* or in his *Breviloquium*. There, Bonaventure is concerned to consider the teaching of Genesis on the days and to consider, in the company of the fathers, problems that emerge from the text about creation itself and its distinctions and embellishment. Here, the six days provide the scaffolding for a magisterial account of understanding in its various forms, as part of the movement to God through Christ. Each understanding has a role to play in noetic ascent, and Bonaventure wants to make clear what is involved in each understanding and how each might contribute to human flourishing. For Bonaventure, through these six understandings, the microcosm will come to perfection, just as the macrocosm has in the six days of creation.

In the *Collations*, Bonaventure insists on the centrality of Christ, or, in the preferred terminology in this writing, on the centrality of the Word.[27] The Word is characterized in three ways, and each makes a decisive contribution: as the *uncreated Word*, who is the Word of the Father and the "center" of the Trinity, and by whom all things are brought forth; as the *incarnate Word*, by whom all things are restored; and as *inspired Word*, by whom all things are revealed. The Word is essential to full understanding; as Bonaventure puts it, "No one can have understanding unless he considers where things come from, how they are led back to their end [that is, by the redemptive and revelatory work of the incarnate Word], and how God shines forth in them [by the inspiring Word, who proclaims God's truth and illuminates within, guiding the learner in apprehending that truth]."[28]

The discussion of the understanding of the first day—that of the natural intelligence, which has to do with the world, the world that God freely and wisely makes—is layered and nuanced. Bonaventure looks at this knowing in the collations professedly devoted to it; but he returns to this knowing in later collations, in the course of his consideration of the knowing of faith and of scripture read in its depth of meaning. Knowing the world by natural intelligence can bear great fruit when it brings a true knowledge of God. But this way of knowing has its limitations and its risks; several wrong assessments of the world have been made, with accompanying error about God. What, then, distinguishes the correct, fruitful use of intelligence in reading the world from a faulty one? A fruitful reading of the world is one in which Christ is prominent and informs the reading as uncreated, as incarnate, as inspiring Word; this is the reading that, when natural intelligence is aided by faith and informed by the Word, is achieved according to Bonaventure by the "true metaphysician." A poor reading of the world, by contrast, will not be in the Word and will fixate on sensible reality, will stick with the essences of created things and not view them as vestige of the God who intentionally creates. Such a Word-less reading has indeed led to several errors (not least of which is thinking the world to be eternal). From Bonaventure's language, in distinguishing the poor metaphysician from the true, he would seem to be thinking of the pagan philosophers and their errors; but it may be that he also has some contemporaries in view. At any rate, one who knows the world as God intends and Bonaventure promotes will study the world but not linger on it; the world, as in the *Itinerarium*, is sign of God, provided by God to come in this distinctive way to know God.

CREATION AND SALVATION: AQUINAS

There is nothing like the *Collations*—or, for that matter, the *Itinerarium*—in the Thomistic corpus. Preferring other genres, Aquinas has not written any treatises in spiritual theology (although I would think that his theological writing, with its care and precision, would be helpful to those pursuing God). Nor is Aquinas as interested as Bonaventure in the "inspiring Word," in the sense of Christ as interior Teacher; Aquinas has other ways to talk about learning and growing by God's spiritual aid. But, in his own way Aquinas is equally committed to "Christ the Center," and his own Christology attends well to what Bonaventure calls the "uncreated Word" and the "incarnate Word." For Aquinas, too, there is a journey of people to God; and as he says very early in the *ST*, Christ *secundum quod homo*[29] is the way to God, the triune God who is end as well as beginning. That is, the Word has become human, without loss to itself as Word; and through the incarnate Word's doing and suffering, people can be brought to eternal life.

Aquinas's handling of a particular topic in Christology will serve here to illustrate his skills in weaving creation into an account of Christology, including soteriology, and rooting all in Trinity. It is the second person of the Trinity who became incarnate. Why? Why the Word? Why is it fitting that this divine person took up human nature? In *Summa contra gentiles* (*ScG*) IV.42, Aquinas suggests three arguments for the fittingness of the incarnation of the Word; I proceed in reverse order.[30] The second and third arguments for fittingness point to the creative activity of the second person. In the third argument for fittingness, Aquinas notes that the Word has a kinship with the whole of creation, since the Word (as eternally generated by the Father) contains the essences of all things created by God. Thus, all creatures are nothing but a kind of real expression and representation of those things which are comprehended in the conception of the divine Word. Hence, it was suitable that it be the Word who took up human nature, one of the creaturely natures patterned on the Word.

The second argument for fittingness in the chapter homes in on the particular kinship of the Word for human nature, which gets its proper species from being rational; and in scripture the human is said to be the "image of God." The "Word" (Logos) is kin to reason, and the second person is indeed the Image (capital "I") of the Father. Most appropriately then was it the Word who was united to reasonable nature.

In the first reason of the chapter, incarnation is tied to salvation. Salvation means the full, direct knowing and loving of God, the First Truth, in the next life, and in that direct knowing, the human person is perfected in his highest, the intellective, part. The Word proceeds from the Father in an eternal, intellectual generation. If the assumption of human nature is ordered to the salvation (fulfillment of humans, in knowing God) of humans (and it is), then it is fitting that it be the Word who becomes incarnate.

In the parallel discussion in the *ST* (in III.3.8),[31] the link between incarnation and salvation is reasserted, with an important gloss, one that factors in the sin that frustrates the journey of humans to God as beatifying end and so needs to be overcome through the work of the incarnate One. Thus, Aquinas writes (ad 2), "The first creation of things was made by the power of God the Father through the Word; hence the second creation ought to have been brought about through the Word, by the power of God the Father, in order that restoration should correspond to creation." Aquinas, of course, is hardly innovative here; nor should he be. There is ample precedent, in both East and

West, when it comes to upholding the importance of creation, and of a creation *ex nihilo*, and in attending to the particular causality of the Word in the coming to be of things and so to the aptness of that same Word to become incarnate, as geared toward salvation; Athanasius's *On the Incarnation* comes readily to mind as an early example of how all of this goes together. It nonetheless surely is to Aquinas's credit to have assimilated this web of teaching so perfectly and to have restated it with the precision of a scholastic.

Aquinas's teaching on appropriateness in the *ScG* and *ST* is brisk and dense and condenses a whole range of claims—about Trinity, about creation, about incarnation, and about salvation—into a focused meditation. It also gives eloquent expression to Aquinas's conviction that creation and salvation are of a piece, evidence of God's love and wisdom, of God's desire to share what is God's with others. In a few quick strokes, Aquinas has in effect claimed as his own the teaching of John 1, that in the beginning the Word was, and was with God, and was God; and that through him all things came to be; and that it is the Word who was made flesh; and that it is from the incarnate Word's fullness that all have received.

Notes

1. For the list of Aquinas's writings, see the "Brief Catalogue" prepared by Gilles Emery in Jean-Pierre Torrell, *Saint Thomas Aquinas*, vol. 1, *The Person and His Work*, trans. Robert Royal (Washington, DC: Catholic University of America Press, 1996), 330–61. In the present discussion of creation according to Aquinas, I am making particular use of Aquinas's *Scriptum super Libros Sententiarum*, ed. P. Mandonnet and M. F. Moos (Paris: P. Lethielleux, 1933–47), especially *In II*; the *Summa Theologiae*, ed. Instituti Studiorum Medievalium Ottaviensis (Ottawa: Commissio Piana, 1941–); and the late treatise *De aeternitate mundi* in *Sancti Thomae de Aquino Opera omnia iussu Leonis XIII P. M. edita, t. 43*, editori di San Tommaso (Roma: Leonine, 1976), 49–89. There is as of yet no complete English translation of the *Scriptum*. However, for the translation of Aquinas on the Lombard's bk. 2, d.1, see *Aquinas on Creation: Writings on the "Sentences" of Peter Lombard*, book 2, distinction 1, question 1, trans. Steven E. Baldner and William E. Carroll (Toronto: Pontifical Institute of Mediaeval Studies, 1997), 63–109. There are various translations of the *ST*; when quoting the English at length in the text below, I am using that by the

English Dominicans, *The Summa Theologica of St. Thomas Aquinas*, rev. ed. (1920; repr., 5 vols., Westminster, MD: Christian Classics, 1981), also available online at newadvent.org. For the English of the treatise on the eternity of the world, see *St. Thomas Aquinas, Siger of Brabant, St. Bonaventure, On the Eternity of the World*, trans. C. Vollert, L. H. Kendzierski, and P. Byrne (Milwaukee: Marquette University Press, 1964), 19–25. Another translation is available in Baldner and Carroll, *Aquinas on Creation*, 114–22.

2. Bonaventure, *Opera Omnia* (Quaracchi: Editions Collegii S. Bonaventurae, 1882–1902): *Commentarium in Secundum Librum Sententiarum* (vol. 2); *Breviloquium* (vol. 5, pp. 201–91); *Quaestiones disputatae de mysterio SS. Trinitatis* (vol. 5, pp. 45–115). There is as of yet no English translation of the *Commentarium*. For the *Breviloquium*, see *Breviloquium*, trans. Dominic V. Monti, O. F. M., vol. 9 of *Works of St. Bonaventure* (St. Bonaventure, NY: Franciscan Institute Publications, 2005); for the disputed questions on the Trinity, see *Saint Bonaventure's Disputed Questions on the Mystery of the Trinity*, trans. Zachary Hayes, O. F. M., vol. 3 of *Works of St. Bonaventure* (St. Bonaventure, NY: Franciscan Institute Publications, 1979).

3. Both of these writings are found in Bonaventure, *Opera Omnia*, vol. 5 (*Itinerarium mentis in Deum*, 293–313; the *Collationes in Hexaemeron*, 327–454). There are English translations of each: *The Soul's Journey into God* in *Bonaventure*, trans. Ewert Cousins (New York: Paulist Press, 1978), 51–116; and *Collations on the Six Days*, vol. 5 of *The Works of Bonaventure*, trans. José de Vinck (Paterson, NJ: St. Anthony Guild Press, 1960).

4. For the statement of faith issued at Lateran IV, see the Latin text, with facing English translation, in *Decrees of the Ecumenical Councils*, vol. 1, *Nicaea I to Lateran V*, ed. N. P. Tanner (London: Sheed & Ward, 1990), 230–31. (Emphases added in the quotation from this statement proclaimed by Lateran IV [p. 230] that follows in the text.)

5. Peter Lombard, *Sententiae in IV Libris Distinctae*, tomus I, liber I et II, Spicilegium Bonaventurianum 4 (Rome: Editiones Collegii S. Bonaventurae ad Claras Aquas, 1971). For the English translation, see Peter Lombard, *The Sentences*, trans. Giulio Silano, 4 vols. (Toronto: Pontifical Institute of Mediaeval Studies, 2007–10).

6. Bonaventure, *Breviloquium*, pt. 2, ch. 2.

7. For the *ex professo* treatment of creation in the *ST*, as preceding the account of the six days, see *ST* I.44–49. Q. 44 is on God as first cause of things; q. 45, on creation (a. 1 is on creation *ex nihilo*); q. 46, on the beginning of the world's duration; q. 47, on the plurality of things (in general); and qq. 48 and 49 are on evil and on the cause of evil (God, the supreme cause, is not the cause of evil; *ST* I.49.2).

8. See Bernard G. Dod, "Aristoteles latinus," in *The Cambridge History of Later Medieval Philosophy*, ed. N. Kretzmann, A. Kenny, and J. Pinborg (Cambridge: Cambridge University Press, 1982), 45–79; a chart of the chronology of translations of given Aristotelian works is found at 74–79.

9. See, e.g., Augustine, *De civitate dei*, bk. 11, as well as bk. 8. Augustine's report about what the philosophers held about the eternity of the world, e.g., is cited by Aquinas at *ST* I.46.2 ad 1.

10. In his *Freedom and Creation in Three Traditions* (Notre Dame, IN: University of Notre Dame Press, 1993), David Burrell has located Aquinas's approach to creation in medieval Muslim, Jewish, and Christian conversations about God and the world, emphasizing that common to the teachings of significant theologians of the Abrahamic faiths is an insistence on creation as God's free act. That there is anything is due to an activity of God in which God need not engage. Burrell contrasts creation as free with (ancient) views that either simply take for granted the existence of what is not God or portray what is not God in terms of a necessary emanation. There is no doubt that for Aquinas (and these other medieval thinkers) creation is God's free act; and Burrell is correct (here in continuity with Robert Sokolowski, *The God of Faith and Reason* [Washington, DC: Catholic University of America Press, 1995; orig. published 1982]) that the doctrine of God's free creation helps to secure the "distinction" between the transcendent God and the world brought into being and sustained by that God. However, Burrell's rendering of Aquinas on creation, not least the alleged distinctiveness of the teaching of the revealed religions on creation as free act, might with profit be supplemented, and qualified where needed, by reference to the following: John Wippel, "Aquinas on Creation and Preambles of Faith," *Thomist* 78 (2014): 1–36; Wippel, "Thomas Aquinas on God's Freedom to Create or Not," in *Metaphysical Themes in Thomas Aquinas* (Washington, DC: Catholic University of America Press, 2007), 2:218–39; Wippel, "Thomas Aquinas on the Ultimate Why Question: Why Is There Anything at All Rather Than Nothing Whatsoever?," in *The Ultimate Why Question* (Washington, DC: Catholic University of America Press, 2011), 84–106; Mark Johnson, "Did St. Thomas Aquinas Attribute a Doctrine of Creation to Aristotle?," *New Scholasticism* 63 (1989): 129–55; Johnson, "Aquinas's Changing Evaluation of Plato on Creation," *American Catholic Philosophical Quarterly* 66 (1992): 81–88. In his articles, Wippel is concerned with what can be known and proven through reason, according to Aquinas, when it comes to creation. For Aquinas, sacred doctrine—the truths needed for salvation—consists of two kinds of truths: the articles of faith and the preambles of faith. Both are revealed by God. But one can reason to (demonstrate) the preambles of faith. Only few have done so, and only after a long time, and even then, with

error mixed in (and so there is a wisdom to God revealing such truth); but they *are* demonstrable. The other kind of truth falling under sacred doctrine is the article of faith; such transcends the ability of reason to argue to, and must be revealed, and when held, will be held by faith. As Wippel shows, for Aquinas, the greater part of the teaching about creation is a matter of preamble: that there is a creation, that God creates, that God freely creates. All can be argued to. But that God is triune, and so the Creator God triune, is an article of faith; so too, that creation is not eternal, that is, has a temporal beginning. As for the entries by Johnson: these have to do with what Aquinas ascribes to important thinkers dependent on reason alone, that is, not privy to revelation. Over the course of his career, Aquinas comes to ascribe a doctrine of creation to Aristotle (that there is a creation, that God creates in bringing things into being, that God does so freely), and likely to Plato as well. Neither Wippel nor Johnson is concerned to challenge Burrell, at least explicitly; but their research has been well-received and does seem worthy of consideration in assessing Burrell on Aquinas.

(As a point of contrast, here at least Bonaventure would seem to show an even greater confidence in the power of reason: not only can one argue to a creation and a creator God and a free creation; for Bonaventure, one can demonstrate that creation is not eternal. I return to the question of the eternity of the world/its temporal beginning later in the text.)

11. For a discussion of *bonum est diffusivum sui* in Aquinas, see, e.g., Wippel, "Thomas Aquinas on the Ultimate Why Question," 91–106, as part of his response to Kretzmann's claim that Aquinas's teaching on creation as act verges on necessitarian: as good, according to Kretzmann's take on Aquinas, God would have to diffuse God's goodness, in creating. For Wippel, the saying, for Aquinas, is to be taken in terms of final, not efficient, causality. And creating would be figured in terms of means; and such means, when it comes to God, are not indispensable. God would be good whether or not God created; God does not become good, or better, by creating. Pseudo-Dionysian ideas about the good and its communication, not incidentally, reappear in Aquinas in a variety of settings, including a discussion of incarnation (see, e.g., *ST* III.1.1c). And there (too), it is quite clear that God need not become incarnate; all of God's activity ad extra, in communicating goodness, is free, unnecessitated.

12. See *ST* I.20.4.

13. Bonaventure, *Breviloquium*, pt. 2, chs. 1, 3; Aquinas, *ST* I.44.1–4.

14. *ST* I.45.2 ad 2: "Creatio non est mutatio nisi secundum modum intelligendi tantum."

15. Aquinas on occasion will offer assessments of the worth or value of God's various works ad extra. As at *ST* I-II.113.9c, in the context of discussing God's justification of the ungodly, Aquinas will say that one act can be deemed

greater than another divine act in some sense. Here, he says that creating can be said to be the greatest of God's acts in terms of the *ex nihilo*. However, in another sense, justification is greater than creating, in that justification makes possible a share in God's own goodness (as ultimately allowing the justified to participate in the beatifying God himself).

16. For what follows in the text, see *ST* I.45.1 ad 3.

17. See, e.g., *In I* Sent.d.14, q.1, a.1 sol.

18. For Aquinas's teaching in the *Scriptum*, see G. Emery, *La Trinité créatrice: Trinité et creation dans les commentaires aux "Sentences" de Thomas d'Aquin et de ses précurseurs Albert le Grand et Bonaventure* (Paris: J. Vrin, 1995). As Emery observes, Aquinas had access to Bonaventure's slightly earlier commentary on the *Sentences* in developing his own Trinitarian teaching of creation. For Bonaventure, see Luc Mathieu, *La Trinité créatrice d'après saint Bonaventure* (Paris: Les Éditions Franciscaines, 1992).

19. The passage from *ST* I.32 that follows in the text is quoted, for example, by David Burrell, "Creation in *Super Evangelium S. Joannis Lectura*," in *Reading John with St. Thomas Aquinas*, ed. Michael Dauphinais and Matthew Levering (Washington, DC: Catholic University of America Press, 2005), 123, and John P. Yocum, "Aristotle in Aquinas's Sacramental Theology," in *Aristotle in Aquinas's Theology*, ed. Gilles Emery and Matthew Levering (Oxford: Oxford University Press, 2015), 227. For an illuminating discussion of the connection between immanent and economic Trinity, and its import for Aquinas's theology, see G. Emery, "*Theologia* and *Dispensatio*: The Centrality of the Divine Missions in St. Thomas's Trinitarian Theology," *Thomist* 74 (2010): 515–61. As a reminder, the question on the mission of the divine persons (*ST* I.43) comes immediately before the *ex professo* discussion of creation in the *ST* (I.44–49).

20. See Joseph Wawrykow, "Franciscan and Dominican Trinitarian Theology (Thirteenth Century): Bonaventure and Aquinas," in *The Oxford Handbook of the Trinity*, ed. Gilles Emery and Matthew Levering (Oxford: Oxford University Press, 2011), 185–90.

21. For an orientation to high medieval discussions, see Richard C. Dales, *Medieval Discussions of the Eternity of the World* (Leiden: Brill, 1990); J. B. M. Wissink, ed., *The Eternity of the World in the Thought of Thomas Aquinas and His Contemporaries* (Leiden: Brill, 1990). On Bonaventure, see also S. Baldner, "St. Bonaventure and the Demonstrability of a Temporal Beginning," *American Catholic Philosophical Quarterly* 71 (1997): 225–36.

22. *ST* I.46.3c.

23. Augustine, *De doctrina christiana* 1.10.10, ed. and trans. R. P. H. Green (Oxford: Oxford University Press, 1996), 20 and 22: "Quasi ambulationem quondam et quasi navigationem ad patriam esse arbitremur."

24. For a fine introduction to Bonaventure's teaching about the movement to God by knowing and loving, made possible by what God has done in creating and in Christ, see Marianne Schlosser, *Saint Bonaventure: La joie d'approcher Dieu*, trans. J. Gréal, coll. Initiations au Moyen Age (Paris: Cerf, 2006). The main features of Bonaventure's worldview are spelled out in J. A. Wayne Hellmann, *Divine and Created Order in Bonaventure's Theology*, trans. with an appendix by J. M. Hammond (St. Bonaventure, NY: Franciscan Institute, 2001). Hammond's appendix focuses on the *Itinerarium*.

25. For an exchange about the upshot of sacramentality, see S. Vanni-Rovighi, "La vision du monde chez S. Thomas et chez S. Bonaventure," and J. Chatillon, "Sacramentalité, beauté et vanité du monde chez S. Bonaventure," in *1274, année charnière: Mutations et continuités* (Paris: Éditions du centre national de la Recherche Scientifique, 1977), 667–78, 679–85. Does insisting on sacramentality entail ignoring the intrinsic worth and meaning of things other than God?

26. See C. Colt Anderson, *A Call to Piety: Saint Bonaventure's Collations on the Six Days* (Quincy, IL: Franciscan Press, 2002).

27. For a useful orientation to Bonaventure's Christology, see Zachary Hayes, *The Hidden Center: Spirituality and Speculative Christology in St. Bonaventure* (New York: Paulist Press, 1981).

28. Bonaventure, *Collations* 3 (p. 42 in the de Vinck translation).

29. See the prologue to *ST* I.2, where Aquinas is sketching the overall organization of the *ST*.

30. Thomas Aquinas, *Liber de veritate catholicae fidei contra errores infidelium, seu Summa contra gentiles*, ed. C. Pera, 3 vols. (Turin: Marietti, 1961). For the English translation of bk. IV: *Saint Thomas Aquinas, Summa contra gentiles*, bk. IV, *Salvation*, trans. Charles J. O'Neil (Notre Dame, IN: University of Notre Dame Press, 1975). Bk. IV, ch. 42, belongs to a set of chapters (chs. 27–49) that constitute an examination of the incarnation of the Word. The particular arguments of the chapter, however, assume and build on what is found in *ScG* IV, chs. 11–13, where the focus is on the Word eternally spoken by the Father, who thus is, by appropriation, the Wisdom of God. Those chapters in turn presuppose and extend the discussion in *ScG* I, chs. 44–88, about the essential divine operations of understanding and willing; those chapters from bk. I, too, undergird the presentation of creation in *ScG* II.

31. I have discussed *ST* III.3.8 at length in "Wisdom in the Christology of Thomas Aquinas," in *Christ among the Medieval Dominicans*, ed. Kent Emery Jr. and Joseph Wawrykow (Notre Dame, IN: University of Notre Dame Press, 1998), 175–96.

CHAPTER 9

Creator, Text, and Law
Torah as Independent Power in Rabbinic Judaism

Tzvi Novick

The doctrine of *creatio ex nihilo* can involve (at least) two distinct theological claims. The first claim concerns divine omnipotence and directs itself against a cosmology in which God fashions the world out of preexistent matter. *Creatio ex nihilo* in the first sense insists that there is nothing coeval with or, still less, prior to God, such that it might in one way or another limit his power, or such that its inherent imperfections might mar the quality of the final product. Rather, everything is posterior and therefore subordinate to God, and the world, as it is, is precisely how God wished it to be. The second claim centers on divine providence and emerges in opposition to an Aristotelian perspective in which the world is eternal and God plays no direct role in creating or guiding the world. The doctrine of *creatio ex nihilo* in the second sense asserts in contrast that God willed the world into existence and, as a corollary, remains engaged with it.

It is only in the medieval period, and especially in the figure of Maimonides, that *creatio ex nihilo* in the second sense becomes a matter of debate in rabbinic Judaism and the notion of an unchangeable God who cannot be implicated in any *novum* gains a hearing.[1] In the classical period, denial of *creatio ex nihilo* in the second sense is beyond the pale.[2] A passage from the foundational legal code of rabbinic literature, the Mishnah, refuses a portion in the world-to-come to a person who denies providence (the "Epicurean").[3] A law that appears to exclude from the legal category of Israel a Jew who desecrates the Sabbath in public may rest on the assumption that such a course of action amounts to denying God's role as creator.[4] We will see below, however, that genuine engagement with the theological issue underlying *creatio ex nihilo* in the second sense—namely, the extent to which God plays a direct, providential role in the world—does occur in the classical period itself in connection with elements of creation discourse.

The situation with respect to *creatio ex nihilo* in the first sense is somewhat more complicated. Only one rabbinic text explicitly and emphatically rejects the notion of creation out of matter. It occurs in Genesis Rabbah, a Palestinian amoraic commentary on the book of Genesis. A "philosopher," evidently not Jewish, contends before Rabban Gamaliel that the Jews' God, while a "great artist," enjoyed the benefit of "good dyes" that "assisted" him. Rabban Gamaliel refutes this view by identifying verses in which these "dyes"—the formlessness and the void, the darkness and the water, the wind and the deep—are objects of verbs of creation.[5]

But in a nearby passage in the same work, another rabbi appears to countenance *creatio ex hylis* (creation out of uncreated matter), albeit with trepidation.

> R. Huna in the name of Bar Kappara decoded [or opened; *patah*]: "Let lying lips be stilled [that speak haughtily against the righteous with pride and contempt]" [Ps. 31:19 NJPS, slightly modified]. Let them be crushed, let them be rendered mute, let them be silenced.[6] . . . "That speak haughtily [*'ataq*] against the righteous." Against the righteous one, the eternal, [they speak] things that he removed [*he'etiq*] from his creatures.[7] "With pride." So as to become prideful and say: I am expounding the work of creation. "And contempt." He contemns my honor. For R. Yose b. R. Hanina said: Anyone who seeks honor through the shame of his friend has no portion in the world to come. How much more so concerning the

honor of the Holiness, blessed be He. And what is written after it? "What [*mah*] abundant good have you stored for those who fear you!" [Ps. 31:20 NJPS, modified]. Said Rav: Let him have nothing from that [*mah*] abundant good. In the ordinary course of things, a king of flesh and blood builds a palace in a place of gutters and garbage and refuse. One who comes and says: This palace is built in a place of gutters and garbage and refuse, does he not impugn? Likewise, one who comes and says: This world was created from the midst of formlessness and void and darkness, does he not impugn? Said R. Huna in the name of Bar Kappara: Were the thing not written, it would be impossible to say it: "God created the heavens and the earth" [Gen. 1:1] from what? From "and the earth was [formless and void, and darkness etc.]" [Gen. 1:2].[8]

In lieu of a thorough unpacking of this complex passage, which contains multiple parts and coordinates multiple voices, let me make two observations.[9] First, while the position that Bar Kappara, at the end of the passage, feels compelled to find in Genesis 1:1–2 is likely *creatio ex hylis*, it is not impossible that he in fact construes the matter out of which God formed the world as itself a work of God. In the context of the passage as a whole, the most immediate problem with the formlessness, the darkness, and the void is not that they are coeval with God but that they are ugly, unsightly. If the distinction between the ugliness of primordial matter and the independence of primordial matter from God is tenable and significant, then the fact that the passage is on its face concerned with primordial matter's ugliness rather than its independence should be given due weight.

Second, the passage offers some insight into one reason that we find so little discussion in rabbinic literature of the question of *creatio ex nihilo*, whether for or against. While R. Yose b. R. Hanina's comment and the material that follows it imply that the problem with inquiring into the "work of creation" lies in the fact that it will expose something shameful, the beginning of the passage in itself suggests instead that such inquiry is bad per se, because it represents a manifestation of pride. Reticence about the "work of creation" has deep, prerabbinic roots, and indeed played a role in defining emergent rabbinic Judaism against the apocalyptic circles from which it distanced itself.[10]

Despite this tradition of reticence, rabbinic texts sometimes speak of creation and primordial things, not in philosophical but in mythic terms. Indeed, there is a pronounced preference in rabbinic discourse for myth over philosophy, and it is probably this preference, more than any specific reservation about the "work of creation," that is most responsible for the paucity of texts that directly confront the question of creation out of nothing versus creation out of matter.[11] Jon Levenson has observed about the Hebrew Bible that while Genesis 1 erases the mythic forces of chaos—but not, as Bar Kappara observes, the primordial matter, no doubt because the author of Genesis 1, like most rabbis, saw no challenge to God in it—these mythic forces not only survive but positively thrive elsewhere in the Hebrew Bible, especially in laments. God *once* defeated the forces of chaos, but now they hold sway again, in the form of Israel's enemies, while God appears to sleep.[12] The same holds true to perhaps an even greater extent in rabbinic literature, where the Leviathan and the sea become real personalities, and God dwells with Israel in its exile, his hands tied.[13]

In this paper I explore the ramifications and resonances of a mythic motif that rabbinic and pararabbinic texts draw out of biblical sources and that bears on *creatio ex nihilo* in both senses. In a number of passages we are told that the world was created by or (more often) by means of the Torah, a position that we may call *creatio ex Torah*. The following passage occurs near the very beginning of Genesis Rabbah.

> "[And I was with him] *'amon*" [Prov. 8:30]. A craftsman [*'uman*]. The Torah says: I was the implement of workmanship [*'umanut*] of the Holiness, blessed be He. In the ordinary course of things, when a king of flesh and blood builds a palace, he doesn't build it on his own counsel but on the counsel of a craftsman, and the craftsman doesn't build it on his own counsel, but has parchments and tablets to know how to make the rooms and the entrances. So the Holiness, blessed be He, would look into the Torah and create the world. And the Torah says, "In/with the beginning [*reshit*] God created" [Gen. 1:1], and "beginning" is nothing other than the Torah, as it says: "The Lord created me [as] the beginning [*reshit*] of his way" [Prov. 8:22].[14]

The passage begins by citing from the monologue spoken by Wisdom, personified as a woman, in Proverbs 8. In this monologue, Wisdom declares that God created her at the beginning, when nothing else yet existed. In the biblical text, Wisdom claims no role in the subsequent creation of the world. It is God who acts, and she is with him, according to Proverbs 8:30, *'amon*, perhaps "faithfully," serving as a source of "delight" for him, but nothing more. The rabbinic reader, however, interprets *'amon* in relation to the word *'uman*, "craftsman." Wisdom, which the passage identifies with the Torah, thus becomes the blueprint or model after which God the craftsman patterns the world.[15]

A similar view is attested in tannaitic literature. R. Akiva is said to have proclaimed: "How beloved are Israel, that they were given the implement with which the world was created."[16] The following passage draws out a practical implication of this characterization of the Torah.

> R. Eleazar b. R. Sadoq says: Do things for the sake of their [intended] action; speak about them [i.e., words of Torah] for their own sake. He would say: If Belshazar, because he used the Temple implements—though they were only profane implements—found his life uprooted from this world and from the next world, one who uses the implement with which the world was created, how much more will he find his life uprooted from this world and from the next world.[17]

R. Eleazar b. R. Sadoq reasons that if the Torah is God's implement for creating the world, then a mortal may not use the Torah as an implement, that is, for ulterior purposes. To do so would be to trespass, and thus to meet the same fate as Belshazar, who, according to Daniel 5, ate and drank from implements from the temple, implicitly figured here (as often elsewhere) as a microcosm. One may therefore only study the Torah for its own sake.[18]

While the above passages single out the Torah for a special role in the creation of the world, others identify the Torah of Proverbs 8—the prooftext for *creatio ex Torah* in the Genesis Rabbah passage—as one of a number of things that arose before the world.[19] But even in this context, the Torah has pride of place, as in the following passage, the most conceptually sophisticated discussion of this topic.

Six things preceded the creation of the world, some of which were actually created, and some of which arose in [God's] thought to be created. The Torah and the throne of glory were created: the Torah, as it is written, "The Lord created me [as] the beginning" [Prov. 8:22]; the throne of glory, as it is written, "your throne was prepared from then" [Ps. 93:2]. The patriarchs arose in thought. . . . Israel arose in thought. . . . The temple arose in thought. . . . The name of the Messiah arose in thought. . . . R. Ahavah b. R. Ze'ira says: Also repentance . . .[20]

In the continuation of the passage, R. Abba b. Kahana argues that of the two items actually created before the world, the Torah was first. Yehoshua Granat suggests that the very distinction between real precreation and theoretical precreation may have been introduced in order to set up the favorable comparison of the Torah to the throne of glory, so as to express the superiority of the sage, the student of Torah, over the mystic, who contemplates God's throne.[21]

Having reviewed some of the key texts and contexts in which the motif of *creatio ex Torah* arises, we may now consider more closely the nature of the primordial Torah. As a successor to personified Wisdom of Proverbs 8, the Torah is a person, but as the Torah, it is also a text. The Torah qua text is, in turn, both an object and a set of propositions. The parable in the Genesis Rabbah passage, which speaks of parchment and tablets, highlights the Torah text as written artifact.[22] Working from the same wordplay as in the latter passage (*'amon*/*'uman*), a later midrash attends instead to the content of the Torah text.

And she was a craftsman for all of the work of creation, as it is said, "[And I was with him] *'amon*" [Prov. 8:30]. Do not read *'amon* but rather *'uman* [a craftsman]. Through it he stretched the heavens and founded the earth, as it is said, "As surely as I have established my covenant with day and night—the laws [*huqot*] of heaven and earth" [Jer. 33:25 NJPS]; and through it he sealed the ocean, that it not go out and flood the world, as it is said, "Will you not fear me, says the Lord? [Will you not tremble before me, who placed the sand as a boundary for the sea, an eternal border (*hoq*) that it not pass over? And they stormed but were not able, and its waters roared, but did not pass over!]" [Jer. 5:22]. And through it he suppressed the deep, that it not flood the world, as it is said, "when he inscribed [*be-huqo*] a horizon upon the face of the deep" [Prov. 8:27]. And through it he created the sun and the moon, as it is said, "Thus says the Lord, who furnishes the sun to illuminate the day, [the laws (*huqot*) of the moon and the stars to illuminate the day]" [Jer. 31:34]. Thus you learn that the earth was founded on nothing other than the Torah.[23]

The passage mingles different visions of creation, from the crafty to the violent. What unifies it is the root חק״ק, which can indicate a boundary or a law, and occurs in all of the prooftexts. For the exegete, this root signals the role of the Torah, the book of laws.

A parallel to the last text occurs in a *piyyut* (liturgical poem) composed by the seventh-century liturgical poet Eleazar be-rabbi Qillir for the festival of *Shavuot* (Pentecost), which in rabbinic Judaism celebrates the giving of the Torah at Sinai. The first half of the piyyut is an extended monologue by the Torah that is built upon but greatly expands Wisdom's words in Proverbs 8.

> "When the springs of the deep grew strong" [Prov. 8:28]
> My springs were stronger than the springs of the deep.
> When the water grew strong my waters grew stronger than the
>   waters of the deep.
> When the strong things grew strong I was strong upon all the deep.
> "In placing upon the sea his limit [*huqo*]" [Prov. 8:29a] / there
>   was my placing on them my limit [*huqi*].
> "And the waters will not transgress his command [lit. mouth]"
>   [Prov. 8:29b], / likewise they will not transgress my command [lit. mouth],
> And the world was completed by the word of my mouth / for I
>   was in his mouth.[24]

As Granat notes, the last line combines the motif of the primordial Torah with the tradition of the creative Logos, the divine word through which (as in Gen. 1) the world comes into being.[25] But even as Qillir subordinates the Torah to God by placing the Torah in God's mouth, he separates the Torah from God by boldly using the verses that describe God's creative acts (e.g., "In placing upon the sea his limit" [Prov. 8:29a]) to generate equivalent acts by the Torah ("there was my placing on them my limit").

In Qillir's piyyut, the Torah is not (or not only) a text, but a person, with a speaking role. The Torah as a personality—and a rather more distinctive one than Wisdom in Proverbs 8—emerges more strikingly still in the second half of the piyyut, which is composed of a dialogue between the Torah and God in which God attempts to find a spouse for the Torah, who thus takes on the role of God's daughter. God puts forward various suitors—Adam, Abraham, Isaac, Jacob—whom the Torah rejects because of their sins. Finally, at Sinai, she is introduced to Moses, whom she accepts.

> And the Torah said: "This is Moses who was called humble
>   [Num. 12:3] from of old.[26]
> 'And the Lord spoke with Moses' is recorded in me from of old.
> He will possess me as an eternal inheritance,
> And he will take me as an eternal gift,
> And everyone in the world / will believe in me forever."[27]

This speech brings the piyyut to an end in a manner that recollects its beginning, through its references to creation ("of old"). The universalism of the last line, with its reference to "everyone in the world," is at first glance surprising, but it is conditioned by the same envelope structure. If the first part of the piyyut has the Torah create the world, then the second part cannot leave the world behind. The Torah finds a match in Moses, but the marriage finds its ultimate end in the world as a whole.[28]

The question of immediate relevance posed by the motif of the primordial, personified Torah text is this: Does the Torah become a rival to God? Does it become a rival god? If Rabban Gamaliel will not allow uncreated elements to assist God in creating the world, will he tolerate such a role for the Torah? Need a monotheist worry that God must use the Torah to suppress the deep, or is it enough to note that the Torah is God's creature? The same question could be asked of Wisdom herself in Proverbs 8, but it becomes more pressing in relation to the Torah because of two aspects of the conception of Torah in rabbinic Judaism, both of which have arisen in the passages analyzed above: first, the Torah is a text, and second, the Torah is law. I turn now to explore the ramifications of both of these features, the first briefly and the second at greater length.

It is of the nature of a text to detach itself from its author. The independence of the Torah qua text from God becomes manifest most clearly in the classical rabbinic corpus in the exegetical school associated with R. Ishmael. This school interprets the Torah as a literary work, like the epics of Homer.[29] The maxim famously propounded by the school of R. Ishmael, that "the Torah speaks in the language of people," may be taken as a figure for the way in which the Torah, conceived of as a text, achieves a certain distance from its divine author. This maxim anchors the position that an interpreter cannot treat the Torah text as maximally meaningful to the point that he ignores the text's stylistic conventions. If biblical Hebrew expresses the imperative by combining the imperative form with the infinitive absolute form, then the interpreter should treat the two forms as a unit, and not attempt to derive separate meaning from each.[30] More generally, the Torah, for the school of R. Ishmael, is conceived of as closing in upon itself, insofar as it serves as the guide to its own interpretation.[31] The Torah comes from God, but, as a text, it has its own integrity. Thus the textual character of the Torah underwrites an independence from God of a sort unavailable to Wisdom of Proverbs 8.[32]

As law, too, the Torah achieves a distinctive measure of independence from God. The status of the Torah as law raises a question that is structurally parallel to the one surrounding *creatio ex nihilo* in the second sense. In her recent book, Christine Hayes sets in contrast two different conceptions of divine law in late antiquity. On one conception, law is divine insofar as it is perfect: perfectly rational, perfectly wise, perfectly true, perfectly in accord with nature. There is, on this conception, an inevitable gap between the divine law, which is unwritten, and the written laws of any human society, which are imperfect. On the other conception, a set of laws is divine insofar as it issues from God, that is, is an expression of God's will. It is the rabbis' innovation, according to Hayes, to identify the Torah as divine law according to the second conception to the exclusion of the first conception. The Torah is not natural law, nor is it perfectly true or rational, but it is divine all the same, because it is legislated by God.[33] Put differently, the Torah is law in the ordinary, human sense of the word "law," even though it is divine.[34]

Hayes marshals an enormous array of sources in support of her claim, but here one must suffice. The following passage, from the Tosefta, a tannaitic compilation that mirrors the Mishnah, concerns the law (Deut. 23:19) that an animal given as payment to a prostitute may not be offered as a sacrifice in fulfillment of a vow.

> If he gave her consecrated animals, these are permissible [for the altar]. Now it stands to reason that they should be prohibited. For if a bird, which is not rendered invalid on account of a blemish, is subject to [the invalidation of] the [prostitute's] hire . . . , then [in the case of] consecrated animals, which are rendered invalid on account of a blemish, does it not stand to reason that they should be subject to [the invalidation of] the [prostitute's] hire . . . ? Hence it says [Deut. 23:19]: "for any vow," to exclude something already vowed.[35]

If the client gives the prostitute an already consecrated animal, the animal does not become invalid for the altar as a prostitute's hire. The Tosefta compares this rule to that governing an ordinary, profane bird. If the client pays the prostitute with such a bird, the bird acquires the status of a prostitute's hire and may not be offered as a sacrifice. The Tosefta ventures that the two rules do not cohere. For birds, unlike consecrated animals, are valid for the altar even if blemished. They are therefore less susceptible to invalidation. And yet it is precisely the bird, and not the consecrated animal, that is rendered invalid as a prostitute's hire.[36]

The reason that the Tosefta argues that a consecrated animal ought logically to be rendered invalid for the altar as a prostitute's hire is, in immediate terms, that it wishes to give meaning to a biblical text ("for any vow"). If the validity of a consecrated animal offered as a prostitute's hire could be deduced from logic alone, the biblical text would be superfluous, and run afoul of the assumption that the Torah does not waste words. It is also true that the notion that the validity of the consecrated animal rendered to a prostitute runs counter to reason does not preclude the possibility it makes sense according to a "higher reason," in the mind of God. But the crucial point is that the Tosefta—which in this respect is entirely typical of rabbinic literature in general—makes no reference to such a higher reason, and is content to let the Torah stand in opposition to reason.

It is trivially true that by making divine law a matter of God's will rather than of truth or wisdom, rabbinic Judaism binds the Torah closer to God, or, from a different perspective, binds God closer to the Torah. The Torah is a sign of God's direct intervention in the world, or in Qillir's mythological terms, the Torah is something like God's daughter. But there is a dialectic at work here. Because the Torah, on this approach, is divine specifically in virtue of its genesis, and not in virtue of its substance, its connection to God *after* the moment of its genesis becomes severely attenuated. In this regard, the characterization of the Torah as God's daughter is misleading, for while a daughter carries within her the traces of her father, the Torah is *not* inherently divine—not perfectly wise, or perfectly rational, or the like—but only genealogically divine. The dialectic by which the Torah, having been authored by God, loses its connection with God is canonized in that most famous of rabbinic stories, the story of the oven of Aknai in the Babylonian Talmud.[37] This story asserts the authority of the rabbis to interpret the Torah even if God interprets it to the contrary, on the ground that "it is not in heaven" (Deut. 30:12). Were the Torah to be divine in virtue of its content, it would remain in heaven, as it were, even after it was given. Ironically, it is the fact that the Torah's authority lies exclusively in God's will that separates it from God.

There is, to my knowledge, no direct interaction between the motif of *creatio ex Torah*, on the one hand, and, on the other, the exegetical and legal texts alluded to above that assume and thematize the Torah's status as a text (as in the maxim, "The Torah speaks in the language of people") and the Torah's dialectical relationship with God as law (as in the Aknai story). While I have drawn mainly from Genesis Rabbah and piyyut for the motif of *creatio ex Torah*, I have introduced texts from other parts of the rabbinic corpus to illustrate the ramifications of the textual and legal character of Torah. Indeed, the Babylonian Talmud, wherein the Aknai story occurs, appears to have almost no interest in the primordial Torah and says next to nothing about Wisdom's monologue in Proverbs 8.

I venture, nevertheless, that the different valorizations of the Torah described above mutually reinforce, to yield a Torah that is in important ways a serious rival to God, not, of course, as an enemy, like the primordial chaos, but as a distinct locus of authority, an entity that underwrites creation and stands, in important ways, apart from God. The synthesis of these treatments of the Torah occurs not in a single passage, nor even in a single work, but holistically, in the rabbinic ethos that emerged from late antiquity and helped shape subsequent Jewish thought.

What function does the Torah's role in creation have in this synthesis? In Proverbs 8, the fact that Wisdom plays alongside God when he creates the world is a way of giving voice to the belief that the world operates on the principles of wisdom, which is the same as righteousness, so that, should we notice a wicked (= foolish) man prospering, or a righteous (= wise) man suffering, we may be confident that their circumstances will change, that the wicked man (or his progeny) will meet his comeuppance, and the righteous man (or his progeny), his reward. This entire framework depends on the absence of a ramified and complex afterlife in which a final accounting of reward and punishment is made. For the rabbis, who have just such an afterlife, and for whom the Torah is, as Hayes argues, something quite different from wisdom as Proverbs understands it, *creatio ex Torah* has, I believe, a different and more expressive function, namely, to convey the Torah's unparalleled, cosmic importance. God may be greater than the cosmos, but the Torah is almost as great, and it is, in a fundamental way, other from God.

We may reframe this conclusion in terms of the two senses of *creatio ex nihilo* that I put forward at the beginning of this paper. The role of Wisdom in Proverbs 8 speaks most directly to the question underlying *creatio ex nihilo* in the second sense; that is, did God will the world into existence, and does he actively govern it? While Proverbs 8 explicitly identifies God as creator of the world, its conception of a world in which reward for the wise and punishment for the foolish occur almost automatically, almost like operating principles, works to distance God from the world. There is love in Proverbs, but chiefly the love of the wise for wisdom, and Wisdom's love of the wise.[38] God does not figure importantly in the book of Proverbs in a relationship of love. The common mischaracterization of the book Proverbs as "secular" arises from the correct intuition of this absence.[39]

When rabbinic Judaism substitutes the Torah for Wisdom, it does not mean to take a position on this dynamic. The rabbis do not envision God standing aloof from the world as a whole, and still less from his people, Israel. On the contrary, as noted in passing above, the rabbinic God binds himself to Israel in the most concrete and intimate ways. The Torah's role in creation figures rather in the framework addressed by *creatio ex nihilo* in the first sense: Is there a power that can rival God? To say that the world emerged from the Torah is to place the Torah alongside God as a cosmic figure. To insist at the same time on the textuality of the Torah, and to insist at the same time that it represents divine law in origin but not intrinsically, is to give the Torah real independence from God.

NOTES

1. For Maimonides' views on this topic see Moshe Halbertal, *Maimonides: Life and Thought*, trans. Joel Linsider (Princeton: Princeton University Press, 2013), 202–8.

2. On creation and providence in rabbinic thought see Ephraim E. Urbach, *The Sages: Their Concepts and Beliefs*, trans. Israel Abrahams (Cambridge, MA: Harvard University Press, 1979), 184–213, 255–85.

3. M. Sanh. 10:1. On the figure of the Epicurean in rabbinic literature see Jenny R. Labendz, "'Know What to Answer the Epicurean': A Diachronic Study of the 'Apiqoros' in Rabbinic Literature," *Hebrew Union College Annual* 74 (2003): 175–214.

4. The law appears in t. 'Erub. 5:18. In H. S. Horovitz and I. A. Rabin, *Mechilta D'Rabbi Ismael*, 2nd ed. (Jerusalem: Shalem Books, 1997), 234 (*ba-Hodesh* 8), one who desecrates the Sabbath denies that God rested on the seventh day, but on every witness except the *editio princeps*, he does not deny that God created the world in six days. All translations of texts other than the Bible are my own.

5. J. Theodor and Ch. Albeck, *Midrash Bereshit Rabba: Critical Edition with Notes and Commentary* (Jerusalem: Shalem Books, 1996), 8 (Gen. Rab. 1:9). On this passage see Menahem Kister, "*Tohu wa-Bohu*, Primordial Elements, and *Creatio ex Nihilo*," *Jewish Studies Quarterly* 14 (2007): 247–53.

6. Bar Kappara renders the verb תאלמנה ("let [them] be stilled") in three ways. I have elided the prooftexts that he supplies for each rendering.

7. Perhaps the exegesis is inspired by the two subsequent verses, Ps. 31:20–21 (partially quoted in the continuation of the passage), which use four words whose root meaning involves concealment. Admittedly, the reference, in context, is to the reward and the sheltering of the righteous.

8. Gen. Rab. 1:5 (Theodor-Albeck ed., 2–3).

9. For fuller discussions see Maren Niehoff, "*Creatio ex Nihilo* Theology in *Genesis Rabbah* in Light of Christian Exegesis," *Harvard Theological Review* 99 (2005): 55–60; Peter Schäfer, "Bereshit Bara Elohim: Bereshit Rabba, Parashah 1, Reconsidered," in Empsychoi Logoi: *Religious Innovations in Late Antiquity*, ed. Alberdina Houtman et al. (Leiden: Brill, 2008), 269–75 (and esp. 271n17).

10. See Yair Furstenberg, "The Rabbinic Ban on *Ma'aseh Bereshit*: Sources, Contexts, and Concerns," in *Jewish and Christian Cosmogony in Late Antiquity*, ed. Lance Jenott and Sarit Kattan Gribetz (Tübingen: Mohr Siebeck, 2013), 39–63.

11. Note in this connection that Rabban Gamaliel's interlocutor in the Genesis Rabbah passage summarized above is a philosopher.

12. See Jon D. Levenson, *Creation and the Persistence of Evil: The Jewish Drama of Divine Omnipotence* (New York: HarperCollins, 1988), 3–50.

13. See Michael Fishbane, *Biblical Myth and Rabbinic Mythmaking* (Oxford: Oxford University Press, 2003), 112–249.

14. Gen. Rab. 1:4 (Theodor-Albeck ed., 2).

15. On the resonances in this passage with Origen's remarks on the creation of the world see Niehoff, "*Creatio*," 60–64. By populating the parable with both a king and a craftsman, the passage appears to imply that God the creator works at the behest of another being, as in Platonic distinction between the inferior demiurge and the superior God. According to Michael Fox (*Proverbs 10–31: A New Translation with Introduction and Commentary* [New Haven: Yale University Press, 2009], 961–92), the parable was in fact originally formulated with this view in mind. I think it more likely that the parable's implied distinction between an inferior creator and a superior divinity is in fact unintended, and represents an incidental result of the rabbis' use of the king as a stock character in parables. Cf. the parable that R. Ammi offers (Gen. Rab. 8:3 [Theodor-Albeck ed., 59]) to explain whom God consulted with in Gen. 1:26 ("Let us make a person"): "He consulted with himself. It is comparable to a king who built a palace by the agency of an architect. He saw it and it did not appeal to him. Against whom is the complaint to be lodged? Is it not against the architect? Thus, 'And he was grieved at his heart' (Gen 4:6)." The formal distinction between God and his heart allows R. Ammi to make God both king and architect. Note should also be taken of a possible disjunct between

the initial comment in Gen. Rab. 1:4, which appears to identify the Torah as the craftsman, and the continuation of the passage, which instead makes the Torah the craftsman's plans.

16. M. Avot 3:19. For the text see Shimon Sharvit, *Tractate Avoth through the Ages: A Critical Edition, Prolegomena and Appendices* (Jerusalem: Bialik Institute, 2004), 137, and for a discussion of the complex textual history of this passage see Sharvit, *Language and Style of Tractate Avoth through the Ages* (Beer-Sheva: Ben-Gurion University of the Negev Press, 2006), 90–93. Although R. Akiva does not cite Prov. 8, his dependence on it is supported (albeit weakly) by the fact that in the continuation of his statement he cites a verse from Prov. 4.

17. Louis Finkelstein, *Siphre ad Deuteronomium* (New York: Jewish Theological Seminary of America, 2001), 114 (Sifre Deut. 48).

18. The fit between the two parts of R. Eleazar b. R. Sadoq's statement is somewhat imperfect, for on the basis of the second, one might conclude that one should not study Torah for its own sake, but rather not study it at all. The passage in Sifre Deut. 48 is clearly related to m. Avot 4:5: "R. Sadoq would say: Don't make them a crown, so as to become great through them, nor a spade, so as to eat from them. And so would Hillel say: One who makes use of the crown passes on." For the text see Sharvit, *Tractate Avoth*, 152–53. The curious absence of an antecedent for the pronoun "them" in the beginning of R. Eleazar b. R. Sadoq's statement in Sifre Deut. 48 ("Speak about them for their own sake") probably has something to do with its genetic link to the statement attributed to his father in m. Avot 4:5, which likewise involves the same underdetermined pronoun ("Don't make them . . ."). Note, too, that the end of the paragraph that precedes R. Eleazar b. R. Sadoq's statement in Sifre Deut. 48 (Finkelstein ed., 113–14) speaks of the glory that accrues to the student of Torah, and also refers to the Torah as a crown. The beginning of the same paragraph speaks of the importance of "doing" Torah after learning it, and so echoes the statement attributed to R. Ishmael the son of R. Yose that precedes R. Sadoq's statement in m. Avot 4:5. While R. Eleazar b. R. Sadoq's selection of Belshazar, hardly a popular exemplar in tannaitic literature, was probably motivated, first and foremost, by the prevalent association of the temple with the world, perhaps it also reflects the fact that R. Sadoq relies on Hillel's statement, which occurs, like the Belshazar story, in Aramaic. On Hillel's statement— whose more original context is m. Avot 1:13; and it is by no means clear that R. Sadoq interprets it according to its original sense—see Aaron Koller, "Learning from the *Tāg*: On a Persian Word for 'Crown' in Jewish Aramaic," in *Shoshannat Yaakov: Jewish and Iranian Studies in Honor of Yaakov Elman*, ed. Shai Secunda and Steven Fine (Leiden: Brill, 2012), 237–45.

19. The lists of such items, their prehistory in Second Temple literature, and their reception in piyyut are the subject of a penetrating dissertation by Yehoshua Granat, "Preexistence in Early Piyyut against the Background of Its Sources" (PhD diss., Hebrew University, 2009).

20. Gen. Rab. 1:4 (Theodor-Albeck ed., 6).

21. Granat, "Preexistence," 60. On the precreated throne in a mystical context see *2 Enoch* 25, and on the latter passage see Andrei A. Orlov, "Adoil outside the Cosmos: God before and after Creation in the Enochic Traditions," in *Histories of the Hidden God: Concealment and Revelation in Western Gnostic, Esoteric, and Mystical Traditions*, ed. April D. DeConick and Grant Adamson (Durham, England: Acumen Publishing, 2013), 32 and 48n7. For a distinctive view about precreated things that is at best only partially determined by exegetical considerations and evidently draws upon outside sources—perhaps, to judge from the references to birthing and to wisdom, gnostic sources—see Exod. Rab. 15:22. On rabbinic borrowings from such sources, but without reference to this passage, see Alexander Altmann, "Gnostic Themes in Rabbinic Cosmology," in *Essays in Honour of the Very Rev. Dr. J.H. Hertz*, ed. J. Epstein et al. (London: E. Goldston, 1942), 19–32.

22. For other examples see Granat, "Preexistence," 181.

23. *Tanhuma* (Warsaw) Gen. 1. The text is from Cambridge, University Library, Add. 212, as transcribed in the online *Historical Dictionary of the Hebrew Language*, published by Maagarim, http://maagarim.hebrew-academy .org.il). On the passage see Fishbane, *Biblical Myth*, 129.

24. Shulamit Elizur, ed., *Rabbi El'azar Birabbi Kiliri: Hymni Pentecostales* (Jerusalem: Mekize Nirdamim, 2000), 106, lines 210–16. See also Joseph Yahalom, "Shiur Qomah in a Misidentified Qalirian Poem for Pentecost," *Kabbalah: Journal for the Study of Jewish Mystical Texts* 32 (2013): 130.

25. Granat, "Preexistence," 183–85. The allusions to the same motif in Elizur, *Hymni*, 98, line 86; 215, line 106 may indeed depend, as Elizur suggests, on Song 5:16, but it is also possible that they depend on Prov. 24:13–14. See Joseph Yahalom, *Priestly Palestinian Poetry: A Narrative Liturgy for the Day of Atonement* (Jerusalem: Magnes, 1996), 70, line 59, and the note thereto.

26. The Torah alludes to Num. 12:3. Perhaps Qillir introduces this verse because, with its reference to all of humanity and the entire earth ("And the man Moses was very humble, more than any person on the face of the earth"), it has something like a cosmic purview.

27. Elizur, *Hymni*, 114, lines 339–42. Some manuscripts (ibid., 288) have "in him" in the last line, per Exod. 14:31; 19:9, which speak of the people believing in Moses.

28. It is not impossible that in opening up the Torah to "everyone in the world," Qillir loses control of the poem, i.e., that Qillir's authorial intent is de-

feated by the poem's structure. I raise this possibility because in the immediate continuation (ibid., 115, line 351) Qillir distinguishes sharply between the nations (who hear "an angry voice") and Israel ("a pleasant voice").

29. On the relationship between tannaitic midrash and the interpretation of Homer in late antiquity see the groundbreaking dissertation of Yakir Paz, "From Scribes to Scholars: Rabbinic Biblical Exegesis in Light of the Homeric Commentaries" (PhD diss., Hebrew University, 2014).

30. See ibid., 96–115.

31. See ibid., 37–47. On this point see also, especially, Azzan Yadin, *Scripture as Logos: Rabbi Ishmael and the Origins of Midrash* (Philadelphia: University of Pennsylvania Press, 2004).

32. From a broader perspective the matter becomes more complicated, as it is the character of the Torah as (written) text rather than (oral) performance that gives rise to the biblical narrator, who in his omniscience is a figure for God. See Robert S. Kawashima, *Biblical Narrative and the Death of the Rhapsode* (Bloomington: Indiana University Press, 2004).

33. Christine Hayes, *What's Divine about Divine Law? Ancient Perspectives* (Princeton: Princeton University Press, 2015).

34. Cf. Ron Naiweld, "The Discursive Machine of Tannaitic Literature: The Rabbinic Resurrection of the Logos," in *Les judaïsmes dans tous leurs états aux Ier-IIIe siècles: Les Judéens des synagogues, les chrétiens et les rabbins*, ed. C. Clivez et al. (Turnout: Brepols, 2015), 405–34, esp. 413 ("For the rabbis, the organizing principle that predated the world was the very text of the Torah, and not an immaterial and invisible divine Word represented by [scil. *merely* represented by (TN)] the Holy Scripture").

35. T. Tem. 4:19 (MS Vienna).

36. Hayes discusses this case in the fifth chapter of her book. Cf. m. Ter. 6:4.

37. B. Bava Mesi'a 59b. No self-respecting scholar of rabbinics can cite this shopworn story without apology. Mine is simply that I have not seen it invoked in connection with the doctrine of *creatio ex Torah*.

38. See Michael V. Fox, *Proverbs 1–9: A New Translation with Introduction and Commentary* (New Haven: Yale University Press, 2000), 294–95.

39. On the (partial) mischaracterization of the book of Proverbs as secular see Fox, *Proverbs 10–31*, 946–50.

CHAPTER 10

Reason, Will, and Purpose

*What's at Stake for Maimonides and His Followers
in the Doctrine of Creation?*

DANIEL DAVIES

Maimonides states that the doctrine of creation is a central foundation
of the Mosaic law. In the *Guide of the Perplexed*, he emphasizes its importance in a variety of contexts and states that "everything is bound
up with this problem" (2:25, 330).[1] Furthermore, he dedicates a major
part of the work to establishing that creation is possible. His stated aim
is to show that those who deny creation cannot demonstrate with certainty that their position is true. However, if creation *ex nihilo* is a doctrine teaching that the whole of creation depends on God, who is the
only uncaused, necessary being, which alone is entirely simple, Maimonides' discussion of creation has no bearing on the issue. He agrees
that God is the only necessary being, and that all things depend on God
for their existence, and he also argues that this is accepted both by those
who accept creation and those who deny it. Instead, Maimonides' discussion centers on the disagreement over whether the world is created
de novo. The doctrine is important, he argues, because the alternatives

have implications for what can be said of divine volition. Those who deny creation, in Maimonides' terms, deny that God creates through an act of will, and therefore understand God's activity to be the result of natural necessity. This chapter will briefly explain Maimonides' reasoning when he defends creation, arguing that it is bound up with his comments about God's knowledge. But his discussion leaves open a number of questions. I will therefore proceed to address some interpretative difficulties that were raised in the wake of Maimonides' work and continue to be discussed today. Many argue that there are two separate and irreconcilable theological strands in the *Guide*. One emphasizes the role of God's will in creation and is aimed at the general masses, while the other argues that God creates through wisdom and is aimed only at the elite. I will explain a view advanced by Isaac Abravanel, which attempts to reconcile the two strands by considering what Maimonides means by saying that God creates through will. Abravanel was not satisfied to assume that Maimonides' arguments could be incoherent. In order to square them, he needed to make distinctions that do not appear explicitly in Maimonides' text, and he argued that "will" can be used with different senses. Since he adheres to both claims that Maimonides makes, that God creates through will and through wisdom, his exposition should be considered a serious interpretation of Maimonides, as well as being important in its own right. Ultimately, Maimonides is concerned both to distinguish creation from any natural activity, preserving human ignorance of particular theological points, and also to preserve the integrity of scientific investigation.

REASON'S ROLE IN ARGUMENTS ABOUT CREATION

When Maimonides explicitly addresses the doctrine of creation, the issue in question is whether or not the world is everlasting. Was there an absolute beginning to time, in which case the world is created *ex nihilo* and *de novo*, or has there always been a world? His stated aim is to show that neither position can be posited with certainty: neither is demonstrable. Nevertheless, he prefers the view that the world is created *de novo* and says that this is the position of the Mosaic law. Those who argue that time is without beginning are known as "the philosophers," and they are Aristotle and his followers.[2] Maimonides divides the philosophers' arguments into two kinds. One is those that argue from the nature of the world, and another is those that argue from the nature of God. Maimonides tries to show that these arguments are not decisive.

So, for example, the philosophers claim that if the world began to exist, there must have been a potential for it to begin existing. But every potency must be brought into actuality by something that is already actual. Therefore there would have to be an action that brought about the move from potency to act, which move is the beginning. In that case, the beginning would be preceded by a prior act. That is absurd, so the world cannot have had a beginning.[3] In Maimonides' view, this and the other arguments based on the nature of the world fail because they use arguments that are true of things in our world and apply them to the generation of the world as a whole, and we have no evidence that they are also true of the world's origination. Maimonides' claim is that the philosophers make a category mistake when they apply the arguments in such a way.

The same is true of arguments that begin from God's nature. One example is as follows. If God were to begin acting at a certain time, there must be some cause that moved God to create. But since God is immutable, a creation cannot be initiated by any change in God. An alternative might be to say that there was an impediment prior to creation, preventing its occurrence, but this would also be impossible if creation is genuinely *ex nihilo*. If there was nothing, there could not be an impediment nor a way of removing one. In short, if God is eternal and immutable, the world cannot begin to exist after not having existed because there needs to be a cause that would bring about such a change. Here too, Maimonides says, there is an assumption that what is true of causes in the world is also true of creation.

Altogether, then, Maimonides' strategy is to oppose those who argue that it was everlasting. He says that the arguments themselves are not decisive because they are based on our experience of the world, but we have no experience of a creation *de novo*, so we cannot know that the arguments apply. But arguments for creation *de novo* fare no better. Maimonides states that creation cannot be demonstrated (2:17, 294). Later on in the *Guide*, he argues that human faculties are simply incapable of representing creation *de novo*, neither through the imagination nor through the intellect (3:15, 460). In that chapter, he distinguishes creation from any other type of coming to be and also from matters that can be shown to be impossible. For the former, there is always something that passes away, out of which the thing generated comes. In the case of creation *de novo*, that is denied. Nothing can be presupposed and there is no temporal priority to creation. Those who claim to be able to show that such a creation is possible are depicting it along the same lines as other kinds of coming to be. But since creation must be an entirely unique event, it cannot be so depicted. What they say is possible must therefore be something else entirely. Creation *de novo* is not something that can be imagined. One can imagine a butterfly emerging from a chrysalis, or a horse giving birth to a unicorn. It is possible to try to understand whether these are possible or not because the imagination can depict what is asserted to be possible or otherwise. But since no sort of image of creation absolutely *de novo* is possible, it cannot be asserted to be possible.

And the opposite position, that such a creation is not possible, also presents creation along the lines of created being. Specifically, adherents to this view say that creation out of nothing is impossible in the same way that a square with a diagonal equal to one of its sides is impossible. The philosophers argue that creation out of nothing is a logical impossibility. But in order to know that a combination of two things is impossible, like a square circle, one would have to know what both of those things are. There is no problem in saying that a square circle is logically impossible, and that God therefore cannot create one, because square and circle are incompatible. Asserting that an object is one involves denying that it is the other, because they are different sorts of the same category, shapes. The philosophers' error, Maimonides argues, is to say the same about creation *ex nihilo*. Such a creation cannot be logically impossible in the same way because absolute nonbeing is not in a category with anything and therefore cannot oppose existence in the same way that a square opposes a circle. We cannot know that a genuinely *ex nihilo* creation is like such an impossibility, because we have no conception of what *nihil* is. The only way we can think of such a creation is by comparing it to creation from relative nonbeing. That is, a thing that did not exist can come to exist, but only from a prior existing being, not from absolute nonbeing. The upshot is that creation *de novo* cannot be said to be either possible or impossible. There is simply no way to grasp or depict it.

THE MOSAIC LAW AND EVIDENCE FOR CREATION

All that Maimonides has argued so far is that whether or not the world is created *de novo* cannot be decided rationally. He has not yet explained why the Mosaic law is in favor of creation *de novo* and why it is important. He interprets the opening words of Genesis to be teaching causal rather than temporal priority (2:30, 348). Everything depends on God for its existence and only God depends on nothing else. This could be the sort of priority of the sun to its light, or the sort that the motion of a hand has to the motion of a ring it wears. The ring's motion is caused by that of the hand, while the reverse is not true, but the hand's motion does not precede the ring's in time. There is no disagreement between the philosophers and the law on the question of causal priority of God to the world, so the opening of Genesis is compatible with either view. At any rate, in common with the Islamic thinkers of the time, Maimonides states that the texts have both internal and external meanings. If the explicit meaning is obviously false, it must be a metaphor or an allegory. And he states that "the gates of figurative interpretation are not shut in our faces" (2:25, 327). That statement occurs in a chapter on creation, in which Maimonides explains that any demonstrably true scientific opinion must be accepted—one cannot choose to disbelieve something that one knows for certain is true—and the texts have to be interpreted in line with that view. On the other hand, if an opinion has not been demonstrated, there is no obligation to believe it and, therefore, no need to interpret the texts to be teaching that view. Since there is no conclusive argument about creation, what the inner meaning of the texts must be is uncertain.[4]

Instead, the view of the Mosaic law must be taken into account. Maimonides states that the consequence of asserting that the world is everlasting would be to undermine the law, with the result that miracles would be impossible. This is an odd claim for Maimonides to make since he usually seems concerned to interpret miracles metaphorically, in naturalistic terms.[5] And many, perhaps most, of his readers seem to have difficulty accepting that Maimonides cares so much about them. Maybe there is an assumption that belief in miracles accompanies an antiscientific or superstitious worldview. I suggest that it can involve a commitment to scientific inquiry, tempered by an acknowledgment that human understanding might not cover every single event. In order to explain why, it will be helpful to consider what Maimonides says about two related issues: the heavenly motions and God's knowledge. The first introduces the idea that God particularizes events, and the second extends particularity to all individuals.[6]

The motions taking place above the moon offer some evidence that tips the scales in favor of creation *de novo*, Maimonides argues, even if there is no decisive proof. He claims that "particularity" in the heavens indicates that they are created through will and choice. Briefly put, there are phenomena that we witness in the superlunar realm that we do not understand. As far as we can tell, these phenomena don't seem to follow any rules, and certainly not those that govern the sublunar world. In such cases, no reason can be found to show that they behave in the way that they do rather than in another way. It therefore seems possible that they could have been otherwise than they are, since they are not apparently caused to behave exactly in the way that they do. They do exist in a particular way, even though it is not the case that they must exist in such a way. There is therefore grounds to argue that they are the product of choice on the part of one who causes them to exist in a particular manner, and therefore particularized, because they might not be necessary. If the heavens do not follow an inevitable, set pattern, but behave in a particular fashion, they seem to be either random or chosen through will, which is able to select alternatives. Unless somebody can show otherwise, Maimonides argues, it makes sense to think that God must create every discrete member of the superlunar world to behave in a particular way. The disorder of the superlunar world is therefore taken as evidence that God particularizes the heavens, and therefore as evidence that God creates through will.[7] Maimonides also presumes that if God creates through will, God creates the world *de novo*. These two claims are inextricable in his presentation, and I will return to the issue of divine volition below.

The second, related issue helps explain why particularity is important and why it opens up the possibility of contingency. There are similarities between the way in which Maimonides approaches the question of an absolute beginning and the way in which he addresses God's knowledge. In both cases, he opposes the philosophers' doctrine to that of the law, and argues that both positions are reasonable, and suggests that there is no way to decide conclusively in favor of one position or the other. Moreover, "with regard to all problems with reference to which there is no demonstration, the method used by us with regard to this question—I mean the question of the deity's knowledge of what is other than he—ought to be followed. Understand this" (3:21, 485). This comment ends a chapter in which Maimonides explains that God's knowledge should be thought of as creative, and that it can therefore include individuals. The philosophers, on the other hand, argue that God does not know individuals. Maimonides states that the method followed here, arguing that God's knowledge is creative, should be used when no position can be shown to be true, as is the case with regard to creation. Once the two doctrines are connected, the relevance that miracles hold for creation can be made evident.

The particularity of the heavens, that each individual heavenly body behaves according to God's will rather than according to fixed laws, is considered evidence that God creates *de novo*, and therefore through will. Miracles are also considered evidence for God's creating through will, since Maimonides' reason for asserting that one ought to believe in creation *de novo*, which entails creation through will, is that not doing so makes the miracles impossible. Miracles must also depend on God's knowledge of particulars in our world. Belief in miracles involves the belief that God knows particulars and can arrange them or, in the term that Maimonides uses, particularize them. If miracles are to be possible, God must be able to bring about aberrations. They must be events that are not traceable to any chance cause. In principle, a chance occurrence can be understood by following the chain of events that led to its happening, even though that chain was not foreseen or previously known to be connected to the outcome. Maimonides explains that a miracle changes the recipient of the miracle without changing its nature, so it cannot be explained by natural philosophy. A miracle is a singular occurrence that does not follow the usual order of events (2:29, 345). Now, if such events are to happen, they must be caused to happen by God, which means that God must be able to cause individual occurrences.

There is an important difference between these two realms of particularized events. Whereas the heavens might offer empirical evidence of particularization, so their disorder is prior to and evidence of particularization, the claim that miracles are possible is made possible by and posterior to particularization. To assert that miracles are possible is not to say that they are witnessed in everyday life. There might not be evidence for particularization from miracles, as there is from the heavens. Rather, particularization would be the ground for thinking that miracles could occur. But if the law asserts that miracles are possible, the law asserts that the sublunar world is particularized, and therefore it must be created through will. Since Maimonides connects creation through will with creation *de novo*, denying creation *de novo* "gives the lie to every miracle" (2:25, 326). Therefore, belief in the possibility of miracles is bound up with belief in creation *de novo*.

In sum, Maimonides makes the point that there is no demonstration for the law's view of God's knowledge after explaining that God can know all things because God knows them as their creator. So a precondition for miracles, which are caused by God's creative knowledge, is that God knows individuals. If God is to cause singular events that do not follow the usual order, God must be said to know those individuals and to particularize them, that is, to create them in a certain way that might not follow the way in which the world generally exists. Maimonides' position therefore emphasizes our uncertainty of scientific matters. Just as we seem to be unable to understand the heavenly realms, since they are apparently particularized, the possibility that there might be aberrations in the sublunar world limits the level of certainty we can have in our scientific understanding of this world. In the Aristotelian worldview, intellect grasps universals rather than particulars, which are perceived by the senses. Scientific investigation deals with generalities and attempts to explain universal rules. If a miracle is caused by God, and there is no way for us to understand its causes because it does not follow scientific laws, we must accept that even if we should perfect our intellects and scientific understanding, it remains possible that we would not be able to understand everything in the sublunar realm.[8] Similar to the way in which creation cannot be understood, then, Maimonides' account of God's knowledge indicates that there are certain aspects of our world that are not scientifically intelligible.

RECEPTION: *EX NIHILO*, *DE NOVO*, AND GOD'S WILL

Until this point, the questions of creation *de novo* and creation *ex nihilo* have not been distinguished. Maimonides treats the two as if they are inseparable. He seems to argue that with an everlasting world, God cannot have the same sort of relationship with the world as *de novo* creation would allow. Why he combines the two different notions of creation is uncertain, but the conflation has caused confusion since many think the two should be distinguished. The philosophers can still hold that the world is created *ex nihilo* by emphasizing its absolute dependence on God, the only being that is itself existence, while maintaining that it is not created *de novo*. Among Maimonides' medieval Hebrew commentators, some argued that this was his real view.[9]

Medieval philosophy written in Hebrew became common only after Maimonides' time, and was greatly facilitated by his first translators, Samuel ibn Tibbon and the ibn Tibbon family. Much of ibn Tibbon's project was dedicated to expanding Maimonides' exegetical agenda and bringing Maimonides' ideas to a non-Arabic-speaking audience. Simply translating the *Guide* would be insufficient, however, as it is a highly allusive work and presumes knowledge on the reader's part of Arabic science of the time. Along with other members of his family, ibn Tibbon set about translating many works of Arabic-Islamic philosophy. One of the most important philosophers for this Hebrew tradition was Averroes, whose commentaries on Aristotle Maimonides praises in a letter to ibn Tibbon.[10] Averroes argued that the world did not have a beginning, and a number of his Jewish readers were convinced.

The fourteenth century saw Averroist readers consciously interpreting the *Guide* in line with Averroes and Aristotle. Their goal was not purely academic, to explain Maimonides' arguments, but to explain the truth, as they understood it, of the doctrine considered. One example is that of Moses of Narbonne. Since he was convinced that the world is everlasting, he interpreted the *Guide* to be teaching that the world is everlasting, in line with the philosophers.[11] In light of the distinction between *de novo* and *ex nihilo*, Narboni was one of a number of the *Guide*'s commentators who seemed to think that, as creation *ex nihilo* does not entail creation *de novo*, Maimonides could not really have believed the two to be necessarily connected. Questions about this very issue constitute a substantial amount of the scholarship on Maimonides written in the past few decades. Many scholars today also hold that line, and they argue that apparent inconsistencies in the way he presents his arguments indicate his hidden position.[12]

Some important evidence for this view is taken from passages in the *Guide* in which Maimonides discusses the role of divine volition and appears to undermine his own claim that it is crucial. Recall that Maimonides argues that if the world is everlasting, it is necessary, and that if the world is necessary, it cannot be created through God's volition. He also argues that if God creates through will, the world must be created *de novo*. On the other hand, if Aristotle is right, and the world is everlasting, God's will is limited because the world is necessary. Aristotle's undermining the law involves denying that God's will plays a role in creation by positing an everlasting world. However, in a number of passages Maimonides appears to indicate that an everlasting world would not limit divine volition. First, with regard to the future, he argues that God could voluntarily create a world that will never pass away, so it is not a fundamental doctrine of the law that the world will end. The idea that everything that comes to be must pass away, which seems to be connected to the statistical understanding of necessity when expressed as "what is always is necessary," simply does not apply here. The world will always exist, but it is not necessary. Moreover, when explaining the activity of the intelligences, Maimonides says that they eternally create through will and choice (2:7, 266).[13] Additionally, when explaining Aristotle's position, he states that Aristotle believes that God brings into existence an everlasting world through an act of will (2:13, 284). From these passages, it seems that Maimonides did not consider divine volition to be incompatible with an everlasting creation.

WISDOM VERSUS WILL?

The two apparently opposed attitudes that Maimonides adopts would seem to fit well with those who argue that two fundamentally incompatible approaches to God pervade the *Guide*. One of those is said to emphasize the role of God's will in creation, and the other stresses God's wisdom. The view that God creates through will allows for miracles; highlighting God's wisdom involves asserting that God works through ordered natural law, and this approach produces science rather than belief based on fantasy and the impossible.[14] On this reading, creation entails a world of miracles and folk religion, while an everlasting world rules out miracles and "popular" religious doctrines. If Aristotle is right, and the world is everlasting, science is upheld because the world follows necessary laws that, once understood, can be seen to apply everywhere equally. Since God works through nature, humans must develop their own capacities to understand creation so far as is humanly possible, rather than hoping for miraculous intervention.

Such an interpretation appears to be supported by Maimonides' discussion of the purpose of creation. On the one hand, Maimonides asserts that God creates because it is God's will to do so. In this context, he appears to distinguish his own view from Aristotle and the philosophers, since Aristotle does not give any final cause for creation, whereas it is proper to believe that God's will is the final cause, or purpose, of creation. On the other hand, several chapters later, he identifies with Aristotle against the view that the world is created according to God's will alone, and asserts very forcefully that everything that God does is wise and good. A good action, he says, is one that aims at a worthy goal and achieves that goal. Everything that God does is good, and creation is God's action, so creation must have a final cause, a purpose which is attained. Moreover, he's extremely dismissive of people who say no reasons aside from God's will should be given for creation. So there are two obvious points of opposition between these chapters. One is in how Aristotle is portrayed. In the earlier chapter he is said to present no final cause for existence whereas in the later one he is said to assert that everything has a final cause. The second opposition is in Maimonides' claim in the earlier chapter that God creates through will and in the later chapter that God creates through wisdom, and not through will. These are the sorts of apparent contradictions that lead scholars to argue that Maimonides tried to indicate to his discerning readers that he was uncomfortable with the traditional position of the law, which he ostensibly defends.[15]

A bald opposition between will and wisdom seems simplistic and lacking in philosophical sophistication. It might be popular because Maimonides does not go into the same philosophical detail as others with whom he is often mentioned, philosophers like Avicenna and Aquinas, to name two of the most obvious.[16] One commentator who defended Maimonides' arguments by elaborating them in ways that are not explicit in the *Guide* was Isaac Abravanel. From the start of the sixteenth century, Abravanel's work looks back over the three centuries of Hebrew philosophy and theology that followed Maimonides, and he also takes into account Christian writers, including Aquinas, whom he calls "the wisest of their sages and the greatest of their intellectual giants."[17] He argues that both passages in which Maimonides considers creation's final cause are correct, but they make quite different points. His explanation extends beyond Maimonides' explicit statements in order to show how the statements cohere.

Abravanel considers whether or not it is right to seek a final cause other than God's will for the whole of creation, concluding that in one sense it is not and in another it is. He states that there are two approaches. One is adopted by those who argue that there is no final cause for the whole of existence. This is plainly false, says Abravanel, and it is disproved by the philosophers. He cites two arguments purporting to show that there is no final cause. One is as follows. All things have their own proximate causes, and they are ultimately united in the final cause, which is the sphere of the world as a whole. But there is nothing external that could count as its final cause, and in view of which it could be created. Although the argument in Abravanel's text is not entirely clear, it seems to build on a distinction between internal and external causes. Efficient and final causes can be considered external. For example, a carpenter, who is the efficient cause of a chair, is external to the chair, as is her idea of the chair she makes, or the chair's purpose, which is the final cause. The material and formal causes, however, are intrinsic to the chair. They are both constituents of the chair. So the sphere as a whole can be the final cause of individual parts of the world, which all tend toward the sphere, because it is extrinsic, but there is nothing that could count as the sphere's own final cause because there's nothing outside of it for it to tend toward. A second argument is that God is the world's agent, its maker. When an agent acts for a purpose, it seeks to attain something that it did not already possess. Were God to act for a purpose, that would imply that God lacks something and tries to attain it. But since God is absolutely perfect in all respects, and therefore lacking nothing, there cannot be an end that God is trying to achieve in creating the universe. God can therefore not be said to act for any purpose.

A second group holds that it is necessary to seek a final cause for the whole of existence. In this case God must be said to act for a purpose. In this context, Maimonides pours scorn on those who say that God acts only through will (3:25, 504). In view of their final causes, he divides actions into four types: futile, frivolous, vain, and good. A futile action has no aim; a frivolous action has an unnecessary or relatively useless aim; a vain action fails to achieve its aim; a good action aims at a worthy goal and achieves that goal. All of God's actions are good, says Maimonides: "A man endowed with intellect is incapable of saying that any action of God is vain, futile, or frivolous" (3:25, 503). To say that God's creation has no aim would be to label it frivolous, but God cannot be said to act frivolously. Therefore, creation has a final cause. The problem is not only that God would be said to act for no discernible purpose, but also that human understanding relies on created things having final causes. Natural science investigates the final causes of individual things, since the intellect understands things primarily through their final causes.

Both of these positions seem to have good arguments in their favor. Abravanel identifies them as apparently competing aspects of Maimonides' view and tries to explain how both are correct. From one point of view, it is appropriate that we say that the final cause is nothing other than God's will. From another, the final cause must be God's wisdom. In order to make this claim, Abravanel distinguishes between two different ways of asking about a final cause. The first asks about the goal of the agent and the second asks about the goal of the artifact. To illustrate the difference, he uses the example of a builder and a house. One can ask why someone builds a house from different points of view. First, the answer to what motivates the builder could be "to make money to feed his family," or "to satisfy a boss." This is the builder's goal. Secondly, one can ask about the goal of the activity: what is the final cause of the thing made? The answer to this question would be "to act as a shelter."

Abravanel argues that this distinction can also be made with regard to questions about the world as a whole. In the first case, when Maimonides states that nothing other than God's will can be the purpose of creation, Abravanel argues that the question is asking about the first of these. The question concerns what moves God to create. Here, the answer would have to be of a kind completely different from that given when the question is asked of the builder. For the builder, unless he acts purely out of love for the activity, the aim is something external. He aims to acquire something that the builder does not already possess, whether that's expertise or material goods. But since God lacks nothing that creation would complete, God's purpose in creating cannot be in order to fulfill some need. God is absolutely perfect, bestows perfection on created things, and is not perfected by anything external. God acts through essence, rather than through an accidental feature, whereas the builder builds qua builder rather than through his essence (1:52, 119).

The philosopher's response to the question "Why does God create?" is therefore, at least in Maimonides' presentation, to say "Nothing." God is not moved to create: it is simply something that happens, a corollary of God's nature. So creation is necessary, because God's existence is necessary and God's nature is to bestow existence. And Maimonides states that, on this view, there is no point asking a question about why God created the heavens with the size and number they have. It was not something chosen, but is a result of God's nature. Things have to be how they are and the question is therefore simply redundant.

The position that Maimonides says is "the law's" agrees with the philosophers' point of view, inasmuch as God does not need to achieve any goal, so there is no external motive for God to create. The final cause of creation, God's purpose, can only be internal to God. However, he disagrees that creation is something that God does out of necessity; it is not something that naturally happens. Creation does not proceed from God simply because God is. God is under no compulsion to create from an external motive *or* from nature. So, instead, creation has to be an act of will on God's part. This is why creation is said to be entirely free and a result of God's purposive activity.

Maimonides states that the nature of will is to be able to choose opposites. That is, God could create or not create. If creation is natural, that is not the case, because a natural action has a single end point. Natural things tend toward a single action, and they fail to fulfill this activity only if there is some impediment. For example, the steam in my kettle will naturally rise upward unless the lid prevents it from doing so. If the law's position teaches that God creates through will, God must be able either to create or not create, as Maimonides puts it, "to will and not to will," even without an impediment (2:18, 301). He reports that Aristotle's God is not able to wish otherwise than to create, so the sense of "will" that the philosophers give to creation is not the same as that which Maimonides himself gives it. They can say that God wished to create in a similar way to that in which I wish to have been born with a nose. I'm glad to have been born with a nose, and want to have one, but it is not the result of a voluntary action that I could have made otherwise (2:20, 314). The philosophers' God is free, in the sense that it acts through its own intellect and according to its own nature, rather than an external cause, but it is not free *not* to act and overflow.[18]

Since God's will is inscrutable, Maimonides argues that in an important sense the law offers no extra knowledge of why God creates. Saying that the world is a product of God's will does not provide greater understanding of why the world exists than the philosophers, who say that there is no point even asking the question. But to say that the world is the result of God's will does not necessarily make God capricious. It simply teaches, firstly, that there is no compulsion on God to create and, secondly, that creation is not a natural process. Neither does it indicate that God's actions do not have goals in themselves, simply that the purposes of created things are not the reason that God creates. So Maimonides emphasizes that no final cause should be sought for creation other than God's will.

That cannot be the whole story, though, since Abravanel says that the philosophers and the law are in agreement that all of God's actions have a final cause. Since God is rational, and therefore all the divine actions aim at a particular end that they achieve, all of God's actions are good. So in the later chapter, in which Maimonides emphasizes that all created things are good, Abravanel claims that he is considering the second question, the final cause of each of the created things. Individual things, or individual classes of things, must have their own final causes. These are proximate causes. Those who believe that created things do not have final causes undermine science altogether. Understanding something involves identifying its characteristic behavior. By identifying what a natural thing tends toward, one understands its nature. However, if its activities depend solely on God's will, and therefore cannot be investigated because the thing does not have a particular characteristic sort of behavior, the basis of scientific investigation collapses. So each created thing has a final cause, an end toward which it moves. But there is also an ultimate final cause that is shared by all things, to which they all tend, which is God. From this point of view, the perspective of created being, the final cause of God's action must be an ordered, intelligible end.

So Abravanel's solution to this apparent inconsistency is to say that there are different senses given to the word "will" when used of creation. He has tried to argue that in the two chapters that appear to support opposing positions, different issues are at stake, and that explains why the two chapters appear to conflict. Ultimately, the final cause in both cases is God. When God is said to create through will, Abravanel understands this to mean that creation is an expression of God's free choice. When God is said to create through wisdom, there is no conflict because God creates an ordered cosmos. He agrees that there is an important sense in which God is free to create even if the world is everlasting, and if God has no other choice but to create. Inasmuch as God is not caused to create by anything external, God's motivation can only be internal, which is to say that God creates because God wants to do so. When the philosophers say that the world is brought into being by an eternal and everlasting act of divine volition, they are, quite rightly, pointing out that God is not determined by any external motive. Nothing compels God to act, and there is nothing that God lacks, and therefore requires, in order to achieve the divine goal. In this sense, the philosophers are entitled to say that the world is brought into being through an act of volition.

However, for Maimonides, this is insufficient since such a creation could be construed as too close to natural inclination.[19] The position that Maimonides says is "the law's" agrees with the philosophers' point of view, inasmuch as God does not require anything, does not need to achieve any goal, so there is no external motive for God to create. The final cause for creation, God's purpose, can only be internal to God. However, he disagrees that creation is something that God does out of necessity; it is not something that naturally proceeds from God simply because God is. So, instead, creation has to be an act of will on God's part. This is why creation is said to be entirely free and a result of God's purposive activity. Ultimately, Abravanel and, if he's right, Maimonides too, seem to think that only this stronger sense of will allows for God to know and particularize creation. The philosophers' account of divine will implies a single activity, like a natural motion. Only the stronger sense would allow for creating multiplicity, rather than the single activity that results from a natural event, and for God to will change while remaining unchanging.

AN ONGOING PERPLEXITY

Maimonides' extensive discussion of creation continues to intrigue even in our times. He insists that a genuinely *ex nihilo* creation must be entirely different from any sort of generation that humans can experience. Whether creation *ex nihilo* entails an absolute beginning to time is subject to disagreement, but Maimonides' arguments assume that a creation that is the result of divine volition and purpose must be a *de novo* creation. He also argued that along with such an understanding of creation, if God causes time to begin, temporal events that are not necessitated by natural causes, but are attributed to divine will, become possible. Like creation itself, such events would be inaccessible to scientific understanding, so both place limits on human knowledge. Discussions inspired by the *Guide* reflect the complexity of Maimonides' own presentations, and also how the issues pervade his entire thought. Many find the different emphases to be irreconcilable, but they need not be. They do, however, require commitment from the reader to engage in independent thought. What is clear is that he goes to some length to emphasize that any attempt to explain creation will automatically misconstrue it and that asserting that creation is true, together with other theological doctrines, limits the reach of human intellect. But notwithstanding his claims, he insists that the scientific approach to created being embodied by the philosophers is correct.

NOTES

1. References are to part, chapter number, and page number in the English translation by Shlomo Pines, *The Guide of the Perplexed* (Chicago: University of Chicago Press, 1963). For the Judeo-Arabic see Joel-Munk, *Dalālat al-Ḥā'irīn* (Jerusalem: Azrieli, 1929).

2. As Herbert Davidson has pointed out, Maimonides attributes to Aristotle doctrines that are actually Avicenna's. *Moses Maimonides: The Man and His Works* (New York: Oxford University Press, 2005), 115.

3. Maimonides' presentation of these arguments is somewhat brief, but Avicenna's position is explained in more detail by Jon McGinnis, who also explains that "for Avicenna, either the existence of the world is eternal or its existence would have been impossible." "The Ultimate Why Question: Avicenna

on Why God Is Absolutely Necessary," in *The Ultimate Why Question: Why Is There Anything at All Rather Than Nothing Whatsoever?*, ed. John Wippel (Washington, DC: Catholic University of America Press, 2011), 83.

4. It is possible that al-Ghazālī is in the background here. Frank Griffel, "Al-Ghazālī at His Most Rationalist: The Universal Rule for Interpreting Revelation (*al-Qān n al-Kullī fī t-Ta'wīl*)," in *Islam and Rationality: The Impact of al-Ghazālī*, ed. Georges Tamer (Leiden: Brill, 2015), 89–120.

5. Hannah Kasher, "Biblical Miracles and the Universality of Natural Laws: Maimonides' Three Methods of Harmonization," *Journal of Jewish Thought and Philosophy* 8 (1998): 25–52.

6. For more on the idea of particularity and on the arguments in the following paragraph, see Kenneth Seeskin, *Maimonides on the Origin of the World* (Cambridge: Cambridge University Press, 2005), 122.

7. Seeskin, *Maimonides on the Origin of the World*, 122.

8. Tzvi Langermann, "Maimonides and Miracles: The Growth of a (Dis)Belief," *Jewish History* 18 (2004): 147–72.

9. Aviezer Ravitsky, "The Secrets of Maimonides: Between the Thirteenth and Twentieth Centuries," in *Studies in Maimonides*, ed. Isadore Twersky (Cambridge, MA: Harvard University Press, 1990), 159–207.

10. "Arabic into Hebrew: the Hebrew Translation Movement and the Influence of Averroes upon Medieval Jewish Thought," in *The Cambridge Companion to Medieval Jewish Philosophy*, ed. Daniel H. Frank and Oliver Leaman (Cambridge: Cambridge University Press, 2003), 258–80.

11. Charles Manekin makes the case convincingly: "To put Moses of Narbonne's principle more crudely: if some passages of the Guide assume Aristotle's position and others don't, reinterpret the latter to conform to the former." "Response to Kreisel," in *Jewish Philosophy: Perspectives and Retrospectives*, ed. Raphael Jospe and Dov Schwarz (Boston: Academic Studies Press), 218.

12. "The majority of those studying Maimonides in academic settings today are convinced that when he argued for creation, he meant that the world was *not* created after not existing—or, in some nuanced versions, he was surreptitiously expressing doubts as to whether or not the world was created. . . . Members of the academic community who cannot shake off the eerie notion that Maimonides may actually have meant what he said hesitate to 'come out' lest they be viewed as gullible and naive." Davidson, *Moses Maimonides*, 398.

13. Howard Kreisel advances these two arguments in "Maimonides on the Eternity of the World," in Jospe and Schwarz, *Jewish Philosophy*, 157–84.

14. Explaining the way in which Maimonides is often read, Moshe Halbertal sets up the opposition between those passages in the *Guide* in which

God is presented in a traditional way and others, in which God is presented in a way that is acceptable to the supposedly more philosophically sophisticated. *Maimonides: Life and Thought* (Princeton: Princeton University Press, 2013), 312–21.

15. Kreisel, "Maimonides on the Eternity of the World," 176: "Belief in creation is necessary for belief in the divine origin of the Law only in the case of the average believer, since his commitment to the Law hinges on viewing the revelation of the Law as a supernatural phenomenon."

16. "Of the three main areas in which he wrote, rabbinics was plainly the one in which his scholarly preparation was most thorough, and philosophy—surprisingly—the one in which it was the least." Davidson, *Moses Maimonides*, 121. Perhaps Maimonides was not a great philosopher, or simply did not pay as much attention to writing the *Guide* as is usually thought. But maybe such a negative appraisal is unnecessary, since he states that he does not intend to write a scientific text. Maybe the purpose was to leave an enigmatic work that would force its readers to think through the issues he raises and follow his pointers while studying works by Arabic philosophers alongside the traditional Jewish texts. See, for example, Joel Kraemer, "Maimonides, the Great Healer," *Maimonidean Studies* 5 (2008): 1–30.

17. Isaac Abravanel, *The Deeds of God* (Lemberg: S. Back, 1863), 6:3. For the discussion that follows, see 7:4. There is another statement of these arguments, with some variations, in Abravanel, *New Heavens* (Rödelheim: B. Heidenheim, 1828), 4:6.

18. Norman Kretzmann calls this "willingness," which, he explains, is "compatible with the necessity of natural order." "A General Problem of Creation: Why Would God Create Anything at All?," in *Being and Goodness: The Concept of the Good in Metaphysics and Philosophical Theology*, ed. Scott Charles MacDonald (Ithaca, NY: Cornell University Press, 1991), 216.

19. Aquinas agrees that an absolute beginning, even if not required by creation *ex nihilo*, makes the doctrine more evident. See David Burrell, *Faith and Freedom: An Interfaith Perspective* (Oxford: Blackwell, 2004), 153.

CHAPTER 11

Spinoza and the Eclipse of Creation from Nothing

CYRIL O'REGAN

In genealogies of modernity we have become used to Descartes being posited as the origin of the modern conceived as the search for certitude.[1] Spinoza may or may not figure in the story. If, however, Spinoza does become part of the story, he is routinely constructed as a thinker who continues the philosophical search for certitude by other means and more specifically as the philosopher who closes conceptual loopholes in the Cartesian scheme, which is still compromised by Christian metaphysical and theological commitments.[2] The exception to this historiographical rule is Jonathan Israel,[3] who gives an exhaustive account of Spinoza's reception in the seventeenth and eighteenth centuries. The particular emphasis of Israel's work, however, should be underscored: its focus is largely on Spinoza's articulation of the relation between faith and reason and the proper mode of biblical interpretation, and not on the God-world relation. While it is true that the issue of pantheism has often been treated in the secondary literature on Spinoza, there is no corresponding general genealogy of the exclusion of creation-from-nothing in the modern period, in which story it would be Spinoza rather than Descartes who would be the main protagonist.[4] The aim of this essay is to provide an outline of a genealogy in which the role of Spinoza is pivotal in two respects: as a critic of the entire gamut of premodern religious and philosophical construals of the relation between God and world, and particularly of the creation-from-nothing view, who at the same time proposed an internally coherent form of naturalism that could sanction the empirical study of nature while at the same time pointing beyond it. Of course, the central text is the *Ethics* (1677) rather than the *Tractatus Theologico-Politicus* (1677).

Interpretively demanded, therefore, is a compendious interpretation that focuses on that text's basic vision and isolates the band of metaphysical convictions that make it revolutionary. Equally important, from my point of view, is "the history of effects" (*Wirkungsgeschichte*) of Spinoza's articulation of the God-world view, particularly how it generates two lineages which both serve as alternatives to the *creatio ex nihilo* view and constitute blocks against the prospects of it assuming a preeminent position regarding the God-world relation. The first of these is an exemplary rationalist heritage convinced that when it comes to explaining the world, God, and more especially God's creative power and act, are theoretically unnecessary. The task of philosophy as well as that of science is to provide an account of the world without appeal to transcendent forms of causality. The second is Romantic and/or Idealist in vintage, which in its "natural supernaturalism" allows nature or the world to have some self-transcendent momentum beyond what can be accounted for by science.[5] Crucially, however, both naturalism and what for convenience we are calling "natural supernaturalism" are allied against the transcendent God of Jewish and Christian faith and any view of the natural world considered as being contingent and as the mere expression of divine will.

The argument will proceed in three stages. Concentrating especially on book 1 of the *Ethics*, in the first section of the essay I provide an outline of the negative and positive agendas of the text. If the negative agenda is to oppose all premodern construals of the God-world relation, with a particular emphasis on the *creatio ex nihilo* view, the positive agenda of the text is to elucidate an alternative account that is putatively irrefutable because articulated after the model of the most rigorous forms of thought available to us, that is, mathematics. In the second section I argue that while in his articulation of the God-world relation Spinoza in fundamental ways represents a radical departure from the premodern tradition when it comes to articulating the God-world relation, in significant respects he is anticipated by a group of Renaissance Christian Neoplatonic thinkers, above all Giordano Bruno (1548–1600).[6] In the third, and from my point of view, the most important section of the essay, I outline the forms of naturalism and natural supernaturalism that filter and disseminate Spinoza's ideas in modernity that contribute to the displacement of the creation-from-nothing view and its replacement by an immanentist alternative, or better put, set of alternatives. Central to this section will be my all-too-brief discussion of German Romanticism and Idealism. My treatment of these incredibly important cultural and discursive phenomena in the modern period, which effect a rage against naturalist reduction, help to bring out some of the real consequences of the structural correspondences between Spinoza's and Bruno's understandings of the God-world relation, which are both decisively set against traditional forms of theism. While the discourses of German Romanticism and Idealism followed Spinoza in his leaving behind of the traditional religious and metaphysical notions of God as sovereign cause of the world and the world as a contingent effect, they also demonstrated an interest in linking Spinoza with prior thinkers who did not subscribe to *creatio ex nihilo*. While this allowed a host of Neoplatonic thinkers to reassume significant status (Proclus, Philo),[7] arguably, the work of Giordano Bruno, which polemicizes against the standard theistic account at the beginning of the modern period, is privileged. I would especially like to draw attention to how this history of Spinoza in both its naturalist and supernaturalist modes continues to be effective in twentieth- and twenty-first-century theology when it comes not only to arguments against theism in general and *creatio ex nihilo* in particular, but also regarding their very thinkability. In the modern or postmodern world, one is dealing in effect with nothing less than the eclipse of the *creatio ex nihilo* view. With regard to the world and its ground the inquirer as well as believer finds not only a bewildering variety of options, but that traditional views of divine alterity and creation are no longer ready at hand. What one might call the grammars of naturalism and natural supernaturalism enjoy considerably more prestige than the premodern view of *creatio ex nihilo* with its insistence both in the registers of revelation and philosophy on a radically transcendent God and the gratuity of the created order.

Spinoza's *Ethics*: The Defeat of *Creatio ex nihilo* and Its Traditional Rivals

Both in formal and substantive terms, the publication of Spinoza's *Ethics* in 1677 represents a watershed in modern philosophical thought. Formally, it represents a watershed in two related ways: first, although the commitment to mathematical form or the *more geometrico* is influenced by the increasingly successful use of mathematics in science (Copernicus) and is anticipated in some significant respects by Renaissance thinkers such as Cusanus and Giordano Bruno, in terms of the putative range of reality covered and its logical rigor it should be considered a *novum*. Spinoza supposes to do nothing less than set up a logical system which draws out the consequences of certain axioms— probably better called fundamental propositions—consequences that pertain to the reality that believers and philosophical theists call God, the entire physical and mental world, and the relation between them. Second, the mathematical or "paramathematical" form of the *Ethics* can be construed as a development and correction of Descartes's *mathesis universalis*.[8] Descartes's avowed aim of a *mathesis universalis* has often struck genealogists as one of the supreme forms of intellectual hubris in the modern period. In hindsight, however, one is struck by Descartes's relative modesty. Reducing geometry to mathematics, Descartes conceived of nature in completely mechanistic fashion. Nature is a machine susceptible to mathematical treatment. Importantly, however, Descartes was not entirely convinced that mathematics would be absolutely sufficient to account for all reality: it was possible that gaps in explanation might prove to be structural. In any event, with regard to scope the mathematical method is regional rather than universal; it is truly applicable only to nature considered as extension (*res extensa*). Neither in the case of the cogito nor God is such a method applicable. Indeed, in the *Regulae* Descartes goes so far as to make the intelligibility of the method depend upon God as the creator of the laws of nature.[9]

Materially, and relatedly, although the mathematical form of the *Ethics* dictates quite literally a constructive view of the relation of mind and matter to God or Substance, it is clear that the entire vocabulary of God-world views in the Western tradition is being subverted. This includes especially standard forms of theism in Christianity and Judaism,[10] informed by the biblical text, but also the various forms of emanationism (largely Neoplatonic), the view of prime matter, and the view of the kabbalah where the emergence of the physical world is construed as event even if the physical world has nonphysical conditions.[11] It is evident from his letters that Spinoza was especially aggravated by the *creatio ex nihilo* view, to which, from his perspective, Descartes's thought represents a cowardly regression.

By far the more important of the two *nova* is Spinoza's break with the standard set of Jewish and Christian philosophical and theological options concerning creation and emanation within the Western tradition, and accordingly we will concentrate on this, even as we underscore its imbrications in Spinoza's peculiar philosophical method. To get matters going, I will concentrate on Spinoza's fundamental outbidding of the four influential forms of the God-world relation in *Ethics* book 1, especially propositions 1–8 and select features of his own constructive position as articulated in the remainder of book 1.[12] It is evident, from Spinoza's perspective, that all traditional Western views of the God-world relation, and the view of creation from nothing in particular, are based on two fundamental assumptions: (a) the contrast between God and the world, with God being immaterial, the world material; (b) some form of causal mediation between the immaterial God and the material world. In propositions 1–5 of book 1 of the *Ethics* Spinoza relentlessly cuts off the retreat of the traditionalist by successfully challenging the cogency of mediation, and proceeds to exclude causal mediation by proposition 6. These propositions are cumulatively devastating to the view of *creatio ex nihilo*; this is particularly true of propositions 3 and 6. Proposition 3 reads: things which have nothing in common cannot be one the cause of the other; proposition 6 reads: one substance cannot be produced by another substance. We know from his letters of Spinoza's antipathy to the theory: "Nothing," he says, "comes from nothing" (*ex nihilo nihil fit*).[13] One might think of this expression itself—despite its Parmenidean evocation[14]—as also a watershed moment in modernity which functions as the white noise in positivistic exclusions in the twentieth and twenty-first centuries of why questions such as the metaphysical question, why is there something rather than nothing?, or why is the world an infinitely organized whole or totality?[15] Spinoza sets in place a prohibition that both generates and supports a sensibility that determines that the questions of structure of the world or events in the world make sense and that the question of the origin or cause of the world does not.[16] In contrast, the prime-matter theory still retains a kind of half-life after proposition 6. Unlike the other theories and especially that of creation from nothing, it does not suppose a mediation between immaterial and material substance. Insofar, however, as this theory supposes two infinities or—to say the same thing—two substances, it is ruled out by the stipulation in note 2 of proposition 8 which has it that "everything which may consist of an individual must have an external cause." Translated: Prime matter is a determinate reality—even if a somewhat indeterminate one—and consequently has to have its cause in an original at once more aboriginal and less determinate.

Spinoza's elaboration of the basic features of the divine or substance from proposition 9 to the end of book 1 of the *Ethics* represents his constructive alternative that complements his act of outmaneuvering of the creation-from-nothing view as well as its traditional alternatives in both the Christian and Jewish spheres of reflection. The basic outline of this constructive complement, in which Spinoza articulates his essentially monistic view of God or substance, consists of three elements. These are (i) God or substance necessarily exists and is one; (ii) all things—mental as well as physical—derive from God or substance (*Deus sive Natura*) and are manifestations of divine power;[17] (iii) God or substance acts solely by the necessity of its own nature; and at the same time God or substance is a free cause. Each of these three aspects will be treated in turn.

(i) *God or substance as one*: A crucial concept of Spinoza's monism is what Spinoza calls *realitas* and what, later in the sphere of German Idealism, is called *Wirklichkeit*.[18] Spinoza introduces *realitas* into his system in proposition 9 (bk. 1), where it is stated that the greater the reality a thing has, the greater the number of its attributes. The philosophical yield becomes clear in proposition 11, which reads:

> God or substance, consisting of infinite attributes, each of which expresses eternal and infinite essentiality, necessarily exists.[19]

God or substance, then, is infinitely expressive. In this lies its perfection.[20] It is important here to distinguish Spinoza's reality from the divine simplicity supported by Maimonides and Aquinas,[21] who both think of it as a foundational metaphysical attribute that corresponds to the God disclosed in Jewish and Christian scripture. Of course, this correspondence is not only of no importance for Spinoza, but, given his view of Jewish and Christian scriptures, actually mischievous. The Bible operates in the language of devotion, not metaphysics; and as the *Tractatus Theologico-Politicus* has it, the Bible is a practical text intended for the improvement of behavior rather than understanding.[22] It moves by exhortation and illustrates by example. In any event, on the one hand, unlike simplicity, the infinity of reality demands an infinite number of means for expression, and, on the other, reality is as much consequent as antecedent and proscribes any thought of a reality that would separate a substratum from what flows from it. Although German Idealism's much more obviously Christian and dynamic metaphysical system will validate final causes, essentially it adopts Spinoza's basic logic of the inseparability of antecedent and consequent,[23] or what Spinoza comes to term (bk. 1, prop. 29), after a Renaissance thinker such as Giordano Bruno, *natura naturans* and *natura naturata*.[24]

I will turn my attention to this famous distinction shortly, but at least in passing I should make the point that although for Spinoza thought and extension are the two preeminent attributes, he does not entirely rule out that there might be others.[25] Given the fundamental expressiveness of the attributes, it also follows that each of the attributes will exhibit itself in an infinite number of individuals or modes (bk. 1, prop. 16). This exhibition of divine expressivity in physical and psychic individuals (covered in bks. 2–4) flows naturally and without gap from the inherent infinity of attributes in general and from the attributes of extension and thought in particular.

(ii) *The identity of power, essence, and act in God*: Here two of the crucial propositions are propositions 34 and 35 in book 1 of the *Ethics*, where the first speaks to the identity of God's essence and power, and the second to the equivalence of power and act.[26] There is nothing innocuous about these particular identifications and especially the latter. Traditional views of the God-world relation, and in particular theistic views in the Jewish and Christian tradition, depend upon an excess of power over act in the act of creation. However expressive the world is of God in Christian and Jewish philosophy and theology, it is understood that at the minimum there is an indivisible remainder of power in that even the entire order of nature does not exhaust the creative capacity of the divine. Otherwise put, what is expressed is necessarily metaphysically deficient vis-à-vis expressive origin.[27]

(iii) *The identity of freedom and necessity in God*: The dependence of this identification on the principle of God or substance being reality or perfection is clearly stated in proposition 33 note in book 1 of the *Ethics*. There Spinoza maintains that it follows from God's perfection that things could not have been created other than they are nor in a different order. Nonetheless, he argues, it is still philosophically legitimate to speak of God or substance as a free cause. Of course, the truth value of that proposition hinges on the definition of freedom. In proposition 32 and following Spinoza provides a definition of freedom, which corrects the definition operative throughout the Jewish and Christian philosophical traditions, and especially to the fore in Jewish and Christian medieval reflection anxious to buttress the incommensurability of the created order with its divine source by underscoring the former's gratuity. For Spinoza, although it is true to say that God or substance cannot act contrary to its nature, at the same time, it is only in the case of God or substance that we can properly speak of freedom, since it is only in this case that we are dealing with a reality that is not constrained by external causes. For Spinoza the definition of freedom is the absence of constraint. All natures other than God or substance are so constrained; therefore it follows that no nature other than God or substance is free in the strict sense.

Given his commitment to logical sequence, Spinoza does not deal with objections to his constructive view in the context of the *Ethics* itself. Outside of his *magnum opus*, however, he has to deal with two frequently lodged objections with a significant degree of persuasiveness: (a) freedom and necessity are contraries, and thus it is illogical to equate them; (b) a singularly uninviting consequence of the equation of necessity with freedom is that necessity presides over everything that has its source in the divine, and thus presides over all physical and psychic objects or individuals. The answers to both of these serious objections can be found in Spinoza's *Correspondences*. In Letter 60 Spinoza replies to the first objection by arguing that the objection is ill-conceived: the real contraries are not freedom and necessity, but rather chance and necessity.[28] Given his first principles Spinoza's objection is entirely predictable. Although it is true that all things follow with necessity from God, God is not subject to fate, since this would imply that God is subject to external constraint, which God is not. Spinoza's reply to the second objection is more subtle and involves denying some intermediate reality such as fate having power over mental and physical particulars. Things and relations between things are just irrefragably what they are.

Strictly speaking, then, Spinoza's articulation of a monist system at once answers and rules out a metaphysical question such as, why is there something rather than nothing?, and a theological question such as, what sparked the divine will to create the world that depends totally on his fiat? Spinoza responds to the first question by providing a metaphysical proof—governed by logic—for the existence of an infinite number of physical and psychic particulars. In short, the *Ethics* seems to give an answer to the philosophical question as to why there is something rather than nothing, albeit one that does not appeal to mystery or myth after the manner of traditional metaphysics or get caught up in sophisticated—but ultimately sophistical—analyses of nothing as the origin of something.[29] In another sense, however, in the *Ethics* Spinoza can be thought to refuse the why question on the grounds that it suggests that God or substance had the option of doing anything other than expressing itself in infinite attributes and finite mental and physical particulars. God or substance does what God or substance does. Here Spinoza anticipates Heidegger's attack against the natural default of the deepest metaphysical question, that is, there is a reason anterior the fact of the existence of finite particulars. The why question undergoes subversion in the asking: one answers "because" (*Weil*) rather than give a why (*Warum*), that is, provide reasons.[30] The theological question of why God created the world is also both answered and subverted as a question. Spinoza's account of God or substance can be regarded as answering the why question by his articulation of *realitas* (and perfection), thereby suggesting that the world as a whole corresponds without remainder to God or substance. Equally, however, the theological question can be seen to be subverted insofar as it is impermissible to think of the world as contingent, that is, as capable of not-being. Thus the proof of the eternity of the world by other means—truly logical and philosophical means—a position that Maimonides had entertained even if he left it open that the view might have to be qualified if one brought the Torah into consideration.[31]

Spinoza's prohibition against a contingent creation (in addition to a prohibition against a view of the world as metaphysically deficient vis-à-vis its putative divine origin) is intrinsically connected with his proscription against theological voluntarism, which, in the Jewish and Christian philosophical and theological traditions, had grounds in Jewish and Christian readings of their scriptures.[32] The world does not follow automatically from God, precisely because there is no need for God to have a creation in order to be God. The commitment to divine aseity was resolute in both traditions. [33] If a world is to be, God must will or choose to create it. Theological voluntarism may be strong (Crescas, Ockham, Luther) or weak (Maimonides, Aquinas). Aseity is often supported in the Jewish and Christian philosophical traditions by some form of appeal to divine will. This is so even when the Christian (Aquinas) or Jew (Maimonides) tends to share the view of the coextensivity of will and reason in the divine, and not separate them as is the case in Crescas on the Jewish side and Ockham, Biel, and Luther on the Christian side. Given that there is a world at all, the emphasis falls on divine will. Spinoza sees this implication in a way that the historical Luther does not, who imagines that to suggest such coextensivity is to subject God to reason and ultimately to the logic of human beings. No matter what the emphasis on reason in both the premodern Jewish and Christian philosophical and theological traditions, in the final analysis divine will is a supervening reality. In addition, in the Jewish and Christian theological traditions more specifically, wherever the discrete exercise of divine will is implied, the personhood of the divine is also implied. But from Spinoza's point of view, this is the excrescence of anthropocentrism, which, if understandable, is nonetheless philosophically invalid. Spinoza's commitment to the impersonal nature of the ground of reality is built into his series of prohibitions on the traditional views of the God-world relation and of the theistic view in particular, whose latest and perhaps most bastardized rendition had been supplied by Descartes.

One extraordinarily interesting consequence of Spinoza's monism is his articulation of a justification of God or substance against the complaints of injustice or unintelligibility, although in a strict sense his peculiar theodicy also represents the subversion of theodicy. The model for this affirmation-subversion is supplied, of course, by Spinoza's acceptance and subversion of metaphysical and theological why questions that serve as the ultimate backdrop of rationalist and positivist embargoes which echo and reecho throughout the modern period down to this day. For Spinoza there are two objections to the theodicy question as commonly asked and answered in the metaphysical and theological traditions. At one level, Spinoza's account of the God-world relation articulates a theodicy: God or substance is exonerated from blame in that things—however negatively we perceive them—are necessarily. The question, why is there evil and pain in a world that is an expression of either a personal God or an impersonal divine principle?, is judged not to be as deep as it might appear to be. It admits of an answer that is at once therapeutical and theoretical: we are enjoined to rise to the disinterested point of view in which we come to see that states of affairs in the world do not admit of being otherwise. At the same time, the question is not as compelling: if one compares Spinoza's *Ethics* with Leibniz's *Theodicy*, one sees that Spinoza's articulation of the God-world relationship also subverts theodicy. To question why things are as they are and not otherwise is incorrigibly anthropocentric and thus, from Spinoza's point of view, irredeemably self-serving.[34] Put another way, the theodicy question inverts the only valid perspective on the God-world relation which, as book 5 of the *Ethics* makes clear, is the divine point of view. Relatedly, the question why things are as they are and not otherwise suggests that there is some end or purpose to the world beyond what actually transpires. While this is a common assumption, it cannot be philosophically sustained. A further factor, which prevents the theodicy question from getting off the ground, is that for Spinoza the terms "good" and "bad" and "good" and "evil" are products of the imagination.[35] They cannot refer to axiological-metaphysical properties of the world, since there are no such properties. They might admit, however, of translation into the more naturalistic properties of "pleasure" and "pain."[36] As with his considerations of whys concerning origin, so also regarding whys with respect to the order of things, there is an affirming and subversive side to Spinoza's answers. Again Spinoza's rebuttal of the answers supplied by the Jewish and Christian tradition sets the stage for its replacement by a naturalistic necessitarian alternative. Yet at the same time this necessitarian alternative to the answers provided by the Jewish and Christian philosophical and theological traditions is also a subversion of the question of why there is anything at all and why things are the way they are and not otherwise—to avail of Leibniz's formulation. Metaphysically there is no gap between is and ought, nor can there be.

SPINOZA AND THE PROXIMITY TO RENAISSANCE NEOPLATONISM

In the first section of the essay I have been concerned to show how Spinoza's metaphysical system is revolutionary in that it departs from the entire Western religious and philosophical articulations of the God-world relation and that it deals with what was considered by many of his followers a final death blow to the theistic position which found its most hyperbolic expression in the doctrine of *creatio ex nihilo*. Perhaps it is only a slight exaggeration to claim that the *Ethics* subverts the standard Jewish and Christian grammars of creation. The mathematical form of Spinoza's articulation of his radically new view of the God-world relation in the *Ethics*, focused in the elaboration of the relation between *natura naturans* and *natura naturata*, is essential to its revolutionary character, even if subsequently, as Jonathan Israel points out,[37] the Spinozist paradigm came to be regarded as uselessly apriorist and hostile to experimentation deemed essential to discovery and the broadening of knowledge. For Spinoza, the advantage of the mathematical model was that it enabled one to sideline polemics, which for him was unphilosophical in spirit in addition to being personally disagreeable. The *more geometrico* was both an alternative to the *more rabbinico*, which in formal structure was disputatious, and also to the high level of polemical exchange that characterized philosophy in the wake of Descartes and scientific discovery. As indicated already, however, despite Spinoza's aversion to polemic, his *Ethics* enacted a deconstruction of the entire vocabulary of Western theological and philosophical parsing of the God-world relation. In his *Dictionary* Pierre Bayle[38]—who, though critical of Spinoza on some points, was one of his most effective apologists—made sure to remind the public of readers of the array of options.[39] The intention was to relativize the standard theistic option, expressed and buttressed by the doctrine of creation from nothing. Arguably, Bayle understood himself to be making explicit what was already implicit in Spinoza. In his *Dictionary*, as well as elsewhere, he tended toward the deflationary: appearances to the contrary, Spinoza's view of the God-world relation is not doing battle with a consensus Jewish and Christian view of the God-world relation. No such consensus existed; rather, throughout the Western intellectual tradition there were a multiplicity of views, many of which themselves were alternatives to the creation-from-nothing view. However different Spinoza's view was from everything that preceded it—and for many purposes Bayle wanted to highlight its novel character—nonetheless, its uniqueness did not consist in its contestation of the creation-from-nothing view. There always have been contenders, even if Spinoza's alternative could be regarded as first among equals because of its logical rigor.

Under "Spinoza's *Ethics*," above, while I highlighted Spinoza's outmaneuvering of the theistic understanding of the God-world relation, I also considered Spinoza's outmaneuvering of the prime-matter view, which, of course, itself has a wide vocabulary given the effective history of the *Timaeus* in Christian and non-Christian Neoplatonism throughout the centuries. I did not attempt to illustrate Spinoza's rejection of kabbalistic speculation, or search for the clues to this being an interest of Spinoza. Whatever the state of evidence brought forward regarding Spinoza's actual knowledge of the Kabbalah, had it been presented to him Spinoza would have had little time for kabbalistic modes of allegorical and mystical exegesis and even less for its speculation, which, from Spinoza's rationalist point of view, would have smacked pejoratively of imagination. Almost certainly he would have found fanciful that the ground of everything, that is, divine attributes and material-temporal expressions, could be characterized as "nothing."[40] What was really shortchanged in that first section of the essay was an analysis of how Spinoza dealt with the emanationist view of the God-world relation that was the main rival of the *creatio ex nihilo* view since the early centuries of the common era.

Now I suggested earlier that standard versions of emanationism are intentionally subverted in the logical movement between proposition 1 and 8 of book 1 of the *Ethics* and replaced in the remainder of the book by an articulation of the God-world relation much more radical than anything found in classical Neoplatonism or its Jewish and Christian varieties. Recall that the first group of propositions rule out mediation between God and world: but mediation is essential to the emanationism of Philo, the classical Neoplatonism of Plotinus and Proclus, and for Jewish and Christian thinkers who borrow from either. One may read the *Ethics* as providing a knockdown argument against emanationism or not. Still, however we judge the success of Spinoza's argumentation, the issue of the relation between Spinoza's monistic system and Neoplatonic emanationism raises its head in proposition 9 with Spinoza's characterization of God or substance as *realitas*. Now to define *Deus sive Natura* as infinitely expressive cannot but recall the philosophical characterizations of the One in Plato's *Parmenides*, Plotinus's *Enneads*, and Proclus's *Elements* and religious philosophical characterizations of the God of monotheistic faith in Philo, in Pseudo-Dionysius, and Johannes Scotus Eriugena. The ultimate foundation of reality in each case is cast as self-expressive and self-communicative.

If this correspondence justifies reopening the issue of the relation between Platonic and Neoplatonic emanationism and Spinoza's logical system, our parsing of proposition 9 and the remaining propositions of book 1 of the *Ethics*, however, give us grounds to shut it down. There are essentially three reasons. The first is that Platonic and Neoplatonic emanationism, whether philosophically or theologically tinctured, presupposes a gap between divine power and divine expression. There is an implied reserve in that expression at the very highest metaphysical level, the Nous in Plotinus, the Henad in Proclus, the hierarchies in Pseudo-Dionysius—not to mention Nature in Plotinus or the physical world of Pseudo-Dionysius—does not exhaust the expressive capacity of the divine. This capacity is always in excess of the manifestation of the maximally real divine origin at all the various ontological levels. As we saw under "Spinoza's *Ethics*," Spinoza does more than close the gap; he removes it entirely: expression exhausts the full reserves of the power of expression of God or substance. Thus, while standard forms of Platonic and Neoplatonic emanationism represents a detour around the divine will and a block against all forms of decisionism, from a Spinozist perspective, they share with theism, scriptural or otherwise (Cartesian), the questionable commitment to ontological reserve in expression. Second, while there is a marked emphasis in non-Christian and Christian emanationism to disturb the absoluteness of the contrast between divine freedom and necessity, at the ultimate level of reality the expressivity of the divine usually bespeaks a providential economy held to be the antithesis of logical or ontological necessity. In Middle Platonism and in Plotinus, and as amplified in Jewish (Philo) and Christian thought (Augustine, Pseudo-Dionysius), the contrary of chance—unlike in Spinoza—is not necessity but rather providence. Third, and finally, while the texts of non-Christian and Christian Neoplatonism routinely advise that human beings, whatever their estate and whatever the particular stresses in life, should rise to the disinterested point of view, nonetheless, they fairly consistently and straightforwardly argue that if blame is to be assigned for the emergence of evil, it must be placed on nature or human being and not on the origin of all.

In Platonic and Neoplatonic forms of emanationism there are a number of features to the theodicy defense, beginning with identifying the origin of everything not only as unitary but also as good. One can expect to find this articulated in Jewish and Christian Neoplatonism, given basic convictions about the God who presides over the physical universe. Yet Plotinus and subsequent Neoplatonists tended to think of the originary oneness and goodness as coextensive. The physical universe as a whole expresses the goodness of origin. There are two other aspects of note. First, when seen aright, the world posited by both classical and nonclassical Neoplatonism contains just enough imperfection to set off the perfection, just enough dark to set off the light. When Augustine articulates the aesthetic theodicy of his early years, he is thoroughly dependent on the "Platonists" in doing so. And second, as a further indemnification that the universe can be validated when imperfection is experienced as posing a challenge to the presumption of its basic goodness, support for theodicy is provided by the notion of evil being the privation of the good, of evil being regarded from the ontological point of view as empty.[41]

Given that Spinoza's metaphysical systems differs from Neoplatonic emanationism in all the above respects, it would seem that this concludes the quest for a truly positive correspondence between Spinoza's articulation of the God-world relation and any and all forms of emanationism in premodern Western religious and philosophical thought. And this would be so if there were not forms of Neoplatonic emanationism in late medieval and early modern thought that seem to emend classical Neoplatonism in ways that anticipate the metaphysical articulation of the *Ethics*. Although the credentials of Nicholas of Cusa are by no means insignificant, the test case has to be Giordano Bruno. This point would be agreed on by those commentators on Spinoza who think that acknowledging the revolutionary character of his thought does not mean that every feature of his thought is novel.[42] Setting aside any effort to establish genetic links between Spinoza and the unfortunate Bruno, who was burned at the stake in 1600 for his putative denial of Christian doctrines, and who, like Spinoza, saw in Copernicus's use of mathematics the dawn of a brave new world, it is worthwhile inquiring whether Bruno's emendation of classical Neoplatonic emanationism brings him into the close proximity to the overall metaphysical structure of Spinoza.

Needless to say, even if the general answer to the question is yes, for Bruno mathematics functions more as an incentive to throw off the old than as the rigorously deductive argumentative ground for the new, as is the case with Spinoza. Furthermore, the high-flown, allusive, and tendentious style of the philosophical thinker from Nola (Italy) differs *toto coelo* from the lean and noncontentious style of the *Ethics*. Featuring texts such as *De la causa, principio et uno* (1584) and *De l'infinito universo et mundi* (1584) among others,[43] I will explore a number of dimensions of excess in the emanationist protocols of Bruno's thought that suggest something like a mutation of the standard form of Neoplatonic emanationism. They are in turn (a) a radicalized use of the standard Neoplatonic trope of self-expressivity of the divine; (b) the coincidence in the divine infinity of constitutive creative power and creative expression; (c) the identification of freedom with necessity and vice versa; (d) a necessitarian theodicy. I begin with the first of these four points.

The locus classicus of Bruno's disruption of the standard use of the Platonic and Neoplatonic trope of the "non-enviousness" of the divine and consequently of divine expressivity is to be found in *On the Infinite Universe*:

Why should we, or could we, imagine that divine power were otiose? Divine goodness can indeed be communicated to infinite things and can be infinitely diffused: why then should we wish to assert that it should choose to be scarce . . . ? Why do you desire that center of divinity which can extend indefinitely to an infinite sphere, why do you desire that it should remain grudgingly sterile . . . ? Why should you prefer that it be less, or by no means communicated rather than that it fulfill the scheme of its glorious power and being? Why should infinite amplitude be frustrated, the possibility of infinite worlds defrauded?[44]

As is obvious from the above quotation, Bruno's version of Neoplatonic emanationism is innovative in two ways: whereas previous regimes of Neoplatonic emanationism did not draw the above conclusion, from the principle of expressivity, or what Arthur Lovejoy referred to as the "principle of plenitude," they could have; one could put it even more strongly: whereas previous regimes did not draw the radical conclusion that Bruno is drawing, they ought to have done so. They introduced an uncalled-for stinginess into the unrestricted self-communication and self-expressivity of origin. In addition, in the above text Bruno makes clear not only that the world is constituted by an infinite number of particulars; he also suggests that the divine attributes, which are the forms and conduits of the expressivity of the henological origin,[45] are also infinite,[46] although he neither identifies these attributes nor feels inclined—as Spinoza does—to insinuate that they could be infinite in number.

One hugely important corollary of Bruno's radicalization of the Neoplatonic trope of the self-expression or self-communication of origin is the one-to-one correspondence between the power or potency of expression and actual expression. Bruno rules that there is no surplus of power over act, or no deficiency of actual expression over the power or potency of the infinite to express itself. In contrast, the traditional view of the relation between power of expression and its realization, whether in its classical or Christian forms, is indicted as being incoherent. Bruno argues that a power or potency that does not or cannot become actual cannot, strictly speaking, be granted the dignity of being called "potency." "Potency" is a meaningful term if and only if it implies a content to be actualized. [47]

Another corollary, but following in particular from the identity of actual expression and expressiveness in origin, is the identity of freedom and necessity. Although the argumentative connection is drawn in *De l'infinito*, arguably the clearest expression is found in another text, *De Immenso*: "Necessity and freedom are one: whence it is not to be feared that that which is done with the necessity of nature is not done freely. But rather I may certainly say that by acting otherwise than necessity and the necessity of nature require would not be acting freely."[48] A crucially important consequence of the identity of freedom and necessity in the divine origin, and in particular the act of will with will as such and with being, is that it excises succession from God. Although Bruno lacked Spinoza's clarity, nonetheless, in a more than rudimentary way he grasped that holding to the distinction between infinite creative potency and act implies the introduction of successiveness and thus time and finitude into the divine will. This antipunctiliar stance finds one of its more eloquent expressions in the following passage in which Bruno personalizes what elsewhere is referred to more metaphysically as one or cause: "Jove . . . does all things together without effort, without solicitude, and trouble; because he provides for innumerable species and infinite individuals by giving them order, not only by a certain successive process, but instantaneously and all at once. He does not create things according to particular efficient causes one by one, by means of many actions; but with one simple and singular act, he creates all of the past, present, and future."[49]

With this we come to the fourth point of discrimination of Bruno's thought from the standard forms of non-Christian and Christian Neoplatonism and its cementing its candidacy as a peculiar prolepsis of Spinoza which operates within an entirely different, that is to say, Cartesian episteme. This follows indirectly from Bruno's view of the expressivity of the divine and directly from the connection between freedom and necessity in the divine origin. The divine act is at once general and infinitely specific without being infinitely discrete. Thus everything is within the ambiance of the divine, the small as well as the great, for absolutely everything follows from God as an effect of God as cause or origin. The infinite effect exhibits distinction regarding place, time, mode, and subject. In God, however, these distinctions exist without distinction. The divine infinite is without differentiation, says one text;[50] unity is the implicit infinite, says another.[51] As there is an implicit infinite, there is also an explicit infinite, which in line with Pythagoreanism and Neo-Pythagoreanism is identified with number. Bruno, however, somewhat confusedly seems to identify the articulation of the universe with both providence and necessity.[52] As we saw in the case of Spinoza, these categories are distinguished. Of course, they are also distinguished in the classical examples of non-Christian and Christian Neoplatonism. The only question to be asked of Bruno's work is whether providence interprets necessity or necessity interprets providence. On balance it seems to be the latter. The order of things is intrinsically justified since it cannot be otherwise. And the divine is justified since it cannot but express itself in the way it actually does. Given this dominant, there is in advance of Spinoza something like a subversion of the theodicy question, as well as the provision of an answer that refuses to appeal to the goodness of the divine origin and some kind of finality in the natural order.

Spinoza and the Double Blockage of the Traditional Doctrine of Creation

The discussion of the relation between Bruno and Spinoza, and more generally between Neoplatonic emanationism and Spinoza, might appear to be merely of historical interest. There can be no doubt that in his own day and for the best part of a century afterwards Spinoza was seen as the apostle of atheism. I want to suggest, however, that the kind of associations between Spinoza and specific forms of Neoplatonic emanationism allowed thinkers in the second half of the eighteenth century and early nineteenth century to have another option besides that of pure naturalism for redressing the classical understanding of the God-world relation. While in one sense this form of Spinozism, tinctured by emanationism, derogated from naturalism, it added another item to the vocabulary of challenge to the classical theistic view in the modern world, thereby further compromising its prospects.

Of course, Spinoza's intellectually demanding *Ethics* was not entirely responsible for the displacement of and replacement for the classical theistic view, even if it was a major destroyer of the premodern philosophical and theological accounts of divine-world relation. Plausibly,

Spinoza's other classic text, that is, the *Tractatus Theologico-Politicus* (1677), was even more responsible for critical leverage against the theological tradition,[53] since it more overtly attacked the Bible as an evidentiary warrant for belief in the creation, fall, and redemption of human beings. From Spinoza's point of view the Bible is rationally deficient, since it is riddled with ambiguity and contradiction. Still, the deconstruction of the biblical text as a source of authority represented a major victory for reason in general and scientific reason in particular. Those who were either unable or unwilling to follow the grinding logic of the *Ethics* could take advantage of the opportunity of this more accessible and transparently critical opportunity. As Bayle, at once a Spinoza apologist and the author of friendly critique, put it, Spinoza's presumed atheism made him the most hated man in Europe at end of the seventeenth century. Bayle, however, also thought that Spinoza's remarkably ascetic private life should be counted at the very least as an extenuation when it comes to judging him.[54] Famously, he opined that Spinoza was "God intoxicated" even if not precisely doctrinally correct. In his view this was sufficient to make the argument between Spinoza and traditional forms of Christianity internal rather than external.

Bayle's apology for Spinoza had little effect in his own day. Arguably, however, it becomes central in the pantheism debate in Germany in the 1770s,[55] which in turn sets the stage for German Romantic and German Idealist appropriations of Spinoza. A century after Spinoza's writings naturalism has made huge inroads on traditional Christian and Jewish understanding of the God-world relation with their suggestions of opposition and superiority and inferiority between what is cast as originary and the physical material world. By and large, however, this naturalism is of the more experimental and practical variety than the highly speculative form that Spinoza advances. This form of naturalism, however, in turn becomes as questionable as the theistic view that it displaces, given the devastating effects of empirical science and technology on the environment and the reductive understanding of human being considered as an individual and as actualized in the community. What is interesting is that after the pantheism debate in the 1770s, overall Spinoza is more nearly regarded as part of the solution than part of the complex problem constituted by bad forms of emergent naturalism together with anachronistic and recidivist forms of biblical and metaphysical theism.

Spinoza becomes acceptable for a number of reasons. (i) Whatever the emerging problems with aggressively reductive forms of naturalism,[56] in the case of both Romanticism and Idealism the assumption is that the classical view of the God-world relation has been intellectually refuted and, as Charles Taylor, would put it, ceased to be a constitutive feature of "the social imaginary." (ii) The corrective labeling of Spinoza as "God intoxicated" acquired some philosophical and theological substance. Spinoza—in contradistinction from Kant—comes to be regarded as a visionary in a generic and specific sense. On the generic level, while just about no German Romantic or Idealist has time for Spinoza's mathematical method, Goethe and Hölderlin, Schelling and Hegel,[57] all understood the universe of Spinoza to be dynamically alive and to differ entirely from Descartes's mechanistic view of the world as *res extensa*, but also the view of Newton's *Principia Mathematica*, which attempts a mathematical understanding of the physical universe. Romantic and Idealist readings of Spinoza might with some justification be cited as creative interpretations of the *natura naturans–natura naturata* pair in the *Ethics*.[58] A second and more specific interpretive correction takes account of Spinoza's epistemology of the three kinds of knowledge and especially Spinoza's reflections on *scientia intuitiva* in some of the concluding propositions of the concluding book 5 of the *Ethics* (props. 29–36). In the body of the *Ethics* Spinoza distinguishes between first and second kinds of knowledge, the first being confused knowledge in and through the imagination, the second being discursive knowledge, where thought follows a trail of logical implication. While in its broad pattern the distinction is fairly traditional, its specific form is Cartesian in that clarity of ideas functions as the basic criterion of distinction. Spinoza, however, also claims there is a third, truly adequate kind of knowledge that is not discursive and is characterized by immediate apprehension of first principles. It is this form of knowledge, which first appears in book 3 of the *Ethics*, which is renamed—if not necessarily repurposed—in book 5 as *scientia intuitiva*. It is by means of intuitive knowledge that material temporal human beings are enabled to participate in adequate knowledge which is nontemporal and also nonindividual (bk. 5., prop. 36). For Spinoza, such participation was nothing less than blessedness (bk. 5, prop. 42).

Although the articulation of *scientia intuitiva* is very much Spinoza's own, there is broad Platonic and Neoplatonic precedent for this modality of knowledge. One can find a precedent in both Plato's *Republic* and *Parmenides* for a form of transdiscursive knowledge appropriate to the very foundation of reality, whether regarded as the Good or the One. This is true also of Plotinus, who insists that while discursive knowledge is relatively adequate and gets at the truth of penultimate layers of the metaphysical hierarchy, only a mode of nondiscursive knowing (*katanoesis*) is appropriate when it comes to the One, which is not divided into subject-object.[59] This pattern continues in Proclus and is readily adopted by Pseudo-Dionysius, who thereafter becomes a standard for Christian theology, both Eastern and Western. Nearer to the time of Spinoza, one can find the distinction between discursive and transdiscursive knowledge in Cusanus, who thinks that mathematics— and especially mathematics considered with the notion of infinity— provides a symbol of the transdiscursive knowledge which is often accompanied by paradox or the appearance of paradox.[60] And even more pertinently—again with mathematics used more as a critical cipher against a received cosmological, philosophical, and theological tradition—Giordano Bruno also promoted a distinction between transdiscursive and discursive knowledge, suggesting, like the classical Neoplatonists, who preceded him, and Spinoza, who followed him, that only a transdiscursive form of knowledge gives the prospect of a fully adequate grasp of the truth of divine origin, world, and their relation.[61]

Of course, like just about every Neoplatonist, Bruno distinguished also between opinion and discursive knowledge, and reproduced a Platonic and Neoplatonic hierarchy in which there were three kinds of knowledge. What is interesting about Bruno is not so much the repetition itself, but the explicitness and vehemence of the recall at the turn of the seventeenth century.[62] Without in any way suggesting genetic dependence on Bruno or Platonic or Neoplatonic models of knowing in general, one can see that Spinoza refigures a Neoplatonic epistemological hierarchy within a Cartesian or post-Cartesian episteme regulated by the contrast between ideas connected to sensation and perception, which are neither clear nor distinct, and clear and distinct ideas typical of conceptual formation. The post-Cartesian episteme, however, exacts a significant price on Spinoza's thought, which sets it off from non-Christian and Christian Neoplatonic traditions. Specifically, Spinoza is not prepared to insist, as Plato and Plotinus did, on the one hand, and

Pseudo-Dionysius, Cusanus, and Bruno, on the other, that essential to the character of transdiscursive knowledge is that while it is rightly cast as the highest form of knowledge, it is not necessarily the clearest.[63] In the case of Spinoza intuitive knowledge is intellectual clarity without reserve; in principle there is no remainder of substance that has proven inaccessible to the third kind of knowledge or proven to be incapable of being conceptually articulated.[64]

While there may have been some sense at the dawn of German Romanticism that Spinoza had been unfairly reviled and that there was a time for a new estimate, a number of features of his thought had become more evident. First, and crucially, there were intimations that Spinozist thought represented the future of the construal of the God-world relation, and that by contrast the traditional view with its sovereign God who creates the universe out of nothing and who subsequently—and arguably consequently—presides over it, is the view of the past. The stakes are clearly set forth in Goethe's watermark poem *Prometheus* (1776), which in turn is used by Jacobi as the litmus test whereby to assess whether Lessing's thought involves an implicit renunciation of the traditional view of the God-world relation, if not an outright expression of pantheism. The discussion prompted is, arguably, more interesting than the accusation itself. Moses Mendelssohn's intervention, whereby he characterizes Lessing's position as a soft rather than hard form of pantheism[65]—what might now be nominated as panentheism—in which there remains some distinction between the divine and its worldly expression, is especially interesting in light of Mendelssohn's Judaism and the common assumption that Judaism rigorously supports the theistic view. For J. G. Herder,[66] however, if what he regarded as the fable of an atheistic naturalist and mechanistic Spinoza were set aside, then one might more properly regard Spinoza as providing an internal correction of a Christianity that has taken too long to slough off its deficient view of the livingness and majesty of the physical world and the essential dignity of human being.

With Spinoza as a herald the premodern model of creation of the world, whether biblical, traditional, or Cartesian, necessarily had to make way for a construal of the relation between divine origin and its worldly and human expressions that considerably deemphasizes the gap between creative source and created expression, if not removes it entirely. This is certainly the view of the three luminaries who were friends in the Stift at Tubingen in the 1790s, Hölderlin, Hegel, and Schelling. Basing himself on Fichte, whom Hölderlin thinks of as a kind of Spinozist,[67] in the philosophical work that precedes his emergence as a poet Hölderlin considers that reality does not consist of a discrete God as creator and a discrete world as created. Rather, reality is the whole in which, if the divine is originary, nature and human beings are also constitutive. The law of reciprocal dependence applies.[68] This philosophical perception is carried forward in his poems, which serve as an unparalleled apology for nature and for the poet as a paradigm of human being. But it is not simply in his invocation of the Parmenidean *hen kai pan* that Hölderlin indicates a broader allegiance to an immanentist alternative to the theistic tradition.[69] His dynamic view of an inspirited rather than mechanistic nature is redolent of classical Neoplatonic views of *anima mundi* and Renaissance Neoplatonic views of nature as the dynamic manifold of *natura naturans–natura naturata*, which receives an unsurpassable expression in the controversial writings of Giordano Bruno.

What is implicit in Hölderlin is made explicit in emerging German Idealism in general and in Schelling in particular. This is first achieved in Schelling's *System of Transcendental Idealism* (1799), in which he adopts Fichte's assertion of the thesis of reciprocal dependence between God and nature and between God and humanity. This thesis completely disturbs the assumption of asymmetry which in the metaphysical and theological tradition found its clearest expression in Aquinas's famous article in the *Summa Theologica* (I.13.7) to the effect that the world has a real relation to God (is dependent on God), whereas God does not have a real relation to the world (is not dependent on it). After this 1799 text it gradually becomes more and more clear that if Schelling subscribes in any way to the pantheism of Spinoza, it can only be the "refined" variety supported by Lessing and Mendelssohn and articulated by Herder, that is, a form in which there might be some measure of distinction—if only residual or perhaps only analytic—between God and the world. This in large part accounts for the attraction of Neoplatonism to Schelling. Largely under Schelling's guidance, Hegel will be inspired to see the associations between his philosophy, which takes a strong stand against the biblical and classical doctrines of creation, and Neoplatonic emanationism.[70] But it is Schelling whose allegiance is more systemic and whose knowledge of Neoplatonism is more thorough. Moreover, it is Schelling who brings the more radical Renaissance form of Neoplatonism into conversation with Spinozism, in which conversation Renaissance Neoplatonism serves both as an ideological support of Spinozism and a modifier of it to the degree to which some parts of Spinoza might suggest that nature is spiritless. The pivotal text appropriately is called *Bruno* (1804). Importantly, the text does not simply evoke the shade of a martyr to the obscurantism of Christianity and the rigidity of its views on nature and the God-world more generally. In this sense, Schelling's short but demanding book is quite different from Hölderlin's poem on Vanini (1585–1619), who was martyred because of his pantheistic views. Rather than dramatizing the clash between the new and the old, *Bruno* recommends a particular form of thinking to displace the outdated view of the God-world relation calculated to alienate human beings both from the divine and nature, and to replace the new view that affirms the minority tradition of unity of and connection between human being, nature, and the divine that was never fully lost throughout the centuries of metaphysical darkness and religious myopia.

Schelling is obviously familiar with the corpus of Bruno and especially the works that the Nolan wrote in Latin. He recurs to them—especially *The Cause, Principle, and Unity*—in order to vindicate a view of the God-world relation arrived at through his reflections on Spinoza being an alternative to Fichte's subjective Idealism and Kant's procedural agnosticism. Whatever the perception of the relative failure or success of Schelling's *Naturphilosophie* elaborated in the same period, it managed to put a kind of modified Spinozism in play against theism to go along with the other, arguably more mechanistic, treatments of the world that were reductionist in kind.[71] For German Romanticism and Idealism Kant was figured as more nearly part of the problem than the solution. As one would expect from the author of the first two critiques, discovery of the laws of nature, of cause and effect, was the only sure means of coming to know the world—the appeal to God throwing no light on these laws. In addition, human beings were at once covered by these laws and exempted, or in Kant's language, human beings were phenomenally determined and noumenally free. Not only Schelling,

but also Hegel and Hölderlin, found both Kant's methodologism regarding nature and his anthropological dualism equally disagreeable.
Granting Schelling's role in working through the complex relation be-
tween Spinoza and Neoplatonism as a double block against the biblical
and classical view of the God-world relation, nonetheless, at the cusp of
the nineteenth century he is not singular. In his respect Schleiermacher's
On Religion (1799) bears consideration not only for its obvious recall of
Spinoza's language and its consistent preference for the language of the
"One" and "Whole" over "God" and "creature," but also for the latent
Platonic metaphysical commitments accompanying Schleiermacher's
application of the maieutic method which he self-consciously borrows
from Plato. Schelling's preeminence lies in his offering a fully worked-
out and highly differentiated metaphysical-religious proposal that
unites Spinozism and Neoplatonism and repurposes the latter for the
nineteenth century and beyond.

To privilege the German trajectory is not to deny that English Romanticism in the shape of Wordsworth, Shelley, and Coleridge was
alive to the ideological value of Neoplatonism as a form of natural supernaturalism and supernatural naturalism. Wordsworth performs a
Neoplatonic commitment throughout the *Lyrical Ballads* and especially in the *Prelude*; such a commitment is the substance of much of
Shelley's finest lyric poetry and is fully self-conscious in the poetry of
Coleridge, whose writing career was launched by an attack against traditional theism and its violent God (1795). Of course, Coleridge differs
radically from both Wordsworth and Shelley in his German learning.
This is not simply because of his tremendous knowledge of Schelling in
particular, whose reflections on imagination in *The System of Transcendental Idealism* Coleridge uses copiously in the *Biographia Literaria*
(1817), but also because of his knowledge of Spinoza and his awareness
of the productive contributions Neoplatonism makes with regard to
forging a view of nature and of human being compatible with the most
modern instincts regarding their value.[72] Interestingly, the Neoplatonists with whom the extraordinarily erudite Coleridge is familiar include
Giordano Bruno.[73] And it is through Coleridge, and the knowledge of
the alternate tradition to theistic tradition that he supplies, that Emer-
son comes to advance his proposals about divinity as expressed in nature and humanity in manifestos such as "Nature" (1836) and "Over-
Soul" (1843) as well his reflections on human genius.

The above is a sketch and hardly does justice to an incredibly complex history of reception of Spinozism in the late eighteenth and early nineteenth centuries. Still, the genealogical point should be clear. If at the end of the seventeenth century and for three quarters of the eighteenth the naturalist Spinoza served as a bracing alternative to the traditional view of the God-world relation, by the end of the eighteenth century a more "refined" form of Spinozism is in circulation—one which allows very limited distinction between God and nature and between God and humanity, for which Neoplatonism was the lingua franca. This in turn will permit Neoplatonism in general, and especially radical Neoplatonism, put into play because of new cosmology and the rise of mathematics, to be recurred to whenever the main interest is proposing an alternative to the premodern understanding of the God-world relation.

The appeal can occur in odd contexts.[74] By the end of the eighteenth century there are a number of alternatives to the classical philosophical views of the God-world relation and the theistic proposals advanced by Descartes and Leibniz in the wake of criticism. Although influential, neither the thought of Descartes nor of Leibniz could really stem the tide. Even those thinkers unsympathetic to Spinoza's particular form of naturalism would have agreed that Descartes's expositions of the relations between God, cogito, and nature are unsatisfactory, if not entirely incoherent. In addition, Leibniz's efforts to rescue the traditional view of the God-world relation suffered from systemic philosophical difficulties that ran deeper than Leibniz's attempt to convince all that the actual world we experience is the best of possible worlds. Voltaire's pastiche of the view in *Candide* (1759), as well as the more moving ethical querying in his poem on the Lisbon (1756), only touches the surface of problems which depict a God arraying before himself possible worlds and choosing the best one. Here God seems to be both anthropomorphized and given durational and discursive properties. Moreover, while Leibniz does indeed recall the classical medieval coincidence of reason and will, the emphasis seems to fall on will. Thus the voluntarism of which early moderns such as Cusanus and Bruno complained, and which it was one of the ambitions of the *Ethics* to refute, is reintroduced into a world at once grown more skeptical and less inclined to entertain anthropomorphic views of divine being and action. Even less convincing again was Leibniz's reintroduction of classical thought's axiom of the gap between infinite power and finite expression questioned at the cosmological level by Bruno and at a truly deep metaphysical level by Spinoza.

The theological situation had also changed. The Christian confessions could continue to insist on biblical and/or traditional views of the God-world relation as a matter of belief. Yet to the degree to which theology was open to the modern world, it entered an environment in which there was a felt demand to give more space to nature and more honor to human being ,where a condition of doing so involved reducing the gap between God and world and between God and human being. If for late-nineteenth- and much of the twentieth-century theology the latter was the dominant concern, perhaps latterly the former has come into view. Although the contribution of process philosophy and theology as well as numerous forms of feminism cannot be ignored, it is also true that some forms of theology interested in renovating a Christian doctrine of creation hark back to Romanticism and Idealism to find their arguments. Jürgen Moltmann (1926–) is one such influential example. Fairly early in his career the Reformed theologian essentially enlists the Idealist principle of reciprocal determination when he argues for a divine who is constituted by relation to the world and humanity,[75] just as the world and humanity are constituted by their relation to God. In a variety of texts he denounces theological voluntarism illustrated in the late medieval theology but also in Karl Barth, and counterintuitively claims that no authentic biblical theology supports divine sovereignty.[76] He wants, however, to avoid both a reduction of God to the world or human being and a logic of necessity, defining the latter in Spinozist-Idealist fashion as the absence of compulsion. The conception of divine expression in and as world is further refined in and through appeal to the Platonic-Neoplatonic trope of divine expressivity.[77] This is a key feature of his construal of the God-world relationship throughout his systematic theology, although he falls short of suggesting, as Bruno as well as Spinoza did, that creation is so expansive that there is no remainder of creativity in excess of what is actually created.

In addition, Moltmann shows also that modified forms of Idealism have a negative capability of making an ecological turn and joining forces with eco-feminism, thereby further imbricating as well as ramify-

ing ideas that crowd out classical theism.[78] The crowding out of the theistic view in turn permits—if not encourages—the tehomic views of the
order of creation such as one finds in the work of Catherine Keller,
which, if it is sympathetic to the work of Moltmann, has its philosophical foundations in process rather than Idealist thought. [79] The Tehom is
what is given aboriginally. Even if Genesis in one way tries to repress
this truth, it is unable to.[80] Although it is a postmodern speculative
metaphysics that is the vehicle for reflection on Tehom, it behooves the
commentator to point out that this issue is alive exegetically and finds
support in scholars of the Hebrew Bible (Jon Levenson), and is provided an opening at the very least by Karl Barth's famous reflection on
the Tehom under the auspices of *Das Nichtige*. Keller's view most certainly parses neither. Not only is there the methodological divide between the speculative metaphysician and the biblical scholar when it
comes to Tehom; compared with a biblical scholar like Levenson, she
both holds a view much more nearly monistic than his and, by the same
token, has a comic rather than tragic register. Keller supposes that
Tehom is the underside to a shaping and thus the contrary to the shaper
only to deconstruct the binary. In the beginning, which is also the end,
there is only the self-organization and destruction of Tehom. The deconstruction changes the tragic valence of the agon between shaping
and recalcitrant material that is the implication of the aboriginal binary.
The refusal of Levenson's reading of Tehom is by the same token the refusal of Barth's exegesis of Tehom in *Church Dogmatics*, which constructs it as setting a chaotic limit on divine power, only to insist in the
end—whether coherent or not—on divine sovereignty.

To sum up the basic drift of Keller, then, is to say that the tehomic
view that she elaborates in *The Face of the Deep*—whose theoretical
engine is supplied by process thought, whose ethos is feminist, and
whose style is literary—definitively cuts against absolute divine sovereignty and forecloses the possibility of *creatio ex nihilo* being anything
other than a masculinist attempt to indemnify an irresponsible divine
sovereignty and by implication to indemnify whatever political sover-
eignties are operative. On a higher order of reflection, the tehomic
view also points to the return of the repressed of the *khora* of the
Timaeus, which is neutralized as prime matter, even if as late as Augustine it remains an alternative to the *creatio ex nihilo* view to which he

pledges his allegiance.[81] Keller's *khora* neither is nor can be domesticated; that is, it does not and cannot submit to form and shaping.[82] In this sense, Keller is not simply bringing *khora* back into theological and philosophical circulation, but refiguring *khora* in a view that troubles all metaphysical binaries, those between God and world and those between human being and nature.

Importantly, Moltmann and Keller are simply two examples of modern theologians who are so critical of Jewish and Christian monotheism as basically to think it devoid of any contemporary purchase. They are quite literally exemplary in that one could find a myriad of other theologians who would repeat the pattern of refutation and constructive neglect. Again, typically, neither of these theologians has any time for crude naturalism. One could expect it to be treated with the same obloquy as straightforward species of theism. Moreover, it would not matter whether the naturalism was sponsored by Spinoza or the scientific positivism of the new atheists. One can notice a general tendency in contemporary theology that when it is not being apologetic vis-à-vis the modern scientific mentality, its construction of alternatives owes a considerable amount to the supernaturalistic inflection of naturalism—more precisely its emanationist inflection—which harks back to German Romanticism and Idealism.

Spinoza as Event

In this essay primarily I wanted to speak to a moment, that is, the seventeenth century, and a particular figure, Benedict de Spinoza, in which the tide turned against *creatio ex nihilo*. What is crucially important about Spinoza is not that he simply advocated a naturalistic view of the world, but that in his *Ethics* he provided a metaphysical legitimation of such a view. This is a key element of the genealogical case prosecuted in this essay. But it is not the only element. Even though the *Ethics* argues against both emanationist and prime-matter views of the divine-world relation as well as against *creatio ex nihilo*, in the reception of the *Ethics* the defeat of the traditional theistic view, whether couched in the provocative language of creation from nothing or simply insisting on creative fiat, makes these views once again contenders, though necessarily they will have to be refigured given modern assumptions about nature. Although Bruno's peculiar form of emanationism antedates Spinoza's work by almost a century and has a metaphysical antitheistic core that can be regarded as anticipating metaphysical positions argued in book 1 of the *Ethics*, nonetheless, it is Spinoza who makes the reception of such an emanationism possible in a world that has made a naturalist turn. This is particularly evident in the trajectories of German Romanticism and Idealism, although, arguably, Spinoza could also be thought of as making credible in the modern world an appeal to forms of emanationism less radical than that of Bruno even if he is not directly responsible for them.

Of course, how a Spinoza, initially perceived to be a reductive rationalist and an atheist, came to be perceived as supporting a natural supernaturalism or supernaturalism is a story which is as interesting as it is antecedently unlikely. The point is that it did happen, and thereafter in philosophy and theology Christian views of *creatio ex nihilo* not only have to contend with Spinozistic and non-Spinozistic forms of naturalism, but also with refigured forms of emanationism and, as we saw in our closing section with Keller, even views of prime matter. One is tempted to suggest that the field of discourse itself has become tehomic and that the classical view is simply one of many in an unceasing production of views in which it is by no means obvious that it is the dominant. But even if we shake off the hyperbole of chaos, though the *creatio ex nihilo* view or weaker analogues are difficult to extirpate from the Christian confessional traditions, at the very best they find themselves squeezed between and fighting against both reductive and elevated forms of naturalism (emanationism and even prime-matter theories). Given the history of successful challenge against *creatio ex nihilo*, which features Spinoza, it is evident not only that it is not generally accepted but that it has been structurally weakened—a weakening further aided and abetted by questions as to whether the doctrine of *creatio ex nihilo* is, strictly speaking, a biblical teaching. While recourse to articulations of creation from nothing in Nyssa, Augustine, and Aquinas in Christian thought and reflections in Jewish thinkers such as Philo and Crescas on divine activity that is not logically necessary still have their place, I want to suggest that Spinoza and his complex history of effects have entirely changed the basic field of argument. Spinoza and his theological and philosophical fallout have achieved this, on the one hand, by elevating naturalism and, on the other, by providing a set of alternatives to naturalism that still operate in terms of the logic of naturalism in forbidding absolute divine alterity and a view of the cosmos as fiat depending upon the "good pleasure" or the sheer goodness of God. The argumentative burdens have shifted: whereas in the premodern episteme the burden seemed to be on those who would argue against *creatio ex nihilo*, now the burden seems to be entirely on those who would argue for it.

NOTES

1. Arguably, from a genealogical point of view Hegel is foundational here and is followed in turn by Husserl and Heidegger, who themselves bear complicated relations to Hegel. If in the *Phenomenology* Hegel implies the revolutionary status of Descartes, he makes this status fully explicit in his lectures on modern philosophy. Although on the one hand, Husserl's transcendental phenomenology can be regarded as in line with Descartes's subjective turn, it is also evident that he has considerable reservations regarding it. His 1936 text on the crisis of European sciences gives the best evidence of it. The subjectivist turn inaugurated by Descartes, which ironically preserves rather than dismantles metaphysics, is a node in Heidegger's telling of the history of metaphysics. For succinct versions of this thesis, see Martin Heidegger, *The End of Philosophy*, trans. Joan Stambaugh (Chicago: University of Chicago Press, 2003). See also Heidegger's famous essay "Age of the World Picture," in *"The Question concerning Technology," and Other Essays*, trans. William Levitt (New York: Harper & Row, 1977), 115–54. This essay dates from the 1950s and had an incalculable effect on Richard Rorty's own major genealogical contribution, *Philosophy in the Mirror of Nature* (Princeton: Princeton University Press, 1981).

2. This might well have been Spinoza's own self-interpretation. Perhaps Cornelio Fabro is a genealogist who thinks of Spinoza in this way. See his *God in Exile: Modern Atheism* (Westminster, MD: Paulist Press, 1968).

3. Jonathan Israel, *Radical Enlightenment: Philosophy and the Making of Modernity (1650–1750)* (Oxford: Oxford University Press, 2001), 157–74, 23–57, 341–51; Israel, *Enlightenment Contested: Philosophy, Modernity, and the Emancipation of Man, 1670–1752* (Oxford: Oxford University Press, 2006), 43–50, 164–73, 444–70.

4. The forerunner in terms of giving the big picture of the shift of per-spective is Alexandre Koyré. See his still useful *From the Closed World to the Infinite Universe* (Baltimore: Johns Hopkins University Press, 1957). Perhaps the most comprehensive account of the shift to naturalism is provided by Hans Blumenberg. See his *The Genesis of the Copernican World*, trans. Robert M. Wallace (Boston: MIT Press, 1989).

5. I am borrowing this locution from M. H. Abrams, the great scholar of Romanticism. See his *Natural Supernaturalism: Tradition and Revolution in Romantic Literature* (New York: Norton, 1973).

6. Scholars of Spinoza, on the one hand, and Giordano Bruno, on the other, have drawn attention to the similarities. So also have a number of intellectual historians. Yet no one is actually suggesting a genetic link. For Spinoza, see Leon Roth, *Spinoza* (London: Ernst Benn LTD, 1929), 223; Harry Austryn Wolfson, *The Philosophy of Spinoza: Unfolding the Latent Processes in his Reasoning*, 2 vols. (Cambridge, MA: Harvard University Press, 1934), 388; also 285–86. For Bruno, see Lewis McIntyre, *Giordano Bruno* (London: Macmillan, 1903), 337–38. See also the introduction to Arthur D. Imerti's translation of *Spaccio de la bestia trionfante*, that is, *The Expulsion of the Triumphant Beast* (New Brunswick, NJ: Rutgers University Press, 1964), 37n285. The intellectual historian who has been most invested in making the connection between Bruno and Spinoza has been Arthur Lovejoy. See his *The Great Chain of Being* (Cambridge, MA: Harvard University Press, 1936), 116–21.

7. Philo is of particular importance, since his views on creation greatly influenced both Jewish and Christian thought. For Philo the Platonic prime-matter view matched up best with the creation account of Genesis. The crucial text is *De opificio mundi*.

8. The term "paramathematical" has been used regarding Bruno's work to differentiate the ideological function the appeal to mathematics serves in his case from the rigorous use of mathematics in the likes of scientists such as Galileo and Copernicus. Bruno is not the only practitioner. He is anticipated by Nicholas of Cusa. While a number of Cusa's books have mathematical ti-tles, more importantly he uses mathematical symbols such as "infinity" to a make important metaphysical and theological points.

9. One of the great paradoxes in Descartes is that having secured the foundation of certainty in the cogito, Descartes feels that the fundamental laws of nature are not autonomous and depend upon the will of God. Spinoza thinks that this is an act of intellectual cowardice. In general he is against any trace of what he construes of as theological voluntarism.

10. Wolfson established in his groundbreaking two-volume work on Spinoza that in addition to being engaged in a critical conversation with

Maimonides' views of the God-world relation as articulated in *The Guide of the Perplexed*, Spinoza is also involved in critical conversation with one of Maimonides' main critics on this point, that is, Hasdai Crescas (c. 1340–1411). What disturbed Crescas was Maimonides' apparent commitment to Aristotle's view of the eternity of the world and, more generally, his granting of philosophy prerogatives over the Torah, which would view creation as an act of a sovereign God.

11. Gershom Scholem still provides the best account of the variety of kabbalistic presentations of creation from the twelfth to the sixteenth century. See his *Major Trends in Jewish Mysticism* (London: Thames and Hudson, 1955).

12. See *Ethics*, trans. Edwin Curley (London: Penguin, 2005).

13. The most famous expression is to be found in a letter to Simon de Vries. For a convenient compilation of Spinoza's correspondences, see *Spinoza: The Letters*, trans. Samuel Shirley (Indianapolis: Hackett, 1995).

14. The other side of Parmenides' identification of being and thinking is that "nothing" (*me eon*) cannot be thought or spoken. See G. S. Kirk and J. E. Raven, *The Presocratic Philosophers* (Cambridge: Cambridge University Press, 1969), 269.

15. Leibniz's question "Why something rather than nothing?" was given a dramatic turn in a parallel structure: Why is there something, why nothing is not? (*Warum is überhaupt Etwas, warum ist Nichts nicht?*). See Karl Jaspers, *Schelling* (München: Piper, 1955), 124.

16. While for the most part modern scientists ignore the question of why anything at all, a physicist such as Stephen Hawking dismisses why questions as spurious, precisely because it is not a question that can be answered by science. This repeats the positivist circle that has been in operation since the beginning of the twentieth century.

17. As it operates in *Ethics*, bk. 1, the formula *Deus sive Natura* is not intended to suggest a strict equivalence between the biblical God and nature properly understood, but intended to suggest that nature plays the same role in being the explanation of mental and physical life without the handicaps of anthropomorphism.

18. While the term *Wirklichkeit* is deployed widely in German Idealism, it is a particular favorite of Hegel in different dimensions of his philosophy. It is used in Hegel's logic, for example, to point to the excess of actualization over mere potential. The location of *Wirklichkeit* is more consequent than ground as *Realitas* is in Spinoza, even if Hegel argues throughout both of his logics that the consequent is more nearly the ground than the would-be ground itself.

19. Quoted from *The Collected Works of Spinoza*, trans. Edwin Curley, vol. 1 (Princeton: Princeton University Press, 1985), 417, slightly modified.

20. In *Ethics*, bk. 2, def. 6, Spinoza identifies *Realitas* with perfection. In his letter to Louis Mayer (Letter 3), he identifies both with eternity properly thought. Spinoza is attempting to provide a definition of eternity that is positive and that is not entirely dependent on its contrast with time.

21. In bk. 1 of *Moreh Nebuchim* (*The Guide of the Perplexed*) Maimonides tries to remove all anthropomorphisms from God and to get to the fundamental attributes of the divine. Both the critique and the result had a significance influence on the thought of Aquinas, but also on Spinoza, who so readily dismisses imagination. Spinoza refuses, however, Maimonides' tendency to insist that the attributes of God are only relatively adequate.

22. On Spinoza's account in the *Tractatus* the proper function of the biblical text is practical rather than alethic: the Bible does not secure truth; it secures piety.

23. For the relation between Spinoza and German Idealism on the priority of wholeness, see Paul Franks, *All or Nothing: Systematicity, Transcendental Arguments, and Skepticism in German Idealism* (Cambridge, MA: Harvard University Press, 2005).

24. Here Spinoza's importance relative to this pair is not that he invented it, but rather that he gave it a new meaning. It surfaces in *Ethics*, bk. 1, prop. 29 note. *Natura naturans* refers to God and substance and the infinite attributes which are expressive of free causality. In contrast, *naturata* indicates the expression itself, which consists of infinite modes, thought and extension, and the finite physical and mental particulars or modes. Used in Renaissance Neoplatonism—especially in Bruno—to distinguish the dynamic force that transcends nature and that yet inheres in it, the pair corresponds pretty much with the relation-distinction of world soul–nature of classical Neoplatonism, which is below Nous and the One (or equivalent). In the *Ethics* there is no longer any ontological hierarchy. There is nothing above *natura naturans–natura naturata*.

25. See *Ethics*, bk. 2, prop. 7 note.

26. See also ibid., prop. 3 proof.

27. It is Leibniz who later validates this premodern point of view of the asymmetry of expression and ground against Spinoza's strict equivalence.

28. A more than usual amount of information about Spinoza's positions can be garnered from his letters. In Letter 60 Spinoza argues that necessity and freedom are not so much opposites as necessity and chance.

29. At one level, one could think of the kabbalistic view of the *Ain Sof* as providing a provocation. But throughout the philosophical tradition beginning with Plato in the *Sophist* 248–52, *mē ōn* is not absolute nothing. Aristotle tries to reverse in a Parmenidean direction by disambiguating senses of nothing and insisting in *De generatione et corruptione* and elsewhere that "nothing" be

used in an absolute sense. Maimonides is in the Aristotelian mode when in *The Guide of the Perplexed* (2:13) he suggests that since the essential cause of the problem is grammatical, specifically the preposition "from," there is good reason to substitute "after." This is a position followed by Aquinas. See *Summa Theologica* I.41.3 ad 3.

30. Although he makes no mention of Spinoza, Heidegger abjures Leibniz as well as Descartes. Leibniz is a prominent interlocutor when Heidegger writes his habilitation on the medieval doctrine of categories, and also in his 1928 reflection on the metaphysical foundation of logic, which focuses somewhat on Leibniz's principle of sufficient reason. Perhaps the sharpest critique of Leibniz is to be found in a post–*Being and Time* text. See *The Principle of Reason*, trans. Reginald Lilly (Bloomington: Indiana University Press, 1996).

31. In *The Guide of the Perplexed* Maimonides regarded Aristotle's view of the eternity of the world to be superior philosophically to the voluntarist and punctiliar view of creation by thinkers in the tradition of the Kalam anxious to remain true to the picture of the God-world relation depicted in the Qur'an.

32. Theological voluntarism, the view that God's will is decisive in creating the world, is definitely illustrated by the Reformers, who emphasize God's "good pleasure" in creation. Of course, the Bible and more particularly a commitment to literal interpretation are major factors in this outcome. For example, in his interpretation of the Genesis creation narrative Luther angrily dismisses Augustine's attempt to remove temporal-narrative indices from the act of creation, which indices reinforce the view of creation as entirely an act of God as the agent of agents. On the theological level proper, Luther's voluntarism was anticipated by William of Ockham, who departed from the position of Aquinas by insisting that will was higher than reason in God, not coextensive with it.

33. In forms of theology influenced by Neoplatonism, aseity admits of a positive definition as the unsurpassable plenitude of being. In significant part, however, from the medieval into the modern philosophical and theological tradition the functional definition was more negative: with respect to God nothing is needed for existence (*nulla rei indiget ad existandum*).

34. Spinoza radicalizes Descartes's view of imagination, which is connected with passion. Imagination constructs a world that does not correspond to the world as it really is. While the construction is a palliative in the short run, in the long run it really cuts against self-interest, since its falseness leads to frustration. Scholars are right to point to the Stoic heritage of Spinoza, which also implies that he thinks philosophy is a form of therapy. Important in this respect is the treatise *The Improvement of the Understanding* (1659).

35. See *Ethics*, bk. 4, preface; also bk. 1, appendix.

36. See *Ethics*, bk. 4, props. 8 and 9; also bk. 3, prop. 39 note.

37. Jonathan Israel, *Radical Enlightenment*, 242–57.

38. Pierre Bayle, *Dictionaire Historique et Critique*, 4 vols. (1684–88).

39. Bayle was anxious to bring to attention that the fact that forms of du-alism (Manichaean and otherwise) and the prime-matter view of creation had been sidelined in the Western tradition by no means proved that they were any less credible from a conceptual point of view. In fact Bayle thought that when it came to the problem of evil, both of these views enjoyed advantages over the theistic view in that God was not directly responsible for evil. Hume's *Dialogues concerning Natural Religion* (1776) depends on Bayle's account both for the sense of the variety of live options when it comes to thinking of the origin of the physical order and of evil and the relative disadvantages of the theistic position.

40. This is a tendency in the classical Kabbalah in which the inexpressible divine ground—the *Ain Sof*—is associated with *ayin* or nothing.

41. The crucial philosophical thinker is Plotinus, who in the *Enneads* (1.6; 2.9) generates the notion of evil being the privation of good in his attempt to rebut the gnostics, who make evil into a substance (material substance). As is well known, Augustine depends on Plotinus for his notion of evil as privation as he finds himself in an analogous situation of refuting the Manichaeans, who also made evil into a principle and imagined it to be a substance of some sort.

42. Among scholars drawing attention to the correspondence between Spinoza and Bruno from the side of Spinoza, see H. A. Wolfson, *The Philosophy of Spinoza*, 33ff., 285–86; Leon Roth, *Spinoza*, 223. Independents such as Arthur Lovejoy also see a close connection. See his famous text *The Great Chain of Being*, 116–21.

43. These are perhaps the two most important texts in addition to *Spaccio*, which has been cited already. Two other texts in which Bruno's appeal to mathematics rather than use of it to change our cosmological picture are *De monade numero et figura* (1591) and *De innumerabilibus, immenso, et infigura-bilii* (1591). For convenient English translations of these texts, see *Cause, Principle, and Unity: Five Dialogues*, trans. Jack Lindsay (Castle Hedingham, Essex: Damon Press, 1962); and for *De l'infinito*, see the translation provided by Dorothea Waley Singer in her *Giordano Bruno: His Life and Thought* (New York: Henry Schuman, 1950).

44. See Singer, *Giordano Bruno*, 260.

45. Bruno's notion of infinite worlds certainly unsettled the received cos-mology and on its own would have drawn similar ire to that shown to Galileo and Copernicus. But Bruno added to the provocation by insisting on an ab-solute origin that he showed no inclination to identify with the triune God of Catholic faith.

46. See Singer, *Giordano Bruno*, 257.

47. See ibid.

48. Bruno, *Opera latine conscripta*, vol. 1, pt. 1 (Charleston, SC: Nabu Press, 2010), 72.

49. Bruno, *Expulsion of the Triumphant Beast*, 135.

50. Bruno, *Cause, Principle, and Unity*, 136.

51. Bruno, *Expulsion of the Triumphant Beast*, 135.

52. Ibid., 135–36.

53. Israel's treatment of the effect of the *Tractatus* is exemplary. See *Radical Enlightenment*, 218–27, 275–85. See also Brayton Polka, *Between Philosophy and Religion: Spinoza, the Bible, and Modernity*, vol. 1, *Hermeneutics and Ontology* (Lanham, MD: Lexington Books, 2007).

54. Israel makes much of this point. See *Radical Enlightenment*, ch. 18, "Bayle and the 'Virtuous Atheist,'" 331–41.

55. See Gérard Vallée, *The Spinoza Conversations between Lessing and Jacobi*, trans. G. Vallée et al. (Lanham, MD: University Press of America, 1987).

56. Here a crucial role is played by Friedrich Schiller, who long before Marx speaks to technology demanding a differentiation of labor that was alienating. Schiller also offered a solution in which art played more of a role of healing than either religion or philosophy. The pivotal text is *Über die ästhetische Erziehung des Menschens in einer Reihe von Breifen* (1794). For an English translation, see *The Aesthetic Education of Man*, trans. Reginald Snell (New York: Dover, 2004; first published by Yale University Press, 1954).

57. In his attack on Lessing, Jacobi pointed to Goethe's 1776 poem on this figure as constitutive of the relay of Spinozistic thought in the late eighteenth century. See Vallée, *Spinoza Conversations*, 21–23, 25, 26, 48–51. Hans Blumenberg seems to underscore the importance of this poem in a major shift of ideology from standard theism to a more world-affirming ideology. See his *Work on Myth*, trans. Robert M. Wallace (Cambridge, MA: MIT Press, 1985). Although surely, like Hegel, Hölderlin is interested in Greek religion as an alternative to Christianity, he is not beyond thinking through the philosophical basis of a movement beyond theism. See my essay "Aesthetic Idealism and its Relation to Theological Formation: Reception and Critique," in *The Impact of Idealism: The Legacy of Post-Kantian German Thought*. vol. 4, *Religion*, ed. Nicholas Adams (Cambridge: Cambridge University Press, 2013), 142–66.

58. Still it is interesting that some of the best scholarship of the twentieth century, as well as some of Spinoza's most creative interpreters such as Gilles Deleuze, concur. For Deleuze, see *Expressionism in Philosophy: Spinoza*, trans. Martin Joughin (New York: Zone Books, 1992). See also, Peter Hallward, *Out of This World: Deleuze and the Philosophy of Creation* (London: Verso, 2006).

59. See Plotinus, *Enneads* 3.8, "On Nature, Contemplation, and the One."

60. I am referring here to Cusa's famous notion of coincidence of opposites of maximum and minimum, which mathematical model he applies to God. *De docta ingnorantia* (*On Learned Ignorance*) (1440) provides just one example of a pattern of extrapolation and instruction that pervades Cusanus's large corpus.

61. Bruno is perhaps clearest on transdiscursive knowledge in his highly allusive and elusive *De gli eroici furori*, which was translated into English by the great Renaissance man of letters Sir Philip Sidney. See Charles Nelson, *The Renaissance Theory of Love: The Context of Bruno's "Eroici Furori"* (New York: Columbia University Press, 1958), 190–92, 204.

62. In fact in *Eroici furori* Bruno distinguishes between three kinds of knowledge, each associated with a mythological figure: the realm of sense knowledge is associated with Circe; knowledge of nature is associated with Diana; knowledge of the invisible power in nature with Apollo. While the second and third are closely connected as in Spinoza in *Ethics*, bk. 5, the third form of knowledge involves a qualitatively higher apprehension of reality.

63. In *Eroici furori*, in line with Cusanus and more generally with the classical and Christian Neoplatonic traditions, Bruno thinks that because of lack of separation between subject and object, transdiscursive knowledge is not necessarily the clearest. Spinoza thinks otherwise.

64. The distinction between Bruno and Spinoza on this point is also the distinction between Hegel and the Schelling of the *System of Transcendental Idealism* (1799). This is also Schelling's position in his Identity-Philosophy book of 1804, which has the name Bruno in the title. While this is not an exegetical work, it does use Bruno's *Cause, Principle, and Unity* as a frame for philosophical reflection. See *Bruno, or On the Natural and Divine Principle of Things*, ed. and trans. Michael Vater (Albany: State University of New York Press, 1984).

65. See Vallée, *Spinoza Conversations*, 36–45.

66. For Herder the key text is *Gott: Einige Gespräche* (1787). For an English translation, see *God, Some Conversations*, trans. Frederick H. Burkhardt (Indianapolis: Bobbs-Merrill, 1940). Burkhardt in his fine introduction sums up Herder's position historically as a Romantic kind of Spinozism and systematically as a form of Spinoza that has been modified by Leibnizian ideas of infinity (3–64).

67. I am thinking here of Hölderlin's philosophical fragment "Being and Judgment" ("Sein und Urteil"). For discussion of the early philosophical orientation of Hölderlin, see Dieter Henrich, *Between Kant and Hegel: Lectures on German Idealism* (Cambridge, MA: Harvard University Press, 2003), 279–95; *The Course of Remembrance and Other Essays on Hölderlin*, ed. Eckhart Förster (Stanford, CA: Stanford University Press, 1997), 104–8.

68. This insight, basic to German Idealism, and crucial later in process theology of the sort found in Hartshorne, is the discovery of Fichte. See his *Wissenschaftslehre* (1794).

69. The commitment to a self-transcending nature is characteristic of all of Hölderlin's poetry, but perhaps receives its most vehement expression in early verse dramas such as *Hyperion* and *The Death of Empedocles* (c. 1800).

70. See G. W. F. Hegel, *Lectures on the History of Philosophy*, vol. 2, *Plato and the Platonists*, trans. E. S. Haldane and Frances H. Simson (Lincoln: University of Nebraska Press, 1995). See especially section 2 on the Neoplatonists (374–453).

71. For a good account of Schelling's *Naturphilosophie* and its struggle with the more empirical orientation toward science in Germany in the nineteenth century, see Joseph L. Esposito, *Schelling's Idealism and Philosophy of Nature* (Lewisburg, PA: Bucknell University Press, 1977).

72. Coleridge's knowledge of Spinoza is considerable. He is reported to have read his works, and Coleridge also followed with great interest Spinoza's reception in Romantic and Idealist Germany. Perhaps the scholar who has plumbed deepest into Coleridge's interest in, but resistance of, Spinoza is Thomas McFarland. See his *Coleridge and the Pantheist Tradition* (Oxford: Clarendon Press, 1969).

73. Coleridge was perhaps the most knowledgeable person in England on what Frances Yates refers to as the "hermetic tradition." He likely had read Bruno in Latin. In any event, as is apparent from his comments in *The Friend* (1809), he had read Bruno in the translation of Sidney.

74. Jonathan Israel sees Spinoza's view of science still having influence with the philosophes, despite the general victory of the empirical method in science. See *Radical Enlightenment*, ch. 37, "From La Mettrie to Diderot," 704–13. One could complement what he says by observing that Neoplatonism plays a major role in the *Encyclopédie* in two different ways: (i) Formally, in that quite literally the "encyclopedia" is imaged as a circle of knowledge at least in terms of aspiration. The recall of the *exitus-reditus* pattern of Neoplatonism is not accidental. (ii) More substantively, even in the very materialist D'Alembert nature is not reductively materialistic. There is at the very least the ghost of *anima mundi*.

75. This is certainly the case with *The Crucified God*, written in 1972 and translated into English in 1974. The clearest expression, however, is to be found in a somewhat later text, *Trinity and the Kingdom*, trans. Margaret Kohl (San Francisco: Harper & Row, 1981), 57–60.

76. Moltmann, *Trinity and the Kingdom*, 52–56.

77. Ibid., 57.

78. See Moltmann, *God in Creation* (London: SCM Press, 1986); also Moltmann, *The Spirit of Life: A Universal Affirmation* (London: SCM Press, 1992).

79. Catherine Keller, *The Face of the Deep: A Theology of Becoming* (New York: Rutledge, 2003).

80. Keller bears a close relationship to the biblical scholar Jon Levenson here. Levenson has written persuasively of the "agonistic" view of creation in the Bible, a view in which *tehom* represents a limit on God's power. See his *Creation and the Persistence of Evil* (San Francisco: Harper & Row, 1986).

81. See Augustine, *Confessions*, bks. 12, 13.

82. Keller confesses that she is indebted to Derrida's highly formal interpretation of *khora*, which does not assume that it is part of a pair. In the end, however, she also leaves Derrida behind precisely because the formality of his view gets in the way of an activist politics, but also in the way of the process metaphysics to which she subscribes.

CHAPTER 12

The Doctrine of Creation and the Problem of the Miraculous in the Modern Theology of Friedrich Schleiermacher

RUTH JACKSON

AN ETERNAL TREATY?

In his opening contribution to a collection of essays titled *Creation 'ex nihilo' and Modern Theology*, David Burrell—a scholar long preoccupied with the doctrine of creation and its theological consequences—contended that modern Western philosophy has "found it necessary to render *creatio ex nihilo* obsolete." Whereas medieval theologians stressed the presence of an absolutely free creator (a move that distinguished them from the ancients), modern philosophy, Burrell explains, sought to "distinguish itself by eliminating the theological overtones of the 'scholastics,' [and] proceeded by avoiding reference to a creator."[1] Such avoidance, he continues, was exemplified by the critical philosophy of

Immanuel Kant, for whom questions about the origins of the universe were designated as lying beyond the grasp of reason and rational enquiry, and were thus also understood to be outside of the boundaries of responsible and constructive discourse. If Thomas Aquinas emphasized the "non-reciprocal relationship of dependence"[2] that takes place between worldly creatures and their Almighty Creator, then by contrast, Burrell writes, the stress within the philosophy of the Enlightenment was upon human autonomy and the deductive and constructive power of individual thinking. By the nineteenth century, philosophical minds had ceased to rely upon appeals to a creator, and thus *creatio ex nihilo* "was nearly totally eclipsed."[3]

The modern theologian-philosopher that we will study in the present essay—Friedrich Daniel Ernst Schleiermacher (1768–1832)—could very well be used in order to buttress Burrell's broad narrative about the modern philosophical disposal of creation "*ex nihilo*." For as he developed the method and approach of his dogmatic theology, Schleiermacher did indeed take seriously the stringent limits that Kant's critical philosophy placed upon human reason. He stressed that Christian faith cannot be founded, premised, or sustained as a communal endeavor upon the notion of the "existence of God," as if the latter were a rationally demonstrable fact.[4] He was also careful to teach that Christian doctrines themselves—including that of creation—cannot be proved or established by the light of human reason,[5] and that the task of dogmatics is not a constructive endeavor driven by systematic argumentation. Instead, Schleiermacher understood dogmatics as a branch of constructive historical theology,[6] and as a discipline concerned with ordering, arranging, and elaborating teachings. We should not expect to see poetic or metaphorical language deployed in his *Glaubenslehre*, nor do we find the sort of rhetorical language that he would employ in the task of preaching.[7] This is because for Schleiermacher, dogmatics is a technical task, which has a "dialectical" character and concerns the constant refinement of statements about the Christian faith.[8] "Dogmatic propositions are doctrines of the descriptively didactic type," he wrote, "in which the highest possible degree of definiteness is aimed at."[9] And dogmatics itself is "the science," he continues, "of the relations between the doctrines in a Christian church society at a given time."[10]

Schleiermacher also understood dogmatics to be a closed discipline, insofar as it is reserved for those who possess the faith of the church in question—in his own case the Prussian Evangelical (Protestant) Church. There is an inner experience to which all dogmas can be traced, he wrote: "They rest upon a *given*, and apart from this they could not have arisen, by deduction or synthesis, from universally recognized and communicable principles."[11] Far from resting merely with the collection and expression of that which is inward, Schleiermacher construed dogmatics as a social task, which proceeds in service of the church's teachers and members in their capacity as preachers and hearers of the gospel.[12] And yet in sum, Schleiermacher's approach to dogmatics was such that he insulated his own *Glaubenslehre* from the non-confessional domain of speculative philosophy.[13] Whereas he opened the former with the doctrine of creation, and with a commitment to the received language of God as Almighty—as "theon pantocratora"—within the sphere of philosophy he would expect no such appeals to a transcendent creator.

Schleiermacher's tendency to carefully differentiate the work of dogmatics from the methodological approach and interests of other disciplines continued in his dealings with the natural sciences. Again, and as was the case with philosophy, Schleiermacher did not conceive theology and science to be necessarily antagonistic. In an oft-quoted letter to his friend Dr. Lücke, published in 1829 (the second edition of his great dogmatic work, *The Christian Faith*, would follow in 1830–31), Schleiermacher spoke of the need to establish an "eternal covenant," or "treaty" (*ewiger Vertrag*) between the Christian faith and scientific enquiry, according to which "faith does not hinder science and science does not exclude faith."[14] The stress here seems to be on the freedom of both disciplines: Schleiermacher communicates the idea that theology and science should proceed independently from one another, and that each should not presume to shape or to ground the activity of the other. He then turns to qualify this, however, with the point that the two disciplines should not seek to define themselves in isolation or opposition to each other, so as to promote a dichotomized view of their intentions and practices. "Shall the tangle of history so unravel," he demanded, "that Christianity becomes identified with barbarism, and science with unbelief?"[15]

A major reason why Schleiermacher raised the matter of the relation between theology and science, it emerges, is that he was anxious about the impact of scientific discourse upon the language and imagery available to Christian theologians, as the latter seek to work through and communicate the content of their faith in a fruitful and coherent manner. And in this same letter to Lücke, we find that his anxiety about science's influence is particularly evident in regard to the idea of creation and the suggestion of the world's absolute beginning "out of nothing." Indeed, conscious that the theology of creation is called into question both by scientific modes of enquiry (the methods through which scientists study the world as well as the types of questions they have about it) and the body of knowledge that science has wrought about natural processes and objects, Schleiermacher admits the following:

> I can only anticipate that we must learn to do without what many are still accustomed to regard as inseparably bound to the essence of Christianity. I am not referring to the six-day creation, but to the concept of creation itself, as it is usually understood, apart from any reference to the Mosaic chronology and despite all those rather precarious rationalizations that interpreters have devised. How long will the concept of creation hold out against the power of a world view constructed from undeniable scientific conclusions that no one can avoid, especially now, when the secrets of the experts concern only the method and detail of the sciences, but their great results will soon be accessible to every enlightened and knowledgeable person throughout the general public?[16]

In his line about the "power of a world view" threatening the conceptual viability of "creation," we infer that Schleiermacher's concerns here stem from his perception that science provides a narrative about the world's structure and character that, in the hearts and imaginations of the Prussian public, could potentially compete with or undermine the Christian narrative. As the natural sciences "increasingly develop into a comprehensive knowledge of the world," Schleiermacher writes, and if this knowledge is disseminated as some sort of a "map," then "what do you suppose the future holds," he asks, "not only for our theology, but for our evangelical Christianity?"[17]

In light of this pressure from science, which has established itself in the popular mind-set as a distinct authority on the world and its nature, Schleiermacher's recommendation to Christian dogmaticians is that they should refrain from trying to fence in church teaching from the "assaults of sound [scientific] research." Instead, he writes, they should make themselves ready for inevitable changes in the way that they will have to think about and communicate their faith. They must, in other words, "make do with history as it develops."[18]

What Schleiermacher is proposing here is not a deferral to sheer theological liberalism. He taught that in order for doctrine to be sound, it must be consistent with scripture[19] and must not be informed or led to a "significant" extent by "pressures from outside of the Church."[20] With his recommendation that theologians "make do with history as it develops," then, and his suggestion that they attend to difficult scientific data as they emerge, he does not address church doctrine as if it were an ancient body of teaching that is *now* ripe for change, at this very point in time and in relation to scientific enquiry, in order to save Christianity for the people and to keep its teaching "relevant" to modern concerns. Rather—and returning to what we noted above about his view of dogmatics as a "historical" discipline—the assumption behind Schleiermacher's words here is that church doctrine has never actually been "fixed," in the sense that the content and structure of its formulations has never been isolated from the world, from the practice of reinterpretation, or from the historical development of language and human culture. Indeed, such is the complexity and detail of doctrine for Schleiermacher, and such is the historical and social nature of human knowledge, that his suggestion, we remember, is that "a dogmatic presentation confines itself to the doctrine existing at a certain time." And although this much is "seldom expressly avowed" about the nature of doctrine, Schleiermacher explains, "it nevertheless seems to be a matter of course; and this seems, for the most part, to be the only possible explanation of the large number of dogmatic presentations which follow upon one another."[21]

Schleiermacher is critical of dogmaticians who seek to shield theology from the results of scientific enquiry, then, because for him, this willingness to cloister the task of dogmatics reveals a preparedness likewise to ossify doctrine—to freeze it in time and to fail to acknowledge its intrinsically *mobile* quality. Such dogmaticians, he writes, risk making doctrine "appear to everyone outside [the church] as an unreal ghost to which they must pay homage if they want to receive a proper burial."[22] To understand the properly "mobile"[23] quality of Christian orthodoxy, by contrast, means for him that the church must not only "hold fast to what is already generally acknowledged" but also "make room for still other modes of apprehension." This is his way of stating that the Christian faith itself is living: that it is a diachronic "consciousness" of God, whom Christians recognize as the eternal "*Whence*" of all receptive and active existence—the Supreme Being upon whom they depend absolutely.[24] And since Schleiermacher construes such faith precisely as a temporal response to the love of God—love he believes to be consummated in the incarnation[25]—in his view, it does not make sense to say that the content of Christian faith can be fixed or pinned down by a single generation of church members. If modern scientific discourse threatens to render the conceptual currency of "creation" obsolete, then, just as it also calls into question those miracles that scripture attributes to Jesus and the apostles, Schleiermacher encourages dogmaticians to respond to such "threats" by seizing them as an opportunity for rediscovering and reasserting that which is essential to the Christian faith, and that which cannot be overwritten by science. In the following passage, taken from the same open letter to Lücke, he hopes that he has been able to achieve this mode of approach in his own dogmatics. We read:

> I thought I should show as best I could that every dogma that truly represents an element of our Christian consciousness can be so formulated that it remains free from entanglements with science. I set this task for myself especially in my treatment of the doctrines of creation and preservation. This latter doctrine influenced in this regard my account of miracles and even the miracle of miracles, the appearance of the redeemer. I hope that even this teaching has been elaborated in such a way that it will not endanger the faith and that science need not declare war against us. . . . As long as we do not need to draw boundaries between what is natural and what is absolutely supernatural in actual reality (and I see nothing that requires us to do so), we can also allow science the freedom to take into its crucible all facts of interest to us and to see what kinds of analogies it discovers.[26]

KEEPING CREATION

Thus far, I have sought to introduce Schleiermacher as a theologian for whom the language of creation had been rendered contentious both by the researches of natural science, which had problematized the notion of miraculous, and the activity and outlook of the discipline of speculative philosophy, which emphasized the autonomy of rational human individuals. Having noted this about the pressures operating on Schleiermacher as he developed his theology of creation, however, in the remainder of this piece I will seek to demonstrate that although these pressures *are* evident in his work (as he himself recognizes), they did not prevent him from developing a fruitful doctrine of creation—a doctrine that not only was consistent with received Christian teaching but also functioned as the frame or scaffolding for his dogmatic project as a whole.

The distinctive nature of Schleiermacher's attention to the doctrine of creation and its influence upon the rest of his dogmatic theology are topics that have already preoccupied Anglo-American scholars like Katherine Sonderegger, Brian Gerrish, and Robert Sherman.[27] All three have drawn attention to the fact that Schleiermacher is not interested in creation as a cosmogenic question, and that he does not construe it in his dogmatics as a distant, merely originary "event"—as a "big-bang," or the flicking of a trigger-switch which is spatiotemporally removed from the here and now of present human experience. Instead, Schleiermacher's way of narrating creation is interesting not least because he stresses the indelible unity of this divine act with the divine purpose both in preserving the world and redeeming it. To put it another way, Schleiermacher articulates creation as a single, steadfast and eternal act—one with which God not only causes or initiates the created order but also sustains it in being, according to the eternal generosity, love, and wisdom of his Word.[28] Divine creation, which Schleiermacher thus teaches is identical in its scope and compass to the act of divine preservation, is *the* act which underwrites and informs Christian doctrines about divine action in general. In Schleiermacher's view, to affirm that God creates "out of nothing" means affirming that the totality of finite being is absolutely dependent upon God for its existence, and that this is the case always and at every moment of human history.[29]

Like Gerrish, Sonderegger, and Sherman, I am convinced that Schleiermacher's doctrine of creation has a foundational and structurally

significant role in his dogmatic scheme as a whole, and that it also reflects (as Sonderegger in particular points out) his approach to the task
of theology more broadly conceived, revealing his perspective on the
nature of faith and the limits of human knowledge.[30] In order to draw
this out further, then, let us now turn to the question of how, in his
Glaubenslehre, Schleiermacher harnesses creation as a means for speaking of God as creator and for portraying the relation between him and
his creation.

ALL THAT GOD KNOWS, IS

Having spent four whole sections introducing the doctrine of creation (§36–39) by insisting on its confluence with that of divine preservation, Schleiermacher proceeds to elaborate the doctrine proper over
the course of only two, slim sections (§40–41). And across these two
sections, his emphasis is on establishing the transcendent otherness of
God as creator and God's sovereignty over the world that he has made.
In the first, for instance, Schleiermacher tells his readers to deny "every
representation of the origin of the world which excludes anything whatever from origination by God, or which places God under those conditions and antitheses which have arisen in and through the world."[31] The
latter part of this imperative is set against anthropomorphizing the object of Christian worship. Nothing of the finite should be projected
onto God, Schleiermacher avers, or attributed to his nature. God's will
to create is determined neither by time nor space, nor by any other
worldly category, and his nature and identity as creator is beyond the
boundaries of human knowledge and linguistic categories. Yet with the
first part of his imperative, where he defines God alone as the sovereign
creator of the world, Schleiermacher also avoids rendering God—as a
factor of this stated unknowability—merely as a "mystery," or a vague
otherness. Here we find God appealed to as an actor. He is named as
the author of all that.

Schleiermacher's resistance to anthropomorphism continues in his
second section on creation, where he switches to the language of divine
agency or action in order to describe the concept. "The origin of the
world must be traced entirely to the divine activity," Schleiermacher
explains, "but not in such a way that this activity is thought as resem-

bling human activity."[32] It is at this point that Schleiermacher also confirms the specific teaching that God created "out of nothing," a teaching according to which divine creation is "raised above mere formation," he writes, so long as we refrain from thinking in terms of the Aristotelian category of "ἐξ οὖ," which gives the impression of a craftsman working upon preexistent matter. By affirming the doctrine of creation "out of nothing," Schleiermacher also resists the idea that creation was a necessary event—an automatic issuing or extension "*ex deo*," brought about by that which "comes naturally" to God. And in the postscript to this section he pushes this point further, as he articulates creation instead as an act which God wills absolutely freely and gratuitously, eternally and steadfastly, without limit or qualification.[33]

Of course, this language Schleiermacher introduces concerning God's "absolute freedom" in creation prompts a raft of secondary questions about the nature of such freedom, including what it implies about God's moral responsibility for that which he has made "*ex nihilo.*" It is beyond the scope of the present essay to deal with Schleiermacher's treatment of natural evil, or to detail his final teaching (which shapes this treatment) that God is love or his perspective (which issues from this) on the doctrine of election. What we must make clear here, however, is that Schleiermacher thinks there can be no "possible" room for God to act outside what is real, for if this were the case it would mean that God was in fact constrained in his agency—that in acting he was forced to choose one single and thus limited route over myriad postulated others. A little later in his dogmatics, Schleiermacher will clarify this point on freedom by asserting that divine agency could never be fruitfully described according to Leibniz's speculative notion that an omniscient, omnipotent, and omnibenevolent God will of his very nature create the "best of all possible worlds." Leibniz's formulation is problematic, Schleiermacher notes, because it elicits the idea of divine "selection" or deliberation—it suggests that the divine mind distends itself through a series of judgments of practical reason before electing to act this way or that.[34] With this in mind, the teaching about God's "free" agency that Schleiermacher approves is thus that "everything for which there is a causality in God happens and becomes real."[35] And as he does this, Schleiermacher also resolves that when trying to refine one's language about the nature of divine creation and agency, it is prudent in the end to hold *both* "freedom" and "necessity" as terms that sit in unresolved dialectical tension with one another. Only by deploying them together like this, Schleiermacher suggests—thereby suggesting a rich and ungraspable reality "behind" their distinction from one another—can these terms get us closer to fruitful imagery about God's creative agency. He writes:

> We must . . . think of nothing in God as necessary without at the same time positing it as free, nor as free unless at the same time it is necessary. Just as little, however, can we think of God's willing Himself, and God's willing the world, as separated the one from the other. For if He wills Himself, He wills Himself as Creator and Sustainer, so that in willing Himself, willing the world is already included; and if He wills the world, in it He wills His eternal and ever-present omnipotence, wherein willing Himself is included; that is to say, the necessary will is included in the free, and the free in the necessary.[36]

With Schleiermacher's points here about the constancy of the divine will, we return full circle to his insistence that the divine act in creating and preserving the universe is a single and unified fiat. In this eternal divine act, Schleiermacher teaches—which in the above excerpt he encourages us to call *both* free and necessary—the whole of nature, its organisms, processes, and products, is taken up into the knowledge and purpose of God, who in his steadfastness has known and willed all of these things that he creates from eternity. And indeed, it is not just a "cold," abstract, or disinterested knowledge of the world that Schleiermacher indicates God has of his creation. By clarifying that God's willing himself always already includes his willing the world, in the above passage Schleiermacher maintains God's sovereignty over the world as its creator. Yet far from *alienating* God from nature and natural processes, God's sovereign and eternal act, we are taught, is one which allows for such radical *intimacy* with the world that—as Saint Augustine put it in his *Confessions*, and as Saint Paul wrote to the Christians in Rome—God knows his creatures better than they are able to know themselves.[37] "God knows all that is," Schleiermacher concludes, "and all that God knows is, and these two are not twofold but single; for His knowledge and His almighty will are one and the same."[38]

A final thing to note here concerning Schleiermacher's presentation of God's agency is that this intimacy he recognizes between God and world translates into a firm rejection of the idea that there is any opposition or resistance between eternal divine causality and the temporal and material nature of worldly causality. Indeed, having stipulated that "the origin of the world must be represented as the event in time which conditions all change, but *not* so as to make the divine activity a temporal activity,"[39] Schleiermacher notes the following passage from Luther's commentary on the book of Genesis: "Everything which God has willed to create He created at that moment when He spake, though certainly everything does not at once appear before our eyes. . . . I am indeed something new . . . but . . . for God I have been born and preserved even from the beginning of the world, and this word when He said, 'Let us make man,' created me as well."[40] Luther's words here run counter to any image of God as needing to interrupt natural processes in order to govern his creation. And as Schleiermacher himself clarifies: we have a fruitful conception of what it means for God to create and to sustain the world "so long as we do not conceive of [God's] act as having ceased, and consequently imagine on the one side, in God, an alternation of activity and rest relatively to the world, and on the other side, in the world, an alternation between a determination of the whole through God and a determination of all single individuals through each other."[41]

THE ONE GREAT MIRACLE

We have seen that in his *Glaubenslehre*, Schleiermacher affirms God's absolute freedom as the creator of the universe and God's absolute sovereignty as an agent unbounded by time, space, or by the idea of that which is "possible." According to Schleiermacher there is nothing in excess of God's creation—whether actual or possible—and no stone is left unturned by him: everything God wills has been made actual. It is by extending this last point, furthermore, that Schleiermacher teaches that according to his absolute freedom, God's agency in the world is not opposed to natural causality or disruptive for natural processes. Eternity working on temporality, Wisdom drawing out purpose, and

Love outpoured in absolute gratuity—in Schleiermacher's view, God's creative and preservative action *perfects* nature, as Saint Thomas would say.[42] God communicates his grace to his creatures in and through creation, giving himself to creaturely eyes, whereas creaturely eyes could not see him as he is in himself.[43] Such is the nature of God's work, Schleiermacher explains, that "it has always been acknowledged by the strictest of dogmaticians that divine preservation, as the absolute dependence of all events and changes upon God, and natural causation, as the complete determination of all events by the universal nexus, are simply one and the same thing simply from different points of view, the one being neither separated from the other nor limited by it."[44]

To extend this point about Schleiermacher's vision of the relation between divine causality and natural causality, we note that this vision reflects his tendency—alongside his contemporaries in the Early German Romantic movement, of course[45]—to think of the natural world in terms of organic wholes. As Brian Gerrish has pointed out, according to this mode of thinking, Schleiermacher depicts God as a causal agent over and within the world *in its entirety*, and only as "cause" of particular events, objects, and processes, in terms of their emergence as part of this greater whole. And certainly, Schleiermacher anticipates the modern language of ecosystem, as he refers to the interdependence of the natural world—its "hanging-togetherness," or "Zusammenhang"— whereby each rock, tree, plant, and animal makes its way through a complex system of giving and taking from the world around it. Gerrish writes:

> Schleiermacher will not allow us to think of God as producing, like the human self, individual acts of will. His entire case for the coextensiveness of divine and natural causation seems, in fact, to have a very important implication for the idea of providence, one that puts him at loggerheads with Calvin: the unit of divine care, so to say, is the whole rather than its parts. If we may put the question a little crudely: Does it not follow that God ordains everything in general and nothing in particular? In a sense, I think the answer has to be yes. . . . The particular event, for Schleiermacher, is *included* in the activity of providence in the sense that it is a part of the whole system of nature.[46]

Having come thus far, then, we have the necessary material to anticipate Schleiermacher's approach to miracles and miraculous activity—to venture how he (to quote his letter to Lücke) ensured that his account of divine action "remains free from entanglements with science."[47] Schleiermacher's conclusion here is simple. When they are defined as an interruption in the laws of nature, or understood as an absolute in-breaking of the supernatural into the natural, then miracles hinder rather than help faith. Such "miracles," Schleiermacher claims, cannot be guaranteed as proofs either of the divine will or of the existence of God,[48] and in a number of cases, he laments, supernatural activity is attributed to a particular event or phenomenon simply in the absence of a "natural" explanation, which the work of science will no doubt eventually provide. If we are to avoid such pitfalls in faith—and if we are also to avoid denigrating nature itself, whose beauty can inspire piety even as and when it can be explained and "understood" by science,[49] then "as regards the miraculous," Schleiermacher writes: "The general interests of science, more particularly of natural science, and the interests of religion seem to meet at the same point, *i.e.* that we should abandon the idea of the absolutely supernatural, because no single instance of it can be known by us, and we are nowhere required to recognise it."[50]

Of course, the way that Schleiermacher treats the category of miracle in his dogmatics raises questions about his understanding of human redemption. This is firstly because the Christian tradition wishes to say that something *new* happens within creation with the coming of Christ, the savior of humanity. It teaches that in the incarnation God bestows an abundance of grace on the people he has created, who have all fallen away from him, and who must overcome sin and death in his love if they are to come into relationship with him again. Not only this, however, but Schleiermacher is also confronted with the orthodox Christian teaching that in the person of Christ we *are* dealing with the supernatural.[51] In Christ it is God himself who comes into the worldly and the natural, in order to heal and transform it.

In his aforementioned desire to avoid conflict with science, Schleiermacher does not neglect this radical teaching, which is the very core of the Christian gospel. Instead, Christ's redemptive mission is in fact the only place in his *Glaubenslehre* where he is willing to use the category of the miraculous in a straightforward and confident manner. Indeed, calling the incarnation *the* "one great miracle,"[52] he thereby indicates that God's graceful work in Christ is in a very real sense extra or surplus to the work of creation. And he also indicates, indeed, that what occurs in the incarnation is radical and transformative: it "interrupts" the natural course of worldly life. Yet as he preserves the category of miracle in this one, privileged sense, what Schleiermacher does not lose is his commitment to the idea that God enjoys an intimacy with the world, as well as to the notion that the divine will is brilliantly unified. "The maxim everywhere underlying our presentation [of Christ's work]," Schleiermacher explains, is "that the beginning of the Kingdom of God is a supernatural thing, which, however, becomes natural as soon as it emerges into manifestation."[53] And maintaining that God's will to redeem is the secret and ever-historically-unfolding center of his original and steadfast will to create, Schleiermacher also states the following: "That one great miracle, the mission of Christ, has, of course, the aim of restoration, but it is the restoration of what free causes have altered in their own province, not in that of the nature-mechanism or in the course of things originally altered by God."[54] For in Christ and through Christ, Schleiermacher suggests, there is a wonderful purpose written into every particle, cell, and plant of nature itself—a purpose given in God's original act of creation. Christ is eternally the one in whom and through whom all are created, and is eternally the one through whom all are saved. This is, in other words, Schleiermacher's reading of the prologue of John's Gospel: "All things came into being through him, and without him not one thing came into being" (John 1:3). And at the close of Schleiermacher's dogmatics, we read, accordingly, that "everything in our world would have been disposed otherwise, and the entire course of human events would have been different, if the divine purpose had not been set on the union of the Divine Essence with human nature in the Person of Christ, and, as a result thereof, the union of the Divine Essence with the fellowship of believers through the Holy Spirit."[55]

THE SAME SHARED WORLD

In the above we have suggested that Schleiermacher developed a sound doctrine of creation—a doctrine which attested divine freedom, and which retained the idea that something *new* is achieved and brought forth as God wills the redemption of humanity through his Son, Jesus Christ. Furthermore, we have also shown that Schleiermacher maintained a framework for thinking about divine agency whereby God is not rendered absent from the world, nor is he separated from natural causality or opposed to nature. Instead, Schleiermacher taught that God gives himself to his creatures *through* the world, and that this world of nature, as Calvin famously put it, is thus "a theatre for God's glory."

Schleiermacher's assertion that the seen, spoken of, and inhabited world cannot be a locus for the "purely" supernatural is of course perfectly consistent with orthodox Christian teachings about the radical transcendence of the divine and the finite limits of human perception. In Schleiermacher's particularly *modern* case, however, we have seen that this assertion leads him to the insight that the eyes of faith share and delight in the same real and true world which is studied by the natural sciences, and the same world which is also abstracted from by practitioners of speculative philosophy. Indeed, for Schleiermacher, confessional theology can happily coexist alongside these other disciplines, and this is the case not least because God himself will never become an "object" for scientific enquiry—whose tools are not sharpened so as to see him—and nor will his agency within the world become such an object. Instead, Schleiermacher's point is that if an individual takes up a life of faith, then this means it has been given to him to take up a "higher" way of inhabiting the world—a higher way of appreciating the world's inherent value, as that which has been made by God.[56]

It is important to emphasize this notion that science and faith share a world and a reality for Schleiermacher. For in light of the notorious way he describes faith in his *Glaubenslehre*, as "the *feeling* of absolute dependence" (*das schlechthinnige Abhängigkeitsgefühl*), it is all too commonly received and taught about him that he is a subjectivist theologian—a thinker who focuses on the inner and the emotional and who reduces religious belief to a function of individual human self-consciousness.[57] In our attention to his doctrine of creation, however, we have prepared the ground to resist this prevalent idea that Schleiermacher understands and portrays religious faith merely as the outward projection of subjective, inwardly cultivated feelings. Indeed, given his depiction of God as sovereign creator, we are led to suggest instead that when he speaks of a "feeling of absolute dependence," Schleiermacher is in fact highlighting the self's recognition that it is finite, and finite in the sense that it cannot ground itself, but is grounded instead in him who creates all things. To put it another way: Schleiermacher takes God to be the source and life of individual consciousness, and the "feeling" he speaks of is the self's passive appreciation of this fact.[58]

In the following passage this much becomes clear, because here Schleiermacher explains that what an individual believer recognizes and appreciates in this "feeling of absolute dependence" is in fact a condition common to all human life. We read: "The feeling of absolute dependence [*das schlechthinnige Abhängigkeitsgefühl*], in which our self-consciousness in general represents the finitude of our being [cf. §8.2], is not an accidental element, or a thing which varies from person to person, but is a universal element of life; and the recognition of this fact entirely takes the place, for the system of doctrine, of all the so-called proofs of the existence of God."[59] Here, then, Schleiermacher teaches that Christian faith begins with a gesture of the precarious self—the fragile and *absolutely dependent* subject—who recognizes that everything she has and is has come to her from without, as a gift.

The World Is Not the Ground of Human Action

I have sought to demonstrate that a significant advantage of Schleiermacher's doctrine of creation is its admission of Christianity's unavoidable "worldliness"—its message that believers must find God *through* his creation. What I want to do in closing, however, is to attach a qualifier to this statement, and one we take on from our last point about Schleiermacher's understanding of faith. The qualifier is simply the following: that with his definition of faith as a "feeling of absolute dependence," Schleiermacher is in a position to take up a more radical stance on the relation of faith to science, or on the nature of miracles, than he actually does.

For stated in Schleiermacher's definition of faith is that the world itself is not the ground of human thought or action—the world, he asserts, is not what provides stability or truth for hearts and minds. Rather, the world in the totality of its causal relationships is ever-changing, and it thus has a radical provisionality to it. In the first part of his *Glaubenslehre*, Schleiermacher writes:

To be one with the world in self-consciousness is nothing else than being conscious that we are a living part of this whole; and this cannot possibly be a consciousness of absolute dependence; the more so that all living parts stand in reciprocal interaction with each other. . . . The feeling of absolute dependence, accordingly, is not to be explained as an awareness of the world's existence, but only as an awareness of the existence of God, as the absolute undivided unity.[60]

With his attestation not merely that the self cannot ground itself, but also that the world alone cannot ground the self, Schleiermacher thus surely highlights a deeper difference between, on the one hand, approaching the world in faith, as a *created* world, and then, on the other hand, attending to nature precisely *as* "nature"—that is, as an organic body of interconnected creatures and causal influences, which is not necessarily created, but merely taken as a given. For written into the fabric of his scheme, framed as it is both by the doctrine of creation and by his appeal to "absolute dependence" (teachings, in other words, that claim God is greater than the finite and provisional world), is the sense that Christian believers must inhabit the world in such a way that they are open to surprise. They should not seek simply to be comfortable in and with the world, and their guiding light for searching for God's action in the world should never be the dictates of scientific opinion—current ideas about the materially possible and the materially actual. Instead, the faith of a finite creature, anchored in love and fear of the Almighty, should be a faith ready to witness a "miracle." A miracle not in the sense that this would mean a stark disruption or interruption of nature—we have suggested that Schleiermacher, after Aquinas, is wise to forestall this idea. Yet a miracle nevertheless, in the sense of an event which is unthinkable, remarkable, unexpected. There is too little of this in Schleiermacher's scheme, which stresses the intimacy between God and the world.

It would be possible to contend that Schleiermacher's faults in this regard are healed and completed in Kierkegaard's theological vision and his famous reference to the faith of Abraham—Abraham who believed in a God who "gives life to the dead and calls into existence the things that do not exist" (Rom. 4:16–17). Instead of looking elsewhere, however, it is perhaps more rewarding to turn back to the resources offered in Schleiermacher's own theology. Schleiermacher's attentiveness to the *absolute dependence* of creatures should impel him to take on a radical sense of the world's provisionality at the same time that it helps him to attest the lack of opposition between Christian faith and science.

Notes

The research for this chapter was supported by funding from the European Research Council under the European Union's Seventh Framework Programme (FP7/2007–2013)/ ERC grant agreement no. 295463.

1. David Burrell, "*Creatio ex Nihilo* Recovered," *Modern Theology* 29, no. 2 (2013): 5–6. The collection was edited by Janet Martin Soskice.

2. Burrell regularly employs this phrase, which was coined by Sara Grant. See her *Towards an Alternative Theology: Confessions of a Non-dualist Christian* (Notre Dame, IN: University of Notre Dame Press, 2001).

3. Burrell, "*Creatio ex Nihilo* Recovered," 18.

4. Friedrich Schleiermacher, *The Christian Faith*, ed. H. R. Mackintosh and J. S. Stewart, trans. D. M. Baillie, W. R. Matthews, Edith Sandbach-Marshall, A. B. Macaulay, Alexander Grieve, J. Y. Campbell, R. W. Stewart, and H. R. Mackintosh (London: T&T Clark, 1999) (hereafter *TCF*), §33 (133–37). All references are to sections and pages. Unless otherwise noted, all translations of *TCF* in this essay are from this edition.

5. See *TCF* §2.1 (3) and §13 (67).

6. Friedrich Schleiermacher, *Brief Outline on the Study of Theology*, §196–231 (72–82).

7. Cf. *TCF* §18.2 (86).

8. *TCF* §28.1 (118).

9. *TCF* §16 (78).

10. Friedrich Schleiermacher, *Der christliche Glaube nach den Grundsätzen der evangelischen Kirche im Zusammenhange dargestellt*, Hrsg. Rolf Schäfer, 1 Abt. Band 13/1 der *Friedrich Schleiermacher Kritische Gesamtausgabe* (Berlin: De Gruyter, 2011), p. 143: "§19. Dogmatische Theologie ist die Wissenschaft von dem Zusammenhange der in einer christlichen Kirchengesellschaft zu einer gegebenen Zeit geltenden Lehre." Translation mine.

11. *TCF* §13 (67).

12. *TCF* §19.1 (88).

13. See Brian Gerrish, "Friedrich Schleiermacher," *Nineteenth Century Religious Thought in the West*, vol. 1, ed. Ninian Smart et al. (Cambridge: Cambridge University Press, 1985), 123–56.

14. F. D. E. Schleiermacher, *On the Glaubenslehre: Two Letters to Dr. Lücke*, trans. James Duke and Francis Fiorenza (Chico, CA: Scholars Press, 1981), 64.

15. Ibid., 61.

16. Ibid.

17. Ibid., 60.

18. Ibid.

19. Schleiermacher, *Brief Outline on the Study of Theology*, §209 (75–76).

20. Ibid., §179 (67): "Only in a diseased condition of the Church can the personal persuasion of individuals or, for that matter, even pressures from outside the Church exert any significant influence upon the course and results of doctrinal study."

21. *TCF* §19.1 (89).

22. Schleiermacher, *On the Glaubenslehre*, 60.

23. Schleiermacher, *Brief Outline on the Study of Theology*, §203 (74).

24. *TCF* §4.4 (16–18).

25. Schleiermacher, *On the Glaubenslehre*, 59: "I would have wished to construct [my *Glaubenslehre*] so that at every point the reader would be made aware that the verse John 1:14 is the basic text for all dogmatics, just as it should be for the conduct of ministry as a whole."

26. Ibid., 64–65. Cf. also *TCF* §46.1 (171): "As the human soul is just as necessarily predisposed towards a knowledge of the world as towards a consciousness of God, it can only be false wisdom which would put religion aside, and a misconceived religion for love of which the progress of knowledge is to be arrested."

27. Katherine Sonderegger, "The Doctrine of Creation and the Task of Theology," *Harvard Theological Review* 84, no. 2 (1991): 185–203; Brian Gerrish "Nature and the Theater of Redemption: Schleiermacher on Christian Dogmatics and the Creation Story," *Ex Auditu* 3 (1987): 120–36; Gerrish, "Providence and Grace: Schleiermacher on Justification and Election," *The Cambridge Companion to Friedrich Schleiermacher*, ed. Jacqueline Mariña (Cambridge: Cambridge University Press, 2005), 189–208; Robert Sherman, *The Shift to Modernity: Christ and the Doctrine of Creation in the Theologies of Schleiermacher and Barth* (New York: T&T Clark, 2005).

28. Cf. *TCF* §164–69.

29. Cf. *TCF* §37.

30. My approach in this essay as a whole is indebted to Sonderegger's excellent article.

31. *TCF* §40 (149–50).

32. *TCF* §41 (152).

33. *TCF* §41 (156).

34. *TCF* §59, postscript (241).

35. *TCF* §54 (211).

36. *TCF* §54.4 (217).

37. See Rom. 8:27; Augustine, *Confessions* 10.1–2.

38. *TCF* §55.1 (222).

39. *TCF* §41 (152).

40. Luther on *Genesis* 2:2, §7. Cited in *TCF* §41 (152), and translated by W. R. Matthews and Edith Sandbach-Marshall.

41. *TCF* §38.2 (147).

42. Thomas Aquinas, *Summa Theologiae* I.1.8.

43. Katherine Sonderegger identifies this insight as the core to what she calls Schleiermacher's "theology of indirectness." See Sonderegger, "Doctrine of Creation and the Task of Theology," 198–99.

44. *TCF* §46.2 (174).

45. See James Benziger, "Organic Unity: Leibniz to Coleridge," *PMLA* 66, no. 2 (1951): 24–48. Hans Eichner describes the Early German Romantic vision of worldly life in the following way: "Nature, according to [the Romantics], is not a mere 'nonego' but unconscious, visible spirit striving toward consciousness. The world is not a 'Great Engine' resting in God's hand but a great organism, a 'cosmic animal' or 'All-Tier,' as the Romantic physicist Ritter calls it. . . . Romantic philosophy sought to explain all phenomena, including so-called dead matter, by freedom, by conscious or unconscious mental processes, and by the analogy of organisms." "The Rise of Modern Science and the Genesis of Romanticism," *PMLA* 97, no. 1 (1982): 15.

46. Brian Gerrish, *Tradition and the Modern World* (Chicago: University of Chicago Press, 1978), 108–9. Emphasis added.

47. Schleiermacher's treatment of miracles in his *Glaubenslehre* can be found in §14 and §47–48. See also Schleiermacher's lectures entitled "Das Leben Jesu" (given in 1819/20; 1823; 1829/30; 1832), selected notes from which have been published in English as *The Life of Jesus*, ed. Jack C. Verheyden, trans. S. Maclean Gilmour (Mifflintown, PA: Sigler Press, 1997).

48. *TCF* §14, postscript (71): "Scripture itself bears witness that faith has been produced without miracles, and also that miracles have failed to produce it. . . . Hence if the purpose of miracles had been to produce faith, we should have to conclude that God's breaking into the order of Nature proved ineffectual."

49. *TCF* §47.3 (184).

50. *TCF* §47.3 (183).

51. Schleiermacher's treatment of the "supernatural" is explored at length by Kevin Vander Schal in his book *Embedded Grace: Christ, History, and the Reign of God in Schleiermacher's Dogmatics* (Philadelphia: Fortress Press, 2013).

52. *TCF* §47.1 (180).

53. *TCF* §100 (430).

54. *TCF* §47 (180).

55. *TCF* §164.1 (723).

56. My use of the comparative "higher" here is a nod to Schleiermacher's reference to religion as a "higher realism," in his *Speeches* (1799). He is contrasting religion here with the discipline of speculative philosophy, and writes that "Idealism will destroy the universe by appearing to fashion it; it will degrade it to a mere allegory, to an empty silhouette of our own limitedness." See Friedrich Schleiermacher, *On Religion: Speeches to Its Cultured Despisers*, trans. Richard Crouter (Cambridge: Cambridge University Press, 1996), 107.

57. For literature on the "subjectivist" reading of Schleiermacher, see Edward Farley, "Is Schleiermacher Passé?," in *Christian Faith Seeking Historical Understanding: Essays in Honor of Jack Forstman*, ed. James Duke and Anthony Dunnavant (Macon, GA: Mercer University Press, 1977), 9–27; Julia A. Lamm, "The Early Philosophical Roots of Schleiermacher's Notion of Gefühl (1788–1794)," *Harvard Theological Review* 87, no. 1 (1994): 67–105; Andrew Dole, *Schleiermacher on Religion and the Natural Order* (Oxford: Oxford University Press, 2010).

58. Schleiermacher's portrayal of God as the ground of individual consciousness is what interests Kathryn Tanner in his doctrine of creation. See her *God and Creation in Christian Theology: Tyranny and Empowerment* (Minneapolis: Fortress Press, 2004), 65–68.

59. *TCF* §33 (133–34).

60. *TCF* §33 (132).

CHAPTER 13

The Devil's March

Creatio ex nihilo, *the Problem of Evil,*
and a Few Dostoyevskian Meditations

DAVID BENTLEY HART

BEGINNING AND END

Within the bounds of our normal human experience of nature and history, no claim seems more evidently absurd than that creation is—in any but the most qualified, conditional, local, and inconstant sense—something good; and no piety seems more emptily saccharine than the one that exhorts us to regard our own existence as a blessing, or as grace, or as anything more than a sheer brute event (and a preponderantly rather horrid one at that). Yes, lilacs are lovely, puppies delightful, sexual intercourse (ideally) ecstatic, and every pleasure of the flesh and mind an invitation to the delirious dance of life. But all the things about the world that enchant us, viewed in proper proportion to the whole, are at best tiny flickers of light amid a limitless darkness. The calculus of our existence is quite pitilessly exact in the end. Children die of monstrous diseases, in torment; nature is steeped in the blood of the weak, but then also of the strong; the logic of history is a gay romp through an endless abattoir, a succession of meaningless epochs delineated only by wars, conquests, enslavements, spoliations, mass murders, and all the empires of the merciless. The few happy savages among us whose lives pass in an unbroken flow of idyllic contentment and end in a final peaceful sleep are so rare that their good fortune, posed against the majestic immensity of the rest of humanity's misery, looks like little more than one of fate's more morbid jests. Everything we love vanishes, and so do we; every attachment is merely the transient prelude to an enduring bereavement; every accidental happiness terminates in an essential sorrow. And, if the teachings of most religions are correct, even death offers most of us no respite from our misery, but only new dimensions and amplitudes and ages of suffering—ceaseless karmic cycles of transmigration, interminable torments in hell, and so on. The *conatus essendi* or *tanha* or whatever else it is that binds us to this world has plenty to feed upon, of course, as many good things are contained within the compass of the whole; but certainly the whole is nothing good. If, as Thomas and countless others say, nature instructs us that we owe God our utmost gratitude for the gift of being, then this is no obvious truth of reason, but a truth more mysterious than almost any other—rather on the order of learning that one is one's own father or that the essence of love is a certain shade of blue. Purely natural knowledge instructs us principally not only that we owe God nothing at all, but that really we should probably regard him with feelings situated somewhere along the continuum between resigned resentment and vehement hatred.

And yet Christians must, of course, believe in the goodness of all being, with a certitude that even the most sanguine Platonist could not match, because they are committed to the doctrine that all things are created from nothingness by a God of infinite power, wisdom, and benevolence. And so certain affirmations—metaphysical, moral, and narrative—prove inevitable for any coherent Christian reflection on the problem of evil, not only to answer the question of evil's origin, but also to defend the innocence of God against the evidences of finite experience. One of these affirmations is that evil possesses no proper substance or nature of its own, that it exists only as a *privatio boni*, that though it is real—exorbitantly and ubiquitously real—it is so only in the way that cancer is real: as a corruption and perversion of something that in its own proper nature is essentially good. Thus we may say that, in a purely metaphysical sense, God is implicated neither as substance nor as direct cause in the existence or effects of evil. Another equally indispensable claim is that evil possesses a history, one composed entirely of contingencies and comprising both a first and a last moment. Thus we may say that evil, in all its cosmic scope, is still only an episode, with no share in God's eternity. Another is that the proximate cause of sin lies in the mysterious difference between rational creatures' natural wills (which necessarily seek the one Good in which all things have their true beginning and end) and their deliberative wills (which, under the transcendental canopy of the Good, can nevertheless be diverted toward lesser goods and false ends). Thus we may say that evil is the creature of our choices, not of God's creative will. Yet another is that the moral apostasy of rational beings from the proper love of God is somehow the reason for the reign of death and suffering in the cosmos, that human beings—constituting what Maximus the Confessor called the priestly "*methorios*" (the boundary or frontier) between the physical and the spiritual realms—severed the bond between God's eternity and cosmic time when they fell. Thus we may say, as fantastic as it seems—and as fantastic as it truly is when reduced to fundamentalist literalism regarding the myth of Eden—that all suffering, sadness, and death, however deeply woven into the fabric of earthly existence, is the consequence of the depravities of rational creatures, not of God's intentions. Not that we can locate the time, the place, or the conditions of that event. That ours is a fallen world is not a truth demonstrable to those who do not believe; Christians can see it only within the story of Christ, in the light cast back from his saving action in history upon the whole of time. The fall of rational creation and the conquest of the cosmos by death is something that appears to us nowhere within the course of nature or history; it comes from before and beyond both. We cannot search it out within the closed totality of the damaged world because it belongs to another frame of time, another *kind* of time, one more real than the time of death—perhaps the divine or angelic *aeon* beyond the corruptible sub-sidereal world of *chronos*, or perhaps the Dreamtime or the supercelestial realm of the pure forms or the Origenist heaven of the primordial intelligences, or what have you.

In any event, this (or something roughly like it) is the story that orthodox Christianity tells, and it can tell no other. From the outset, Christian doctrine denies that suffering, death, and evil in themselves have any ultimate value or spiritual meaning at all. They are cosmic contingencies, ontological shadows, intrinsically devoid of substance or purpose, however much God may, under the conditions of a fallen order, make them the occasions for accomplishing his good ends. It may seem a fabulous claim that we exist in the long grim aftermath of a primaeval catastrophe—that this is a broken and wounded world, that cosmic time is a phantom of true time, that we live in an umbratile interval between creation in its fullness and the nothingness from which it was called, and that the universe languishes in bondage to the "powers" and "principalities" of this age, which never cease in their enmity toward the kingdom of God—but it is not a claim that Christians are free to surrender. There is a kind of "provisional" cosmic dualism within the New Testament that simply cannot be evaded: not an ultimate dualism, of course, between two equal principles, but certainly a conflict between, on the one hand, a sphere of created autonomy that strives against God and, on the other, the saving love of God in time. The explicit claim of Christian scripture is that God's will can be resisted by a real and (by his grace) autonomous force of defiance, and that his purposes can be hidden from us by the history of cosmic corruption, and that the final realization of the good he intends in all things has the form—not simply as a dramatic fiction, for our edification or his glory, nor simply as a pedagogical device on his part, but in truth— of a divine victory.

Very well, then. But once all of this has been established, curiously enough, the question of the moral meaning of a created realm in which evil is possible has not been answered, but has in fact been made all the more troublingly acute. For no picture of the autonomy of secondary causes can by itself entirely exonerate an *omnipotent* and *omniscient* primary cause of the things that those secondary causes accomplish. Thus the doctrine of creation still necessarily entails an assertion regarding the eternal identity of God. Of course, chiefly it is an affirmation of God's absolute dispositive liberty in all his acts: the absence of any external restraint upon or necessity behind every decision of his will. And, while one must avoid the pathetic anthropomorphism of imagining God's decision to create as an arbitrary choice made after deliberation among options, one must still affirm that it is *free*, that creation can add nothing to God, that God's being is not dependent on the world's, and that the only necessity in the divine act of creation is the impossibility of any hindrance upon God's expression of his goodness. Yet, paradoxically perhaps, this means that the moral destiny of creation and the moral nature of God are absolutely inseparable. For, as the transcendent Good beyond all beings, he is also the transcendental end of any action on the part of any rational nature; and then, obviously, the end toward which God acts—he who is the beginning and end of all things—must be his own goodness. And this eternal teleology, viewed from the vantage of history, is a cosmic eschatology. As creation is an eternal act, its term is the divine nature; within the orientation of time, however, its term is a "final judgment." And so, no matter how great the autonomy one grants the realm of secondary causes, two things are certain. First, as God's act of creation is free, constrained by neither necessity nor ignorance, all contingent ends are intentionally enfolded within his decision. And, second, precisely because God in himself is absolute, "absolved" of every pathos of the contingent, his moral "venture" in creating is infinite. For all causes are logically reducible to their first cause. This is no more than a logical truism, and it does not matter whether one construes the relation between primary and secondary causality as one of total determinism or utter indeterminacy, for in either case all "consequents" are—either as actualities or merely as possibilities—contingent upon their primordial "antecedent," apart from which they could not exist. Moreover, the rationale—the definition—of a first cause is the final cause that prompts it; and, if that first cause is an infinitely free act emerging from an infinite wisdom, all those consequents are intentionally entailed—again, either as actualities or merely as possibilities—within that first act; and so the final end to which that act tends is its *whole* moral truth. The ontological definition of evil as a *privatio boni* is not merely a logically necessary metaphysical axiom about the transcendental structure of being, but also an assertion that when we say "God is good" we are speaking of him not only relative to his creation, but (however apophatically) as he is in himself; for in every sense being *is* act, and God—in his simplicity and infinite freedom—*is* what he does. And for just this reason the final "solution" to the mystery of evil in a world created by a good, loving, and omnipotent God must be sought in eschatology; for everything depends not only on whether God will be victorious—we cannot doubt that he shall be—but also on what the nature and terms of that victory are.

Regarding this, however, actual history can tell us nothing. History, after all, being a mere succession of contingencies, cannot be redeemed by any *merely* historical event, as no event can ever constitute anything more than one relative and episodic good among all other events. Even the incarnation of the divine Son and the death and resurrection of Christ appear as saving truths only in the light of their ultimate meaning, as the invasion of history by the kingdom that lies beyond history. But neither can the totality of historical events be vindicated by some sort of higher logic of the whole, which "redeems" the transitory evils of life by figuring them into some ultimate sum that merely balances the accounts, absorbing evil within itself as a necessary part of the equation. Between the ontology of *creatio ex nihilo* and that of emanation, after all, there really is no metaphysical difference—unless by the latter we mean a kind of gross material efflux of the divine substance into lesser substances (but of course no one, except perhaps John Milton, ever believed in such a thing). In either case, all that exists comes from one divine source, and subsists by the grace of impartation and the labor of participation: an economy of donation and dependency, supereminence and individuation, actuality and potentiality. God goes forth in all beings and in all beings returns to himself—as, moreover, an expression not of God's dialectical struggle with some recalcitrant exteriority, but of an inexhaustible power wholly possessed by the divine in peaceful liberty. All the doctrine of creation adds is an assurance that in this divine outpouring there is no element of the "irrational": something purely spontaneous, or organic, or even mechanical, beyond the power of God's rational freedom. But then it also means that within the story of creation, viewed from its final cause, there can be no residue of the pardonably tragic, no irrecuperable or irreconcilable remainder left at the end of the tale; for, if there were, this too God would have done, as a price freely assumed in creating. This is simply the logic of the truly absolute. Hegel, for instance, saw the great slaughter-bench of history as a tragic inevitability of the Idea's odyssey toward *Geist* through the far countries of finite negation; for him, the merely particular—say, the isolated man whose death is, from the vantage of the all, no more consequential than the harvesting of a head of cabbage—is simply the smoke that rises from the sacrifice. But the story *we* tell, of creation as God's sovereign act of love, leaves no room for an ultimate distinction between the universal truth of reason and the moral meaning of the particular—nor, indeed, for a distinction between the moral meaning of the particular and the moral nature of God. Precisely because God does not determine himself in creation—precisely because there is no dialectical necessity binding him to time or chaos, no need to forge his identity in the fires of history—in creating he reveals himself truly. Thus every evil that time comprises, natural or moral (a worthless distinction in this context, really, since human nature is a natural phenomenon), is an arraignment of God's goodness: every death of a child, every chance calamity, every act of malice; everything diseased, thwarted, pitiless, purposeless, or cruel; and, until the end of all things, no answer has been given. Precisely because creation is not a theogony, all of it is theophany. It would be impious, I suppose, to suggest that, in his final divine judgment of creatures, God will judge himself; but one *must* hold that by that judgment God truly will *disclose* himself (which, of course, is to say the same thing).

I learned this very early in my theological wanderings, I believe, from Gregory of Nyssa. At least, it was from him that I learned how very important it is for anyone who truly wishes to understand the Christian doctrine of creation not to mistake it for a merely cosmological or metaphysical claim, but rather to recognize it as also an eschatological claim about the world's relation to God, and hence a moral claim about the nature of God in himself. In the end of all created things lies their beginning, and only from the perspective of the end can one know what all things are, why they have been made, and who the God is who has called them forth from nothingness. And in Gregory's thought, with an integrity found only also in Origen and Maximus, protology and eschatology are a single science, a single revelation disclosed in the God-man. There is no profounder meditation on the meaning of creation than Gregory's eschatological treatise *On the Soul and Resurrection*, and no more brilliantly realized eschatological vision than his *On the Making of Humanity*. For him, clearly, one can say that the cosmos has been truly created only when it reaches its consummation in "the union of all things with the first good," and that humanity has truly been created only when all human beings, united in the living body of Christ, become at last that "Godlike thing" that is "humankind according to the image." It is an unambiguously universalist vision of the story of creation and redemption, and one that I am certainly content to accept in its entirety without hesitation or qualification. In a sense, I think it the only plausible Christian vision of the whole. But I also know that, before I can embrace it with quite as unclouded a conscience as I should like, there is at least one obstacle that I have to clear away, or surmount, or circumvent. And it is an imposing obstacle. And no Christian thinker ever saw it with greater clarity than did Dostoyevsky, or described it more powerfully than he did, in the voice of Ivan Karamazov.

Vanya's Devils and Vanya's Devil

The first point probably worth making about *The Brothers Karamazov* is that nowhere in the novel does Dostoyevsky provide a full and convincing riposte to Ivan's arguments. Christian readers who want to believe that the book in the end provides the answers to the theological questions it raises almost inevitably fasten upon the figure of the Staretz Zosima, and upon his mystical discourses; but they are wrong to do so, or at least wrong to imagine that Zosima offers anything more than a necessary but still altogether limited qualification merely of the way in which the question has been posed. He provides nothing remotely like a solution. Nor is there reason to think that Dostoyevsky intended Zosima's teachings as a sufficient counter to Ivan's arguments. Really, trying to identify anything like a final and comprehensive theological proposal amid the ceaseless flowing and halting, advances and retreats, of what Mikhail Bakhtin called Dostoyevsky's "polyphonic poetics" is fruitless in the end.

Rather, the principal contribution the novel makes to moral reflection on creation and evil lies in all the avenues of facile theodicy that it entirely cuts off—all the false, preposterous, ill-formed answers it precludes. Some of these, of course, the novel does not directly address at all. The "antinomian" answer provided by high Reformed tradition, for instance—which elevates a thoroughly modern and voluntaristic concept of divine "sovereignty" over any rationally consistent understanding of divine goodness, and so dispels the quandary by effectively inventing a God beyond good and evil—appears nowhere in the book's pages. But this is a positive strength of the text: even if the Reformed position were not so curious a theological aberration, or were not so logically incoherent in itself (the way any voluntarist theology is), or were not dependent upon so huge a catalogue of exegetical ineptitudes, or were not so obviously morally repellant, it would still never have occurred to an Orthodox Christian like Dostoyevsky as a plausible variant of Christian faith. Instead, in the novel he starts from a genuinely Christian understanding of God as infinite love, willing only the salvation of all his creatures, and then forces himself (and his readers) to ask whether, even from that vantage, the claim that God is good can ever be reconciled with the terms apparently included in the decision to create the world we know. In fact, much of the singular power of the argument made by Vanya (Ivan) to Alyosha in the chapter entitled "Rebellion" lies in its rejection not merely of the worst and most morally repugnant versions of the Christian story—after all, any sane soul already knows that Calvinism is nonsense—but of what appears to be very nearly the most radiantly hopeful. Late-nineteenth-century Russia was one of those places where a perennial Eastern Christian sympathy for universalist eschatologies had resurfaced among educated believers, and in many quarters had become almost the standard view. Certainly it is as far as Ivan is concerned, though in his case it is also a view mingled with a quasi-Hegelian optimism regarding the rationality of history. He begins from the assumption that the true Christian story is that, in the end, "all shall be well, and all manner of thing shall be well," and that the kingdom of God will be a reign of perfect harmony in which all souls will be reconciled with one another, and the greatest sinners will seek forgiveness from their victims and receive it, and all persons will together join in an everlasting hymn of praise to the God who made them, and none will doubt that all the evils of the former things have not only passed away, but have also made an indispensable contribution to that final heavenly music. At one point he briefly considers the possibility of an eternal hell for the reprobate, but immediately dismisses it, correctly recognizing that simply "squaring accounts" with sin's victims through the superaddition of a yet greater and more abysmal quantity of suffering atop all the sufferings that time already comprises would in no way either recompense the innocent for their pains or achieve a true kingdom of peace and harmony.

And therein lies the peculiar subtlety and nearly irresistible force of Ivan's unrelenting, tortured, and haunting case for "rebellion" against "the will of God" in worldly suffering. For him, *even if* something like Gregory of Nyssa's vision of the last things should prove true, it will still be a happiness achieved as the residue of an inexcusable cruelty. Ivan allows himself no simple answers. He does not waste his time or ours by discriminating between the impersonal evils of nature and the personal evils of human malice, or by attempting to explain either away in terms of their immediate occasions or causes, or by struggling with the metaphysical puzzle of how evil arises within a good creation. Instead he concentrates all his attention upon the sufferings of the innocent, of children, and merely demands to know how, within any providential scheme whatsoever, those sufferings could ever really be an acceptable price to pay for the glory of creation.

Ivan, it must be noted, does not represent himself as an atheist; he refuses to take a firm position on whether God is the creator of humanity or humanity the creator of God, in part because the very idea of God would be so implausibly wise and holy an achievement for a vicious animal intellect like ours that he is loath to treat it as a trifle or mere fantasy. That said, he insists that God (if God there be) has supplied humanity with finite "Euclidean" minds, bound to the conditions of time and space, unable to grasp those transcendent designs by which God undoubtedly guides all things toward their final harmony with him and with one another. It is better not to worry, then, about ultimate things; our minds are conformed to the circumstances of this world, which are all that we can meaningfully judge. So, he says, he accepts that there is a God and even that there is an eternal plan that will, in its consummation, bring about a condition of perfect peace and beatitude for all creation; but it is creation, in fact, that Ivan rejects. This is the splendid perversity and genius of Ivan's argument, which makes it indeed the argument of a rebel rather than of a mere unbeliever: he willingly grants, he says, that all wounds will at the last be healed, all scars will disappear, all discord will vanish like a mirage or like the miserable invention of finite Euclidean minds, and that such will be the splendor of the finale of all things, when that universal harmony is established, that every heart will be satisfied, all anger soothed, the debt for every crime discharged, and everyone made capable of forgiving

every offense and even of finding a justification for everything that has
ever happened to mankind; and still he rejects the world that God has
made, and that final harmony along with it. Ivan admits that he is not a
sentimentalist, that indeed he finds it difficult to love his neighbor, but
the terms of the final happiness God intends for his creatures are greater
than his conscience can bear.

To elucidate his complaint, he provides Alyosha with a grim, un-
remitting, remorseless recitation of stories about the torture and murder
of (principally) children—true stories, as it happens, that Dostoyevsky
had collected from the press and from other sources. He tells of Turks
in Bulgaria tearing babies from their mothers' wombs with daggers, or
flinging infants into the air to catch them on their bayonets before their
mothers' eyes, or playing with babies held in their mothers' arms—
making them laugh, enticing them with the bright metal of their
pistols—only then to fire the pistols into the babies' faces. He tells a
story of two parents regularly savagely flogging their seven-year-old
daughter, only to be acquitted in court of any wrongdoing. He tells the
story of a "cultured and respectable" couple who tortured their five-
year-old daughter with constant beatings, and who—to punish her, al-
legedly, for fouling her bed—filled her mouth with excrement and
locked her on freezing nights in an outhouse; and he invites Alyosha to
imagine that child, in the bitter chill and darkness and stench of that
place, striking her breast with her tiny fist, weeping her supplications to
"gentle Jesus," begging God to release her from her misery, and then to
say whether anything—the knowledge of good and evil, for instance—
could possibly be worth the bleak brutal absurdity of that little girl's
torments. He relates the tale of an eight-year-old serf child who, in the
days before emancipation, was bound to the land of a retired general
and who accidentally injured the leg of his master's favorite hound by
tossing a stone; as punishment, the child was locked in a guardroom
through the night and in the morning brought out before his mother
and all the other serfs, stripped naked, and forced to run before the entire pack of his master's hounds, which were promptly set upon him to
tear him to pieces. What can a finite Euclidean mind make of such
things? How, with anything like moral integrity, can it defer its outrage
to some promised future where some other justice will be worked, in
some radically different reality than the present?

Ivan says that he does indeed want to see that final harmony, and to hear the explanation for why such horrors were necessary, but not so as to assent to either; for, while he can go some distance in granting the principle of human solidarity—in sin and retribution—he cannot figure the suffering of children into that final equation without remainder. What makes Ivan's argument so novel and disturbing is not that he simply accuses God of failing to save the innocent; in fact, he grants that in some sense God still will "save" them, in part by rescuing their suffering from sheer "absurdity" and showing what part it had in accomplishing the final beatitude of all creatures. Rather, Ivan rejects salvation itself, insofar as he understands it, and on moral grounds; he rejects anything that would involve such a rescue—anything that would make the suffering of children meaningful or necessary. He grants that one day that eternal harmony will be achieved, and we will discover how it necessitated the torments endured by children. Perhaps mothers will forgive the murderers of their children, and the serf child, his mother, and their master will all be reconciled with one another, and all will praise God's justice, and all evils will be accounted for; or perhaps the damnation of the wicked will somehow balance the score (though how then there can be that final harmony, when the suffering of the victims has already happened and the suffering of their persecutors will persist eternally, Ivan cannot guess). But, still, Ivan wants neither harmony nor the knowledge of ultimate truth at such a cost: "For love of man I reject it"; even ultimate truth "is not worth the tears of that one tortured child." Nor, indeed, does he want forgiveness: the mother of that murdered child must not forgive her child's murderer, even if the child himself can forgive. And so, not denying that there is a God or a divine design in all things, he simply chooses (respectfully) to return his ticket of entrance to God's kingdom. After all, Ivan asks, if you could bring about a universal and final beatitude for all beings by torturing one small creature to death, would you think the price acceptable?

The chief reason that no Christian should ignore or seek to evade Ivan's argument is that, at base, it is so profoundly, even prophetically, Christian—though Ivan himself may have no awareness of this. His ability to imagine a genuinely moral revolt against God's creative and redemptive order has a kind of nocturnal grandeur about it, a Promethean or Romantic or gnostic audacity that dares to imagine some spark dwelling in the human soul that is higher and purer than the God who governs this world; but, in that very way, his argument also carries within itself an echo of the gospel's vertiginous annunciation of our freedom from the "elements" of the world and from the power of the law. And, if nothing else, Ivan's argument provides a kind of spiritual hygiene: a solvent of the semi-Hegelian theology of the liberal Protestantism of the late nineteenth century, which succeeded in confusing eschatological hope with progressive social and scientific optimism, and a solvent as well as of the obdurate fatalism of the theistic determinist, and also of the confidence of rational theodicy, and—in general—of the habitual and unthinking retreat of most Christians to a kind of indeterminate deism. And this, again, marks it as a Christian argument, even if Christian *sub contrario*, because in disabusing Christians of facile certitude in the justness of all things, it forces them back toward the more complicated and subversive theology of the gospel, with its "provisional dualism" and its militant language of divine victory. Ivan's rage against explanation arises from a Christian conscience, and so—even if he cannot acknowledge it—its inner mystery is an empty tomb, which has shattered the heart of nature and history alike (as we understand them) and fashioned them anew. And yet, even so, even when all the bracken and weeds have been cleared away—the seventeenth century's rational theodicies, with their vacuous cant about cosmic balance and the best *possible* world, the eighteenth century's vapid deist moralism, the nineteenth century's sublimely impersonal dialectical teleologies—Ivan's protest still remains unanswered. For, even if the empty tomb of Christ is the secret "sedition" hidden deep within Ivan's rebellion, one must still ask whether one can reconcile that *divine* subversion of the present frame of *fallen* reality with the story of God creating all things freely out of nothing, and do so in such a way as to reduce the "price" of that little girl's tears to nothing.

This is why it is I say, again, that it is a mistake to regard the discourses of the Staretz Zosima as the novel's answer to Ivan's complaint. They never even address the problems he raises. The old monk is a figure of extraordinary imaginative gracefulness, a kind of idealized distillate of everything most luminously beautiful in the Eastern Christian contemplative tradition, equal parts Macarius the Great, Isaac of Ninevah, Serafim of Sarov, and Tikhon of Zadonsk. As such, he represents not the contrary position to Ivan's, but rather an entirely different orientation of vision and moral intention. It is true that his posture is a necessary corrective to Ivan's in various senses. Whereas Ivan claims that it is impossible to look from God's vantage upon the whole of creation, and that therefore we can judge our experience of the world only from a finite and Euclidean perspective, Zosima claims just the opposite: that by love we can indeed see the world as God sees it; that, by looking with a burning charity upon all our neighbors, despite their sins, and by looking with that same charity upon all creatures whatsoever, we can in fact know the glory and the truth of God's love in creating all things for himself. And whereas Ivan's seemingly intensely personal rebellion is in fact essentially an abstract moral interrogation of the universal rationality of the world, Zosima's seemingly cosmic vision of a creation utterly pervaded by divine love is in fact an essentially intensely personal "suffering with" all creatures that refuses to assume a detached universal perspective. And very much at the heart of Zosima's vision is a radical acknowledgment of personal responsibility for the whole of reality, and of (however mysterious this may be) a personal complicity in all creature's sufferings. Before all else, he says, one must not presume to judge, but must instead recognize oneself as the only proper object of judgment, whose own sin is somehow the ground of the sin and torment of all. Thus one must not only pour oneself out in love for all creatures, but must do so as a penitent, seeking the forgiveness not only of one's fellow human beings, but of animals and plant-life as well. This is splendid, and is so in large part because it is sustained by a genuinely humble and ascetic refusal to look to the horizon of the absolute for answers, or to seek out some total rationality of history that will make the pains and disaffections of the present moment tolerable.

Yet, in another sense, not only does all of this fail to answer Ivan's argument; it in fact sharpens and refines it. For, while it tears away any possible presumption on the part of any human being that he may judge God from a position of moral superiority or purity, and so momentarily might seem to render Ivan's posture of defiance a little ridiculous, in truth it accomplishes quite the opposite: Zosima's teachings merely show that, though God is to be "judged" only against himself—"Who are you, O man . . . ?"—this nevertheless means that God and his works must therefore pass the judgment of a love capable of embracing all things without wrath or condemnation, and without indifference to any particular being. And so, still, the question remains: How can the tears of that little girl be an acceptable price for the drama of creation? After all, would Staretz Zosima himself—with his exquisite counsels on the necessity of loving children with the fullness of one's heart—create a world on such terms if he had the power to do so?

I do not know whether Dostoyevsky intended Zosima's final mystical discourse on hell to provide some sort of clarity on this point. In some sense, of course, it does, insofar as it expresses the dominant Eastern Christian mystical tradition of reflection on damnation, which tells us that the flames of hell are nothing more than the transfiguring glory of God experienced by someone who, having sealed himself within himself, "interprets" it as an exterior chastisement. Hell, Zosima insists, is not God's wrath visited upon sin, but the self-condemnation of a soul that can no longer love, and that has therefore placed an impassable chasm between itself and all others. Nor can those who have subjected themselves to such torment be delivered from it, for it is all within themselves; even if dragged into paradise they would be more miserable there than in the heart of hell, for they could never reciprocate the love of the blessed. Their hatred for God and his creation is boundless, "and they shall everlastingly burn in the fires of their own hatred, and shall long for death and nonexistence; but death shall not be granted them. . . ." Thus hell is always and only the free choice of the damned, and in no way detracts from or dilutes the infinite love of God. It is much the same picture provided in more colorful form by Grushenka's tale to Alyosha of the wicked crone whose guardian angel tried to rescue her from the lake of fire by pulling her out at the end of a spring onion she had once given a beggar (the only good deed she had ever performed), but who tried to kick away the other desperate souls clinging to her in hope of salvation, and thereby cast herself back into the flames. If we are damned, it is because we damn ourselves, and indeed wish to be damned rather than to submit to love. It is a powerful notion. It is also utter nonsense.

Not, that is to say, nonsense as a psychological truth: certainly whatever hell there may be is self-imposed, and in this life already we know that the rejection of love is a torment unlike any other, and we know also how easy it is for someone to cling obsessively to hate and resentment despite the misery they induce in him. What is nonsense is that such a condition is any meaningful sense truly free, or that it could ever eventuate out of true freedom, or that it could be sustained "everlastingly" as a free act of the creature that would in no way inculpate God. Among more civilized apologists for the conventional concept of eternal damnation, the most popular defense has long been an appeal to creaturely freedom and to God's supposed respect for its dignity. But there could scarcely be a poorer argument; whether made crudely or elegantly, it invariably fails. It might not fail if one could construct a metaphysics or phenomenology of the will's liberty that was purely voluntarist, purely spontaneous; but that is impossible. For one thing, there is no real sense in which an absolutely libertarian act, obedient to no ultimate prior rationale whatsoever, would be distinguishable from sheer chance, or a mindless organic or mechanical impulse, and so any more "free" than an earthquake or embolism. On any cogent account, free will is a power inherently purposive, teleological, primordially oriented toward the good, and shaped by that transcendental appetite to the degree that a soul can recognize the good for what it is. The "intellectualist" understanding of the will is simply the only one that can bear scrutiny. Any act not directed toward its proximate object as "good," at least as "good for me," within a constant transcendental intentionality toward the Good as such, would be by definition teleologically irrational, and so not an act of the rational will at all. Thus no one can *freely* will the evil as evil; one can take the evil for the good, and even know that in doing so one is choosing what others condemn as evil, but for a rational spirit this cannot alter the prior transcendental orientation that makes all desire and action possible. Even God could not create a rational will directed to the evil as evil; evil is not a substance, and reason is nothing but a teleological orientation toward the Good. To see the Good truly is to desire it insatiably; not to desire it is not to have known it, and so never to have been free to choose it. Thus it makes no more sense to say that God allows creatures to damn themselves out of his love for them or out of his respect for their freedom than to say a father might reasonably allow his deranged child to thrust her face into a fire out of a tender respect for her moral autonomy. Freedom as a rational condition is nothing but the inability to mistake evil for, or prefer it to, the Good. And freedom as an irrational impulse, therefore, cannot exist. And the argument for hell as an eternal free choice of the creature becomes quite insufferable when one considers the personal conditions—ignorance, mortality, defectibility of intellect and will—under which each soul enters the world, and the circumstances—the suffering of all creatures, even the most innocent and delightful of them—with which that world confronts the soul.

We simply cannot in this way evade the shattering force of Vanya's question: if universal harmony and joy could be secured by the torture and murder of a single innocent child, would you accept that price? And once the question has been posed with such terrible clarity, we find its logic goes all the way down to the last lingering residue of unredeemed pain. Let us say that somehow, mysteriously—in, say, Zosima's sanctity, or Alyosha kissing his brother, or the tale of the callous old woman's onion—we could find an answer to the question that might make the transient torments of history justifiable in the light of God's everlasting kingdom. Very well then, perhaps we might. But *eternal* torments, *final* dereliction? Here the price is raised beyond any calculus of relative goods, and into the realm of absolute—of infinite—expenditure. And the arithmetic is fairly inflexible. One need not imagine, in traditional fashion, that the legions of the damned will far outnumber the cozy company of the saved. Let us imagine instead that only one soul will perish eternally, and all others enter into the peace of the kingdom. Nor need we think of that soul as guiltless, like Vanya's helpless child, or even as mildly sympathetic. Let it be someone utterly despicable—say, Hitler. Even then, no matter how we understand the fate of that single wretched soul in relation to God's intentions, no account of the divine decision to create out of nothingness can make its propriety morally intelligible, or make whatever good it accomplishes anything other than relative and incomplete. This is obvious, of course, in predestinarian systems, since from their bleak perspective, manifestly, that poor, ridiculous, but tragically conscious puppet who has been consigned to the abyss exists for no other purpose than the ghastly spectacle of divine sovereignty. But, then, for the redeemed, each of whom might just as well have been denied efficacious grace had God so pleased, who is that wretch who endures God's final wrath, forever and ever, other than their surrogate, their redeemer, the one who suffers in their stead—their Christ? Compared to that unspeakable offering, that interminable and abominable oblation of infinite misery, what would the cross of Jesus be? How would it be diminished for us? And to what? A bad afternoon? A temporary indisposition of the infinite? And what would the mystery of God becoming man in order to effect a merely partial rescue of created order be, as compared to the far deeper mystery of a worthless man becoming the suffering god upon whose perpetual holocaust the entire order of creation finally depends?

But predestination need not be invoked here at all. Let us suppose instead that rational creatures possess real autonomy, and that no one goes to hell save by his or her own industry and ingenuity: when we then look at God's decision to create from that angle, curiously enough, absolutely nothing changes. Let us imagine merely that God created *on the chance* that humanity might sin, and that a certain number of incorrigibly wicked souls might plunge themselves into Tartarus forever; this still means that, morally, he has purchased the revelation of his power in creation by the same horrendous price—even if, in the end, no one at all happens to be damned. The logic is irresistible: for what is hazarded has already been surrendered, entirely, no matter how the dice fall; the aleatory venture may be indeterminate in terms of God's intention, but the wager is itself an irrevocable intentional decision, wherein every possible cost has already been accepted; the irrecuperable expenditure has been offered even if, happily, it is never actually lost, and so the moral nature of the act is the same in either case. To venture the life of your child for some other end is, morally, already to have killed your child, even if at the last moment Artemis or Heracles or the Angel of the LORD should stay your hand. And so the revelation of God's glory in creatures would still always be dependent upon that sacrifice of misery, even if at the last no one were to perish. Creation could never then be called "good" in an unconditional sense; nor God the "Good as such," no matter what conditional goods he might accomplish in creating. And, here too, the losing lot might just as well have fallen to the blessed, given the stochastic vagaries of existence: accidents of birth, congenital qualities of character, natural intellectual endowments, native moral aptitudes, material circumstances, personal powers of resolve, impersonal forces of chance, the grim encumbrances of sin and mortality . . . Once again, who would the damned be but the redeemers of the blessed, the price eternally paid by God for the sake of the kingdom's felicity?

Hence, Zosima's qualification of Ivan's argument must itself be qualified if the terms entailed in God's act of creation are truly to be vindicated. And if, anywhere in the novel, a final answer (or hint of an answer) is given to the quandary, it is provided by the devil with whom the febrile Ivan converses on the night of his collapse. It is all too easy to fail to recognize this when reading the novel; perhaps its author did not see it either. Vanya's devil is one of Dostoyevsky's most inspired creations, one in which the combination of antic absurdity and deeply intelligent pathos is every bit as accomplished as in the figure of the Underground Man, but within a much more confined space. The conceits are all in such perfect balance—the devil's philosophical detachment, his world-weariness and amused nonchalance, his theatrical humility, his faded gentleman's attire, the appearance he wears of a penurious petty noble dependent on the hospitality of others, his rheumatism and bronchitis, his professed longing to be reincarnated as the obese wife of a merchant, his silly self-justifications ("I was marked out by some prehistoric decree that I have never understood to epitomize negation. . . . Man cannot live by Hosannas alone. . . . If everything earthly were governed by reason, nothing would ever happen")—that they can render the scene's subtle undertones of moral gravity almost inaudible.

Not that I intend to dilate on those here. I wish merely to call attention to the devil's admirable air of *fatigue*: with human and cosmic history, with the imponderable pointlessness of his own role of sending souls to perdition, with the self-importance of those who construct grand theories, and especially with the hilarious folly of the young radical philosopher who dreams of a future man-god beyond good and evil, beyond God. He seems to grasp that whatever truth this world might serve must lie altogether beyond the violence and imbecility of its immanent logic. He certainly would never be tempted to consider the problem of evil as a question regarding the universal rationality of history, as Ivan feels compelled to do. Nor certainly would he be tempted to imagine that he could view the spectacle of cosmic suffering from outside, without involvement or responsibility—even if he cannot quite assume the penitential approach to creation of Zosima. He claims to believe that there is, no doubt, some great secret behind it all that he cannot divine; but he does not speculate on some final resolution of evil in which the kingdom of God will emerge from the dialectic of history or from the cosmic drama of a necessary suffering. What he does do, however, is tell a delightfully silly story: that of the materialist philosopher who repudiated all law, conscience, and faith, but who on dying found himself in the next world and was so indignant at this contradiction of his deepest convictions that he was promptly condemned to a quadrillion-kilometer march through the void; at one point along the way, he even refused to continue walking and obstinately lay down for a thousand years; but in the end he was admitted through the gates of paradise and within two seconds declared it worth every step of his journey, and worth a journey of even a quadrillion quadrillion kilometers to the quadrillionth power, and joined in the heavenly chorus of praise. And then a little later, quite casually, the devil also remarks that he will himself someday have to surrender his post of negation, make his own quadrillion-kilometer march, and at last utter those hosannas he has felt constrained by his role within the drama of history to withhold. Perhaps one can make too much of the tale, of course, and certainly one ought to be suspicious of the devil's sincerity. Even so, it is worth noting that the tale he tells is not one regarding a universal harmony somehow necessarily premised upon the unanswered tears of a little girl weeping in misery in the night. It is simply a story of a soul's pilgrimage out of the shadows and into the light, and of a forced rescue from a self-imposed ruin. It is not about a kingdom achieved by way of time, through Spirit's diremption in the finite or the rational labor of history, but of a salvation graciously granted altogether beyond history. And it is a story that—at least, so it is obliquely suggested—leaves not even the devil out, not as a necessary force of dialectical negation, but as yet another rational spirit called to union with God.

Why is this interesting? Does it answer Ivan's argument for rebellion? No, not exactly. As even the devil's tale suggests, only the final vision of the kingdom could possibly do that. Nevertheless, the problem Ivan poses is radically altered when the story of creation and redemption is told not as a narrative of the rational meaning of the whole, nor as a grand epic whose denouement somehow depends upon a tragic drama of eternal loss, but rather as the tale of the "rescue" of all creatures from nonbeing, and then also from sin and ignorance, and finally even from themselves and their illusory "freedom," so that they may be drawn on to the God who will not abandon even those who abandon him. Seen from that vantage, the question of whether it was all "worth the price" is reduced from the status of a logically irrefutable arraignment of creation's goodness to that of a powerful intuitive moral anxiety. The time of sin and death, which we call history, cannot be—and this is the truth that Ivan sees so clearly—the foundation of God's kingdom, as then it would be a final harmony sustained by an unredeemed injustice. Rather, it is the last residue of the darkness of nonbeing that God conquers in creation and salvation. That being so, the question of the price of that victory is not one of the rational calculation of relative goods, but one whose final answer is entirely the province of—and this is Zosima's truth—one who can see the whole of creation with the eyes of perfect love: that same little girl, though now lifted up into the eternity of the kingdom, divinized, glorified, capable of a love like God's, which can forgive perfectly and thereby triumph over all evil. Yet even this forgiveness cannot bring the kingdom to pass unless—and this is the truth to which the devil attests, even if only inadvertently—eternity reduce the price of evil to absolutely nothing. For if anything were to be eternally lost—the least little thing—then the goodness of creation could never be more in the end than a purely conditional goodness, a mere relative evaluation, rather than an essential truth. And then neither could God be the Good as such.

Again, the issue is the reducibility of all causes to their first cause, and the final determination of the first cause by the final. If Christians did not believe in a *creatio ex nihilo*—if they thought God a being limited by some external principle or internal imperfection, or if we were dualists, or dialectical idealists, or what have you—the question of evil would be only an aetiological query for them, not a terrible moral question. But, because they say God creates freely, they must believe his final judgment shall reveal him for who he is. If God creates souls he knows to be destined for eternal misery, in himself he cannot be the good as such, and creation cannot possess any true moral essence: it is from one vantage an act of predilective love, but from another vantage, and one every bit as logically necessary, it is an act of prudential malevolence. And so it cannot be true. And this must be the final moral meaning of the doctrine of *creatio ex nihilo*, at least for those who truly believe that their language about God's goodness has any substance, and that the theological grammar to which that language belongs is not empty: that the God of eternal retribution and pure sovereignty proclaimed by so much of

Christian tradition is not, and cannot possibly be, the God of self-outpouring love revealed in Christ. If God is the good creator of all, he is the savior of all, without fail, who brings to himself all he has made, including all rational wills, and only thus returns to himself in all that goes forth from him. Only thus can it be true that God made the world and saw that it was good; and only thus can we hope in the end to see that goodness, and also to see that he who made it is himself the Good as such.

CHAPTER 14

What Does Physical Cosmology Say about Creation from Nothing?

ADAM D. HINCKS, S.J.

Less than a hundred years ago, the Milky Way was the only known galaxy, and the universe was believed to be static. Today, we know that the universe emerged from a big bang, that it is 13.8 billion years old, and that the Milky Way is one of some hundreds of billions of observable galaxies. Physical cosmology, the branch of astrophysics that has uncovered these and many other facts about the universe on its largest scales of space and time, has made this rapid progress over the past few generations thanks to remarkable improvements in telescope technology coupled to a growing understanding of the relevant physics.

The successes of cosmology,[1] particularly its ability to study the universe in its infancy, have prompted speculation about what, if anything, it reveals about the need for a divine Creator. Some prominent cosmologists eschew such a need. Stephen Hawking, for example, made headlines a few years ago when he claimed that God is "not necessary" to explain the universe.[2] But the conversation between cosmology and theology contains other points of view, and there is a fair amount of academic literature on the subject.[3] In much of the discourse about cosmology vis-à-vis God, the issue of design is emphasized, and the question is whether it is "necessary," in some sense, to invoke an intelligent Creator to explain the makeup of our universe.

In this paper, however, my primary interest is how cosmology relates specifically to creation *ex nihilo* (CEN), or the doctrine that God is not merely a demiurge who imparts intelligibility to matter, but is also the being who makes possible the very conditions of order and intelligibility in the world. Focusing on this topic is fruitful because it provides a distinct perspective that focuses not on design but rather on the metaphysical framework that is common to physical cosmology and the doctrine of CEN.

After giving a brief overview of contemporary cosmology, I shall examine three topics that are often presumed to have some bearing on creation: first, the so-called multiverse theory, in which our observable universe is a minuscule patch of a much larger landscape that can look radically different elsewhere; second, the possibility of a cyclic universe in which the big bang is not the beginning of time; and third, the attempts in quantum cosmology to describe physically how a universe can come from "nothing." I shall take special care to distinguish between the elements that are empirically well-grounded and those that are speculative. What will emerge is that cosmology's real contribution to understanding CEN is not that it proves or disproves it or somehow probes its mechanics, but rather that cosmology can help elucidate and purify its metaphysical framework, particularly notions like matter, nothingness, space, and time.

A Brief History of Contemporary Cosmology

Contemporary cosmology has its origins in the 1920s when Edwin Hubble made a series of observations of galaxies using the powerful new 2.5-meter Hooker telescope in California. He discovered that, on average, all galaxies are moving away from each other.[4] This had, in fact, been independently predicted by Alexander Friedmann and by the physicist-priest Georges Lemaître upon studying Einstein's new theory of gravity, also known as the general theory of relativity. In 1931, Lemaître began proposing that this expanding universe had an explosive, temporal beginning starting with a 'primeval atom,' an idea that eventually became known as the big bang theory.[5]

There is a common misconception that the big bang was like a bomb explosion in which material was ejected outwards from a central point. However, in the expanding universe, space itself is stretching, and the material within space goes along for the ride. A better analogy than a bomb is an expanding rubber sheet. If you imagine that galaxies are points painted on the sheet, what is happening is not that the points are moving relative to the surface of the sheet, but rather that the sheet is stretching and the distance between the fixed points is increasing. Thus, the big bang did not occur at a single point in space, but rather everywhere.

This should make it clear that the question of what space is expanding "into" is nonsensical: expanding into something is already a spatial concept. On the other hand, the question of whether space is infinite or finite is cogent. In the latter case, the universe would have a topology such that if you traveled far enough in a straight line, you would end up where you started, just like on the surface of the earth. However, as far as we can see, there is no such wrapping of space. But this is just as far as we can see. Cosmologists commonly refer to the "observable universe," or the volume of space defined by the distance that light can travel in the age of the universe, or 13.8 billion years—a number we know to a precision of about 3 percent.[6] Beyond these 13.8 billion years,[7] we cannot say with empirical certainty whether space is finite or infinite.[8]

Though Hubble's measurements of receding galaxies were made in the 1920s, it took a few decades for the theory of the expanding universe to be fully convincing. Two other pieces of evidence emerged that helped make the case. First, the big bang theory makes specific predictions about the relative abundances of hydrogen and helium in the universe. These two elements were produced at different rates by the nuclear reactions that occurred soon after the big bang, and their observed relative abundance in the nearby universe is an impressive match to the predictions of nuclear physics.[9] Second, in the 1960s, researchers discovered a background signal of microwaves that is the same intensity everywhere in the sky.[10] It was soon realized that it is the glow of the universe soon after the big bang, at a time when the universe was still small, dense, and hot, and long before the gas had collapsed into stars or galaxies.[11] This microwave background radiation comes from almost 13.8 billion years ago and is the very earliest light that we have access to. By studying it, we learn about the conditions very early on and we are able to connect it to the structure of the local universe, thereby learning how the universe has evolved into its present form.

The basic history of the universe is as follows. In the first few seconds of the universe, everything was so hot and dense that even the simplest elements in the periodic table were not stable against the massive amount of radiation. Within the first few minutes, the universe cooled enough that hydrogen and helium nuclei began forming. About four hundred thousand years later it had cooled further, and the nuclei were able to join with electrons to form stable atoms, at which time the microwave background was produced. Slight overdensities in this neutral gas of hydrogen and helium slowly condensed and collapsed to form the first stars—when precisely this occurred is currently a popular area of research, but it would have been a few hundred million years after the big bang.[12] When the first stars came to the ends of their lives and were destroyed in supernovae, they produced the heavier elements such as oxygen, nitrogen, carbon, and so on. And as gravity continued its work of collapsing structure, galaxies consisting of billions of stars started taking shape.

There are still many open questions in cosmology—not least of which is the fact that only about 5 percent of the universe is made up of atomic matter, with the rest being so-called dark matter and dark energy, mysterious substances that are necessary for understanding how the universe evolved but about which we have virtually no theoretical understanding. But the area of research most relevant to this paper is the attempt to understand the conditions in the very early universe. Remarkably, we can describe the universe back to less than one second after the big bang, but there are still important questions about what occurred even earlier than this and about the big bang itself. It is these issues that we shall examine in depth.

MATTER AND THE MULTIVERSE

A major puzzle in cosmology is the fact that the early universe appears to have been very finely tuned. The cosmic microwave background glows at the same temperature everywhere, but any given region would never have been in causal contact with other regions in the universe in the simple big bang scenario. How, then, could everything have been the same temperature—precise to five decimal places—if there was no time for the temperature to even out on its own? Again, as far as we can measure, the curvature of the universe has always been completely flat: that is, it follows Euclidean geometry—angles in a triangle add up to one hundred eighty degrees and parallel lines never intersect—though there is no a priori reason why it shouldn't be curved negatively (like a saddle) or positively (like a sphere). Finally, there is the somewhat more technical problem that the universe seems devoid of magnetic monopoles, the magnetic equivalents of the electric charge, even though many theories of particle physics predict their existence.

The most popular way to explain these puzzles is via the theory of inflation, which proposes that almost immediately after the big bang, the universe underwent an extremely rapid but brief period of expansion. In figures, it would have grown by a factor 10^{25} in less than 10^{-32} seconds, equivalent to the nucleus of an atom growing to the size of the Solar System in less time than light would take to traverse the width of the aforesaid nucleus.[13] The numbers may sound incredible, but Alan Guth introduced inflation in 1980 after realizing that this simple mechanism explains the fine-tuning problems.[14] The volume that comprises our universe initially was in causal contact, and only after it inflated did different regions fall out of contact: this explains how the microwave background is the same temperature everywhere. The problem of flatness is solved because inflation can smooth out any initial curvature to the point where it is undetectable. The monopole problem is solved because any existing monopoles have been spread out so thin that one would reasonably expect them to be too rare to observe.

Inflation also explains the origin of large-scale structure in the universe. During inflation, quantum fluctuations produced tiny inhomogeneities in the density of the universe that later grew into galaxies under the influence of gravity. We can observe these initial perturbations in the cosmic microwave background, and even better, the distribution and properties of the perturbations are exactly what inflation would produce. Indeed, after the *Planck* satellite released its maps of the microwave background in 2013, Guth, together with colleagues David Kaiser and Yasunori Nomura, reported: "To date, every single one of these inflation-scale predictions has been confirmed to good precision."[15]

However, there is one further prediction that has not been observed. Inflation also produces gravity waves—that is, undulations in space itself. These too should in principle be observable in the microwave background, but their signature is extremely faint. Inflationary theory does not predict exactly how faint they should be, so if we are unlucky, the gravitational waves could be so small that we could never practically observe them. Nevertheless, there are several experiments currently underway designed to detect them, in hopes that they are large enough to be seen. In 2014, the BICEP2 collaboration claimed that they may have made a detection,[16] but subsequent analysis has shown that dust in our own galaxy is very likely responsible for the bulk of the signal,[17] so further observations are still needed.

In the absence of a detection of gravitational waves, inflation is not fully verified, but it remains the leading theory of the early universe. However, it solves the fine-tuning problems only by pushing them back further. To get the early-universe conditions that we observe, inflation needs to last the right amount of time and produce the right kind of expansion. As of yet there is no complete physical theory that naturally predicts the specific form of inflation that our universe requires, and therefore it remains an ad hoc prescription.

One paradigm often invoked to circumvent this difficulty is the so-called multiverse. This is a somewhat misleading moniker because the multiverse is not a collection of radically disconnected realities. Rather, the multiverse consists of a vast expanse of space in which different regions have strikingly different properties, and we live in a tiny patch that happens to be conducive to the formation of galaxies and planetary systems, and therefore to life as we know it.

The idea that there is an intimate link between the multiverse and inflation can be traced to Andrei Linde's work in 1983.[18] He proposed that after the big bang, the energy field responsible for inflation existed everywhere, but took on different, random values in different places. Our observable universe began by inflating in a patch that happened, by chance, to have a suitable value of the inflation field; different patches have undergone different types of inflation that could never lead to a stable universe suitable for life. Fittingly, Linde named his theory "chaotic inflation." One of its unexpected consequences is that most places never stop inflating. Our observable universe, then, is a tiny, safe haven that has stopped inflating amidst a (presumably) infinite landscape, most of which is perpetually expanding at exponential rates. Other "bubbles" that, like our universe, have stopped inflating, would be very sparsely sprinkled throughout.

The multiverse has the added attraction that it may explain other fine-tuning problems that are more or less independent of the puzzles that inflation was invoked to explain. If certain physical constants of nature, such as the strength of the electrical force or the mass of the proton, were altered even slightly, stars would never have formed and the structure of our universe would be so radically different that it would be inhospitable to life.[19] In a multiverse, however, one can postulate that in addition to the inflation field, the other constants of nature take on different values in different patches. Thus, some patches would not only have the right type of inflation to produce our universe, but also the right combination of other physical parameters.[20] Even better, this idea appears to align nicely with current research in theoretical physics. At the high energies of the early universe, the fundamental forces of nature were unified. As universe cooled, the forces split apart into the strong, weak, and electromagnetic forces, each with its own strength and parameters, but how exactly the split occurred would have been a random process varying from place to place. Hence, physical "constants" would vary from patch to patch. In some versions of string theory, which include gravity in this splitting, the number of possible resulting combinations of parameters exceeds the number of atoms in the observable universe. Many physicists view the multiverse as a natural partner or even corollary of this theoretical framework, which would make it more than simply an ad hoc mechanism to explain fine-tuning.

At least two serious criticisms that be leveled at the multiverse hypothesis. The first is based on recent searches for inflationary gravity waves that have made simple versions of chaotic inflation appear quite unlikely.[21] Some cosmologists have maintained confidence that improved theories consistent with observations will emerge.[22] Others, however, have argued that this amounts to adjusting arbitrary theoretical knobs to force ad hoc theories to match the data; they advocate abandoning chaotic inflation altogether.[23]

However, the more serious criticism is that the multiverse theory falls outside the domain of natural science. The multiverse is unobservable because, by definition, it extends beyond the observable universe. The most that can be done is to figure out how likely it is for a universe like ours to arise under the assumption that we live in a multiverse. This probabilistic exercise can then be interpreted as the predictive power of the theory—although nobody currently knows how to calculate such probabilities. But the fact remains that even a complete theory of the multiverse would not be empirically verifiable in any traditional sense. As George Ellis has argued, "The multiverse idea is provable neither by observation, nor as an implication of well established physics. It may be true, but it cannot be shown to be true."[24]

These criticisms notwithstanding, the multiverse concept is relevant to our discussion because it is often invoked as an argument against a Creator. According to Stephen Hawking and Leonard Mlodinow: "Many people through the ages have attributed to God the beauty and complexity of nature that in their time seemed to have no scientific explanation. But just as Darwin and Wallace explained how the apparently miraculous design of living forms could appear without intervention by a supreme being, the multiverse concept can explain the fine-tuning of physical law without the need for a benevolent creator who made the universe for our benefit."[25] Bernard Carr is even more pithy: "If you don't want God, you'd better have a multiverse."[26] The basic argument is that in the multiverse, there is no fine-tuning properly speaking but only random occurrences in an enormous ensemble of options: "In an eternally inflating universe, anything that can happen will happen: in fact, it will happen an infinite number of times."[27] Therefore, there is no Fine Tuner.[28]

However, if it were valid to argue that the multiverse is required if there is no Creator, this would not imply that if the multiverse is real that there is no God. There may even be good reasons to suppose that God would choose to create a multiverse because this makes nature more beautiful and elegant.[29] For instance, Don Page (a former doctoral student of Stephen Hawking) has argued that certain versions of the multiverse may actually have an overall simpler structure than certain versions of a single universe, implying a possible fittingness for the multiverse from the design point of view; he concludes, "God might indeed so love the multiverse."[30]

Despite the importance of understanding the relationship between providence, design, and randomness in nature, the central concern in this paper is CEN. In fact, it is very useful to turn our attention to this doctrine because it cuts across the issue of design in an important way. Namely, CEN is not primarily about how the intelligible structure of the world came to be as it is, but rather about the conditions for it to exist at all. In classical language, CEN does not first and foremost explain why the form of the universe is what it is, but insists that the matter which is actually informed must first be explained. Without matter, there can be no form: and all arguments about the relationship between the Creator and fine-tuning presume that there is matter.

It is essential to be aware that the modern use of the word "matter" is significantly different from the classical[31] meaning that CEN employs. In the modern sense, matter means "stuff": the collections of elementary particles that form atoms and molecules. These particles can be "created" and "annihilated." For instance, in a particle accelerator, colliding electrons and positrons annihilate each other and produce energy. And in a vacuum, particles continually pop in and out of existence on short time scales. Classically, however, matter is that which underlies change; it is the substrate that makes form, or intelligibility, possible in a thing. It is the component in stuff that allows it to be either this kind of stuff or that kind of stuff; it is potency, and as such is functionally related to form. Clearly, matter in the classical sense is a metaphysical concept, whereas in the modern sense it is a physical concept, and therefore the two senses of the word, while different, are not incompatible. This can be illustrated by considering a solid, which, as we all know, is composed of molecules. In classical language, the molecules stand as matter to the form of the solid. But if we were to consider the chemistry of the molecules, then the molecules would be forms of which the matter is atoms and atomic forces. Classically, the molecules are the matter when considering the form of the solid, but they are forms when considering their chemistry. On the other hand, in the modern sense of matter, the molecules are material regardless of which aspect of the solid we are considering.

Of course, one might question whether matter, in the classical sense (which I shall henceforth be careful to distinguish as such), is a useful or even a valid concept. I shall return to this point in the next section when I explore the place of contingency in cosmology. For now, however, I wish to establish that CEN is intimately connected to a basic insight that all form or intelligibility in the universe is contingent: that is, it all has underlying matter—classically speaking, of course—which, because it is the very potential for it to change, also means the intelligible structure is not at all necessary but could very well be different. It is the matter that CEN explains. God is not just a Platonic demiurge that informs preexisting matter; rather, he is the Creator of matter and the author of the very existence of possibility itself. Once this is established, the role of the Creator in the actual informing of matter becomes a secondary question. The issue of fine-tuning is one example of this subsequent question; the multiverse presumes, by definition, that a landscape of possibility preexist. But that landscape, which is the matter of the multiverse (if the multiverse should actually exist) is precisely what CEN explains.

The foregoing is an excellent example of how the contingency of cosmological theories—of the multiverse on the possibility of a landscape of variable physical parameters, in this instance—is what is relevant to CEN. For if something is contingent, it is the result of a possibility, and where there is possibility there is matter, and CEN is the doctrine that form did not simply arise from some preexisting (classical) matter that is just there. If everything is to be explained, then the existence of matter cannot be taken for granted. For potentiality is by definition not actual, and as such does not explain its own existence.

THE CYCLICAL UNIVERSE VERSUS INFLATION: CAN WE SEE THE BEGINNING?

As early as inflation occurred, it still would not have been at the beginning of the universe. Space filled with energy must already exist for inflation to occur. Now, the big bang theory formally says that the universe began in an infinitely dense and energetic state—a "singularity," to use the technical word. In fact, there are a series of theorems that prove that Einstein's theory of gravity under some reasonable physical conditions *requires* that the universe begin with a singularity.[32] However, while it seems that the universe must have a beginning, it is a beginning that we cannot physically describe because it consists in something infinitely dense and hot, and, like philosophers, physicists have trouble with actual infinities. As Hawking puts it, "Classical general relativity brings about its own downfall: it predicts that it can't predict the universe."[33]

The foregoing, however, is strictly true only under classical[34] physics. While classical gravity (i.e., general relativity) tells us how space expands, we need quantum mechanics to describe the matter and energy that occupy that space. And at very high energies—above what is called the "Planck scale"—we have no rigorous knowledge of how to use both theories together. Classical gravity becomes inadequate for describing the universe. Indeed, we know that a new, more fundamental theory is necessary. Therefore, any ideas about what the universe was like at or very soon after the big bang are still necessarily speculative.

One interesting idea that has emerged over the past fifteen years or so is a cyclic universe. A universe that continually dies and is reborn is an ancient concept, but what is novel about the contemporary theory, conceived by Paul Steinhardt and Neil Turok,[35] is that it finds some measure of success in explaining the same data that inflation considers, but with a profoundly different model. In the cyclic model, our three-dimensional universe is embedded in a four-dimensional space, or, in the language of string theory, our universe lives on a "brane" of the higher dimensional space. This brane has a partner brane with which it collides periodically. After a collision, the branes bounce apart, only to slowly be attracted to one another again in the future. It is the energy of the collision that produces the big bang within our three-dimensional universe—or rather, many successive big bangs—and it is the energy between the branes that creates the mysterious dark energy mentioned earlier. Between the big bangs, there are trillions of years of expansion and contraction driven by the dark energy. From the point of view of the higher-dimensional space, the universe grows from cycle to cycle, and its entropy, which determines the arrow of time, also continually increases. But in the three-dimensional world in which we live, and from which we cannot directly see the other dimensions, each cycle appears more or less the same.

The big bang from which we have issued is not the beginning of time in the cyclic model. There is also no singularity at the beginning of a cycle in the three-dimensional universe: everything remains finite and well behaved during the big bang—although there is a large question mark about whether the physics breaks down in the higher-dimensional universe when the two branes collide. This problem aside, however, the cyclic model naturally produces the initial conditions we observe in the universe without requiring inflation. Further, it can be distinguished from inflationary models by the fact that it creates no gravitational waves in the early universe. Hence, if primordial gravity waves are discovered, the cyclic model is ruled out.

It can be asked if the cyclic universe exists forever. The singularity theorems described above that require that the universe not extend infinitely into the past are still valid. However, the situation is subtle, because the enormous expansion of the previous cycle spreads matter out so much that it ends up extremely diluted. This means that the probability of finding a particle that did not originate in the most recent big bang or its predecessor, but in some earlier cycle, is essentially nil. Therefore, in practice there are no particles whose history actually extends back past one or two cycles. For this reason, Steinhardt and Turok "do not attribute any physical significance" to the fact that even the cyclic universe needs initial conditions, simply because those initial conditions get completely erased by all the cycles that have occurred since.[36]

It is significant, in fact, that this "erasing," or perhaps "forgetting," of initial conditions, is not unique to the cyclic model. Inflation too erases information that existed previously, simply by the fact that it stretches everything out so much and so violently. It seems to be a fairly generic feature of primordial cosmological theories that whatever the universe was like initially, its earliest evolution has been made inaccessible to later observers. In this context, Alex Vilenkin opines, "Quantum cosmology is not about to become an observational science. The dispute between different approaches will probably be resolved by theoretical considerations, not by observational data."[37]

Clearly, as with the multiverse conjecture, the nature of empirical science is at stake. The cyclic universe has the virtue that it does not predict gravity waves, and is thus empirically distinguishable from inflation. However, consider the scenario in which inflation did happen but produced gravity waves that are too small to detect. Not detecting gravity waves does not imply that the cyclic model is correct; it implies that we cannot distinguish between inflation with unobservably small gravity waves and the cyclic model with no gravity waves. It would then be unclear whether it is scientifically viable to prefer one or the other of the cyclic or the inflationary models. Although they describe radically different cosmological histories, both would "save the appearances."

Confronted with a potential lack of discriminatory data, cosmologists are somewhat divided. On the one hand, some are comfortable making claims about the origin of the universe based purely on "theoretical considerations," to use Vilenkin's language from above. Guth, Kaiser, and Nomura, who advocate the multiverse paradigm, argue: "The successes that inflation has had in explaining the observed features of the universe give us motivation to explore the speculative ideas about the implications of inflation for questions far beyond what we can observe."[38] Along these lines, Stephen Weinberg is not alone when he muses, "Now we may be at a new turning point, a radical change in what we accept as a legitimate foundation for a physical theory."[39] On the other hand, this kind of logic has been (pejoratively) labelled "postmodern" and "a construct that lies outside of normal science."[40] And George Ellis contends: "It is a retrograde step towards the claim that we can establish the nature of the universe by pure thought without having to confirm our theories by observational or experimental tests. This abandons the key principle that has led to the extraordinary success of science."[41]

This debate is relevant to CEN because of its connection to the contingency I introduced earlier. It often seems at first blush that those who advocate a cosmology relying solely on theory extrapolated to that which is "far beyond what we can observe" are actually expressing a vague conviction that cosmology will eventually become an a priori science. That is, there sometimes appears to be a confidence that our physical theories will one day evince a metaphysical necessity that will make their extension beyond the boundaries of empirical access rigorously valid. If the doctrine of CEN is to be seriously called into question, it must be around this issue. For if cosmology turns out to be not an empirically a posteriori but rather a logically a priori science, then what appears to be contingency in our universe is merely due to our current ignorance. If scientific theory is strictly necessary in all its aspects, then there is no matter (in the classical sense I defined earlier) in the world; or to put it another way, if the world is governed in all its aspects by purely necessary laws, then there is no potentiality properly speaking. CEN claims that matter is created by God; but if there is no matter, there is no CEN.

However, when it comes down to it, I am not aware of any cosmologists that go so far as to propose an approach to cosmology as bald as that caricatured above. All the ideas about the early universe that I am presenting in this paper are ultimately motivated by observations; and everyone insists upon the importance of empirical data. A good example is provided by Hawking and Mlodinow, who, when discussing string theory as a candidate for a complete physical theory explaining everything about the universe, write, "Perhaps the true miracle is that abstract considerations of logic lead to a unique theory that predicts and describes a vast universe full of the amazing variety that we see." But they immediately stress that it must be confirmed by observation before it can be "successful,"[42] thereby effectively conceding that it will never be a purely necessary theory. Further, cosmologists in the so-called postmodern camp still tend to use words like "speculative" or "plausible" to qualify their descriptions, as we saw in the quote from Guth, Kaiser, and Normura above, for instance. It seems, therefore, that the main point of interest is demonstrating not the necessity of theories like the multiverse, but rather their possibility. Hence Lawrence Krauss expresses satisfaction simply in the fact that we can guess at what it *may* have been like: "Plausibility itself, in my view, is a tremendous step forward as we continue to marshal the courage to live meaningful lives in a universe that likely came into existence, and may fade out of existence, without purpose, and certainly without us at its centre."[43]

At the end of the day there does not seem to be any substantial challenge from cosmology to the radical contingency of being in the universe that is premised by CEN. In fact, it is striking just how much of our knowledge about cosmology could not have been predicted. As cataloged earlier in this paper, the last hundred years have seen a series of cosmological surprises: the expansion of the universe, the existence of dark matter and of dark energy and the apparent fine-tuning of initial conditions, to name a few of the more important. Such unexpected discoveries in of themselves are salient indicators of the thoroughgoing contingency I have been emphasizing.

It is important, therefore, to recognize cosmological conjectures, like the multiverse paradigm or the cyclic universe, for what they are. They may be interesting and even worth understanding as possibilities—perhaps even "plausible" possibilities, for what that is worth—but as long as they lack empirical consequences, I would agree with those who caution that they exit the realm of "normal science."[44] Bernard Lonergan has succinctly summarized the latter in a way I find very helpful: "Empirical science rests upon two distinct grounds. As insight grasping possibility, it is science. As verification selecting the possibilities that in fact are realised, it is empirical."[45] This second ground, which was the key advance of modern science over the Aristotelian approach, is what separates conjecture about the physical world from scientific knowledge about the physical world. The commitment to empiricism, which has led to such success in cosmology, entails a commitment to the presence of contingency in the world. In its very philosophical basis, then, cosmology as an empirical science remains open to the possibility of CEN.

Is *EX NIHILO* a Scientific Category?

Our final topic to explore is the notion of *ex nihilo*, particularly because of claims that cosmology can explain how the universe comes "from nothing" without a divine Creator. Popular books such as Lawrence Krauss's *A Universe from Nothing* and Hawking and Mlodinow's *The Grand Design* are recent examples of this atheistic proposal.

Let me preface this section by mentioning that I take it as a matter of course that CEN is not primarily about the beginning of time. It teaches the radical dependence of the contingent being of the universe on God, whose existence is wholly actual and noncontingent. This dependence is clearly not limited to a t equals zero, as though the universe stopped being contingent at t greater than zero. Augustine is at pains to emphasize that although the creation of matter precedes its reception of intelligibility, it is not a temporal precedence, precisely because time is measured by change, which requires form.[46] Saint Thomas argues that the finite age of the universe cannot be demonstrated but is an article of faith;[47] he explains that creation is often associated with the beginning of time not because the beginning encompasses creation, but because time itself was part of creation.[48] What I wish to explore in this section, then, is not the beginning of time as a necessary condition for the possibility of CEN, but rather what *ex nihilo* means with respect to theories of physical cosmology.

The scientific idea that the universe can come from "nothing"—a term we shall certainly examine in due course—is motivated by attempts to circumvent the infinities of the big bang that I introduced in the last section. As I explained, there is currently no viable theory that properly combines quantum mechanics and gravity. Nevertheless, this has not prevented theorists from working on "quantum cosmology," or the introduction of quantum mechanics into the big bang theory in a provisional sort of way. Although it requires sweeping a fair bit of detail under the rug and then arguing that this does not make much difference, quantum cosmology provides what physicists call "toy models": theoretical constructs that we know to be inadequate, but that we hope provide insight into the real world.

One famous model, first proposed by Vilenkin,[49] is that the universe "tunneled" out of nothing. Quantum tunneling is a well-known phenomenon that has been experimentally observed: it means that a system can overcome an energy barrier that it could not do in classical physics. For example, in our sun, nuclear fusion occurs when hydrogen nuclei combine to form helium. Classically, the hydrogen nuclei in the sun are not energetic enough to collide because their mutually repulsive electrical charges are too strong. However, quantum mechanically, there is a probability that hydrogen nuclei will "tunnel" through the electric barrier and fuse to helium. It is one of the consequences of quantum mechanics' uncertainty principle: energy can be "borrowed" if it is "returned" in an appropriate amount of time. In the sun, the extra energy to overcome the repulsion between hydrogen nuclei is promptly returned by the larger amount of energy released when they fuse into helium. Another manifestation of tunneling is the fact that particles can spontaneously appear and disappear in a vacuum. It takes energy to create particles, which the vacuum does not possess, but the uncertainty principle allows two particles appear and annihilate with each other in a brief enough time. Hence particles can tunnel in and out of existence.

Vilenkin proposed that universes may spontaneously appear and disappear like particles, but unlike a pair of particles that appears in a vacuum already embedded in space and time, a spontaneous universe would appear together with its space and time from a state without space and time. According to the uncertainty principle, such a universe would have to quickly disappear. However, Vilenkin calculated that there is actually a nonzero probability for one of these ephemeral universes to tunnel into an inflating universe filled with energy, just like our universe, but only if the total net energy of the resulting universe is zero. This would occur if the positive energy contributed by matter and radiation is precisely canceled out by the negative gravitational energy that obtains when space has a certain geometric curvature. Because the final total energy is zero, no energy would be borrowed, and the universe could persist. Although our own universe appears to be geometrically flat to the best of our observational capabilities, it is possible that inflation stretched space so much that the curvature needed to make the energy zero is present but not detectable. Thus, it is argued that our universe could have emerged from nothing.

Another well-known quantum model is the "no-boundary" proposal of Hartle and Hawking.[50] They make use of the tight-knit relationship between space and time in general relativity. In extreme conditions, such as in black holes, the dimension that we ordinarily label as "time" actually behaves more like what we label "space." Hartle and Hawking argue that the beginning of the universe is best understood not in a geometry consisting of three spatial dimensions and one temporal dimension, such as we are accustomed to, but rather a geometry consisting of four spatial dimensions and no temporal dimension. The universe does "begin" at a point, but this point has no temporal label. "Before" and "after" do not exist, therefore, with reference to this point. Our three-dimensional space with a temporal dimension subsequently emerges from this atemporal four-dimensional space. Hawking and Mlodinow provide the following helpful analogy:

> Suppose the beginning of the universe was like the South Pole of the earth, with degrees of latitude playing the role of time. As one moves north, the circles of constant latitude, representing the size of the universe, would expand. The universe would start as a point at the South Pole, but the South Pole is much like any other point. To ask what happened before the beginning of the universe would become a meaningless question, because there is nothing south of the South Pole.[51]

The no-boundary proposal eliminates the problematic singularity at the beginning of time by reconceptualizing the origin of the universe in an atemporal manner. The universe still comes from nothing (in a sense), but it doesn't "come from" in a conventionally temporal way. On the other hand, whether the mathematical convenience of a spatial dimension switching to a temporal dimension is physically meaningful is not entirely clear.

Their speculative nature notwithstanding, the tunneling and the no-boundary proposals are appealing because the beginning of the universe is physically describable. Physics is not merely given a universe at some early but nonzero initial time before which physics can ask no questions; rather, the universe is intelligible through and through. As Hawking explains of the no-boundary proposal, "[The universe] would quite literally be created out of nothing: not just out of the vacuum but out of absolutely nothing at all because there is nothing outside the universe."[52] Part of what he is expressing here is that his theory, like other quantum cosmological models, includes all of space and time in its purview.

With this brief introduction to quantum cosmology complete, we can return to CEN. Much is made of how quantum cosmology demonstrates that the universe can be created from nothing without God. In their popular book *The Grand Design*, Hawking and Mlodinow conclude: "Spontaneous creation [i.e., as described by quantum cosmology] is the reason there is something rather than nothing, why the universe exists, why we exist. It is not necessary to invoke God to light the blue touch paper and set the universe going."[53] Similarly, in his best seller *A Universe from Nothing*, Lawrence Krauss maintains: "Just as Darwin, albeit reluctantly, removed the need for divine intervention in the evolution of the modern world . . . our current understanding of the universe, its past, and its future make it more plausible that 'something' can arise out of nothing without the need for any divine guidance."[54] In the book's afterword, Richard Dawkins enthusiastically responds: "Even the last remaining trump card of the theologian, 'Why is there something rather than nothing?' shrivels before your eyes as you read these pages."[55]

Of course, the meaning of "nothing" is crucial, and much of Krauss's book is devoted to exploring this question. Despite a fair amount of rambling (e.g., "By nothing, I do not mean nothing, but rather nothing"[56]), he settles on the notion of nothing as physical laws in the absence of space and time,[57] but also indicates there may be a "more fundamental nothingness" than this, by which he seems to mean a preexisting landscape of potential physical theories, such as is envisaged by the multiverse.[58]

Clearly none of these is the metaphysical nothing, or complete absence of being, that is meant by CEN. In the context of a universe tunneling from nothing, Vilenkin is refreshingly frank: "The state of 'nothing' cannot be identified with absolute nothingness. The tunnelling is described by the laws of quantum mechanics, and thus 'nothing' should be subjected to these laws. The laws of physics must have existed, even though there was no universe."[59]

To recast this in the classical language that I employed earlier, even a universe that tunnels from null space-time requires potentiality. And so again we find that matter, in the classical sense, is the crux of CEN in the cosmological context. The *ex nihilo* of CEN is the affirmation that God created even the potential for physical processes to occur in the universe—be it the universe tunneling from a vacuum, emerging from an atemporal state of four spatial dimensions, or entering into an endless cycle of big bangs.

Nonetheless, Krauss resists an exploration of the metaphysical meaning of nothing and of creation—an exercise he characterizes as "abstract and useless" in contrast to the "useful, operational efforts" of physics.[60] He accuses theology of obscurantism because it proposes views on the meaning of nothing "without providing any definition of the term based on empirical evidence."[61] This is highly revealing, because it shows that Krauss operates under a radical scientific reductionism. Being, for Krauss, can be known only through the empirical method. Hawking and Mlodinow are of the same mind. "Philosophy is dead," they claim, for "scientists have become the bearers of the torch of discovery in our quest for knowledge."[62]

This point of view is anticipated by Saint Thomas in the well-known question on "whether God exists": "It seems that everything we see in the world can be accounted for by other principles, supposing God did not exist. For all natural things can be reduced to one principle which is nature."[63] Clearly, the reductionist doctrine is inspired by the fundamental presupposition of the natural sciences that Thomas articulates here, physical cosmology included: the whole of the empirical world is understandable. There is, of course, nothing wrong with this. I for one think it is the most self-consistent position one can have about the physical world. It is therefore fitting for cosmologists not to be content with the notion that there was a time before which physics is impotent; it is very apt that cosmology attempt to explain the whole physical universe including its emergence from a physical nothingness. But as we have seen, a physical nothingness—the absence of space and time and perhaps even of fixed physical laws—is not an absence of potentiality. "Nature itself causes natural things as regards their form, but presupposes matter," as Saint Thomas puts it.[64] Nature is not necessary, but contingent, and as such does not explain itself.

Of course, the crucial question is whether the existence of such a contingent nature needs to be explained by CEN. On the atheistic view there could be contingent facts, such as a quantum wave-function for the universe, that "just are." Ultimately I think this leads to a profound incoherence, for it forces one to hold to the validity of causality and sufficient reason in some cases but not in others. Nevertheless, it is beyond the scope of this essay to defend this position rigorously. My main point is that it is not an issue answerable by physical cosmology. Cosmology as an empirical science presumes that the world is contingent. It cannot, therefore, be used to argue against CEN without destroying its own foundation—a foundation that nobody, including Krauss and Hawking, appears willing to completely abandon. To argue for or against CEN requires moving into the philosophical and theological domains.

What Does Physical Cosmology Say about Creation from Nothing?

In this paper, I have indicated some of the important boundaries between empirical results and speculative conjectures that are present in contemporary cosmology. I have explained that ideas like the multiverse or the spontaneous appearance of the universe are speculative, and in an important sense outside of the traditional domain of empirical science. Additionally, it seems to be a generic theoretical feature that we may never be able to make observations that bear directly on the very beginning of the universe: both the theory of inflation and the cyclic model indicate that information on the prior state of the universe has been erased from our view. The cosmological conjectures I have discussed are indications of what the universe in the totality of its history and extent might *possibly* be like.

Nevertheless, even if they are only possibilities, some cosmologists present scientific theories as alternatives to the theological notion of creation. I have argued throughout this paper that this will not do. The linchpin to my position is the fact that CEN is not merely an explanation for why the universe is as it is, but the claim that the very potential for the universe to be like anything at all must be created: in classical language, God creates matter prior (but not necessarily temporally prior) to the form. I have argued throughout that cosmological theories always presuppose (classical) matter. They do so because they are physical theories, ultimately connected to empirical method, and as such they are possibilities that may happen to be realized, not necessities that must be. Hence, contemporary cosmology actually operates in the same metaphysical framework as CEN, in which the being of the world is thoroughly contingent.

Cosmology will not, therefore, prove or disprove CEN as such, but it still does have something important to say on the subject. For as Lonergan has aptly put it, investigating metaphysical issues without reference to the empirical sciences "exposes the metaphysician to the ever recurrent danger of discoursing on quiddities without suspecting that quiddity means what is to be known through scientific understanding."[65] In the foregoing pages, we have seen important examples of how the science of physical cosmology makes more concrete some of the conceptual framework—the quiddities, so to speak—of CEN. We have seen three important instances of this.

First, cosmology provides insights into how to think of the matter (classically speaking) that CEN explains.[66] The matter of the multiverse is the potential for the inflationary field to take on different values in different places or for the physical parameters of string theory to take on different combinations. The matter of the cyclic universe is the underlying, higher-dimensional space in which the big bang process can occur. The matter of the no-boundary universe or the universe tunneling from a null space-time is an underlying quantum wave-function. These are all concrete (albeit speculative) ways to think about what the matter that is created *ex nihilo* might be like. A topic for further investigation would be how this relates to the classical notion of prime matter. Thus, one might try to determine whether cosmology can probe a fundamental level of intelligibility below which there is *only* matter.

Second, cosmology makes it clear that empty space and time do not constitute nothingness. CEN should not be conceived in a manner in which space and time are a neutral backdrop to the matter of the universe, but rather are part of the empirical world. Einstein's theory of general relativity, which undergirds modern cosmology and has passed every experimental test successfully attempted to date, has at its core the principle that the behavior of space and time is fundamentally connected to the behavior of matter (in the modern sense) and energy; it wholly displaces any Newtonian or Kantian concept of space and time as a priori to the empirical world. Thus, all cosmological theories have space and time as explicitly constitutive elements: the expanse of space containing the multiverse, for instance, or the evolution of branes in the higher dimensions of the cyclic universe. Further, quantum cosmologies, though only toy models, can at least explore the role of space and time in the physical origin of the universe.

Finally, to highlight the latter point in particular, there is an important lesson to be learned from the quantum cosmological attempts to paint a self-consistent picture of how the universe could have a temporal beginning without introducing manifest self-contradictions such as assuming that something happened "before" the beginning. Even if they be speculative, such attempts drive home the Thomistic point I mentioned earlier about time being part of creation. Time is not a supernatural clock that runs the universe from the outside, but is part and parcel with the universe. Hence, even if the universe has not existed forever, it has always existed, in the sense that "always" refers to all possible time, whether it be infinite or finite.[67] Cosmological theory can explore what that might be like physically. Along these lines, I feel that it would be worthwhile exploring with more philosophical rigor the claim of quantum cosmology to be able to describe the spontaneous appearance of the universe in an atemporal fashion. Terms like "spontaneous appearance" or "emergence" seem to denote a kind of change, of which time is normally considered the measure, so one may legitimately ask whether quantum cosmology inadvertently smuggles temporality back into the picture.

In sum, cosmology tells us something about creation not by pushing out theology as a discipline, but rather by elucidating just what the metaphysical terms it employs are like in the world we live in. It is probably not possible for physical cosmology alone to demonstrate that God created everything from nothing. But cosmology can help us to get straight what exactly we might mean by "nothing," and what exactly is included in "everything." True to the traditional metaphor, cosmology is a worthy handmaiden to the theology of creation.

NOTES

1. Henceforth, "cosmology" will be used frequently as shorthand "physical cosmology."

2. E.g., Laura Roberts, "Stephen Hawking: God Was Not Needed to Create the Universe," *The Telegraph*, September 2, 2010, http://www.telegraph .co.uk/news/science/science-news/7976594/Stephen-Hawking-God-was-not -needed-to-create-the-Universe.html.

3. For an overview, see, e.g., Hans Halvorson and Helge Kragh, "Cosmology and Theology," in *The Stanford Encyclopedia of Philosophy*, ed. Edward N. Zalta, 2013, http://plato.stanford.edu/archives/fall2013/entries /cosmology-theology/.

4. Edwin Hubble, "A Relation between Distance and Radial Velocity among Extra-Galactic Nebulae," *Proceedings of the National Academy of Sciences* 15, no. 3 (1929): 168–73.

5. Though Lemaître is credited as being the originator of the big bang theory, the history of the idea's development is complex. See. H. S. Kragh and D. Lambert, "The Context of Discovery: Lemaître and the Origin of the Primeval-Atom Universe," *Annals of Science* 64 (2007): 445–70.

6. P. A. R. Ade et al., "Planck 2015 Results. XIII. Cosmological Parameters," *Astronomy & Astrophysics* 594, id. A13 (2016), http://www.aanda.org /articles/aa/abs/2016/10/aa25830-15/aa25830-15.html.

7. An age of 13.8 billion years corresponds to a *distance* of about 46 billion light years. This is further than the 13.8 billion light years that one would naively infer from the age of the universe for technical reasons stemming from general relativity, but can be calculated very accurately.

8. Technically, this is not quite true. If the universe were finite but only slightly larger than the observable volume, there would be some observable effects (see, e.g., J. Levin, "Topology and the Cosmic Microwave Background," *Physics Reports* 365 [2002]: 290–92 [§4.4]); these have not been detected with current data, however.

9. R. H. Cyburt et al., "Big Bang Nucleosynthesis: 2015," *Reviews of Modern Physics* 88, id.015004 (2016).

10. A. A. Penzias and R. W. Wilson, "A Measurement of Excess Antenna Temperature at 4080 Mc/s.," *Astrophysical Journal* 142 (1965): 419–21.

11. R. H. Dicke et al., "Cosmic Black-Body Radiation," *Astrophysical Journal* 142 (1965): 414–19.

12. For a summary of current constraints on the epoch of the first stars, see L. Koopmans et al., "The Cosmic Dawn and Epoch of Reionisation with SKA," *Advancing Astrophysics with the Square Kilometre Array (AASKA14)* (2015): §2.2, https://pos.sissa.it/cgi-bin/reader/conf.cgi?confid=215.

13. In response to popular presentations of inflation, many ask how the universe could expand faster than the speed of light if the latter is a universal "speed limit." The answer is that in fact during inflation nothing *does* travel faster than light. Just as with the expanding universe, objects are not traveling through space, but space itself is inflating. Hence the speed limit is not violated.

14. A. H. Guth, "Inflationary Universe: A Possible Solution to the Horizon and Flatness Problems," *Physical Review D* 23 (1981): 347–56.

15. A. H. Guth, D. I. Kaiser, and Y. Nomura, "Inflationary Paradigm after Planck 2013," *Physics Letters B* 733 (2014): 112.

16. P. A. R. Ade et al., "Detection of B-Mode Polarization at Degree Angular Scales by BICEP2," *Physical Review Letters* 112, id.241101 (2014), http://journals.aps.org/prl/abstract/10.1103/PhysRevLett.112.241101.

17. P. A. R. Ade et al., "Joint Analysis of BICEP2/Keck Array and Planck Data," *Physical Review Letters* 114, id.101301 (2015), https://physics.aps.org/featured-article-pdf/10.1103/PhysRevLett.114.101301.

18. A. D. Linde, "Chaotic Inflating Universe," *Soviet Journal of Experimental and Theoretical Physics Letters* 38 (1983): 176.

19. B. J. Carr and M. J. Rees, "The Anthropic Principle and the Structure of the Physical World," *Nature* 278 (1979): 605–12; Robin Collins, "The Multiverse Hypothesis: A Theistic Perspective," in *Universe or Multiverse?*, ed. Bernard Carr (Cambridge: Cambridge University Press, 2007), 459–80.

20. Using the criterion that the laws of physics and cosmology must be able to generate a universe like ours, one that is hospitable to life, is usually referred to as *anthropic*. It is a term used with considerable looseness and involves a fair amount of philosophical subtly that is not always fully acknowledged; for this reason, and because it is not necessary to introduce it for the purposes of my paper, I have chosen not to mention it explicitly except in this note.

21. Ade et al., "Joint Analysis of BICEP2/Keck Array and Planck Data."

22. E.g., Guth, Kaiser, and Nomura, "Inflationary Paradigm after Planck 2013."

23. E.g., Anna Ijjas, Paul J. Steinhardt, and Abraham Loeb, "Inflationary Schism," *Physics Letters B* 736 (2014): 142–46.

24. George Ellis, "Opposing the Multiverse," *Astronomy & Geophysics* 49, no. 2 (2008): §2.35.

25. S. Hawking and L. Mlodinow, *The Grand Design* (New York: Random House, 2010), 165.

26. Quoted in Tim Folger, "Science's Alternative to an Intelligent Creator: The Multiverse Theory," December 2008, http://discovermagazine.com /2008/dec/10-sciences-alternative-to-an-intelligent-creator.

27. A. H. Guth, "Inflation and Eternal Inflation," *Physics Reports* 333 (2000): 555–74.

28. Of course, this line of reasoning is not new: it is highly reminiscent, for example, of Epicurean philosophy, which also taught that there is an infinite number of worlds. See, e.g., Epicurus, *Letter to Herodotus* 45, 73.

29. See, e.g., Collins, "Multiverse Hypothesis: A Theistic Perspective."

30. D. N. Page, "Does God So Love the Multiverse?," in *Science and Religion in Dialogue*, ed. Melville Y. Stewart (Chichester: Blackwell, 2010), 380–95.

31. In physics, the word "classical" refers to prequantum theories or concepts. I do not, of course, intend that sense in this paper, but rather use it to refer to the classical period of philosophy which was the original context for CEN.

32. S. W. Hawking and R. Penrose, *The Nature of Space and Time*, Princeton Science Library (Princeton: Princeton University Press, 2000), ch. 1.

33. Hawking and Penrose, *Nature of Space and Time*, 75.

34. Here, of course, "classical" refers to prequantum theory, not to ancient philosophy.

35. P. J. Steinhardt and N. Turok, "A Cyclic Model of the Universe," *Science* 296 (2002): 1436–39; for a popular introduction to their theory, see Steinhardt and Turok, *Endless Universe: Beyond the Big Bang* (New York: Doubleday, 2007).

36. P. J. Steinhardt and N. Turok, "Cosmic Evolution in a Cyclic Universe," *Physical Review D* 65, no. 12 (2002): 8.4.

37. Alex Vilenkin, *Many Worlds in One: The Search for Other Universes* (New York: Hill and Wang, 2006), 193.

38. Guth, Kaiser, and Nomura, "Inflationary Paradigm after Planck 2013."

39. Steven Weinberg, "Living in the Multiverse," in Carr, *Universe or Multiverse?*, 30.

40. Ijjas, Steinhardt, and Loeb, "Inflationary Schism," 145.

41. Ellis, "Opposing the Multiverse," 2.35.

42. Hawking and Mlodinow, *Grand Design*, 181.

43. L. M. Krauss, *A Universe from Nothing: Why There Is Something Rather Than Nothing* (New York: Atria Books, 2012), 147.

44. This is not to claim that the multiverse or the cyclical universe *cannot* have empirical consequences. I simply point out that we currently lack solid empirical data, and I flag the possibility that we may never have them.

45. Bernard Lonergan, *Insight: A Study of Human Understanding* (Toronto: University of Toronto Press, 1992), 101.

46. Augustine, *Confessions* 12.29. As a point of interest, Alex Vilenkin, who developed the notion of the universe tunneling from nothing (see later in this essay), explicitly mentions in one of his scientific papers that Saint Augustine had basically solved the conundrum of what happened before the universe began. A. Vilenkin, "Quantum Origin of the Universe," *Nuclear Physics B* 252 (1985): 141.

47. Thomas Aquinas, *Summa Theologiae* (*ST*), trans. Fathers of the Dominican Province (New York: Benziger Bros., 1947), I.46.2. Thomas notes that because our knowledge of the world is abstracted from the here and now, there cannot be a scientific demonstration of its "newness." An interesting line of inquiry which I do not pursue in this paper is whether this claim is really valid in the light of our ability to see the universe at different times due to the finite speed of light.

48. *ST* I.46.2.

49. A. Vilenkin, "Creation of Universes from Nothing," *Physics Letters B* 117 (1982): 25–28.

50. J. B. Hartle and S. W. Hawking, "Wave Function of the Universe," *Physical Review D* 28 (1983): 2960–75.

51. Hawking and Mlodinow, *Grand Design*, 130.

52. Hawking and Penrose, *Nature of Space and Time*, 83.

53. Hawking and Mlodinow, *Grand Design*, 180.

54. Krauss, *Universe from Nothing*, 147.

55. Ibid., 191.

56. Ibid., 58.

57. Ibid., 170.

58. Ibid., 174, Supplementary Q&A #1.

59. Vilenkin, *Many Worlds in One*, 181.

60. Krauss, *A Universe from Nothing*, xv.

61. Ibid., xvi.

62. Hawking and Mlodinow, *Grand Design*, 5; cf. also 34.

63. *ST* I.2.3.

64. *ST* I.45.2.

65. Lonergan, *Insight*, 533.

66. Matter, of course, is not a quiddity, but it is known when potentiality is realized in form. And the latter can be studied by the natural sciences.

67. I cannot recall for certain, but to give credit where it is due, I believe I received this insight into the meaning of "always" from a colloquium delivered by Roger Penrose to the Princeton Physics Department sometime between 2004 and 2009. Unfortunately, I have not been able to find the date.

CHAPTER 15

Eyesight with Insight

Cosmology and Second-Person Inspiration

ANDREW PINSENT

The story of the origin of the cosmos, as retold in an influential early science fiction novel by Olaf Stapledon, includes the following lines: "Then the Star Maker said, 'Let there be light.' And there was light. From all the coincident and punctual centres of power, light leapt and blazed."[1] Stapledon's novel, written in 1937, clearly alludes both to Genesis 1:3 and to a new theory of cosmology proposed only a decade previously by a Catholic priest and physicist, Fr. Georges Lemaître.[2] This theory, now known as the "big bang," describes the observable universe in terms of an ongoing expansion from a hot and compact state of pure radiation, an account that clearly resonated, for Stapledon and many of his contemporaries, with the text of Genesis.

This pattern of cosmic expansion, from which the term "big bang" derives, raises the obvious questions of why and from what did the expansion originate. Extrapolating back in time, the pattern of expansion also suggests, but cannot prove, a beginning of the cosmos (or at least *this* cosmos). Nevertheless, at every point in space and time at which physical theories can be formulated, there is always *some*thing and never *no*thing, even if the something is described in terms of potential such as a quantum field.³ Similarly, the text of Genesis, prior to the "Let there be light" statement, does not describe a state of absolute nothingness but a formless void with the Spirit of God moving over the face of the waters (Gen. 1:2). Hence the scientific and scriptural narratives to which Stapledon alludes do not begin with nothing but with a state of undifferentiated potential and a first-created state of light or pure radiation from which a vast and differentiated complexity unfolds.

Since Genesis and contemporary science do not begin with nothing, one cannot make simple and direct links with the doctrine of *creatio ex nihilo*. Nevertheless, the doctrine did develop at least in part out of the ancient scriptural texts, and the contemporary account of the cosmos exploding virtually out of a point was seen as consistent enough with the doctrine of *creatio ex nihilo* for Lemaître's theory to be condemned in the Soviet Union for "encouraging clericalism."⁴ One reason for the perceived consonance may be the fact that the primordial states in both the scientific and scriptural accounts lack differentiation into determinate things: a state of being that is not nothing but is also "no things," albeit rich with the potential to generate things. So upon closer examination modern cosmology, the beginning of Genesis, and the doctrine of *creatio ex nihilo* are interwoven in subtle and suggestive ways, even if not in an immediate and simplistic manner.

This chapter explores another way in which the doctrine, the scripture, and modern cosmology are interwoven. *Creatio ex nihilo* did not develop in isolation from other teaching or merely to satisfy intellectual speculation. The doctrine is embedded within a larger theological framework of salvation, notably the principle of a covenant.⁵ In a manner distinct from the classical conceptions of God in ancient philosophy, this covenant is founded on second-person relatedness with God, as "I" to "thou," culminating in divine love or friendship. The question I address in this chapter is how this relationship, at least in principle, may have shaped perception of the cosmos and may be a fruitful context within which to gained new insights. I begin by considering what is meant by insight in ordinary human contexts and the role played by second persons in accelerating insight.

INSIGHT INTO INSIGHT

Whatever the precise relationship between the doctrine of *creatio ex nihilo* and the accounts of creation in Genesis, it is clear that the world of theological discourse about creation is remote from that of current scientific discourse about the early conditions of the observable universe. Theology employs literary genres, whereas papers that follow the conventions of contemporary physics, replete with equations and references to "space-time," "redshifts," "Hubble parameters," and so on, usually epitomize a Cartesian ideal of clear and distinct mathematical laws and categories.

Nevertheless, progress in physics as it is described in papers tends to be rather different from how scientific insight actually works. By the time physics is written up, the formal records have largely been purged of fruitful and fruitless ideas, hunches, inspirations, and so on. In other words, physics as it is reported is an activity that has largely been purged of those judgments of reason that cannot be expressed in mathematical terms. Not only is the story of discovery thereby incomplete but the role of powerful but implicit narratives and influences on the context of theories, such as the notion of space-time as a background, is also overlooked, even when those narratives and influences ought to be challenged.[6]

Even the more prosaic steps of scientific cosmology often rely on intellectual operations that are not strictly justifiable by rational or empirical means. Consider, for instance, Edwin Hubble's famous plot of galactic distance versus recessional velocity.[7] A person who has some familiarity with normal scientific practice "sees" the relationship as more or less a straight line. This linear, proportional relationship between distance and recessional velocity is one of the major pieces of evidence for continuing cosmic expansion from an initial, compact state, now called the "big bang."

As has been investigated many times under the heading of "the problem of induction," however, there is something deeply mysterious about "seeing" an underlying, simple relationship in a scatter of data points, however fruitful this interpretation proves to be.[8] Of course, it is possible to program a computer to find the best fit, but the programmed criteria for success still require a personal judgment based on heuristic guidelines. One such guideline is the presumption of underlying simplicity in the cosmos, a presumption that is not strictly justifiable by rational or empirical means. More subtly, even the objects of empirical study that are modeled as points on a plot, such as galaxies in this case, themselves have to be identified as things that can be placed within a single category, as opposed to being mere patterns of light and dark registered by the pixels of a camera. The intellectual ability to grasp something as a "thing" is deeply mysterious, and not readily explicable from the empirical data and laws of science. As one consequence, the human eye and mind are often superior to computer programs for identifying galaxies in star fields.[9]

Whether one is seeing a group of bright pixels *as* an object, a plot of points *as* a geometric relationship with some random scatter, or the entire universe in one's imagination *as* an ordered whole, such changes do not involve the acquisition of new data. The existing data are instead seen with "new eyes," the very wording of this phrase reflecting the need to resort to strongly evocative metaphors to describe a change in understanding.[10] Such transformations are often given names that denote one or more aspects of their most dramatic instances, such as "epiphany moments," the German "*aha-erlebnis*" (literally, an "aha! moment") and, of course, the "eureka effect" after Archimedes.[11] Accounts of these transformations often also refer to their suddenness, a new ease in solving a problem, positive affect, and a feeling of confidence in being right, although it should also be noted that the more basic and commonplace operations of insight, such as seeing a group of bright pixels *as* a galaxy, may happen without conscious reflection or reaction.[12] Given the widespread use of metaphors of unveiling, illumination, or sight to describe such operations, I refer to the phenomenon that is the main focus of this chapter by the term "insight." As the examples above imply, whatever can be gleaned from eyesight also requires the help of insight, including in cosmology.

Insight, which is also called an "act of understanding"[13] (or more precisely the transition to a new understanding), is clearly indispensable for many of the most significant advances in knowledge. Nevertheless, insight itself remains mysterious and frustratingly resistant to direct study. It is impossible to model insights, which are not the conclusions of arguments,[14] by means of arguments,[15] or to analyze their discrete steps, given their all-at-once quality. Such difficulties are sometimes disguised by the expedient of masking the contribution of insight. For example, the precision of fine-tuning arguments plausibly makes them attractive, at least in part, due to the status of quantitative arguments as the "gold standard" of epistemological value today. Yet quantitative precision often obscures the fact that a judgment is still needed, even if the judgment is "obvious" that there has been a systematic deviation from randomness, as opposed to a remarkable statistical fluctuation.[16] In other words, these cases also require insight, not deduction, to reach the conclusion that God (or something fulfilling a God-like role with respect to the cosmos) is playing with loaded dice. These analytical limitations are compounded by the fact that insights cannot be generated at will and their arrival is not reliably predictable. Instead, insights are often received in a gift-like way, and those who are interested in promoting or studying insights have to resort to heuristic guidelines without guarantee of success, like trying to conduct experiments on lightning.[17]

There are, however, indirect approaches, such as contrasting before-and-after states, possible neural concomitants, and social conditions that promote insights. In particular, although some insights are acquired in social isolation, their quality and rate of acquisition can be increased dramatically in certain social settings. Indeed, good teaching is largely about catalyzing insights, thereby vastly accelerating understanding by others, and plausibly also forming their intellectual dispositions to understand.[18] Theology, as it has developed in Christianity from its Jewish roots, has largely been about relating to God as to a person or to the Trinity of divine persons. Hence it is important to examine more familiar contexts to see how one person can catalyze insights in another. On this basis, it may then be possible to examine how purported personal interaction with a personal God might be expected to modify human understanding, including understanding of the cosmos.

AUSTEN AND AUTISM

For a perceptive account of how a good teacher catalyzes insights, consider the following passage from Jane Austen's *Mansfield Park*:

Kept back as she [Fanny] was by everybody else, his [Edmund's] single support could not bring her forward; but his attentions were otherwise of the highest importance in assisting the improvement of her mind, and extending its pleasures. He knew her to be clever, to have a quick apprehension as well as good sense, and a fondness for reading, which, properly directed, must be an education in itself. Miss Lee taught her French, and heard her read the daily portion of history; but he recommended the books which charmed her leisure hours, he encouraged her taste, and corrected her judgment: he made reading useful by talking to her of what she read, and heightened its attraction by judicious praise. In return for such services she loved him better than anybody in the world except William: her heart was divided between the two.[19]

The use of phrases like "recommending books" and "correcting judgment" in this text indicate at least some of the ways in which one person may help to catalyze the insights of another. As someone who already "sees" the world in relatively more advanced ways, the teacher can provide hints, draw attention to key facts, remove distractions, put questions and praise progress toward the goal that the student cannot perceive in advance of its attainment. In such ways, a second person can vastly accelerate understanding by a first person.

Austen, however, draws attention not only to Edmund's skills as a teacher but also to the love that informs the relationship: "*She [Fannie] loved him [Edmund] better than anybody in the world except William: her heart was divided between the two.*" This use of terms of affection, combined with the description of Edmund's manner of teaching, provides a hint that the effect of his teaching involves more than communication of what is reducible to objective information, expressed as propositions. According to Austen, interpersonal relatedness plays an important role.[20]

What kind of interpersonal relatedness is conducive to this communication? The situation that Austen describes, involving mutual personal presence, is one that has attracted much interest from psychologists and social neuroscientists in recent decades, with many studies emphasizing that much of what is communicated is not easily reducible to propositions. Consider, for example, one of the simplest of all such modes of communication, namely the action of pointing something out to someone in a situation of mutual personal presence. Even this simple action, without words, communicates understanding by abstracting an object from the background of the visual field and indicating to another person that the object is worthy of attention. Moreover, this action is accompanied by at least a momentary shared awareness of shared attention with the other person, often also with a shared "stance" or attitude toward the object of attention.[21]

Although seemingly commonplace, pointing has been described as one of the keys by which an infant begins to unlock the meaning of the world,[22] such actions being instances of a broader range of phenomena called "joint attention" or "second-person relatedness."[23] At a more complex level, the extended dialogue of a teacher and student in a situation of second-person relatedness will often involve the sharing of a complex pattern of stances toward diverse matters, not only by explicit speech (such as pointing out useful books), but also by prosody, nonverbal communication, and a variety of other means.[24] Such exchanges may help to trigger insights, rather as the revelation of fragments of a picture from a new and hitherto unknown perspective may suddenly be interpolated into a whole image from that perspective. Another and possibly complementary way of thinking about this process might be that of two systems coming into harmony and thereby sharing similar cognitive capacities. Whatever the precise means, understanding that is gained from another and shared with another in this context of joint attention could be called *second-person understanding*.

Given the success of teaching at accelerating insights, it seems plausible that there is such a thing as second-person understanding, specifically in the context of "I"-"you" relatedness. Nevertheless, given the wide range of other means of communication and possible causes of insights, it is not straightforward to test this hypothesis. One possibility is to examine situations in which second-person relatedness is atypical and to examine whether there are any unusual and concomitant impacts on a person's capacity to understand. Of the range of such conditions, autistic spectrum disorder (ASD) is especially important for these studies. A person with severe ASD is sometimes described as not seeing persons,[25] although careful studies in fact suggest that ASD does not involve a lack of third-person recognition of a person, that is, as a special kind of object in the world. What is missing or inhibited, rather, is second-person relatedness, as of "I" to "you." This absence is corroborated by the frequent association of ASD with the phenomenon of "pronoun reversal," by which a person makes mistakes in using the correct grammatical forms for second persons.[26] Hence, if second-person relatedness does indeed contribute to the development of understanding of all kinds of matters, including cosmology, then the expectation is that those with ASD will have difficulties in understanding or perhaps have atypical ways of understanding the world.

Is this correlation found in practice? A properly justified response would be a major project in itself, and there would be a need to try to isolate the direct impact of second-person relatedness on understanding from effects that may be due to other factors associated with ASD. Nevertheless, under a variety of terms going back to Kanner's original description of autism,[27] research suggests that there is indeed a correlation with atypical patterns of understanding. To give a few of many examples, those with ASD often focus on local features instead of global patterns,[28] suggesting a difficulty in turning many "trees" into a single "forest" within which the trees stand.[29] Another commonly reported difficulty is being overwhelmed in social situations or crowded places, consonant with an inability to group and set aside details.[30] Other difficulties include a failure to consolidate learning over time and poor predictive abilities, such as a failure to anticipate picking-up by parents and the timing of air puffs to eyes,[31] as well as difficulties in grasping the intentions conveyed by social cues.[32] All these symptoms can be interpreted as an undeveloped capacity to understand, insofar as they involve difficulties in relating parts to wholes, or grasping the underlying regularities of the world, or in comprehending the intentions of others. On the other hand, by way of compensation, those with ASD may display superior performance on local tasks, including reduced contextual modulation or interference.[33]

These many findings suggest that an inability to engage in joint attention or second-person relatedness also inhibits one of the most common ways in which human persons acquire insights in the context of relating to others, and perhaps also inhibits the dispositions to acquire insights. Conversely, teaching by a second person in the context of joint attention can vastly accelerate the rate and quality of the acquisition of insights by a first person. Hence the role of a second person in teaching is not simply as a source of information that is reducible, in principle, to the communication of objective propositions. There is a growing body of evidence in support of the view that shared awareness of shared focus, in the manner of joint attention or second-person relatedness, plays a critically important role in communicating understanding and encouraging the development of the faculty of understanding. This connection between second-person relatedness and the development of understanding is one reason, I suggest, why an impersonal computer cannot replace a personal teacher, or that a child cannot learn language simply by watching videos.[34]

SECOND-PERSON INSPIRATION

What are the implications of second-person understanding for a theologically informed cosmology, in particular, the impact on understanding the cosmos when second-person relatedness is with a divine rather than a human person? Within the context of classical philosophy, the notion of a relationship between God and human beings that could be described as "second-personal" is uncommon to the point of nonexistence. Although Aristotle refers to God in the third person, he does not address God as a second person and even denies that it is possible to be friends with God.[35]

Nevertheless, the account drawn from natural philosophy is not, of course, the whole story of purported human interactions with God. A central theme in the history of the Jewish people (taken up and transfigured by Christianity) is the notion of a covenant with God. The use of terms pertaining to marriage as metaphors for covenants, as well as adultery for breaking them, underlines that they are to be understood in what would today be called second-personal terms, as "I" to "you."[36] In the book of Job, however, a covenant has been made but is not yet wholly efficacious. This separation from God is correlated, according to the book of Job, with limitations of human understanding as seen, for example, in the following passage from chapter 38: "Where were you when I laid the foundations of the earth? Tell me, if you have understanding. Who determined its measurements? Surely you know! Or who stretched the line upon it? To what were its foundations fastened? Or who laid its cornerstone, when the morning stars sang together, and all the sons of God shouted for joy?"[37] In this passage, God communicates with Job, but principally to underline how Job does not understand the cosmos. Moreover, there is a sense that Job, representing natural human perfection, is still cut off from understanding God's interactions with other beings, including the sons of God, the drops of dew (v. 28), the belt of Orion (v. 31), and young lions (v. 38), to whom God relates in a remarkably intimate way. One can gain the impression from the text that there is a kind of playful intimacy between God and creation from which humanity is self-excluded.

Consider, by contrast, the following passage taken from one of the earliest Christian documents outside the New Testament. This text is the work of someone whose whole life revolves around the perception of a new covenant with God revealed in the incarnation, a life in which human beings have themselves received the grace of adoption as children of God, with the gift of the Holy Spirit and the promise of seeing the face of God:

> The heavens, revolving under his government, are subject to him in peace. Day and night run the course appointed by him, in no wise hindering each other. The sun and moon, with the companies of the stars, roll on in harmony according to his command, within their prescribed limits, and without any deviation. The fruitful earth, according to his will, brings forth food in abundance, at the proper seasons, for man and beast and all the living beings upon it, never hesitating, nor changing any of the ordinances which he has fixed.[38]

What is striking in this second passage is the calm confidence of the writer, who perceives order and harmony from the largest to the smallest beings, under the authority of God, who has become known. The cosmos is not perceived as an accidental assemblage, or the operation of some vast, impersonal mechanism, or the work of an unknowable or only partly known divinity (or divinities). On the contrary, this second-person relatedness to God is accompanied by a new understanding of the cosmos as harmonious, law-like, and potentially knowable. Whatever the veracity of the theological claims, one can plausibly attribute a new cultural confidence to this change of perspective, a confidence to uncover this cosmic order with an expectation of success.

Later theological development put this distinction on a systematic basis. The state of second-person relatedness to God, as described in Augustine's *Confessions*,[39] was classified as a "supernatural" *life of grace*. This relation is absent from the Aristotelian *life of nature*, which could be thought of, in contemporary terms, as spiritually autistic from the perspective of grace.[40] Later theological developments also assigned a distinction of two kinds of dispositions (*habitus*) of understanding (*intellectus*): the intellectual virtue that human beings have by nature[41] and, in the life of grace, a new kind of understanding that is a gift of the Holy Spirit.[42] In the work of Thomas Aquinas, all these gifts, including understanding, are interpreted as dispositions enabling what would today be called "joint attention" with God, by which human beings are moved, out of love, to love with God the things that God loves.[43] So theology already has a place reserved for a special kind of understanding that a person gains specifically in the context of second-person relatedness with God, as opposed to other possible sources of revelation, such as words carved into tablets of stone. This account dovetails well with all kinds of stories in which someone suddenly sees the world from a new perspective, a world that has not changed visibly, but is grasped with a new understanding in the perceived presence of a divine person.[44] One might call such insight "second-person inspiration."

Faced with this claim, however, a skeptic would rightly demand whether these purported second-person inspirations have effects that can be discerned by a third person. In other words, besides first-person experiences, attitudes to creation, and theology itself, is there really any observable and significant change in the way that the natural world is understood as a result of such inspirations?

I suggest that the answer is "yes." The evidence for this claim can be seen in a sequence of famous representations of nature that more or less track the decline in the cultural and artistic importance of second-person relatedness to God. Starting with Van Eyck, *The Ghent Altarpiece* or *The Adoration of the Mystic Lamb* (1432), one sees what is arguably the most theologically perfect symbolic painting of the kingdom of heaven that art has ever attempted. A theme of this image is that the focus on the perfection of the divine life of grace, centered on the divine liturgy, is accompanied by the perfection of nature. In the transition from Van Eyck to Joachim Patinir, *The Penitence of St. Jerome* (c. 1518), there is, however, a diminishment of the life of grace in comparison to nature, indicated by the small figure of Saint Jerome in the foreground and the large landscape in the background. This transition is continued with the obscured church in the background of Pieter Bruegel the Elder, *The Harvesters* (1565), and is complete in wholly natural focus of Constable, *The Hay Wain* (1821). A few decades later, however, Van Gogh, *Wheatfield with Crows* (1890), has a road going nowhere, a compressed vertical dimension, and blurred creatures. Finally, in the work of Jackson Pollock, *Enchanted Forest* (1947), there are no discernible features left. Without making a judgment about the comparative value of these works, what is striking is the way in which the loss of second-person relatedness to God, as a first principle of art, artists, and the broader culture, has been followed by an extraordinary decline in the ordered perception of the world.

While those working in physical cosmology today might regard such cultural changes with equanimity, I suggest that art is playing the role of the proverbial canary in the mine, or possibly the dead bird suffocated by an early air pump in the famous painting by Joseph Wright in 1768. The loss of perceived second-person relatedness with God has already had a profound impact on art and may eventually have an impact on science, including cosmology. Lest this claim seem fanciful, it should be noted that some recent influential studies have suggested that much of intellectual life, including that of the hard sciences, is already suffering the effects of the changes anticipated by art. These effects include a paucity of new insights, a loss of coherence and fragmentation,[45] which has also been characterized in terms of an eclipsed right-hemisphere cognition of the world.[46] If this trend continues, the loss of the influence of the theological context that gave rise to the doctrine of *creatio ex nihilo* will presage a more general and widespread cultural descent into nihilism.

FUTURE INSIGHTS

The conclusion that we understand the cosmos in ways that are strongly influenced by our theology is scarcely new and has been explored with great subtlety from at least the time of J. Wisdom's "Parable of the Garden."[47] What is less widely recognized, I believe, is the way in which this understanding is shaped not only by the knowledge of certain things about God as Creator, but by the perception of relating to God as to a second person in the context of a covenant, the ground also of the doctrine of *creatio ex nihilo*. Whatever the precise explanation, it is this relationship that seems to be associated with a cultural confidence for seeing the cosmos as harmonious, law-like, and potentially knowable. Conversely, there is evidence that the decline of a sense of second-person relatedness with God has been associated with a loss of a sense of coherence in nature.

How then can we best hope to accelerate our insights into creation in future? In the case of ordinary insights from other human persons, a good strategy can be to get out more, to spend time mixing with colleagues in other fields, and to listen respectfully and learn from those with different perspectives and expertise.[48] Faced with the sometimes dreary earnestness of the modern academy, we urgently need to rediscover the value of intellectual play, especially in dialogue with others, to break the ice of frozen representations that can form so quickly over our cognition of the world.[49]

Perhaps something similar may be said about the need to spend time with God. After all, if there is a God who created the cosmos and who desires a covenant with human beings, then God is unlikely to be a passive player in the relationship. On the contrary, covenant is enriched by shared understanding, so God will presumably want to accelerate the insights of human persons, including insights into the created cosmos as a whole. As in the case of communicating insights between human persons, the acceleration and communication of these insights is likely to arise principally in the context of lives and cultures that are infused with a strong sense of an "I"-"you" relationship with God. The practices that cultivate this sense of communion include the assimilation of divinely revealed narratives, sacraments, liturgies, sacred art, and perhaps, via harmonization on a subliminal level, sacred music. Above all and in the spirit of a noetic version of Pascal's wager, in which one seeks understanding by venturing a standpoint of faith, one needs to pray.

Notes

I am grateful to the Analytic Theology project at the University of Innsbruck, the intellectual humility project led by Daniel Jayes O'Brien at Oxford Brookes University, and the Department of Theology at the University of Notre Dame for the opportunity to present and receive feedback for ideas presented in this chapter. I am also grateful for the opportunities provided by the "Special Divine Action" project at Oxford University, supported by a grant from the John Templeton Foundation.

1. Olaf Stapledon, *Star Maker* (London: Methuen & Co. Ltd., 1937), ch. 13.

2. Georges Lemaître, "Un Univers Homogène de Masse Constante et de Rayon Croissant Rendant Compte de La Vitesse Radiale Des Nébuleuses Extra-Galactiques," *Annales de La Société Scientifique de Bruxelles* 47A (1927): 49–59. For a history of the work of Georges Lemaître and its reception, see Helge Kragh, *Cosmology and Controversy* (Princeton: Princeton University Press, 1999).

3. There are many reasons why the big bang does not lead directly to the notion of a true beginning of the cosmos, not least the problem that all possible clocks are absorbed into the initial singularity. More generally, the big bang, insofar as it can be expressed as a scientific theory, can only describe how some created things become other created things, and not how things come to be in an absolute sense.

4. Helge Kragh, *Cosmology and Controversy* (Princeton: Princeton University Press, 1999), 262.

5. Justin Stratis, "Unconditional Love: Creatio Ex Nihilo and the Covenant of Grace," in *Theological Theology*, ed. R. David Nelson, Darren Sarisky, and Justin Stratis (New York: Bloomsbury, 2015), 286.

6. For a detailed study of some of the current mysteries and problems regarding progress in physics, see, for example, Lee Smolin, *The Trouble with Physics: The Rise of String Theory, The Fall of a Science, and What Comes Next* (New York: Houghton Mifflin Harcourt, 2006). One theme of the book is the failure to examine background assumptions, such as the treatment of space-time as an invariant background to phenomena.

7. Edwin Hubble, "A Relation between Distance and Radial Velocity among Extra-Galactic Nebulae," *Proceedings of the National Academy of Sciences* 15, no. 3 (1929): 168–73 (fig. 1).

8. The "problem" of induction, made famous by the epistemological framework of David Hume, *An Enquiry concerning Human Understanding*, Oxford World's Classics (Oxford: Oxford University Press, 2007), ch. 4, is another way of expressing the discontinuity between what can be achieved by discursive reasoning and insight. The connection between induction and insight is made, for example, in Bernard J. F. Lonergan, *Insight: A Study of Human Understanding*, ed. Frederick E. Crowe and Robert M. Doran, in *The*

Collected Works of Bernard Lonergan, 5th ed., revised and augmented (Toronto: University of Toronto Press for Lonergan Research Institute of Regis College, 1988), 3:313.

9. See, for example, "Galaxy Zoo," http://www.galaxyzoo.org/. This project involves the public in helping to classify galaxies, on the basis of the reliability and flexibility of the human ability to grasp a pattern of bright pixels as a galaxy, across an extraordinarily wide variety of irregular shapes.

10. Hence those studying insight have also taken a particular interest in psychology, especially *gestalt* psychology. See Ludwig Wittgenstein, *Philosophical Investigations*, trans. by G. E. M. Anscombe (New York: Macmillan, 1953), II.xi.

11. Pioneering work on the "aha! moment," as an "inner illumination," was carried out by Karl Bühler; cf. *The Mental Development of the Child: A Summary of Modern Psychological Theory*, trans. O. A. Oeser, International Library of Psychology, Philosophy, and Scientific Method (London: Kegan Paul, Trench, Trübner, 1930), ch. 14. See also Pamela M. Auble et al., "Effort toward Comprehension: Elaboration or 'aha'?," *Memory & Cognition* 7, no. 6 (1979): 426–34. The term "epiphany" to describe such moments is from the Greek *epiphaneia*, meaning "manifestation" or "striking appearance," a word now associated with the liturgical feast of Epiphany, commemorating the wise men finding the child Jesus (Gospel of Matthew 2:1–11). The term was adapted to a more secular context in literature principally by the work of James Joyce; see, for example, Zack Bowen, "Joyce and the Epiphany Concept: A New Approach," *Journal of Modern Literature* 9, no. 1 (1981): 103–14.

12. Sascha Topolinski and Rolf Reber, "Gaining Insight into the 'Aha' Experience," *Current Directions in Psychological Science* 19, no. 6 (2010): 402–5.

13. The notion that insight is experienced as a new presentation of the world, rather than a manipulation of preexisting representations, is consonant with its other characteristics. For example, the word "insight" and other visual metaphors associated with the phenomenon, like the exclamation "I see," imply the immediate and all-at-once cognition of something new. Moreover, this "seeing" with the mind is often closely associated with the perception of an object, with the eyes or in the imagination. It is plausible, for instance, that what provoked the famous "Eureka!" of Archimedes was not immediate knowledge of the steps required to solve the problem, the details of which were presumably elucidated later, but "seeing" the solution implicitly and inchoately by seeing the water rising up the side of the bath.

14. For such reasons among others, it has proved impossible to program any kind of computer to generate insights, a major frustration to efforts to create artificial intelligence. For an account of the problems that insight presents

to the challenge of artificial intelligence, see, for example, Stuart Shanker, *Wittgenstein's Remarks on the Foundations of AI* (London: Routledge, 1998), ch. 4. This distinction between discursive reasoning, associated with the manipulation of representations of the world, and insights, associated with new presentations of the world, parallels a widely observed asymmetry in the typical operations of the two hemispheres of the brain. Iain McGilchrist has compiled a vast body of evidence that supports the position that use of the left hemisphere (LH) of the brain is biased toward the use of existing representations and models of the world, toward the analysis of parts rather than the perception of wholes, and toward linear, sequential arguments. By contrast, the use of right hemisphere (RH) is more closely associated with *gestalt* perception, new presentations, and metaphor, by which words carry over into embodied experience. See especially ch. 2 of Iain McGilchrist, *The Master and His Emissary: The Divided Brain and the Making of the Western World* (New Haven: Yale University Press, 2009). Insight has been associated specifically with RH activation, mainly the right anterior temporal area, specifically in the right anterior superior temporal gyrus. Where high levels of restructuring are required, there is also activity in the right prefrontal cortex. See Edward M. Bowden and Mark Jung-Beeman, "Aha! Insight Experience Correlates with Solution Activation in the Right Hemisphere," *Psychonomic Bulletin & Review* 10, no. 3 (2003): 730–37; John Kounios et al., "The Origins of Insight in Resting-State Brain Activity," *Neuropsychologia* 46, no. 1 (2008): 281–91; Simone Sandkühler and Joydeep Bhattacharya, "Deconstructing Insight: EEG Correlates of Insightful Problem Solving," *Public Library of Science One (PLOS ONE)* 3, no. 1 (2008): e1459.

15. True insights may even undermine previous, apparently consistent arguments. Galileo's challenge to geocentrism was arguably a case of a true insight, raising problems lacking immediate solution; cf. Paul Feyerabend, *Against Method*, updated ed. with a new introduction by Ian Hacking (London: Verso, 2010).

16. I am thinking here of the following scenario. If I roll one, two, or even three straight pairs of sixes in a game, you would probably just consider that I am lucky. If I roll a hundred such pairs, you would almost certainly judge that I am playing with loaded dice. Yet even a million such pairs in succession would violate no physical laws, even for a perfect pair of dice, and one cannot create a precise mathematical rule, based on the number of sixes rolled in succession, for reaching the conclusion that the dice are loaded. Regardless of the apparent mathematical nature of the problem, a human judgment is required, as is also the case for so-called "fine-tuning" arguments in cosmology.

17. Rule-of-thumb recommendations include attending to connections, coincidences, and curiosities, investigating contradictions, and "creating breakthrough solutions through the force of desperation," according to Gary Klein,

Everything That Follows Is Different: The Disruptive Power of Insight (New York: PublicAffairs, U.S., 2013).

18. "Teaching is a vast acceleration of the process of learning. It throws out the clues, the pointed hints, that lead to insights; it cajoles attention to remove the distracting images that obstruct them; it puts the further questions that reveal the need of further insights to complement and modify and transform the acquired store." Lonergan, *Insight*, 3:315.

19. Jane Austen, *Mansfield Park*, ed. James Kinsley, Oxford World's Classics (Oxford: Oxford University Press, 2003), 18.

20. I use the term "relatedness" rather than "relation" or "relationship" because the latter words convey an intimacy or familiarity that may not be present in all pertinent cases. I am grateful to Peter Hobson for making this point to me.

21. By "stance" I mean what Eleonore Stump has described as a "conative attitude prompted by the mind's understanding"; see Eleonore Stump, "The Non-Aristotelian Character of Aquinas's Ethics: Aquinas on the Passions," *Faith and Philosophy* 28, no. 1 (2011): 41.

22. Clara Claiborne Park, *The Siege: The First Eight Years of an Autistic Child (With an Epilogue, Fifteen Years After)* (Boston: Little, Brown, 1982), 6.

23. Naomi Eilan et al., eds., *Joint Attention: Communication and Other Minds; Issues in Philosophy and Psychology* (Oxford: Clarendon Press, 2005). I explore the close connection, to the point of interchangeability, between "joint attention" and "second-person relatedness" in Andrew Pinsent, *The Second-Person Perspective in Aquinas's Ethics: Virtues and Gifts* (New York: Routledge, 2012), 47–49.

24. There is a vast literature on these matters, the emphasis of which is the need to think about language not simply in terms of symbol use and organization, but as a communicative interaction between persons. See, for example, John T. Nusbaum, "Language and Communication," in *The Oxford Handbook of Social Neuroscience*, ed. Jean Decety and John T. Cacioppo, 1st ed. (New York: Oxford University Press, 2011), 668–79.

25. Park, *Siege*, 93.

26. I describe this connection between autistic spectrum disorder (ASD) and lack of second-person relatedness in Pinsent, *Second-Person Perspective in Aquinas's Ethics*, ch. 2.

27. Leo Kanner, "Autistic Disturbances of Affective Contact," *The Nervous Child* 2 (1943): 217–50.

28. See, for example, Uta Frith and Francesca Happé, "Autism: Beyond 'Theory of Mind,'" *Cognition* 50, no. 1–3 (1994): 115–32; Simon Baron-Cohen, "The Extreme Male Brain Theory of Autism," *Trends in Cognitive Sciences* 6, no. 6 (2002): 248–54; Francesca Happé and Uta Frith, "The Weak Coherence

Account: Detail-Focused Cognitive Style in Autism Spectrum Disorders," *Journal of Autism and Developmental Disorders* 36, no. 1 (2006): 5–25.

29. Ning Qian and Richard M. Lipkin, "A Learning-Style Theory for Understanding Autistic Behaviors," *Frontiers in Human Neuroscience* 5, no. 77 (2011): 4–6. See also Temple Grandin, *Thinking in Pictures: And Other Reports from My Life with Autism*, 2nd ed. (London: Bloomsbury, 2006).

30. John Elder Robison, *Be Different: Adventures of a Free-Range Aspergian with Practical Advice for Aspergians, Misfits, Families & Teachers* (New York: Crown Archetype, 2011).

31. Kanner, "Autistic Disturbances of Affective Contact"; Lonnie L. Sears, Peter R. Finn, and Joseph E. Steinmetz, "Abnormal Classical Eye-Blink Conditioning in Autism," *Journal of Autism and Developmental Disorders* 24, no. 6 (1994): 737–51.

32. Courtenay Frazier Norbury, Helen Griffiths and Kate Nation, "Sound before Meaning: Word Learning in Autistic Disorders," *Neuropsychologia* 48, no. 14 (2010): 4013.

33. See again, for example, Frith and Happé, "Autism: Beyond 'Theory of Mind'"; Baron-Cohen, "Extreme Male Brain Theory of Autism"; Happé and Frith, "Weak Coherence Account."

34. Many studies have highlighted the importance of social interaction to language acquisition. See, for example, Sarah Roseberry, Kathy Hirsh-Pasek, and Roberta Michnick Golinkoff, "Skype Me! Socially Contingent Interactions Help Toddlers Learn Language," *Child Development* 85, no. 3 (2014): 956–70.

35. Aristotle, *Nicomachean Ethics* 8.7.1158b36–1159a3.

36. See, for example, Isa. 54:5; Jer. 3:20; Ezek. 16:15–19; and especially the book of Hosea, in which the adultery of the prophet's wife, Gomer, signifies the sin of the children of Israel (Hosea 2:2–5; 3:1–5; 9:1) in breaking their covenant with God; in the New Testament see, for example, James 4:4–5. Note that many cultural and religious practices in these traditions also serve to encourage, express, or defend the notion of second-person relatedness with God in the manner of a covenant. For example, the notion of a covenant is central to much liturgy and sacrifice, and one can also point to the extensive use of narratives in sacred texts, the unique literary genre that communicates a sense of knowing a person, as well as the emphasis on the face in Christian art, following the incarnation.

37. Job 38:4–7. I have used the New King James translation.

38. The translation is from James Donaldson and Alexander Roberts, eds., *The Apostolic Fathers with Justin Martyr and Irenaeus*, vol. 1, Ante-Nicene Christian Library: Translations of the Writings of the Fathers down to A.D. 325 (Edinburgh: T&T Clark, 1867).

39. See, for example, Augustine, *Confessions* 10.27.38.

40. The phrase "spiritual autism" should, of course, be read as a metaphor, just as "spiritual blindness" has long been a metaphor in theological discourse, without implying that the corporeally blind are spiritually inhibited. As I have argued in detail in Pinsent, *Second-Person Perspective in Aquinas's Ethics*, especially ch. 2, the vast systematic description of this life of grace developed by Thomas Aquinas is not only organized around divine friendship but has, as its root metaphor, the notion of being moved by God in a second-person way, comparable to shared awareness of shared focus with a human person. So one of the most influential and most detailed articulations of the meaning of the life of grace has as its core principle the notion of second-person relatedness with God, a condition in which the innate "spiritual autism" of the postlapsarian human condition is dispelled.

41. Aquinas, *Summa Theologiae (ST)* I-II.57.2.

42. The gift of understanding, in contrast to the homonymous virtue of understanding, is described in *ST* II-II.8. According to Aquinas, all the infused virtues and gifts have the form of divine love (*caritas*) or friendship; cf. *ST* II-II.23.8.

43. See Pinsent, *Second-Person Perspective in Aquinas's Ethics*, ch. 2.

44. As a description of what such moments are like, see, for example, C. S. Lewis, *That Hideous Strength: A Modern Fairy-Tale for Grown-Ups* (London: Bodley Head, 1945), 395.

45. See, for example, Smolin, *Trouble with Physics*. See also McGilchrist, *Master and His Emissary*.

46. See McGilchrist, *Master and His Emissary*.

47. J. Wisdom, "Gods," *Proceedings of the Aristotelian Society*, n.s., 45 (1944): 185–206.

48. Cf. Alex Pentland, *Social Physics: How Social Networks Can Make Us Smarter*, reissue ed. (New York: Penguin, 2015), 26–27: "The most consistently creative and insightful people are explorers. They spend an enormous amount of time seeking out new people and different ideas, without necessarily trying very hard to find the 'best' people or the 'best' ideas. Instead, they seek out people with *different* views and *different* ideas."

49. This situation is depicted in Hans Christian Andersen's "The Snow Queen," in which the boy Kai is trapped in the Snow Queen's palace, where he endlessly rearranges blocks of ice. In the story, he is unable to escape until the love and tears of his childhood friend Gerta dissolve the indifference of his heart, and his eyes are opened to new understanding. For a translation, see, for example, Hans Christian Andersen, *The Complete Fairy Tales and Stories*, trans. Erik Christian Haugaard (London: Victor Gollancz, 1974). For an analysis, see Andrew Pinsent, "Special Divine Insight: Escaping the Snow Queen's Palace," *European Journal for Philosophy of Religion* 7, no. 4 (2015): 173–96.

CHAPTER 16

Looking Back toward the Origin

Scientific Cosmology as Creation ex nihilo
Considered "from the Inside"

ANDREW DAVISON

The origins of the universe have not always been open to us as a topic for scientific investigation. Writing in the late 1260s, Thomas Aquinas judged that "the newness of the world cannot be demonstrated on the part of the world itself."[1] His empirical agnosticism about beginnings, in this case his sense that no form of empirical investigation could determine whether or not the universe had a beginning, remained an accurate assessment of the state of physical cosmology into the twentieth century. Only with Edwin Hubble's confirmation, in the early 1920s, that certain objects in the sky lie outside our galaxy (the Milky Way), and with related observations that allowed him and others to infer the expansion of the universe,[2] was scientific elucidation of the early moments of the observable universe possible.

Today, almost a century later, cosmologists are increasingly able, in scientific terms, to describe the behavior of the universe in its earliest moments. Going beyond scientific considerations, however, this has

sometimes been presented as overthrowing theological (and philosophical) perspectives, and apt to render them obsolete.[3] In contrast, I
will argue here that theologians have every reason to welcome such
scientific investigations as complementary to their own formulations.
The theologian can take any elaboration of the early moments of the
universe that is genuinely cosmological (rather than philosophical)—
even an elaboration of the origination of the universe *as such* (understood scientifically)—as providing a description of what creation *ex
nihilo* looks like "from the inside."

Quantum Fluctuations and Inflation

We can begin by considering some of the principal cosmological proposals that have been under discussion in recent decades concerning the
early universe. Among these potential descriptions of the origination of
the universe in physical terms, one prominent class takes its lead from a
phenomenon that is also observed in the world as we know it today,
albeit indirectly: the momentary production of matter, and therefore
energy (within the already existing arena of space-time), known as quantum (or vacuum) fluctuation.[4] This phenomenon sees particles and anti-
particles emerge momentarily into existence within empty space (on
account of which, no space *can* properly said to be empty). This phenomenon follows as a consequence of Heisenberg's uncertainty principle, according to which quantities of energy are ill-defined over very
short periods of time. Particle-antiparticle pairs can therefore come into
existence for an infinitesimal period of time—too short for them to be
detected directly—without their arrival violating the principle of the
conservation of energy: the difference from zero of the energy associated with these particles falls within the margin of uncertainty described
by Heisenberg's principle.[5] Although this phenomenon, and these particles, cannot be detected directly, because they exist for such a short
period of time, their influence on the properties of otherwise-existing
matter can, which provides indirect but forceful confirmation of such
fluctuations. In particular, the prediction of a feature of the way in
which atoms interact with light—the so-called Lamb shift in atomic
spectra—accords with experiment only when the influence of these
fleeting particles is included in the calculations.

In 1973, Edward Tyron proposed quantum fluctuation as a mechanism for the creation of our universe.[6] On the face of it, this is not a promising phenomenon as an explanation for the existence of the universe as a whole: such fluctuations, as we know them, apply to individual particles and for an infinitesimal duration, whereas Tyron was talking about the whole of the universe, over the whole course of its history, 13.8 billion years (so far). His reply was that the enormous positive energy of the universe (including that associated with its matter) can be said to be canceled out by the formally "negative energy" associated with gravitational attraction.[7] Whatever we make of that, we should note that Tyron was emphatically not attempting, with this proposal, to account for the existence of the whole of reality per se, since he takes his theory to assume the existence of a "vacuum of some larger space in which our universe is embedded."[8]

The phenomenon of quantum fluctuation has gained a stronger standing as a proposal for the way in which the universe emerged by combination with what may count as the most extraordinary proposed feature of the early universe, namely its incomprehensibly rapid initial inflation.[9] The claim is that the universe increased in size by a factor of somewhere between 10^{21} and 10^{43} in the period stretching between 10^{-36} second and 10^{-34} second after the big bang.[10] Hawking and Mlodinow spell those numbers out in full: "according to even conservative estimates, during this cosmological inflation, the universe expanded by a factor of 1,000,000,000,000,000,000,000,000,000,000" over the course of an infinitesimal period of time: a mere "0.00000000000000000000000000000000001 second."[11] Qualitatively, this magnitude of expansion is as if "a coin one centimetre in diameter suddenly blew up to ten million times the width of the Milky Way." After this unimaginably rapid *inflationary* phase was over, the much more moderate business of cosmic *expansion* continued, according to the way it had already been laid out, following Lemaître and others, in the "standard model."

This "inflation scenario" was first proposed by Alan Guth in the early 1980s, as a way to account for what seem to be peculiar initial features of the universe, otherwise unexplained by the standard model up until then, including its seeming high degree of uniformity and flatness (a technical cosmological term to do with the sort of geometry that characterizes the universe). These features could be explained by a period of extraordinarily rapid expansion, through which the universe came to possess a state that was much more favorable, in terms of energy, than the state of its initial existence. (This is comparable, for instance, to a ball rolling down a hill, into a more favorable state of energy.) The vast domain of energy and matter that characterizes the universe as we now know it "crystallized out" during this process.[12] The inflation scenario, while not supported by all cosmologists, is currently generally regarded as the most promising description of the very early universe.

According to the combination of quantum fluctuation with inflation, which I trailed above, the *fluctuation* brought a state of energetic-material being into existence, and *inflation* then followed. After inflation, if need be, the energy associated with the initial quantum fluctuation could be "paid back" with complete impunity, leaving the universe behind. We will consider the theological consequences of these accounts below.

Quantum Gravity and "No Boundary" Proposals

A different approach to the origin of the universe addresses its beginnings by denying or dissolving the very category of a temporal beginning itself. This is the "no boundary" proposal, associated with explorations in theories of quantum gravity.

A helpful mental device here is to discuss the question of the beginning of the universe by a form of mental *approach*, toward the beginning, from later in time: an imaginative journey that traces the course of time backward from the present. As we came very close to what we will for now call the beginning, we would see the four fundamental forces of nature fusing, one by one. First, which is to say *nearest in time* to us imagining backward, we would see electromagnetism and the weak nuclear force coalescing. Further back toward the origin, we would see the resulting "electro-weak force" coalescing with the strong nuclear force. Nearer still to the origin, we would witness the ultimate fusion of forces, when this electro-nuclear force was fused with gravity, as a single, unified force.[13] That would put us in the realm of "quantum gravity": a proposed early state where the universe was so dense, small, and hot that gravitational effects and quantum mechanical effects operated at the same level. This is also often referred to as the Planck epoch, since the scales involved are compatible to the fundamental "Planck" units of time and space.[14] Running forward the story that we have just approached backward, the history of the early universe is seen as a story of emergence and of the unfolding of four forces out of one.

The crucial proposal about the state of the universe during this initial, Planck, epoch is that time would have behaved differently from the way in which it behaves now, functioning in fact as a fourth spatial dimension.[15] According to this account, in that furthest off initial domain of "quantum gravity," when the forces of nature were fused as one, time and space would not have been distinct from one another. Proponents of this approach therefore argue that the initial originatory "passage" of the universe is not one *in* time as much as one by which time itself emerges from something prior (and such a "prior" would not, therefore, be a temporal one). On that account, there would be no "t = 0" (a beginning of time), since at what we might mentally retroject as "t = 0," there would precisely be no "t," or, to put it another way, the nearer one was to approach to "t = 0" (by this process of mental extrapolation backward), the less the concept of "t = " would make sense.[16]

THEOLOGICAL COMPATIBILITY: THE "NO BOUNDARY" OF QUANTUM GRAVITY

We can begin to explore what these accounts of the origin of the universe do, and do not, mean for theology by considering a theological interpretation offered by the cosmologist Stephen Hawking. He begins by sketching what he takes as the theological implications of a commonsense vision of time. Crucially, he takes this vision to involve a temporal "edge" to the universe. Hawking proposes that, on this view, "you would really have to invoke God."[17] To see why, we need to understand how Hawking construes, and contrasts, his "no boundary alternative": "[With] no edge of space-time at which one would have to appeal to God or some new law . . . the universe would be completely self-contained and not affected by anything outside itself. It would neither be created nor destroyed. It would just BE."[18] A temporal edge,

Hawking thinks, raises the question of the origin of being, while the removal of such an edge dismisses that question. Here, the theological tradition of thinking about creation as *ex nihilo* characteristically disagrees, as we will see.

More recently, writing with Leonard Mlodinow, Hawking made a similar contrast: before the proposal of "no boundary" cosmology, time "seemed to be like a model railway track. If it [time] had a beginning, there would have to have been someone (i.e., God) to set the train going."[19] In contrast, Hawking and Mlodinow propose, God would no longer be implied if, with the "no boundary" proposal, "one can get rid of the problem of time having a beginning." In summary, according to Hawking and Mlodinow, while the idea that "the universe had a beginning" in time was for some "an argument for the existence of God," now the "realisation that time behaves like space [in the Planck epoch] presents a new alternative. It . . . means that the beginning of the universe was governed by the laws of science and doesn't need to be set in motion by some god."[20]

Hawking's comments here (in the second analysis joined by Mlodinow) are a useful foil for theological discussion. The incompatibility they propose between theology and a cosmological understanding of the beginning of the universe deploys terms entirely at variance with their meaning within an account of *creatio ex nihilo*. Indeed, from the perspective of that tradition, to propose that God is best understood as an agent at some putative beginning would be fundamentally to misunderstand the meaning of creation altogether, and of God.

To say that creation is *ex nihilo* is principally to say that God is *creator omnium*: the maker of all things, of every kind, in their entirety. It is to say that there is no noncreated reserve to the universe. It contrasts, for instance, with notions of creation out of preexisting matter. Understood this way, God is not simply, or even mainly, seen as an agent at work "at the beginning," as the one who sets procedures in process, or in train. God is equally at work in relation to all moments, not least because the *ex nihilo* proposal holds that *time itself* is created (it is part of that *omnium*). Moreover, we cannot compare creation with any sort of "initiatory moment" that we have experienced within time, since events in time are associated with change, and creation out of nothing is not any kind of change.[21] This stands in direct contrast to the theological vision assumed by Hawking and Mlodinow.

Further still, *creatio ex nihilo* also entails a prohibition on thinking of God as a cause among causes, or as a thing among things. God—the cause of everything about every creature (importantly, including its freedom)—cannot be ranked as one more cause among causes, or thing among things.[22] This is another reason why God does not function in the vision of *creation ex nihilo* as simply some initial cause. Again, this stands in contradistinction to the understanding that is mistakenly assumed by Hawking and Mlodinow as standard and representative of theology. Expressed graphically, *creatio ex nihilo* would not depict God's causal relation to creation as one more "earlier" arrow in a series of causal arrows representing creaturely causes, but as an entirely different sort of cause: the cause or "arrow" holding up the whole chain of creaturely causes from below.

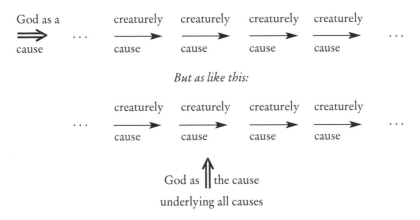

For a theological elaboration of these points, we can consider the proposal, put forward by Aquinas in his *Disputed Questions on the Power of God*, that *creatio ex nihilo* conceives of creation most basically in terms of the *relation* of creatures to God *at all times*, as much now and in the future as at some putative beginning—*if there was one*.[23] (We will return to that last phrase below.) In this text, Aquinas identified two dimensions to creation, as he understood it both on the basis of philosophical reflection and on the basis of his reading of scriptural texts: creation is a "relation" of the creature to God, combined with "inception of existence." However, and significantly for our purposes, he followed this with a caveat: the former aspect ("relation") is definitive in a way that the latter ("inception of existence") is not. The foundational sense of creation is *relation to God*, and, as such, "creation may be understood [as either combined] with newness of existence or without."

Aquinas's reason for including a beginning to time ("newness of existence") within his wider, two-part definition was his conviction that *scriptural sources* imply that creation has not always existed. All the same, he also thought it necessary—for the sake of intellectual integrity—to show that the alternative state of affairs (creation as a relation to God but without a beginning to time) was also possible, meaningful, and not contrary to the more foundational meaning of creation.[24] In particular, he thought, there is no "logical contradiction" in supposing "that something created was never lacking existence." That phrase "putative beginning—*if there was one*" in the previous paragraph is therefore no twenty-first-century gloss on Aquinas's approach to the doctrine of creation: it is his own.

In his short treatise *On the Eternity of the World*, we find Aquinas making this point in terms that bear directly upon our consideration of whether it matters for the universe to have a demarcated beginning in time.[25] In particular, Aquinas discusses the proper meaning of *priority* when applied to thought about creation. The question, as he sees it, is what the relation of one-after-another means, and what it applies to. Two such relations pertain to creation, he writes: in one respect, creation comes "after" God; in another, it comes "after" nothing. If, that is to say, we ask what is "prior'" to creation, we can say both "God" and "nothing." The second response simply reformulates the conviction that creation is *ex nihilo*.

With each of these relations (to God and to nothing), Aquinas wrote, we can distinguish an "order of time" from an "order of nature": one thing can be prior to another in either of these two ways. The central point about creation is the affirmation that apart from God's action no creature would exist: "A creature does not have its existence except from another. . . . Left to itself and considered by itself, it would be nothing." (This weaves together the perspectives that both God and "nothing" are prior to creation in different ways.)[26] The ultimate priority when it comes to where the universe "comes from" is the priority of "nature," not of "time": it is about what is causally or logically prior, rather than what is temporally prior. Once we have said that, he thinks, nothing of ultimate theological freight is then lost by saying either that creation has a beginning to time or that it does not. Both God and, in another sense, nothing are "naturally" prior to the universe, whether the universe has a temporal beginning or not.

Veiling

Hawking supposes that, for the theologian, God dwells at the edge of the universe, from where he "pushes" the "train" of the universe off on its journey along some "track" of space and time (or from where—we might say—he flicks the first domino). In response, the theologian who thinks from the perspective of *creatio ex nihilo* might reply that she is rather little interested in a discussion of any *one* moment, even if that is a *first* moment. Instead she considers the existence of the entirety of created reality at *every* moment and asks of it "why is there anything (track, train, and time) rather than nothing?" She answers that question in terms of God's entirely nonnecessary gift of creaturely being, when there need not have been any such being. The world follows logically after *nothing* because it follows *causally* after God (and that *is the main point*, made before any discussion about a beginning of time, or not, is on the table). Approaching the question of origination that way, the theologian will not be expecting, simply or primarily, to encounter God at some temporal edge of the universe, and there in particular. Consequently, she will be far from disappointed to hear that there may be no such boundary. Indeed, the theologian might find the idea of God encountered *at the edge* intrinsically problematic, and be glad if it is precluded.

The burden of *creatio ex nihilo*—once again—is that God is not a thing among things, nor a cause among causes. At such an "edge" God might *mistakenly* be interpreted as just such an intramundane agent or cause. The removal of any juncture, of any edge, by a "no boundaries" proposal—the removal of any initial moment where God might be confused as one more cause in a chain of causes—can not only be embraced within a scheme of *creatio ex nihilo*; it can be welcomed. If the world's creation is *ex nihilo*, and God does not act as a cause among causes, then the universe's veiling of its origins from a backward gaze from within, on account of a dissolved state for time at the start, seems supremely appropriate.[27]

THEOLOGICAL COMPATIBILITY:
QUANTUM FLUCTUATION AND INFLATION

Turning to the other class of cosmological descriptions of the early universe outlined above, that of quantum fluctuation combined with inflation, we are presented with another significant question for theology in relation to physical cosmology, namely how far one can go in accepting both a physical and a theological account of origins, as possessing their own integrity and place. It will be useful to begin by noting that in recent decades a number of theologians have linked creation *ex nihilo* to a noncompetitive paradigm of relation between divine and creaturely agency. *Ex nihilo*, they insist, demonstrates that God and creatures are not parallel entities (again, that God is not one more cause among causes), and that God's agency or causality does not compete on the same plane as that of the creature. An act can therefore be fully God's and that of the creature, each in its own way. Everything about the creature comes from God (except for evil, which is an attenuation of that reception), including the power and freedom to act. This grounds the creature's action in divine action, such that the divine act empowers the act of the creature, rather than occluding it. David Burrell and Janet Soskice stand among those who have made this connection.[28]

Remaining with Aquinas as our principle interlocutor, in his writings we find not only the elaboration of a scheme by which divine and creaturely agency are not in competition (they do not operate according to a "zero sum," as David Burrell has put it, among others), but even an account as to why God might *characteristically* work through creaturely agency. A representative discussion is found in the *Summa contra gentiles*:

> [It is not] superfluous, even if God can by Himself produce all natural effects, for them to be produced by certain other causes. For

this is not a result of the inadequacy of divine power, but of the immensity of His goodness, whereby He has willed to communicate His likeness to things, not only so that they might exist, but also that they might be causes for other things. Indeed, all creatures generally attain the divine likeness in these two ways. . . . By this, in fact, the beauty of order in created things is evident.[29]

In the later *Summa Theologiae*, Aquinas provides a succinct rationale for why this dynamic of God acting through creatures is an appropriate or fitting scheme for the divine ordering of the universe. If, he writes, the goal underlying the way in which God has structured the causal relations of nature is that everything should be "brought to perfection," then within that frame of reference "it is a greater perfection for a thing to be good in itself and also the cause of goodness in others, than only to be good in itself. Therefore God so governs things that He makes some of them to be causes of others in government; as a master, who not only imparts knowledge to his pupils, but gives also the faculty of teaching others."[30]

Examples of how such a vision can be grounded in scriptural exegesis could be multiplied,[31] but a particularly important case, for our purposes, is found in the opening chapter of Genesis. Here, as Bill T. Arnold has pointed out, we find patterns of delegated or secondary causation: of God acting through or by means of creatures.[32] The creation account in Genesis 1:1–2:4 contains examples of creatures themselves being given a role in the story of creation, so that in some passages God is depicted as creating directly while, in others, God commands the elements to exercise a delegated creativity, commanding the earth to bring forth vegetation (1:11–12) and the sea to "bring forth swarms of living creatures" (v. 20). The passage dealing with the fifth day offers a particularly clear account of this interweaving of primary and secondary causation, of causation divine and creaturely. The waters *themselves* bring forth creatures at God's command, and yet this is also fully attributed to God: "God said, '*Let the waters* bring forth swarms of living creatures.' . . . *So God created* the great sea monsters and every living creature that moves, of every kind, with which the waters swarm" (vv. 20–21). Similarly, with the creation of the sun and moon (vv. 14–19), what had previously been presented as God's work, namely separating day from night (v. 4), is given to parts of his new creation, to the sun and moon: they are "to give light upon the earth . . . and to separate the light from the darkness" (vv. 17–18).

This aligns with the noncompetitive paradigm for causation suggested by *creatio ex nihilo*, which provides for an act being at the same time, but in different ways, the act of the creature and the act of God. That proposal applies not only to actions that are in some sense specially marked out as "religious" or "moral": to the writing of a scriptural text, or to acts of heroic self-sacrifice, for instance. It would also apply to the most mundane of creaturely actions. As Aquinas saw it, even the most ordinary case of creaturely action God is involved in three ways: as the one foreshadowed in the goodness of the *end* on account of which the creature chooses to act, as the one giving the *existence* of the creature, and as the one giving the *nature* of the creature, which undergirds the particular way in which its power to act is exercised.[33]

If divine purposes are fulfilled through creaturely agency, and if to say that an act is creaturely does not cut it off from participation in divine activity, then scientific cosmological accounts of the origin of the universe need not stand in conflict with theological notions of creation. They can be seen and accepted as compatible and complementary with one another. Already, in the opening chapter of the Hebrew scriptures, as we have seen, we find a sense of creation as dignified through its derived, but real, role in the process of its unfolding. The theologian can approach contemporary scientific accounts of the physical story of the universe's origination in a similar way.

Earlier, in discussing suggestions thrown up by explorations of quantum gravity, we deployed the mental device of looking back toward the beginning "from the inside." Indeed, situated as we are within time, there is a sense in which we can *only* approach the beginning in this way, from the inside. Now, turning from quantum gravity to the proposals associated with quantum fluctuations married to inflation, we can point to a second aspect of such a "from the inside" dynamic to cosmological investigation, namely that there was bound to be one. The absolute appearing that is creation *ex nihilo* is going to have some creaturely appearance. Cosmology reflects upon the appearance of that appearing, as—in its own particular and limited fashion—it looks back at what creation *ex nihilo* looks like from the inside.

Cosmological accounts of origins do not dispense with God, however, or with theology, since they offer no description of the origin of being qua being. To say that is not to preclude the possibility and value of an exploration of how that gift of creaturely being looks, again "from the inside," as for instance is proposed by the combination of quantum fluctuation with inflation.

At its weakest, we can say that a physical account of the immanent unfolding of the universe need stand as no threat or competition to a theological account of the universe's origination from God. At its strongest, we might say even that the existence of such an immanent, physical story is to be expected, or perhaps that it is necessary: God is not an agent among agents, and our empirical observations will not apprehend him as such; God is not a cause among causes, to be observed as such. Whatever we can see of creation will be *creaturely*.

PHYSICS AND METAPHYSICS

Cosmological labors to understand the origin of the universe as a scientific story offer no conflict or contradiction to theological accounts of creation, understood as *ex nihilo*. Conflicts do arise, however, if a cosmologist steps out of physics into metaphysics, from a discussion of the particular form that is taken by the universe as we encounter it, into a discussion of the existence of being qua being.

The precise origin of the term "metaphysics" is disputed, and Aristotle did not himself give that name to his foundational treatise in that field, which now bears it. All the same, meta-physics is an apt description of his project there, which is to consider what "follows on from physics" in the course of the human study of reality.[34] In the order of knowing, in the sequence by which we come to know, certain questions "follow on" from physics: once (and however exhaustively) we have studied the questions belonging to physics, such as the motions of beings and their changes, something remains to be considered, which is the nature of being itself—after physics, metaphysics.

For Aristotle, that question did not go so far as to ask about the *origin* of being itself,[35] but for the theologian it can, and does. In that way, what comes *after* physics in the order of knowing (the study of metaphysics beginning where the study of physics ends) is *prior* to physics in the order of being (metaphysics deals with that which underlies all physical behavior). This bears most ultimately upon the question of why there is creaturely being at all.

THE EMERGENCE OF SPACE-TIME:
FROM "ABSOLUTELY NOTHING"?

A recurrent motif in recent cosmological-turned-metaphysical writing is to postulate that an origin for being qua being can be found in "nothing": in a "nothing" now conceived as productive. In the words of Frank Wilczek, for instance, one can answer the question "Why is there something rather than nothing?" with the answer that "nothing is unstable."[36] Alternatively, the philosophical concern that "from nothing, nothing comes" is circumvented—it is claimed—by the observation or contention that the universe "adds up" to "nothing," albeit according to a certain very particular measure. We have already encountered Edward Tyron talking about such balancing. Lawrence Krauss goes further than Tyron, advancing this notional canceling as an explanation for the arrival of the whole of being qua being: "If the total energy of a closed universe [a technical term] is zero, and if the sum-over paths formalism of quantum gravity is appropriate, then quantum mechanically such universes could appear spontaneously with impunity, carrying no net energy."[37] As John Gribbin has put it, adopting the same explanation, this makes the universe "not something for nothing, after all, but *nothing* for nothing,"[38] and therefore something that he can imagine passing from nothing, without a cause. Similarly, in the words of Quentin Smith, "we came from nothing, by nothing, and for nothing."[39] The physical chemist Peter Atkins takes a different, although related, tack when he equates the universe not with nothing but with very little, at least when it comes to complexity: "The creation [understood naturalistically] can generate only the most primitive structures, structures of such simplicity that they can drop out from absolutely nothing."[40]

The reply of the physicist Peter Hodgson (1928–2008) to Atkins's proposal can be taken to respond also to Krauss, Gribbin, Smith, and Wilczek: "Simple or complicated, small or large, the passage from nonexistence to existence is the most radical of all steps. It cannot be glossed over, and no one with any sense of ontological reality could accept this for an instant. However large or small the object may be, the passage from non-being to being is the greatest possible transition [. . . , and] the transition from non-being to being is beyond the power of science to detect."[41]

POTENTIAL AS NONBEING

We can identify the nub of the reason why these forms of argumentation are flawed—with physics seeking to take the place of metaphysics—by considering the relation of actuality and potentiality. At the root of the antitheological cosmological proposals above lies the sense that we can treat potential as "nothing," and nothing as potential, and therefore discard any sense that this potential itself calls for an explanation. Consider a colorful metaphor, deployed by Lawrence Krauss in order to head off the charge that the potential for something requires explanation: "Potential for . . . [something's] existence . . . doesn't define *being* any more than a potential human being exists because I carry sperm in my testicles near a woman who is ovulating, and she and I might mate."[42]

The move in Krauss's procreation simile, put philosophically, is to insist that "being" only means one thing (that the word is only used univocally). On that account, because potential is not being in the same way that actuality is being, potential is therefore not being at all: and not, therefore, something that registers as requiring an explanation. However, as Aristotle famously put it, we use the word "being" to mean more than one thing.[43] To observe, therefore, as Krauss does, that potentiality does not manifest being in the same fashion as actuality does is no basis for an argument that potentiality equates to nonbeing. It simply means that potentiality cannot be equated with being *in the same way* that actuality can.

Aristotle's diagnosis here deserves to be taken seriously, namely that "actuality is prior to potentiality."[44] One aspect of his analysis is based on the observation that act has priority over potential in the sense that any transition from potential to actuality is always a consequence of a particular act on the part of an agent: of something already "in act."[45] Any act that *realizes* potential is the act of something *real*;

the *activation* of potential is the work of something *active* and *actual*.[46] *Pace* Krauss, there is something here that calls for an explanation.

Approached another way, act precedes potency in the sense that *potency itself* is seen to be a positive principle or "actuality": a "power" to be other than what one is (as, indeed, the English word "potency" itself suggests, being related to "power"). Aristotle uses the word *dunamis* here, which he notably applies to the power of one thing *to act upon* another (to change another) as well as—which is relevant here—to the power of a thing *to be acted upon* (to be changed), so as to be different from how it now is (as when a builder turns wood into a house), or *to act upon itself* (as when an acorn grows into an oak tree).[47] Such potentiality is always a characteristic *of actuality*, since only what already and really *is* can have potential. As R. M. Dancy put it, potential is a capacity, and "capacities for becoming things are capacities *of* things. So they depend for their existence on actual things."[48] Again, potential cannot be dismissed as nothing.

This may seem to have been a digression, but it is not. Real change and development is found in the world, and that is always grounded in the potential belonging to an existing act (which makes every part of the internal physical story of the world an *ex*, and never an *ex nihilo*). No scientific exploration backward delivers to us anything that does not itself need an explanation, at least philosophically. Precisely inasmuch as a scientific account must always begin from something that is *in act*— concerning which, the natural sciences cannot give an explanation— such a scientific account will not trespass on a theological one. The theological endeavor, in contrast, takes it upon itself to consider the more absolute origination of all things—potential and actuality among them—in the most absolute of all agents-in-act, namely God, who does not simply "have" being, but "is" being, having it from no other.

Natural science always offers a narrative that begins with something actual, "out of" which (*ex*) its story proceeds, whether that beginning is the paradox of a finite universe without boundaries, a string landscape, a multiverse based on endless inflation, an endless cycle of big bangs and "big crunches," one universe produced from another,[49] or the givenness of the flow of time.[50] To theology, however, it belongs to think of a gift so total that it is *ex nihilo*, and to think of God's act in creating, and of God, who is act itself.

NOTES

1. Thomas Aquinas, *Summa Theologiae (ST)* I.46.2, trans. Fathers of the English Dominican Province (London: Burns, Oates & Washbourne, 1912–36). Jean-Pierre Torrell dates the first part of the *ST* to the period immediately before September 1268. *Saint Thomas Aquinas*, vol. 1, *The Person and His Work*, rev. ed. (Washington, DC: Catholic University of America Press, 2005), 333.

2. As interpreted by Georges Lemaître in the mid-1920s and Edwin Hubble shortly after.

3. Several examples will be given below. Consider also the opening of one of the most significant mediations of cosmology to a wider audience, Stephen Hawking and Leonard Mlodinow's *The Grand Design* (New York: Bantam, 2010), where we read, "Traditionally these are questions [such as 'What is the nature of reality? Did the universe need a creator? Where did all this come from?'] for philosophy, but philosophy is dead. Philosophy has not kept up with modern developments in science, particularly physics. Scientists have become the bearers of the torch of discovery in our quest for knowledge" (5).

4. Or, alternatively, it is an exploration of the qualities of a "quantum vacuum."

5. This behavior can also be understood in terms of a Heisenberg uncertainty principle relationship between electric and magnetic fields (Lee Smolin, *Three Roads to Quantum Gravity* [London: Basic Books, 2002], 83), or between the value of a field and its rate of change (Hawking and Mlodinow, *Grand Design*, 113).

6. Edward Tyron, "Is the Universe a Vacuum Fluctuation?," *Nature* 26 (1973): 396–97.

7. Tyron, "Vacuum Fluctuation," 396. The suggestion is reiterated by Hawking and Mlodinow, *Grand Design*, 180. Expansion is associated with negative energy because energy "has to be expended in separating matter against the force of gravity." C. J. Isham, "Quantum Theories of the Creation of the Universe," in *Quantum Cosmology and the Laws of Nature*, ed. R. J. Russell et al. (Vatican City: Vatican Observatory, 1993), 56.

8. Tyron, "Vacuum Fluctuation," 397.

9. Alan H. Guth, "Inflationary Universe: A Possible Solution to the Horizon and Flatness Problems," *Physical Review D* 23 (1981): 347–56.

10. George Greenstein, *Understanding the Universe* (Cambridge: Cambridge University Press, 2013), 549. The claim in 2014 that the BICEP2 experiment had provided direct confirmation for inflation, through patterns of polarization in the cosmic microwave background radiation, was later retracted once more complete observations were available from the Planck satellite.

P. A. R. Ade et al., "Joint Analysis of BICEP2/Keck Array and Planck Data," *Physical Review Letters* 114, id.101301 (2015), https://physics.aps.org/featured -article-pdf/10.1103/PhysRevLett.114.101301. The earlier observations were put down to the effects of interstellar dust. The best current evidence for inflation rests on the very low curvature of space, the high degree of isotropy at large angular scales, and the spectral index of the initial perturbations. All these parameters are measured with high accuracy by the Planck space mission. The Planck Collaboration, "The Planck Collaboration, Planck 2013 Results. I. Overview of Products and Scientific Results," *Astronomy and Astrophysics* 571, id. A1 (2014), http://www.aanda.org/articles/aa/abs/2014/11/aa21529-13/aa21529-13.html. I am grateful to Marco Bersanelli for discussions of this material.

11. Hawking and Mlodinow, *Grand Design*, 129.

12. This is sometimes described as a transition to a lower "vacuum state." As Lawrence Krauss put it in *A Universe from Nothing* (London: Simon and Schuster, 2012), the very expansion of the universe itself creates matter and light (150–52, 168). The extremely rapid initial expansion is triggered by a large negative pressure generated by a state of "false vacuum": an energy density that remains nearly constant during expansion. When the false vacuum decays, its energy is released and fills the whole space with a hot and uniform swarm of particles (here I again acknowledge my debt to Bersanelli). All the same, as Krauss also notes, "while inflation demonstrates how empty space endowed with energy can effectively create everything we see, along with an unbelievably large . . . universe, it would be disingenuous to suggest that empty space endowed with energy, which drives inflation, is really *nothing*. In this picture one must assume that space exists and can store energy, and one uses the laws of physics like general relativity to calculate the consequences. So if we stopped here, one might be justified in claiming that modern science is a long way from really addressing how to get something from nothing" (152).

13. See, for instance, William R. Stoeger, "The Big Bang, Quantum Cosmology and *Creatio ex Nihilo*," in *Creation and the God of Abraham*, ed. David B. Burrell et al. (Cambridge: Cambridge University Press, 2010), 156.

14. These are the scale of size and time that correspond to the Planck constant, the pivotal constant in quantum mechanics. The length is 1.6×10^{-35} meter and the time 5.4×10^{-44} second (which is the time required for light to traverse the Planck length). During the Planck epoch, the universe was of a comparable size and age (although "age" may be a fuzzy concept here) to these fundamental units. According to some understandings, it would not make sense, on that basis, to speak of an entity of a smaller size or younger age.

15. Stoeger, "Big Bang, Quantum Cosmology and *Creatio ex Nihilo*," 157. At this size, temperature and density, the very nature of spatiality is also consid-

ered to be different from how we know it: it would have been quantized or granular, with what William Stoeger called "discrete, broken-up, foam-like structure": "The fluctuations in geometry [in this period] are so large that the concept of space-time as we usually model it—as a smooth, connected manifold—is no longer valid. Instead we have to find an adequate way of representing this highly energetic state with a discrete, broken-up, foam-like structure . . . a quantum description of space-time and therefore of gravity" (160).

16. An important formulation of this idea is the Hartle-Hawking "No Boundary Proposal." James Hartle and Stephen Hawking, "Wave Function of the Universe," *Physical Review D* 28 (1983): 2960–75. Hawking later produced a formulation of this idea with Neil Turok known as the "Instanton Theory." "Open Inflation without False Vacua," *Physics Letters B* 425 (1998): 25–32. See Stoeger, "Big Bang, Quantum Cosmology and *Creatio ex Nihilo*," 164–65, for a discussion in relation to a parallel proposal by Alexander Vilenkin. Time is seen in these models as initially "imaginary," in the mathematical sense of having tilted onto the imaginary axis.

17. Stephen Hawking, "If There's an Edge to the Universe, There Must Be a God," in Renée Weber, *Dialogues with Scientists and Sages: The Search for Unity* (London: Routledge and Kegan Paul, 1986), 209, quoted by Ted Peters, "The Trinity in and beyond Time," in *Quantum Cosmology and the Laws of Nature*, ed. R. J. Russell et al. (Vatican City: Vatican Observatory, 1993), 276.

18. Stephen Hawking, *A Brief History of Time* (London: Bantam, 1988), 136.

19. Hawking and Mlodinow, *Grand Design*, 134.

20. Ibid., 135.

21. Creation understood *ex nihilo* is not a movement or a change. As Aquinas put it, "What is created is not made by movement, or by change. For what is made by movement or by change is made from something pre-existing. And this happens, indeed, in the particular productions of some beings, but cannot happen in the production of all being by the universal cause of all beings, which is God." *ST* I.45.3.

22. Authors have pointed out in the past couple of decades that this observation (that God is not a thing among things) aligns both with the unutterable difference of God from creation and with the profound intimacy of the world's relation to God. See, for instance, Jacob H. Sherman, "A Genealogy of Participation," in *The Participatory Turn*, ed. Jorge N. Ferrer and Jacob H. Sherman (Albany: State University of New York Press, 2008); David C. Schindler, "What's the Difference? On the Metaphysics of Participation in a Christian Context," *Saint Anselm Journal* 3 (2005): 1–27; Philipp Rosemann, *Omne Agens Agit Sibi Simile: A "Repetition" of Scholastic Metaphysics* (Leuven: Leuven University

Press, 1996); David B. Burrell, *Freedom and Creation in Three Traditions* (Notre Dame, IN: University of Notre Dame Press, 1994). Aquinas expressed this point in his scholastic terminology when he wrote that God is not included within any genus or species. *Compendium of Theology* I.10; *ST* I.3.5.

23. *De Potentia* III.3 ad 6 (dated to 1266–67 by Jean-Pierre Torrell, *Saint Thomas Aquinas*, 1:335), trans. Fathers of the English Dominican Province (London: Burns, Oates & Washbourne, 1932–34). I discuss the conceptualiza-tion of the relation of creatures to God in this way in *Participation: An Explo-ration in Christian Metaphysics* (forthcoming, 2018).

24. He elaborates this point, not least, as a clarification in the face of a tra-dition which thought otherwise—that creation made no sense other than as having a beginning to time—of which a prominent exponent was Bonaventure. For a discussion of Bonaventure on this point, and a list of texts, see Christo-pher M. Cullen, *Bonaventure* (Oxford: Oxford University Press, 2006), 42–43. Texts from Bonaventure are brought together, with English translation, along with others from Aquinas and Siger of Brabant (who held that the universe was definitely eternal) in *On the Eternity of the World*, trans. Cyril Vollert et al. (Milwaukee: Marquette University Press, 1965).

25. It is dated to 1271 by Jean-Pierre Torrell, *Saint Thomas Aquinas*, 1:348.

26. Aquinas deploys a favorite analogy here, of the sun and the sunbeam: "We say that the air is made lucid . . . not because [or not primarily because] the air was once non-lucid or opaque, but because the air would be opaque if the sun did not illuminate it."

27. The idea that the universe veils its beginning—the nakedness of its birth—is encountered, in fact, on several levels. One is empirical obscurity, as for instance with the opacity of the universe to light until around 380,000 years after the big bang. See, for instance, Tarun Souradeep, "Cosmology with the Cosmic Microwave Background," in *Springer Handbook of Spacetime*, ed. Abhay Ashtekar and Vesselin Petkov (Dordrecht: Springer, 2014), 701. On ac-count of this, we cannot observe anything earlier by direct detection of electro-magnetic radiation. Then there is the epistemological provisionality of certain models. An example would be the way in which the regnant model for the gravitational behavior of the universe (the Friedmann-Lemaître-Robinson-Walker, or FLRW, model) points to its own incompleteness by virtue of the in-finitudes that it throws up when applied to the notion of an extrapolated very beginning. As William R. Stoeger has commented, "The fact that [the big bang as predicted by the FLRW model] involves infinite temperature and infinite density serves as a warning that this did not actually happen. It is simply a 'pre-diction' of the model which does not represent what really occurred." "The Big Bang, Quantum Cosmology and *Creatio ex Nihilo*," 158; see also 159, 162.

The model is "very reliable" for describing the behavior of the universe below the Planck-era temperature, "but severely fails in describing its physical state and behaviour during the Planck era itself, or during any era preceding it." Finally, there is the sort of "veiling" of the beginning which we find with the "no boundary" proposal. If the inapplicability of FLRW model to the earliest moments of the universe represents a theory pointing to its own incompleteness, the "no boundary" approach operates differently: it predicts not the absence of a theory about an absolute temporal origin but a theory about the absence of such a temporal origin.

28. See Janet Martin Soskice, "*Creatio ex nihilo*: Jewish and Christian Foundations," 37–38, and David Burrell, "Freedom and Creation in Three Traditions," especially 67–159, both in Burrell et al., *Creation and the God of Abraham*. Jacob H. Sherman, David C. Schindler, and Philipp Rosemann are further examples. See also note 22 above.

29. Thomas Aquinas, *Summa contra gentiles* III.70.7.

30. Aquinas, *ST* I.103.6.

31. For Aquinas, a decisive text, quoted again and again (for instance in *ST* I.105.5) comes from Isa. 26.12: "All that we have done, you have done for us." God acts in and through his creatures, and those actions are both theirs and his. Paul follows this pattern in 2 Cor. 6:1, and possibly in 1 Cor. 3:9 (the precise interpretation of those words is disputed). Discussing the drama of salvation in Phil. 2:12–13, Paul instructs his readers: "Work out your own salvation with fear and trembling; for it is God who is at work in you, enabling you both to will and to work for his good pleasure." There is a close parallel in Heb. 13:21. Revelation itself also stands as an example, as it is understood in Christian theology. It too is a matter of mediation: of *in*, *by*, and *through*. God is manifest as mediated in specific and finite way: through prophets and apostle and their stories, through events and the histories of peoples and nations, and through other creatures of various sorts, including an ass (Num. 22), and a burning bush (Exod. 3). This dynamic reaches its highest pitch in the person and life of Christ, where divine words are given in and as human words, and divine life is revealed in and as a human life.

32. Bill T. Arnold, *Genesis* (Cambridge: Cambridge University Press, 2009), 42–43. Arnold acknowledges his debt to W. P. Brown, "Divine Act and the Art of Persuasion in Genesis 1," in *History and Interpretation*, ed. M. Patrick Graham, William P. Brown, and Jeffrey K. Kuan, Journal for the Study of the Old Testament Supplement Series 173 (Sheffield: JSOT Press, 1993), 24–27. Aquinas does not, to my knowledge, comment on this aspect of the text.

33. Aquinas, *ST* I.105.5. These dimensions align with final, efficient, and formal aspects of causation, respectively.

34. "This science . . . comes after physics in the order relative to us." Alexander of Aphrodisias, second-to-third century AD, *Metaphysics* 171.5–7, quoted in Jean Grondin, *Introduction to Metaphysics: From Parmenides to Levinas* (New York: Columbia University Press, 2013), 269n4, translating Luc Brisson, "Un si long anonymat," in *La Métaphysique: Son histoire, sa critique, ses enjeux*, ed. Jean-Marc Narbonne and Luc Langlois (Paris: J. Vrin, 1999), 45. Aquinas ventures the following interpretation of the term in the prologue to his *Commentary on the Metaphysics*: "It is called metaphysics inasmuch as it considers being and the attributes which naturally accompany being (for things which transcend the physical order [*transphysica*] are discovered by the process of analysis, as the more common are discovered after the less common)." Trans. John P. Rowan (Chicago: Regnery, 1961).

35. See *Metaphysics* 9.6 and the commentary provided by Adrian Pabst on this passage in "The Primacy of Relation over Substance and the Recovery of a Theological Metaphysics," *American Catholic Philosophical Quarterly* 81 (2007): 553–78, 559.

36. "The Cosmic Asymmetry between Matter and Antimatter," *Scientific American* 243 (1980): 82–90, quoted in Christopher Hitchens, *The Portable Atheist: Essential Readings for the Nonbeliever* (London: Da Capo Press, 2007), 327, and, from there, by Krauss, *Universe from Nothing*, 159.

37. Krauss, *Universe from Nothing*, 167.

38. Gribbin, *In Search of the Big Bang* (London: Penguin, 1998), 374, quoted in Paul Copan and William Lane Craig, *Creation out of Nothing: A Biblical, Philosophical, and Scientific Exploration* (Grand Rapids: Baker Academic, 2004), 256. Emphasis original.

39. Quentin Smith, "The Uncaused Beginning of the Universe," in *Theism, Atheism, and Big Bang Cosmology*, by William Lane Craig and Quentin Smith (Oxford: Clarendon Press, 1996), 135, quoted in Copan and Craig, *Creation out of Nothing*, 255.

40. Peter Atkins, *The Creation* (London: W. H. Freeman and Co., 1981), 113. Quoted in Peter Hodgson, *Theology and Modern Physics* (Aldershot: Ashgate, 2005), 193.

41. Hodgson, *Theology and Modern Physics*, 193. Indeed, it is even beyond the power of science to *theorize* this "transition," and the inexplicability of this "transition" relates precisely to the point that it is not a transition: creation is not any kind of change (see earlier in this essay, under "Theological Compatibility").

42. Krauss, *Universe from Nothing*, 146. Krauss makes it clear that he is responding to a theological or philosophical concern at this point (referring the reader back [146] to the discussion of this point in the introduction

[xiii–xv]), the concern that he has not arrived here at a "nothing" so complete that it does not (according to his understanding of the matter) itself call for an explanation: that "if there is the 'potential' to create something [that is, in his terms, for something to emerge spontaneously], then that is not a state of true nothingness" (xv).

43. Aristotle, *Metaphysics* 4.2.1003a; 7.1.1028a.

44. Aristotle, *Metaphysics* 9.8.1049b, trans. W. D. Ross with revisions by Jonathan Barnes, in Jonathan Barnes, ed., *The Complete Works of Aristotle* (Princeton: Princeton University Press, 1984), 2:1657.

45. "For from the potential the actual is always produced by an actual thing. . . . There is always a fired mover, and the mover always already exists actually." Aristotle, *Metaphysics* 9.8.1049b, in Barnes, *Aristotle*, 2:1658.

46. This conviction underlies the first of Aquinas's "Five Ways": "Nothing can be reduced from potentiality to actuality, except by something in a state of actuality." *ST* I.2.3. We can note that Krauss himself adopts a parallel usage when he writes, "As I have defined it so far, the relevant 'nothing' from which our observed 'something' arises is 'empty space.' However, once we allow for the merging of quantum mechanics and general relativity, we can extend this argument to the case where space [and—his argument here implies—time] it-self *is forced into existence*" (*Universe from Nothing*, 161; emphasis added). At least on grammatical terms, the words in italic suggest something prior with the power, or actuality, of being capable of "forcing."

47. "For the one [potentiality] is in the thing acted on. . . . But the other potentiality is in the agent." Aristotle, *Metaphysics* 9.1.1046a, in Barnes, *Aristotle*, 1652. There is a parallel in 5.12.

48. R. M. Dancy, "Aristotle and the Priority of Actuality," in *Reforging the Great Chain of Being*, ed. S. Knuuttila (Dordrecht: D. Reidel, 1981), 73–115, 94. Dancy bases this on an analogy to form and matter: "The priority of form over matter for which Aristotle argues in *Met. Z 3* [*Metaphysics* 7.3, but see also especially 7.17] is, in fact, precisely the priority of actuality over potentiality: a thing's matter is that which might or might not have been that thing, and its form is that by virtue of which the matter is that thing and not whatever it would have been had it been something else" (93).

49. Roger Penrose, *Cycles of Time: An Extraordinary New View of the Universe* (London: Bodley Head, 2010).

50. Lee Smolin and Roberto Mangabeira Unger, *The Singular Universe and the Reality of Time* (Cambridge: Cambridge University Press, 2014).

CONTRIBUTORS

KHALED ANATOLIOS is professor of theology, University of Notre Dame.

GARY A. ANDERSON is Hesburgh Professor of Catholic Theology, University of Notre Dame.

MARKUS BOCKMUEHL is Dean Ireland's Professor of the Exegesis of Holy Scripture, University of Oxford.

JOHN C. CAVADINI is professor of theology and McGrath-Cavadini Director of the McGrath Institute for Church Life, University of Notre Dame.

RICHARD J. CLIFFORD, S.J., is professor emeritus of Hebrew Bible/Old Testament, Boston College.

DANIEL DAVIES is a research associate at the University of Hamburg.

ANDREW DAVISON is Starbridge Lecturer in Theology and Natural Sciences, University of Cambridge.

DAVID BENTLEY HART is a Director's Fellow at the Notre Dame Institute for Advanced Study, University of Notre Dame.

ADAM D. HINCKS, S.J., is a graduate student at Gregorian University, Rome.

RUTH JACKSON is a research associate at the University of Cambridge.

SEAN M. MCDONOUGH is professor of New Testament, Gordon-Conwell Theological Seminary.

TZVI NOVICK is Abrams Chair of Jewish Thought and Culture, University of Notre Dame.

CYRIL O'REGAN is Huisking Professor of Theology, University of Notre Dame.

ANDREW PINSENT is the research director of the Ian Ramsey Centre for Science and Religion, University of Oxford.

JANET SOSKICE is professor of philosophical theology, University of Cambridge.

GREGORY E. STERLING is the Reverend Henry L. Slack Dean and Lillian Claus Professor of New Testament, Yale Divinity School.

JOSEPH WAWRYKOW is professor of theology, University of Notre Dame.

SUBJECT INDEX

Specific works will be found under the author's name. Citations to biblical and other foundational texts are located in the separate Index of Citations.

second person perspective in
scientific cosmology and
theology (*cont.*)
insight, importance of, 349–51,
361–62nn13–16, 361n11
Jewish and Christian thought
on second-person relationship
with God, 355–57, 364n36
salvation and covenant
relationship, creation *ex nihilo*
developing in framework of,
348
Sedley, David, 115n23
*Creationism and its Critics in
Antiquity*, 39
seeming and being distinguished in
Revelation, 79–81
sense-perceptible world. *See*
intelligible and sense-
perceptible worlds
Septuagint (LXX), 17, 78, 112n2,
130
Serafim of Sarov, 309
Sextus Epiricus, 114n19
Shavuot (Pentecost), 201
Shelley, Percy Bysshe, 258
Sherman, Robert, 281
Sidney, Sir Philip, 271n61, 272n73
Siger of Brabant, 386n24
singularity, 328, 329–30, 335,
360n3
Smith, Quentin, 380
Smolin, Lee, 360n6
Sonderegger, Katherine, 281,
294n43
Sorabji, Richard, 117n57
Soskice, Janet, 4, 15, 22, 117–18n74,
376
"soul" sense of biblical text, 158–59,
160, 163
The Sound of Music (film), 164

Spinoza, Benedict de, 9
atheism, viewed as apostle of, 251,
252
on Bible, 252
Bruno and Renaissance
Neoplatonists, 9, 235, 236, 239,
248–51, 254–60, 263, 265n6,
269n42, 271n64
classical Neoplatonism and,
244–48
classical theism, displacement and
replacement of, 233–34, 252–62
Correspondences, 241
Descartes and, 233, 234, 236, 242,
253, 259, 264n1, 265n9, 268n30,
268n34
emanationism and, 237, 245–49,
251, 257, 262–63
Ethics, 234, 236–44, 245, 246, 248,
251, 252, 259, 262–63, 266n17,
267n20, 267n24, 271n62
German Romanticism and
Idealism influenced by, 9, 234,
235, 238, 239, 252, 253, 255–58,
260–61, 262, 263, 267n23,
271n66, 272n72
on God or substance as one, 238–39
on identity of freedom and
necessity in God, 240–41
on identity of power, essence, and
act in God, 239–40
letters of, 266n13, 267n28
Maimonides and, 239, 242,
265–66n10, 267n21
mathematical account of reality, 9,
235, 236, 237, 244, 248, 253, 254,
259
natura naturans and *natura
naturata*, 239, 244, 256, 267n24
naturalism and natural supernaturalism of, 234, 235, 251–63

INDEX OF CITATIONS

8:22	198, 200
8:22, 30	8
8:22–26	72
8:22–31	63, 71–72
8:27	201
8:27–29	69
8:27–31	72
8:28	201
8:29a	201, 202
8:29b	201
8:30	198, 199, 200
19:17	28, 31
24:13–14	210n25

Song of Songs 5:16	210n25

Isaiah   48

24:3–5	93
26:12	387n31
27:1	18
40–55	63, 69–71
40:17	88
43:10, 12	71
43:16–18	70
43:16–21	63, 70–71, 75
43:19–21	70
44:8	71
45:6–7	88
51:9–11	70
51:19	18
54:5	364n36
60	20–22, 27
60:19–20	20–21
Deutero-Isaiah	5
Third Isaiah	32

Jeremiah

3:20	364n36
4:23–26	84
5:22	201
31:34	201
33:25	200

Ezekiel

16:15–19	364n36
40:5–16	86

Daniel

5	199
7	84

Hosea

2:2–5	364n36
2:8	67–68
3:1–5	364n36
9:1	364n36

Habakkuk 2:20	85

Zephaniah

1:2–3	96n22
1:7	85

Zechariah

2:1–5	86
2:13	85

APOCRYPHA/PSEUDEPIGRAPHA

1 Enoch

17–19	98n39
91	97n23
93	96–97n23

2 Enoch

24:2–26:3	116n46
25	210n21

Jubilees 2:2–3	117n54
Judith 16:14	48

CPSIA information can be obtained
at www.ICGtesting.com
Printed in the USA
LVHW012314200721
693264LV00004B/237